THE WILEY BICENTENNIAL—KNOWLEDGE FOR GENERATIONS

*E*ach generation has its unique needs and aspirations. When Charles Wiley first opened his small printing shop in lower Manhattan in 1807, it was a generation of boundless potential searching for an identity. And we were there, helping to define a new American literary tradition. Over half a century later, in the midst of the Second Industrial Revolution, it was a generation focused on building the future. Once again, we were there, supplying the critical scientific, technical, and engineering knowledge that helped frame the world. Throughout the 20th Century, and into the new millennium, nations began to reach out beyond their own borders and a new international community was born. Wiley was there, expanding its operations around the world to enable a global exchange of ideas, opinions, and know-how.

For 200 years, Wiley has been an integral part of each generation's journey, enabling the flow of information and understanding necessary to meet their needs and fulfill their aspirations. Today, bold new technologies are changing the way we live and learn. Wiley will be there, providing you the must-have knowledge you need to imagine new worlds, new possibilities, and new opportunities.

Generations come and go, but you can always count on Wiley to provide you the knowledge you need, when and where you need it!

WILLIAM J. PESCE
PRESIDENT AND CHIEF EXECUTIVE OFFICER

PETER BOOTH WILEY
CHAIRMAN OF THE BOARD

Threats to Homeland Security:
An All-Hazards Perspective

Richard J.Kilroy, Jr.
Virginia Military Institute
Editor

BICENTENNIAL
1807
WILEY
2007
BICENTENNIAL

Credits

PUBLISHER
Anne Smith

DEVELOPMENT EDITOR
Laura Town

MARKETING MANAGER
Jennifer Slomack

SENIOR EDITORIAL ASSISTANT
Tiara Kelly

PRODUCTION MANAGER
Kelly Tavares

PRODUCTION EDITOR
Kerry Weinstein

CREATIVE DIRECTOR
Harry Nolan

COVER DESIGNER
Hope Miller

Wiley 200th Anniversary Logo designed by: Richard J. Pacifico

This book was set in Berkeley Oldstyle Book by Aptara, Inc. and printed and bound by Donnelley/Crawfordsville. The cover was printed by Phoenix Color.

To order books or for customer service please call 1-800-CALL WILEY (225-5945).

ISBN 978-0470-07398-8

Printed in the United States of America

10 9 8 7 6 5 4 3 2 1

PREFACE

College classrooms bring together learners from many backgrounds with a variety of aspirations. Although the students are in the same course, they are not necessarily on the same path. This diversity, coupled with the reality that these learners often have jobs, families, and other commitments, requires a flexibility that our nation's higher education system is addressing. Distance learning, shorter course terms, new disciplines, evening courses, and certification programs are some of the approaches that colleges employ to reach as many students as possible and help them clarify and achieve their goals.

Wiley Pathways books, a new line of texts from John Wiley & Sons, Inc., are designed to help you address this diversity and the need for flexibility. These books focus on the fundamentals, identify core competencies and skills, and promote independent learning. Their focus on the fundamentals helps students grasp the subject, bringing them all to the same basic understanding. These books use clear, everyday language and are presented in an uncluttered format, making the reading experience more pleasurable. The core competencies and skills help students succeed in the classroom and beyond, whether in another course or in a professional setting. A variety of built-in learning resources promote independent learning and help instructors and students gauge students' understanding of the content. These resources enable students to think critically about their new knowledge and apply their skills in any situation.

Our goal with *Wiley Pathways* books—with their brief, inviting format, clear language, and core competencies and skills focus—is to celebrate the many students in your courses, respect their needs, and help you guide them on their way.

CASE Learning System

To meet the needs of working college students, *Wiley Pathways Threats to Homeland Security: An All-Hazards Perspective* uses a four-part process called the CASE Learning System:

▲ *C:* Content
▲ *A:* Analysis
▲ *S:* Synthesis
▲ *E:* Evaluation

Based on Bloom's taxonomy of learning, CASE presents key topics in homeland security in easy-to-follow chapters. The text then prompts analysis, synthesis, and evaluation with a variety of learning aids and assessment tools. Students move efficiently from reviewing what they have learned, to acquiring new information and skills, to applying their new knowledge and skills to real-life scenarios.

Using the CASE Learning System, students not only achieve academic mastery of homeland security *topics*, but they master real-world *skills* related to that content. The CASE Learning System also helps students become independent learners, giving them a distinct advantage in the field, whether they are just starting out or seeking to advance in their careers.

Organization, Depth, and Breadth of the Text

Modular Format

Research on college students shows that they access information from textbooks in a non-linear way. Instructors also often want to reorder textbook content to suit the needs of a particular class. Therefore, although *Wiley Pathways Threats to Homeland Security: An All-Hazards Perspective* proceeds logically from the basics to increasingly more challenging material, chapters are further organized into sections that are self-contained for maximum teaching and learning flexibility.

Numeric System of Headings

Wiley Pathways Threats to Homeland Security: An All-Hazards Perspective uses a numeric system for headings (e.g., 2.3.4 identifies the fourth subsection of Section 3 of Chapter 2). With this system, students and teachers can quickly and easily pinpoint topics in the table of contents and the text, keeping class time and study sessions focused.

Core Content

After the terrorist attacks against America on 9/11, there was a rush to publish new textbooks that responded to the demand on college campuses for classes related to homeland security and terrorism. The first attempts at meeting this void were texts in traditional fields of study, such as political science or criminal justice. Terrorism studies was a little-known field in international studies programs at some colleges, and it still looked at the subject from a theoretical or conceptual construct. Other approaches looked at the topic in terms of policy studies, such as national security policy or foreign policy courses, which expanded to include the subject of homeland security.

When Hurricanes Katrina and Rita struck the Gulf Coast in August and September 2005, there was a similar rush to publish new textbooks on natural disaster response and planning, primarily in the field of emergency management.

New college curricula also developed in areas of "applied sciences," which now placed greater emphasis on studying the role of first responders and state and federal agencies in addressing natural disasters, as opposed to terrorist attacks. Community colleges, four-year undergraduate institutions, and even graduate schools began to develop degree programs related to emergency management and planning. One can thus anticipate that after the next "threat" the United States faces, there will be yet another academic shift to accommodate that new area of study.

Rather than waiting for the next event to occur, the approach taken in this text is to address the subject of homeland security from an all-hazards perspective. In other words, the goal in writing this book is to provide students in a variety of academic disciplines with an integrated approach to security studies and the continuing nature of security challenges through both a theoretical and a practical lens. Through this text, students and practitioners achieve a comprehensive understanding of threats to the United States from an interdisciplinary perspective. They gain an overview of both terrorism and disasters, of the threats posed by each type of hazard, and of the response to those threats. Through this all-hazards perspective, readers gain a better understanding of the threats we face today and those we will continue to face in the future.

In Chapter 1, "The Changing Nature of National Security," John H. P. Williams and Richard J. Kilroy, Jr., provide a historical context for understanding national security and how homeland security today is an extension of previous policy choices. The focus of this chapter is on threats in the twentieth century, from the geopolitical focus on nation-states and the continental balance of power, through the Cold War and the superpower rivalry of a bipolar international system, to the post–Cold War security environment prior to 9/11. Williams and Kilroy further explain the national security decision making that emerged after 9/11 in response to the new threat of global terrorism.

In Chapter 2, "U.S. Homeland Security Interests," Amy Blizzard provides an overview of different dimensions of security. She examines the process of determining what to protect, ranging from the security of individuals to that of critical infrastructure and key assets. Blizzard further notes that in the post-9/11 world, economic activities and societal values have taken on increased significance because the measures enforced by governments to provide for greater security and protection can also have significant trade-offs in areas related to individual freedoms and democratic values.

In Chapter 3, "The All-Hazards Perspective," Richard J. Kilroy, Jr., explores the nature of various threats by discussing them in terms of different categories, such as threats from natural disasters, accidents, and man-made incidents. Kilroy also explores the concept of secondary and tertiary effects and the potential linkages between terrorism and other catastrophic events.

In Chapter 4, "A Conceptual Framework—Assessing Threats and Interests," Amy Blizzard presents a theoretical structure for considering threats to homeland security. Blizzard's analytical perspective provides a matrixed approach to threat assessment, which is applicable across the all-hazards perspective. In addition, Blizzard provides a practical risk assessment tool for emergency managers.

In Chapter 5, "State Actors and Terrorism," Jeannie Grussendorf explains terrorism from a theoretical perspective, exploring the reasons behind the formation of terrorist groups, as well as the role governments play in both fostering the growth of and responding to these groups. She further examines the implications of current U.S. foreign policy with regard to its impact on state-sponsored terrorism.

In Chapter 6, "Non-State Actors and Terrorism," Grussendorf continues her theoretical analysis by exploring the role of non-state actors and their use of terrorism within the inter-state system. She further defines the types of terrorist organizations that exist today, the methods they employ to achieve their goals and objectives, and how the United States has responded to threats from these groups.

In Chapter 7, "Cyber-Terrorism and Cyber-Warfare," Richard J. Kilroy, Jr., examines these unique threats of the Information Age. He explains why both nation-states and terrorist groups would consider using new informational technologies aimed at crippling or disabling a nation's critical infrastructure, economy, and means of response. Kilroy also explains the new organizational roles and missions of the military in responding to threats posed by cyber-warfare and cyber-terrorism.

In Chapter 8, "Weapons of Mass Destruction," Alice Anderson explores the dangers posed by WMDs, focusing on chemical, biological, and radiological threats. She examines what these weapons are and why they pose a threat of catastrophic damage. Anderson also reviews our nation's response in trying to prevent a WMD attack, as well as how to respond if and when such an attack occurs.

In Chapter 9, "Domestic Terrorism," Daniel Masters examines terrorism within the United States. Masters looks at the history of terrorist groups operating within this country, including both foreign and homegrown terrorist organizations. He assesses the domestic threat environment in terms of support for and defenses against the growth of terrorist cells. Masters also provides a compelling case for the reason why terrorism within the United States has historically not been a major threat, as well as why an all-hazards perspective is needed.

Finally, in Chapter 10, "Enablers of Mass Effects," Carmine Scavo explores the unique challenges posed by the ability of terrorist groups to use information in the war of ideas. Scavo looks at the role of the media and the Internet in providing the technology to link terrorist groups around the world today. He further examines the role universities play in teaching about security challenges and developing initiatives to meet the needs of students and practitioners wanting to learn more about threats to homeland security from an all-hazards perspective.

Pre-reading Learning Aids

Each chapter of *Wiley Pathways Threats to Homeland Security: An All-Hazards Perspective* features a number of learning and study aids, described in the following sections, to activate students' prior knowledge of the topics and orient them to the material.

Pre-test

This pre-reading assessment tool in multiple-choice format not only introduces chapter material, but it also helps students anticipate the chapter's learning outcomes. By focusing students' attention on what they do not know, the self-test provides students with a benchmark against which they can measure their own progress. The pre-test is available online at www.wiley.com/college/kilroy.

What You'll Learn in This Chapter

This bulleted list focuses on *subject matter* that will be taught. It tells students what they will be learning in this chapter and why it is significant for their careers. It will also help students understand why the chapter is important and how it relates to other chapters in the text.

After Studying This Chapter, You'll Be Able To

This list emphasizes *capabilities and skills* students will learn as a result of reading the chapter. It prepares students to synthesize and evaluate the chapter material and relate it to the real world.

Within-Text Learning Aids

The following learning aids are designed to encourage analysis and synthesis of the material, support the learning process, and ensure success during the evaluation phase.

Introduction

This section orients the student by introducing the chapter and explaining its practical value and relevance to the book as a whole. Short summaries of chapter sections preview the topics to follow.

"For Example" Boxes

Found within most sections, these boxes tie section content to real-world organizations, scenarios, and applications.

Figures and Tables

Line art and photos have been carefully chosen to be truly instructional rather than filler. Tables distill and present information in a way that is easy to identify, access, and understand, enhancing the focus of the text on essential ideas.

Self-Check

Related to the "What You'll Learn" bullets and found at the end of each section, this battery of short-answer questions emphasizes student understanding of concepts and mastery of section content. Although the questions may be either discussed in class or studied by students outside of class, students should not go on before they can answer all questions correctly.

Key Terms and Glossary

To help students develop a professional vocabulary, key terms are bolded when they first appear in the chapter. A complete list of key terms with brief definitions appears at the end of each chapter and again in a glossary at the end of the book. Knowledge of key terms is assessed by all assessment tools (discussed later in this preface).

Summary

Each chapter concludes with a summary paragraph that reviews the major concepts in the chapter and links back to the "What You'll Learn" list.

Evaluation and Assessment Tools

The evaluation phase of the CASE Learning System consists of a variety of within-chapter and end-of-chapter assessment tools that test how well students have learned the material. These tools also encourage students to extend their learning into different scenarios and higher levels of understanding and thinking. The following assessment tools appear in every chapter of *Wiley Pathways Threats to Homeland Security: An All-Hazards Perspective*.

Summary Questions

These exercises help students summarize the chapter's main points by asking a series of multiple-choice and true/false questions that emphasize student understanding of concepts and mastery of chapter content. Students should be able to answer all of the Summary Questions correctly before moving on.

Applying This Chapter Questions

These questions drive home key ideas by asking students to synthesize and apply chapter concepts to new, real-life situations and scenarios.

You Try It Questions

Found at the end of each chapter, You Try It Questions are designed to extend students' thinking and are thus ideal for discussion or writing assignments. Using an open-ended format and sometimes based on web sources, they encourage students to draw conclusions using chapter material applied to real-world situations, which fosters both mastery and independent learning.

Post-test

The Post-test should be taken after students have completed the chapter. It includes all of the questions in the pre-test so that students can see how their learning has progressed and improved.

Instructor and Student Package

Wiley Pathways Threats to Homeland Security: An All-Hazards Perspective is available with the following teaching and learning supplements. All supplements are available online at the text's Book Companion Website, located at www.wiley.com/college/kilroy.

Instructor's Resource Guide

The Instructor's Resource Guide provides the following aids and supplements for teaching an introduction to homeland security course:

▲ **Sample syllabus:** This syllabus serves as a convenient template that instructors may use for creating their own course syllabi.

▲ **Teaching suggestions:** For each chapter, these include a chapter summary, learning objectives, definitions of key terms, lecture notes, answers to select text question sets, and at least three suggestions for classroom activities, such as ideas for speakers to invite, videos to show, and other projects.

PowerPoints

Key information is summarized in 10 to 15 PowerPoints per chapter. Instructors may use these in class or choose to share them with students for class presentations or to provide additional study support.

Test Bank

The test bank features one test per chapter, as well as a mid-term and two finals—one cumulative and one non-cumulative. Each includes true/false, multiple-choice, and open-ended questions. Answers and page references are provided for the true/false and multiple-choice questions, and page references are given for the open-ended questions. Tests are available in Microsoft Word and computerized formats.

CONTRIBUTING AUTHORS

What makes *Wiley Pathways Threats to Homeland Security: An All-Hazards Perspective* unique among the homeland security texts on the market today is the truly interdisciplinary nature of the work, based on the academic and practical experiences of the authors who contributed chapters. The authors represent diverse academic disciplines in political science, public administration, security studies, environmental health, and emergency planning. Some authors also bring practitioner experience in fields related to homeland security, such as emergency management, security management, military and homeland defense planning, and public health. The end result is a rich, educational contribution to the broader field of security studies as it currently exists today, as well as how it will evolve in the future.

▲ **Dr. Alice Anderson** is an Assistant Professor of Environmental Health and Director of the Graduate Program in the College of Health and Human Performance at East Carolina University. Her expertise is in the area of nuclear radiation effects and the effects of airborne diseases caused by vectors such as mosquitoes. She received her Ph.D. from Bowling Green State University.

▲ **Dr. Amy Blizzard** is an Assistant Professor of Planning in the Department of Geography at East Carolina University. She has taught courses in both political science and emergency planning, as well as had practical experience as an urban planner responsible for developing emergency planning procedures at the local community level. Her Ph.D. is from East Carolina University in Coastal Resource Management.

▲ **Dr. Jeannie Grussendorf** is currently a Lecturer in Political Science at Georgia State University in Atlanta. Her teaching focuses on international relations, specifically the role of international organizations and the politics of terrorism in an international context. She received her Ph.D. in Peace Studies from the University of Bradford in the United Kingdom.

▲ **Dr. Richard J. Kilroy, Jr.,** is Professor of International Studies and Political Science at the Virginia Military Institute in Lexington. Dr. Kilroy teaches courses related to security studies, national security and foreign policy, and Latin American security issues. He is also a retired Army Intelligence and Foreign Area Officer who has served in various positions planning and implementing national security policy, to include creating the Department of Defense's new U.S. Northern Command after 9/11. His Ph.D. is in Foreign Affairs from the University of Virginia.

▲ **Dr. Daniel Masters** is Assistant Professor of Political Science at the University of North Carolina at Wilmington. His area of expertise is national and international security, decision making and foreign policy, international political economy, and Middle Eastern, Russian, and European political systems. His research interests relate to terrorism and security studies, with a particular focus on rebellious collective action. He is currently authoring a text titled *Understanding Terrorist Action and Response*. His Ph.D. is from the University of Tennessee Knoxville.

▲ **Dr. Carmine Scavo** is Associate Professor of Political Science and Director of the Masters in Public Administration (MPA) program at East Carolina University. Dr. Scavo's teaching focuses on state and local politics, as well as intergovernmental relations. His most recent research focuses on the role of local community managers in responding to homeland security issues and challenges to federalism. His Ph.D. is from the University of Michigan.

▲ **Dr. John H. P. Williams** is Assistant Professor of Political Science at East Carolina University. He has taught courses related to comparative politics, foreign policy, international relations, and international studies. Dr. Williams has also served as a research analyst for the Congressional Research Service, as well as a policy analyst for other departments of the U.S. government. His Ph.D. is from the University of North Carolina.

ACKNOWLEDGMENTS

A work such as *Wiley Pathways Threats to Homeland Security: An All-Hazards Perspective* would not be possible without the collaborative efforts of all those contributors involved. Their timely submissions and quick responses to editorial comments allowed this work to come together in a relatively short period of time. A special note of appreciation is due to Dr. Dan Masters, who stepped in at the last minute to fill a critical void in the text when one of the planned contributors could not complete his chapter.

Special thanks are also due to Dr. Todd Stewart, Director of the Program for International and Homeland Security at Ohio State University, whose vision and direction launched the *Wiley Pathways* series of texts on homeland security. I also would like to thank the reviewers of the text for their comments and corrections, which made this text much more readable and more thorough in its analytical and contextual basis:

▲ Vincent Henry, Long Island University
▲ James Jernigan, Albany Technical College
▲ Lynnette Rodrigue, Clark State Community College
▲ D. Shawn Fenn, Ecology and Environment, Inc.

Finally, I wish to thank Laura Town, the overall project editor at Wiley, for her continuing support, direction, and guidance throughout this effort from start to finish. Her constant attention to detail and editorial expertise truly made this work a success, and I have learned much from her efforts.

RJK, Jr.

CONTENTS

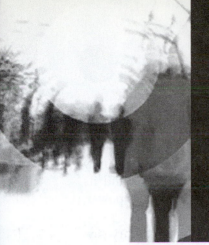

1

THE CHANGING NATURE OF NATIONAL SECURITY

Understanding the Nature of Threats and the U.S. Response

Starting Point

Go to www.wiley.com/college/kilroy to assess your knowledge of the basics of national security.

Determine where you need to concentrate your effort.

What You'll Learn in This Chapter

▲ The definition of national security
▲ The key players who formulate national security policy
▲ How changing national security environments affect national security policies
▲ Current influences in a post-9/11 world that impact national security policy issues

After Studying This Chapter, You'll Be Able To

▲ Analyze security environments and assess national security policy choices during specific historical periods
▲ Distinguish between national security policy players within government and outside government
▲ Appraise the threat situation in the post-9/11 security environment
▲ Examine U.S. national security policy as a response to the changing security environment and threat perceptions

INTRODUCTION

Throughout our nation's history, we have faced a variety of threats from adversaries possessing both capability and intent to do our nation harm. To combat these threats, various policy choices emerged, each reflecting our nation's security interests. These policies serve to protect the United States, its citizens, and its interests through the threatened and actual use of all elements of national power, and can best be understood as **national security** policies.

The security environment during the first half of the twentieth century saw the United States change from a nation with the seventeenth largest military in the world to one of two military superpowers poised to lead the free world against a new kind of threat: communism. This change was not pre-ordained, however, as strong domestic political challenges also shaped foreign policy outcomes. Fifty years after becoming a superpower, the United States again found itself in a new kind of security environment with both domestic and foreign policy implications. At this point, the nation was faced with the new threat of global terrorism.

In this chapter, you will analyze security environments and assess national security policy choices during specific historical periods. You'll also learn to distinguish between the various national security policy players both within and outside government. Finally, you'll appraise the threat situation in the post-9/11 security environment, as well as examine our nation's national security policy as a response to the changing security environment and threat perceptions.

1.1 Foundations of American Security Policy

When our nation's founders were crafting a new system of government based on a republic (versus a monarchy), they struggled over the concept of security. How much power should be vested in the central government versus the state governments? Should we have a standing army, or rely on the state militias alone for our nation's security? The **Federalist Papers** (authored by Alexander Hamilton, James Madison, and John Jay) argued the need for a central government strong enough to protect the nation against the threats it faced at the time, while also protecting states' rights and individual liberties. As James Madison noted in Federalist Paper 41, "The means of security can only be regulated by the means and danger of attack . . . They will in fact be ever determined by these rules and no others" (Hamilton, Madison, and Jay 1961:257).

Upon achieving its independence, our new nation faced the possibility of British re-invasion, attacks by other European colonial powers in the region, and challenges to commerce. Our national security policy reflected George Washington's admonition in his Farewell Address to avoid entangling alliances with European powers, which would draw us into Europe's sectarian wars. Thus, for over a century and a half, **isolationism**, a foreign policy based on avoiding alliances with other countries, produced an American national security policy of limited military force, depending instead on the ocean boundaries, diplomacy, and commerce to keep the country safe.

Prior to our entrance into World War I, U.S. security interests were primarily focused regionally, rather than globally. An example of a security policy reflecting this regional focus was the **Monroe Doctrine** of 1823. Although the United States did not have the military might to back up such a policy, the Monroe Doctrine expressed the principle that the United States should support the desire of the new democratic nations of the Americas to break from their colonial past and exist as free nations, secure from overt European influence. This principle was tested throughout the nineteenth century by various European powers, such as the French occupation of Mexico and the continuing Spanish and British presence, primarily in the Caribbean region. With the U.S. military defeat of the Spanish in 1898, however, the United States displayed the capacity to live up to its principles.

Why did the United States enter these new domains? For most of America's early history, security meant maintaining territorial integrity, but it also involved protecting American trade overseas. As the United States grew economically, so did other countries, and American traders found themselves clashing more frequently with foreign interests over resources and markets. The clashes could be simply commercial competition, but violence could break out with local populations, other commercial enterprises, or governments. Trade was enriching the country, but also redefining the government's duty to protect American citizens to include events that were increasing in both scope and frequency.

1.1.1 Geopolitics at the Beginning of the Twentieth Century

The emergence of American military power (primarily sea power) at the beginning of the twentieth century expanded U.S. national security interests beyond the Western Hemisphere. The capability of the United States to project military power to other regions further increased our nation's capacity to leverage other elements of national power, including the use of diplomacy, economic power, and informational power. The threat of military force therefore broadened the expression of national security interests, leading to a more expansionist role for the United States. Broadening the context of national security further affected U.S. foreign policy interests toward Europe and European affairs. Whereas in the past the United States was comfortable in its isolationist role, in the early 1900s, the changes in the geopolitical make-up of Europe were directly affecting America's security at home.

The causes for World War I were complex, reflecting imperial competition, the rise of industrial economies, the decline of the aristocracy, and the rise of nationalism, anarchism, and communism. Powerful political ideas and movements swept across the European continent, creating conditions for conflict and war. Although Woodrow Wilson ran for re-election in 1916 on the campaign slogan "He kept us out of war," by 1917, he came to the realization that America's security required the United States to join with the **Entente Powers** (mainly France, Russia, Britain, and Italy) against the **Central Powers** (Germany, Austria-Hungary, the Ottoman Empire, and Bulgaria). A German submarine's sinking of the *Lusitania*, an American ship loaded with supplies for Britain, underscored America's inability to cut itself off from countries at war. As Wilson noted, "I made every effort to keep my country out of war, until it came to my conscience, as it came to yours, that after all it was our war a well as Europe's war, that the ambition of these central empires was directed against nothing less than the liberty of the world" (Foley 1969, 12).

World War I completely changed the geopolitical landscape of Europe as empires were dissolved and new nation-states emerged. Wilson pressured the European powers to accept his famous 14 points, which called for **collective security** based on international responses to aggression. This laid the foundation for the League of Nations, the precursor to the United Nations. In effect, Wilson was redefining national security policy from one based on neutrality to one based on continuing international cooperation. The U.S. Senate refused to ratify the resulting treaty, however, and America retreated back to a period of isolationism and avoidance of European affairs. In addition, partly because of American reluctance, but also because of the difficulty of constraining major powers, the League of Nations ultimately failed.

Also after World War I, the United States used naval disarmament as a means to increase international security, without having to enter into a collective security arrangement. Navies allowed the projection of power at that time, so limiting naval power also limited military potential. Proposed as an alternative to the League of Nations, Republicans in the U.S. Senate promoted the Washington Naval Conference (1921–1922), limiting the size and growth of the world's major naval powers: the United States, Great Britain, France, Japan, and Italy. The treaty, however, delayed rather than ended such arms races.

In the 1930s, Congress engaged in another effort to promote isolationism by way of the **Neutrality Acts**, which were laws forbidding American support for or involvement with countries at war. Under these laws, the *Lusitania* might never have been sunk because it could not have carried supplies to Britain or even entered British ports. As a security issue, the laws represented a major challenge to presidential power because they restricted the flexibility the president enjoys as commander-in-chief and as the chief architect of U.S. foreign policy.

Between wars, ocean barriers and relatively secure borders continued to provide security for the United States. Canada to the north was a proven ally, requiring a minimal security presence. To the south, however, Mexico was emerging from a bitter civil war and internal revolution. In fact, before the U.S. entry into World

War I, the Mexican revolutionary Pancho Villa staged a series of attacks into the United States, the most famous being the Columbus, New Mexico, raid of March 19, 1916. This led to the legendary Pershing Expedition into Mexico in pursuit of Villa, and it also included a mobilization of a number of National Guard units to the border to provide security. The Expedition ended in 1917 with U.S. entry into World War I and diplomatic efforts between the American and Mexican governments to avoid further conflict. By the end of World War I, the Mexican revolution had moved toward stabilization under a new regime, which would eventually emerge as Mexico's dominant political party for the next 70 years.

Immediately prior to the start of World War II, the United States began aggressively developing its air and naval capabilities, allowing it to be able to project power where and when necessary. The United States also expanded its military overseas presence in places like the Philippines, Cuba, Panama, Puerto Rico, the Midway Islands, and the Hawaiian Islands. Set up as strategic coaling stations, naval bases at these locations provided the United States forward presence in areas it deemed to have strategic interests. At the same time, Britain and France, still suffering "war weariness," were attempting to pull back from some of their overseas commitments and colonial holdings, leaving power vacuums that were quickly filled by Japan, Italy, and Germany, the countries that would be known as the **Axis Powers** during World War II.

1.1.2 National Security and World War II

World War II began in 1939 with the German invasion of Poland, followed by declarations of war by Britain and France. The United States did not officially enter the conflict until 1941, following Japan's surprise attack on Pearl Harbor. By its end in 1945, World War II had inflicted over 62 million casualties from at least 50 countries. Major operational campaigns occurred in the Atlantic and Pacific theaters, as well as throughout Europe, Eastern Europe and Russia, Asia, China, Africa, and the Middle East. British and German vessels even fought near the tip of South America. The shear magnitude of the conflict impacted people and nations throughout the world such that security took on new meaning for different nations. For the United States, it meant that our nation would never again be able to return to an isolationist foreign policy and our security would be directly linked to that of Europe, Asia, and other regions of the world.

As previously mentioned, from 1939 to 1941, the United States maintained its neutrality with regard to World War II, despite Winston Churchill's pleas for a formal alliance with Britain. America demonstrated this neutrality by avoiding direct conflict, preferring to support the Allies through other means. For example, Franklin Roosevelt's lend/lease program provided Britain with essential war materials to continue military operations against Germany, even though this policy contravened the Neutrality Acts. This security strategy further provided for **prepositioning**, or establishing bases and supplies in foreign countries to prepare a rapid response to future crises, anticipating the time when the United States would eventually join the conflict. For Roosevelt, the United States was the "arsenal of democracy," and it was only a matter of time before the United States would become directly involved in another land war in Europe, given the expanding German threat. Domestic public opinion was mixed, however, as was that of Congress, given the large numbers of German and Italian immigrants in the United States. In fact, until the attack on Pearl Harbor, 64 percent of the American public still thought peace was possible without U.S. intervention. Some revisionist historians argue that knowing this, Roosevelt provoked a Japanese attack to force Congress to declare war against Japan and the Axis Powers (e.g., see Williams 1978). According to this argument, Roosevelt could then support Winston Churchill's "Germany first" strategy to save Europe before opposing the Japanese in Asia. These views are clearly in the minority, however, as most recognized military historians clearly place the blame on Japan for its preemptive strike at the U.S. Pacific fleet, in order to reduce resistance to Japan's imperial strategy to conquer southeast Asia. Roosevelt and his top military advisor, General George C. Marshall, both supported the "Germany first" war plans, recognizing the immediate need for American military intervention in the European theater of operations. Roosevelt, exercising his prerogative as commander-in-chief, set the nation's strategic policies, ordering the military to begin combat operations in North Africa rather than plan for a direct attack on France. Codenamed Operation Torch, this campaign began in November 1942, signaling the beginning of American offensive efforts in the war (Brower 2002).

During World War II, Roosevelt and his successor Harry Truman left the operational wartime decision making to their military commanders. In the European theater, General Dwight D. Eisenhower commanded U.S. and Allied military forces in North Africa, the Italian peninsula campaigns, the crossing of the English Channel on D-Day (June 6, 1944), and forward to Berlin. Eisenhower, as the Supreme Allied Commander, determined security policy during the war in Europe, as did General Douglas MacArthur and Admiral Chester Nimitz in the Pacific. The Army Chief of Staff, General George Marshall, served as the Chairman of the Joint Chiefs of Staff and was the president's principal military advisor at the time. He did not command forces, nor did he set operational policy decisions. Rather, the president and the Secretaries of War and the Navy set strategic security policies, which the military leaders then executed. Only later, during Korean War in the 1950s, when MacArthur challenged Truman's authority by questioning his strategic policies, did the president exercise his role as commander-in-chief to remove MacArthur from command.

U.S. national security policy during World War II was, first and foremost, the defeat of the Axis Powers, Germany and Italy first and then Japan. America applied all elements of its national power to that end. Even domestic politics took a

FOR EXAMPLE

Japanese Internment Camps

During World War II, the United States government took the action of interring Japanese Americans from the West Coast in War Relocation Centers located away from the coastal areas in the west. Over 120,000 men, women, and children were sent to the Centers. Over two-thirds of them were U.S. citizens. President Roosevelt justified the action based on the threat of Japanese spies operating in those communities. The Supreme Court upheld Roosevelt's actions, stating that ethnic groups could be interned during a state of war because "[p]ressing public necessity may sometimes justify the existence of such restrictions" (*Korematsu v. United States* 1944). What is not as well known is that smaller groups of Italians and Germans living in the United States were also interred during the war, classified as "enemy aliens" (Siasico and Ross 2006).

backseat to foreign policy, as every American accepted the sacrifices required of a nation at war, to include certain deprivations of goods and services in support of the war effort. The largest domestic economic impact was the retooling of our industrial base from a consumer-based economy to a war-based economy, as America leveraged its economic and military power to achieve its national security objectives. The American public responded by investing in their country (buying war bonds), working in the factories (women joined assembly lines in record numbers), and collecting salvageable materials (children led collection efforts for scrap iron, rubber, and other items). During World War II, whether they were fighting the war in Europe, the Pacific, or the home front, most Americans felt they were directly contributing to the security goal of defeating our enemies. However, some groups, such as Japanese Americans, were not allowed to help due to fears over their true sense of loyalty to America versus Japan, and thus they were subjected to isolation in special camps during the war.

World War II ended in 1945 with the surrender of Germany, followed by Japan's surrender after the dropping of nuclear bombs on Hiroshima and Nagasaki. The decision to use nuclear weapons for the first time was made by President Truman, knowing that short of a U.S. invasion of the Japanese mainland, the war in the Pacific could drag out for years. Rather than accept the larger loss of American and Japanese lives from such a protracted conflict, Truman's use of this new technology was as much psychological as it was physical. Due to the magnitude of the destruction caused by nuclear weapons, the world was about to enter a new stage of both security and insecurity, as other nations sought to come under the nuclear umbrella and avoid conflict for fear it would escalate into global nuclear warfare.

SELF-CHECK

1. Define national security.

2. Which of the following was not one of the Central Powers during World War I?

   a. Germany
   b. Austria-Hungary
   c. Russia
   d. Bulgaria

3. Italy was not one of the Axis Powers during World War II. True or false?

4. The League of Nations would have replaced a collective security policy with one based on neutrality. True or false?

1.2 Security in the Cold War Era

At the end of World War II, the United States emerged as the strongest military and economic power in the world by virtue of having avoided the direct impact of the war, with the exception of the attack on Pearl Harbor. Most of Europe lay in ruins, however, as did much of Japan. Working with Great Britain and other countries, the United States created the **United Nations (UN)** and, through the **Bretton Woods Agreements**, key economic institutions that were intended to promote political and economic stability throughout the international system, including Europe and Japan. Believing the causes of World War II lay in political, economic, and social instability created by World War I, planners in 1945 sought to prevent the recurrence of those conditions.

Despite agreements made at Yalta between Stalin, Roosevelt, and Churchill, the Soviets moved quickly to fill the geopolitical vacuum of German defeat by occupying those countries they "liberated" during the war. The United States countered the Soviets by seeking to restore a balance of power to Europe through the combination of a continued U.S. military presence in the region, as well as a large amount of direct economic aid to rebuild Europe. Conceived by U.S. Secretary of State George C. Marshall, the **Marshall Plan** provided funds supplied by the United States to help rebuild non-Communist countries after World War II. The Plan provided means for Germany, in particular, to recover from the devastation of World War II and emerge later as an ally in the Cold War.

Initially, President Truman assumed that Stalin, like most political leaders, was a pragmatist and that Soviet security policy would be motivated by a quid pro quo. Truman expected that Stalin would be willing to negotiate (horse trading, as Truman called it), assuming that Soviet behavior could be modified. However, George Kennan, a U.S. government official stationed in Moscow, published works explaining the source of Soviet behavior toward the West and challenging Truman's perception. Kennan argued that the Soviets were not willing to work with the United States and other Western nations to share power. Rather, the Soviet goal was to destroy the West, and the only rational U.S. security policy was one that stood up to Soviet aggression, willing to match force with force if necessary. Whether we liked it or not, America would take on a leadership role in setting the international security agenda, as well as in committing the resources necessary to serve as global guarantor of a new world order. Thus began the period that would come to be known as the Cold War.

FOR EXAMPLE

Mr. X and Containment

George F. Kennan was a U.S. Department of State official who was convinced that the Soviets viewed accommodation with the United States and other Western powers as a weakness and contradictory to their goal of expanding international communism. Kennan sought to communicate his views about the true nature of Soviet ambitions through what became known as his "Long Telegram" back to the State Department. In this official document, Kennan laid out the reasons why the United States needed to take a hard-line strategy toward Moscow and Soviet expansionism.

This official document became public in 1947 when it was published in an article titled "The Sources of Soviet Conduct" in *Foreign Affairs*. The author was called "Mr. X," but experts knew it to be the work of George Kennan. In this article, Kennan explained the motivations behind Soviet behavior in foreign affairs. He argued that the Soviet state was totalitarian in its political structures as well as its ruling ideology, communism. Kennan believed communism to be antithetical to the West and a direct challenge to our nation's democratic principles, free-market capitalist economy, and cultural and spiritual beliefs. He warned that the United States should not regard the Soviets as partners in managing international security, but rather as competitors, always seeking an advantage on the world stage. As Kennan stated, "In these circumstances, it is clear that the main element of any United States policy toward the Soviet Union must be that of long-term, patient but firm and vigilant containment of Russian expansive tendencies." The key word **containment** signified the principal national security policy pursued during the Cold War to prevent the spread of communism and Soviet influence throughout the world (History Guide n.d.).

1.2.1 Bipolarity vs. Multipolarity

Prior to World War II, the international security environment could be characterized as a **multipolar system**, a relationship among countries in the international system where no country dominated, with a number of nation-states (primarily European) possessing military power and capable of acting independently. Hans Morganthau (1978) characterized this system as a balance of power, where nations sought to maximize power either through alliances to compensate for weaknesses or through unilateral means when they perceived it be in their national interest to do so. Morganthau believed that a multipolar system allowed for greater flexibility for nations, who could change alliances as necessary to maximize their power and security.

After World War II, the old vestiges of the European balance of power, based on a multipolar system, disappeared, as two new spheres of military power and influence emerged: the United States and the Union of Soviet Socialist Republics (USSR). Because both powers emerged as victors after World War II, each sought to consolidate its influence over parts of Europe, as well as former European colonial interests. The new security environment that developed was therefore characterized as a **bipolar system**, with other nation-states tending to align themselves with either the United States or the USSR. Those supporting the United States were primarily Western European nations, while Eastern European countries came under the influence of the USSR, mostly by force. Those in the U.S. camp came to be called the First World or Free World nations, while those in the USSR camp came to be called the Second World or Communist-bloc states (see Figure 1-1).

George Kennan's notion of containment was a strategy for handling the bipolar system. Other possible strategies ranged from returning to isolation to initiating total war, where all national resources would be employed to destroy the Soviets. Containing Soviet expansion would be a long-term policy and would be very expensive, but it seemed the best way of pressuring the Soviets while minimizing costs at home. The array of threats included conventional and nuclear war in Europe, direct attacks with nuclear weapons on the United States and the USSR, proxy wars where the two major powers supported competing sides in wars of national liberation, and also espionage and subversion in the two countries.

To manage this bewildering array of threats, Congress passed the National Security Act in 1947. This act turned the Army Air Corps into the U.S. Air Force and merged the War Department and Navy Department, creating the Department of Defense. The act also created a civilian organization, the Central Intelligence Agency (CIA), to manage overseas intelligence gathering and clandestine and covert operations against foreign governments. The Department of Justice's Federal Bureau of Investigation (FBI) received responsibility for domestic counterintelligence. Several influences drove the effort: the new Soviet threat; the intelligence failure that had permitted the attack on Pearl Harbor; and concerns about

Figure 1-1

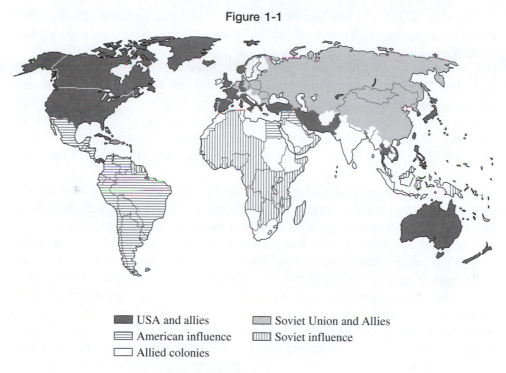

USA and allies
American influence
Allied colonies

Soviet Union and Allies
Soviet influence

The global context of the Cold War in 1959 (White 2003, by permission).

Communist groups operating inside the United States. Finally, some argue that the act was created to reduce turf wars between the Army and Navy.

The primary international security structures that emerged after World War II reflected the interests of these two power blocs representing the bipolar system. To counter the overwhelming conventional military force build-up by the Soviets in Eastern Europe, the United States led the development of the North Atlantic Treaty Organization (NATO) in 1949. This collective security organization was first and foremost a military alliance, with each member nation pledging that an attack on any one of them would bring the collective response of all member nations. The original 12 members of NATO were Belgium, Canada, Denmark, France, Iceland, Italy, Luxembourg, the Netherlands, Norway, Portugal, the United Kingdom, and the United States. Between 1949 and the end of the Cold War in 1991, four other nations would also be admitted to NATO: Greece, Turkey, Germany, and Spain. These 16 nations, led by the United States, comprised the "West" and its military response to the "East," which was led by the USSR. In response to the formation of NATO, the Soviets sought to counter the collective military powers of the West by forming the Warsaw Pact in 1955, composed of Albania, Bulgaria, Czechoslovakia, East Germany, Hungary, Poland, Romania, and the Soviet Union.

Besides NATO and the Warsaw Pact, other regional security alliances also formed during the Cold War, including the Australia, New Zealand, United States Defense Pact (ANZUS), the Southeast Asia Treaty Organization (SEATO), and Organization of American States (OAS). Other Communist countries, such as Cuba, North Korea, and the People's Republic of China (PRC), were also considered to be in the Soviet sphere of influence, but they did not enter into formal alliances such as occurred with those nations under the U.S. sphere of influence. Most third-world countries were faced with a stark choice of association with one or the other superpower, dividing most of the world into two competing camps.

This change from multipolarity to bipolarity was a significant shift in the way international politics worked. The balance of power system described by Morganthau, where countries would make alliances to prevent any one country from gaining too much power, had broken down during World War I. Wilson's idea of collective security, mentioned previously, would have had every country unite against aggression, replacing the balance of power system. Without this system, however, bipolarity arose in the absence of multipolarity. Bipolarity was based on two competing groups of countries, or "blocs." Competition became what the Soviets called managing the **correlation of forces**, a measure of comparative military power of member nations (see Table 1-1), where the two blocs were locked in combat like two wrestlers grappling. Over time, some countries might move from one bloc to the other, changing relative power, until one side had a clear advantage. Throughout this period of Cold War competition, the U.S. and USSR spent lavishly on weapons and political influence to ensure their own success.

Eventually, the bipolar system broke down, not from the direct tensions between the superpowers, but from the internal fragmentation of the two power blocs. The most important changes emerged in the 1960s when France left NATO, and the Peoples' Republic of China (PRC) quarreled with the Soviets. In the latter instance, the two nations fought a low-level border war in the early 1970s. President Nixon visited the PRC around that time, and the resulting relationships moved closer to the shifting patterns of the earlier multipolar system.

1.2.2 Containing Communism

During the Cold War era, Kennan's view of the Soviet Union was essentially correct, but managing the threats posed by the USSR proved difficult. This section examines the different threats mentioned above and subsequent responses. Keep in mind that the choices were highly politicized, reflecting concerns about the desirability of peace and war, and also how best to allocate defense dollars.

Table 1-1: Approximations of NATO vs. Warsaw Pact Military Power—Contrasting Views

	Warsaw Pact Count	*NATO Count*
Tanks		
Warsaw Pact	59,000	52,000
NATO	31,000	16,000
Armored Personnel Carriers		
Warsaw Pact	70,000	55,000
NATO	47,000	23,000
Artillery Systems		
Warsaw Pact	72,000	43,000
NATO	57,000	14,000
Combat Aircraft		
Warsaw Pact	7,900	8,200
NATO	7,100	4,000
Helicopters		
Warsaw Pact	2,800	3,700
NATO	5,300	2,400
Ground Forces		
Warsaw Pact	3,600,000	3,100,000
NATO	3,700,000	2,200,000

(*Source: Soviet Military Power 1989, 99*)

Conventional and Nuclear War in Europe

When tensions with the Soviets began, planners presumed that war would be fought in Germany and surrounding areas. Some planners wanted American forces to be limited, acting as a trigger for nuclear war, while others wanted NATO forces to be adequate for defeating a Soviet invasion. Compromises led to forward-basing substantial amounts of supplies, along with over one million American personnel. Included in this force was a substantial collection of short- and medium-range nuclear weapons, and the order of battle was reorganized for fighting on a nuclear battlefield.

An important part of planning for security was that if America should be fighting a war in Europe, it might be seen by other opponents as an opportunity to attack elsewhere. Just as World War II was fought in several theaters simultaneously, America needed to prepare for similar conditions in the future.

Some of these forces remain in Europe today, available for assignment elsewhere. Their numbers were drawn down over time, and their equipment and munitions were redirected for conflicts elsewhere, including Vietnam and Iraq. In one of the last major threats of the Cold War, the Soviets began basing intermediate-range (1,000 miles) missiles in the early 1980s. American intentions to counter with similar missiles produced a treaty to eliminate these weapons from Europe. This part of the Cold War was finally winding down.

Nuclear Threats to the United States and USSR

In 1945, the United States was the only country with nuclear weapons, but Soviet spies managed to steal the technology. Thus, by the middle of the 1950s, both countries had hydrogen bombs, also known as thermonuclear weapons. The only long-range delivery platforms, though, were bomber aircraft. Suddenly, however, in 1957, the Soviets orbited a satellite, Sputnik, meaning that they had missile technology that would allow an attack on the United States without the use of airplanes. The United States thus developed a nuclear triad, composed of long-range strategic bombers, intercontinental ballistic missiles, and submarines, all of which were capable of delivering nuclear warheads. The U.S. nuclear strategy leveraged technology, increasing its nuclear weapons capability with improved accuracy in striking targets (referred to as reducing the **circular error of probability** or **CEP**) and also the use of **multiple independently targeted reentry vehicles (MIRVs)**, which allowed missiles to have more than one warhead. The Soviets relied more on "throw weight," using a brute force strategy—in other words, the more warheads the better, with accuracy not being as important.

Throughout the Cold War, there was always concern on both sides over how accurate each nation's intelligence assessments were with regard to actual nuclear weapons counts and capabilities. As a result, on two occasions, the two **superpowers**, the United States and USSR, came close to actual nuclear war. In the first instance, during the Cuban missile crisis in October 1962, the Soviets tried to base short-range missiles in Cuba. For many years, it was thought that the United States had forced the Soviets to back down. It has recently been discovered that the crisis was resolved by a quid pro quo of American missiles being removed from Turkey. The second occasion was during the Arab-Israeli War of 1973.

It's important to note that the possibility of nuclear war was the first major direct threat to the United States in decades. Further, it augmented the civil defense planning that began during World War II, which required the creation

of shelters and food stocks for emergencies. Further, the arms race and conse-
quent intelligence-gathering efforts produced dramatic technological advances,
changing perceptions about war and war fighting by adding satellite imagery,
computer analysis, and advanced communications to the mix.

Nuclear war, however, is for many people the worst form of a bad business.
Americans became divided over whether someone could in good conscience use
such weapons, and they pressed for actions through the United Nations (UN)
instead of relying on power politics. Others argued with equal fervor that as long
as someone else had such weapons, the United States must have them as well.
Such fears among the five countries that had nuclear weapons in the 1960s
produced treaties to limit **proliferation**, or the supplying of other countries with
the technology to build their own nuclear weapons. Eventually, using a policy
called **détente** (a relaxation of tensions), the Nixon administration began negotiating treaties that would slow the arms race, and subsequent administrations
would negotiate actual reductions in nuclear weapons. President Reagan achieved
great success in negotiation through a two-track approach. On one side, he
negotiated aggressively, calling for dramatic reductions in stockpiles of nuclear
weapons. On the other, he pressed for advanced technology, including the Strategic Defense Initiative (SDI). Also known as Star Wars, the SDI relied on the
use of ground- and space-based systems to protect the United States from attack
by nuclear missiles. In light of these actions, the Soviets could either negotiate
or face economic failure by trying to keep up with American efforts.

Proxy Wars

The United States and the Soviet Union never actually fought each other during
the 45 years of the Cold War. Military advisors, money, and equipment were
delivered far and wide, however. For instance, the Soviets and the Peoples'
Republic of China supported North Korea's invasion of South Korea, and Cubans
advised in Angola and Central and South America. For a time, Americans were
in Ethiopia and Russians were in Somalia, until civil wars in those countries
caused the two to switch sides. The last major anti-communist operation was in
the island of Grenada, which was being used as a staging area for supplies for
insurgents.

During the Cold War era, the largest commitment of American forces was
in Vietnam, where the conflict dragged on for over ten years, from the Kennedy
administration into the second Nixon administration. Eventually, domestic opposition forced American withdrawal. The Soviets ran into similar problems later
in the 1970s when they invaded Afghanistan, encouraging the rise of radical
Islamic groups, such as al-Qaeda and the Taliban. In fact, when the Soviet Union
collapsed in 1991, a contributing factor was the money spent on such foreign
adventures. Such proxy wars also had profound effects on U.S. domestic politics,
forcing the end of the draft and the move to an all-volunteer military, and

additionally contributing to reluctance among some Americans to engage in overseas operations. Despite this tendency, both Republican and Democratic presidents continued to commit troops overseas.

The proxy wars added a new layer of responsibility for military planners. Now, not only did they need to plan for conventional and nuclear wars, but they were also required to create doctrine to manage low-intensity conflict, counterinsurgency, and circumstances calling for rapid troop deployments. The Green Berets, for example, were created not simply to fight an unconventional war, but to organize local populations against a common enemy.

Espionage and Subversion During the Cold War

The Cold War created difficult times for managing domestic security, as political and normative goals clashed with the needs of security. The Soviet Union operated an active program of spying and subversion in the United States, and the FBI replied with an intense counter-espionage program. In the late 1940s and early 1950s, Alger Hiss and other government officials were convicted of spying for the Soviets. Senator Joseph McCarthy held hearings to investigate how Soviet spies were able to penetrate so deeply into government during the 1950s, and he also pursued subversives in the media and government. Eventually, important political actors concluded that McCarthy was going too far and was ignoring constitutionally guaranteed rights for the accused, and they forced McCarthy to back down. This debate between individual rights and national security remains a hotly contested topic to this day.

As the Cold War continued, the CIA and the Defense Intelligence Agency (DIA) were joined by additional specialized agencies, such as the National Security Agency, which monitors radio and other communications. During the 1960s, these agencies had a fairly free hand in pursuing intelligence problems. In the 1970s, however, Congress set up the Church Commission to draw up rules restraining the intelligence community. According to this commission, **clandestine and covert operations** would require written presidential approval in the future. Although some people use these terms interchangeably, clandestine operations are secret efforts to gather information; covert operations are intended to influence how governments behave. Covert operations could include bribes, subversion and psychological operations, and support for insurgent forces, with the intent not to reveal the source of the operation.

Finally, while the United States was dealing with spies, Europe was struggling with bands of terrorists, such as the Baader-Meinhoff gang and the Red Brigades, operating independently of the Soviet Union. The Weathermen, Symbionese Liberation Army (SLA), Black Panthers, and other extremist groups began plotting terrorist activities in the United States as well. Cooperation between American and European intelligence and police forces became a critical effort for addressing these problems.

1.2.3 Non-Communist Threats

International communism presented the greatest, but by no means the only, threat to the United States during the Cold War. The U.S. government preferred, however, to focus on the major threat, hoping that the others would remain minor problems. Nonetheless, wars of national liberation and revolutions in the developing world drew resources away from the main problem, as did frequent conflicts about religion and territory in the Middle East. Conflicts betweens Arabs and Israelis broke out four times between 1948 and 1973; these conflicts were as much about who controlled Palestine as what religion should be followed. The Carter administration withdrew support for the Shah of Iran in 1978, a move that resulted in Iran being taken over by religious extremists. A group of students seized the U.S. embassy in that country late in 1979, creating the famous Iran hostage crisis. American efforts at negotiation and at rescue failed, though the hostages were released at the beginning of the Reagan administration. These problems caused the government to again rethink how to manage special operations and rapid deployment.

During the 1980s, efforts at projecting power met with mixed success. American intervention in Lebanon in the early 1980s failed after the bombing of the U.S. Marine barracks in Beirut. A terrorist attack on a night club in Berlin was found to have been planned by Libya; President Reagan retaliated by bombing many targets in Libya (called Operation El Dorado Canyon), eliminating Libya's military potential (but not its support for terrorism) for years to come. These and other attacks reflected state-sponsored terrorism, where governments encouraged extremists. An increasing problem, however, were the radical Islamists, consisting of the Moslem Brotherhood in Egypt and the Wahabbists in Saudi Arabia, both of which were factions from the majority Sunni sect of Islam, as well as the followers of the Ayatollah Khomeini in Iran, who are part of the Shiite minority. Osama bin Laden and al-Qaeda come from the Wahabbist movement. They favor efforts to drive Western influences from the Middle East and to replace existing Middle Eastern governments with newer, more radical ones.

Two points are important here. First, although many problems occurred in the Middle East during this time, they were not specifically problems with Islam. Second, although the cases listed here involved conflict, there were also extensive efforts to encourage peaceful resolution to problems. For example, the Camp David Accords of 1979 settled conflict between Israel and Egypt and established a long-term relationship between the United States and Egypt. Although problems with groups and governments in the Middle East were present, those groups and governments did not represent a monolithic threat. However, the Islamic Revolution in Iran in 1979, and the subsequent rise of the Ayatollah Khomeini, did usher in a new era of state-sponsorship of terrorism, with the rise of Hezbollah, Islamic Jihad, and other groups espousing radical Islamic ideologies that have both regional and global impact today.

SELF-CHECK

1. Define balance of power politics.
2. The principal national security policy pursued during the Cold War was called:

   a. containment.
   b. isolationism.
   c. expansionism.
   d. unilateralism.

3. Covert operations seek to cover their sources. True or false?
4. Terrorism is a product only of religious extremism. True or false?

1.3 Security in the Post–Cold War Era, Pre-9/11

The government of the Soviet Union collapsed in 1991, when a coup by communist hard-liners failed. The Soviet economic relationship with Eastern Europe had already been abandoned, and the leader of the new democratic government, Boris Yeltsin, moved quickly to turn the old USSR into the Commonwealth of Independent States (CIS), relieving the Russian Republic of responsibility for governing the Ukraine, Belarus, and other parts of the federal (soviet) union. The Cold War was over, and for a brief moment, some scholars argued that the world had become a **unipolar system** characterized by one superpower—in this case, the United States.

This milestone in history complicated, rather than reduced, the national security debate. Some people foresaw an end to conflict and a "peace dividend" from the reduced need for major weapon systems and a large standing army. Americans could come home. Others argued that the UN would take on a greater role in sustaining world peace, and it would need American and NATO support. Some of these people suggested that NATO's mission, the defense of Europe, should be redefined to engage in worldwide humanitarian assistance. Still others argued that economic globalization would bind together the commercial interests of the entire world, so that the United States would still be heavily involved in world affairs, but not as a military power.

1.3.1 Changing Threats

During the 1990s, most of the old threats from superpower tensions were dramatically reduced or eliminated. New regional organizations had been established to settle conventional disputes in Europe, and NATO was negotiating with former Soviet bloc countries about joining the organization. The United States and the Soviet Union had signed agreements that dramatically reduced their nuclear arsenals. The proxy wars were now simply local and regional conflicts rather than extensions of Soviet and American policy. Espionage remained an issue, but it was the Peoples' Republic of China, rather than the Russia, that was to attract the most frequent complaints.

Non-Communist threats remained, however, and were growing in scope. A number of minor powers sought weapons of mass destruction (WMDs), which included chemical, biological, radiological, nuclear, and explosive (CBRNE) weapons. Such weapons would give them an advantage in regional power struggles and could possibly deter the United States and other powers from threatening them. The availability of these weapons could also make terrorist groups more dangerous, so monitoring was enhanced. In 1998, for example, India and Pakistan both tested nuclear devices, attracting severe criticism from the rest of the world. Likewise, intelligence gathered by several countries indicated that during the 1990s, Iraq, Iran, and North Korea were producing an array of WMDs as well as developing missiles to carry them.

During this period, the intelligence community suffered from certain organizational shortcomings that undermined broad cooperation, so it was fortunate that terrorist groups were unable to acquire WMDs. However, terrorist attacks using conventional explosives and methods on the World Trade Center in 1993, the attacks on American embassies in Tanzania and in Kenya in 1998, the Khobar Towers apartment complex bombing in Saudi Arabia in 1998, and the attack on the USS Cole in 2000 were indications of a growing problem. An attack by homegrown terrorists on a federal office building in Oklahoma and the use of poison gas on the Tokyo subway by Aum Shinrikyo further indicated that it was not just Islam that was the source of extremist threats.

1.3.2 New Conflicts, New Responses

As noted earlier in this chapter, there were many competing perceptions of the proper foundations for American security planning during the post–Cold War, pre-9/11 era. These included joint efforts with the UN and other international organizations, a general reduction of American involvement overseas, and ad hoc coalitions to address specific problems. In choosing a strategy, our government needed to consider domestic concerns, the interests of our allies, and the perspectives of our opponents. Thus, planners needed to consider how a given action might affect voters in Illinois, government officials in Beijing and London, Muslims in Cairo, dictators in Iraq, and insurgents in Colombia. The end of the Cold War made these opinions loom in importance, as the Soviet threat had previously provided an excuse for setting many of these issues aside.

The first test of this situation occurred in 1990, when Iraq invaded Kuwait. Through the UN Security Council, the first President Bush organized an international coalition to drive the Iraqis out of Kuwait. This intervention became only the second instance of the UN using its enforcement powers against an aggressor, the first having been the response to North Korea in the 1950s.

From this point onward, the performance of international coalitions became more erratic. In 1992, American forces joined a UN effort to provide emergency food relief in Somalia. In 1994, fighting in Rwanda turned into genocide, or widespread politically motivated murder, but the United States refused to become involved in or to push for UN intervention in what it thought to be no more than civil war. Despite increasing evidence of genocide, which would eventually leave over 800,000 people dead, governments and key UN officials including Secretary General Kofi Annan sided with the U.S. position. Stung by criticisms of this inaction, in 1995, the United States participated in a UN intervention to stop violence in the breakaway Republic of Bosnia, where Muslims and ethnic Croatians fought Bosnia Serbs who were being supported by the army of the Former Republic of Yugoslavia (now Serbia-Montenegro). American efforts produced the Dayton Accords, a compromise between competing sides that at least stabilized circumstances. Interventions in a political crisis in Haiti in 1995 and against ethnic cleansing in the Serbian province of Kosovo in 1999 were added to the array of interventions. The last began as a UN response to the crisis, but it eventually became a NATO operation.

FOR EXAMPLE

U.S. Intervention in Somalia

As a result of civil war in the early 1990s, over 350,000 Somalis had died and over 1.5 million faced starvation. In December 1992, at the end of his administration, President George H.W. Bush committed 28,000 U.S. military forces to the humanitarian mission to "stop the dying" in Somalia by aiding in relief efforts. However, as a result of the security environment in the country and attacks by armed militia groups, which impeded the mission, the U.S. military took more offensive actions against Somali warlords by attempting to disarm them and capture key leaders, such as Mohammed Farah Aideed. In one military operation, made famous by the movie *Black Hawk Down,* U.S. military forces were caught in a firefight with the Somalia militias, resulting in the deaths of 18 U.S. Rangers and other Special Operations forces flying support missions. French television crews showed one dead U.S. Ranger being dragged naked through the streets of Mogadishu. The impact of those images on the American public eventually caused the Clinton administration to pull U.S. military forces out of Somalia and turn over the mission to a United Nations force. It also contributed to the reluctance of the United States to respond with a military intervention to the genocide that occurred in Rwanda in 1994.

On a positive note, some problems were dramatically reduced during this time. The United States negotiated a trade deal with Mexico and Canada called the North American Free Trade Agreement (NAFTA). Other Central and South American countries began promoting free trade and democratic government as well. Countries were adopting American practices to promote mutually beneficial exchange and general prosperity. Instead of shipping weapons, countries were shipping automobile components. Although drug trafficking and internal violence remained problems in some countries, the future looked promising.

1.3.3 Reorganization of National Security Policy

The reorganization of American security policy that took place during the 1990s actually began in the closing days of the Cold War. Many important changes sprang from the legal reviews required by the Senate Church Commission and also from the 1986 Defense Reorganization Act, also known as the Goldwater-Nichols Act after its two Congressional sponsors. The earlier National Security Act of 1947 had not ended the political competition between the branches of the military, which became evident during the failed hostage rescue attempt in Iran in 1980 as well as military operations against Grenada in 1983. The new Act required systematic joint planning efforts, including a Joint Strategic Planning System, to augment existing defense planning and contingency planning programs. It also required a quadrennial defense review process and eventually led to the establishment of the U.S. Special Operations Command.

A more important change was the requirement for a National Security Strategy (NSS) that would describe strategic concerns to reconcile planning for current and future threats. When the Cold War ended, Congress wanted to know what threats remained, and what the priorities were. The Reagan, Bush, and Clinton administrations provided these documents every other year on average. The 1997 NSS gave a good sense of the transformation in how people perceived security, with a strong focus on the need for interagency integration (e.g., between the CIA and Defense Intelligence Agency) to combat problems like terrorism, drug trafficking, and international organized crime. Thus, the NSS discussed the importance of **non-state actors**, or people or organizations that exercise political influence, either domestically or internationally, even though they do not represent sovereign governments. (Examples include groups such as al-Qaeda.) Promoting democracy, trade, arms control, and the information infrastructure were seen as essential for sustaining peace and stability in the world at large. The security provided by tanks and missiles had become part of a much broader effort.

Finally, during this period, the government began to move away from security planning based on world war–level thinking. A commission was set up to study which military facilities were still needed, withdrawing resources from communities throughout the country. The usefulness of new weapon and support systems also came under scrutiny. These matters became political footballs: The

B-2 bomber looked too expensive, but then it was noted that parts were manufactured in over 400 congressional districts. The Marine Corps' Osprey aircraft was cancelled repeatedly as a technical failure, only to be resurrected by Congress. As these examples show, many of the players involved in security planning may have had different concerns at heart when policy was created.

SELF-CHECK

1. Define unipolarity.

2. Which of the following terrorist incidents against U.S. interests did not occur between 1990 and 2000?

   a. Khobar Towers bombing
   b. First World Trade Center bombing
   c. U.S. embassy bombings in Kenya and Tanzania
   d. Marine Barracks bombing in Lebanon

3. Al-Qaeda is an example of a non-state actor. True or false?

4. Crimes against humanity always result in U.S. intervention. True or false?

1.4 Security in the Global War on Terrorism, Post-9/11

On September 11, 2001, terrorists seized control of passenger aircraft and flew two of them into the two towers of the World Trade Center and a third into the Pentagon. A fourth aircraft crashed in Pennsylvania as passengers sought to overwhelm the hijackers. Several thousand people died in the incident, making it the worst loss of life from an attack inside the United States since the Civil War. For a brief time, most Americans as well as people from other countries were unified by the horror of the attack. How had it happened? Who was responsible? What should be done to prevent similar attacks in the future? The warnings of many specialists in terrorism had come to pass, and Americans needed to rethink national security yet again.

The "how had it happened?" component of the 9/11 attacks proved straightforward. A group of well-financed terrorists had come to America, taken flying lessons, and at an agreed-upon time, boarded aircraft and seized control. The terrorists were identified with a loose association of Muslim extremists called al-Qaeda. Operating under the direction of Osama bin Laden, a Saudi Arabian, al-Qaeda's stated goal was to restore the purity of Islam. This goal requires at the very least driving American interests out of the Middle East, then overthrowing governments in the region. Further, it was believed that al-Qaeda was responsible for many terrorist incidents in the 1990s as well.

Intelligence community analyses from the 1990s indicated that al-Qaeda had substantial financial resources and enjoyed support from several countries. Muslim fundamentalists called the Taliban had seized power in Afghanistan and were providing a safe haven for al-Qaeda. Iraq, though it was under UN sanctions, was sponsoring terror attacks in Israel and was also linked to al-Qaeda. Thus, terrorism reflected more than one group of people, and it presented a variety of targets and dangers.

Other chapters in this book present distinctions among these dangers as well as specific responses. The remainder of this chapter, however, discusses some key considerations regarding understanding threats and preparing responses that will be presented in greater detail later.

1.4.1 Globalization and Geopolitics

In the late 1990s and early 2000s, **globalization**, the increasing economic and social interdependence among countries, created many opportunities for mutually beneficial exchange. As noted earlier in this chapter, many argued that this change would increase stability and peace. Interdependence also creates vulnerabilities, opening countries to short- and long-term risks. For example, if a country has a civil war, any investments from outside may be lost. Further, each country has its own form of government and its own interests. Will interdependence bind a potential adversary to peaceful behavior, or just make it stronger and create more damage when it turns on us? Scholars differ significantly on this question. One issue that they do agree on, however, is that globalization can present a challenge to cultural integrity and national identity, creating a backlash. Terrorism by radical Islamists and other forms of extremism represent this backlash. Finding an appropriate response becomes a matter of building a coalition among seemingly competing views.

First, consider the threats. Terrorism problems are part of a much larger set of challenges that the United States faces, reflecting the "preventing similar attacks" issue. As trade and other forms of international cooperation increase, the importance of specific circumstances also grows. In addition, given the interconnectedness of global economies, trade, politics, and security issues, the ability of a non-state actor to use **asymmetric warfare**, or non-conventional warfare tactics and techniques employed by a less powerful force against a more powerful nation such as the United States, continues to grow as technology creates vulnerabilities.

Second, **geopolitics**, the political impact of geographical relationships, plays a key role in globalization's interdependence. Oceans protected the United States

FOR EXAMPLE

Asymmetric Warfare Isn't New

Asymmetric warfare includes the use of terrorism and could involve the use of various WMDs (or technologies capable of producing a WMD effect). Yet, as Thomas Barnett (2005) and others have argued, asymmetric warfare is not completely new. These tactics and techniques have existed for millennia—remember the Trojan horse? For the most part, they reflect eastern rather than western military thought. What has changed, though, is the belief that we are now entering into a new historical phase of conflict, called Fourth Generational Warfare (Hammes 2004), in which asymmetrical warfare can be understood as "evolved irregular warfare" with a new emphasis on factors other than military power, such as moral force and sociological factors.

Terrorist groups, such as al-Qaeda, apply asymmetrical tactics when they use non-conventional means to attack Western interests (car bombs, suicide bombers, etc.). The "tools" available to terrorists are described in detail in Chapters 7 and 8, with a special focus on those tools that can cause the most damage.

in its early history, but expanding trade links mean many American interests are far from the center of American power. For example, China is far away and still has a Communist government overseeing the capitalist aspects of its economy. If China decided to cut off or dramatically alter its economic relations with the United States, what could we do about it? Further, China sees some of its near neighbors, such as Taiwan and Japan (who are some of America's closest allies in the region), as rivals. An incident early in 2001 underscored this problem: A Chinese fighter aircraft collided with an American reconnaissance aircraft, killing the Chinese pilot and forcing the American plane to land on Chinese territory. The airplane and crew were returned after intense negotiations, but many felt the United States had been forced to concede too much. However, the fact that the event occurred far from the United States and close to China made other alternatives short of war unlikely.

Domestic and international coalitions form around different interpretations surrounding this interplay of geopolitics and globalization. For example, in what is called the Bush Doctrine, national security is based on an aggressive response to perceived threats. Certain repressive regimes that President Bush referred to as "the axis of evil" present significant dangers to the rest of the world. These countries—Iran, Iraq, and North Korea—were suspected of developing WMDs, and they are also located in places where they can harm American interests. North Korea, for example, has been developing missiles that can hit Japan and Taiwan and have the potential to hit the west coast of the United States. Iran and Iraq were both in a position to disrupt the flow of oil from the Middle East and to threaten Israel. One of the more substantial concerns was that WMDs would find their way into the hands of terrorists. Finally, all three countries are close to China and Russia, both of which are potential sources of materials for WMDs.

Another principle of the Bush Doctrine is **preemption**, which is taking action against a state or non-state actor *before* it becomes too dangerous a threat. As always, experts disagree as to when preemption becomes necessary. Also, under this doctrine, moral values are to have a stronger place in evaluating the actions of others. Finally, according to this belief system, the linchpin to world peace is creating peace between the Israelis and Palestinians, something that will require substantial political change among the latter.

The Bush Doctrine enjoyed support at first, but the coalition necessary for successful policy has been weakened by circumstances. Notions such as preemption are questioned by people who see terrorism as a crime to be dealt with by legal processes, rather than a security matter to be dealt with by military force. Also, many observers fear that the doctrine might lead to unilateral actions in which the United States ignores the voices of its friends overseas, undermining the gains in cooperation from globalization. Although President Bush is using a multilateral approach with North Korea, critics fear that the nation's efforts in dealing with Iraq and Iran will leave the United States isolated from its allies. Finally, the absence of WMDs in Iraq seriously undermined the credibility of American efforts there, breaking the domestic coalition that supported the Second Gulf War. Although geopolitical concerns about oil and moral concerns about Saddam Hussein's repressiveness were important, the presence of WMDs made the threat to the United States from Iraq both greater and more direct.

The domestic political debate surrounding these issues continues. If the interdependence of globalization governs national policies, these concerns will ultimately be reduced. If Morganthau's balance of power is the norm, however, these remain significant problems.

1.4.2 Reorganization for the Global War on Terrorism

The 9/11 attacks on the World Trade Center and the Pentagon produced significant changes in the way agencies monitored and responded to potential and actual threats. The 2002 NSS provided direction for responding to terror as an issue, laying the foundation for increased coordination among agencies responsible for security. Later, the 2006 NSS added support for pursuing preemptive war.

In the immediate aftermath of 9/11, the United States planned and executed the first campaign in what has since become called the **Global War on Terrorism**

(GWOT). The target was Afghanistan, the home of the Taliban regime and the base of operations for al-Qaeda. It was also believed to be the last known location of al-Qaeda's leader, Osama bin Laden. The GWOT began in earnest with the start of Operation Enduring Freedom in October 2001, in which military operations commenced against the Taliban regime in Afghanistan. Initially proposed as Operation Infinite Justice, **Operation Enduring Freedom (OEF)** (see Figure 1-2) actually comprised military operations in Afghanistan, the Philippines, and the Horn of Africa, with the target being terrorist groups believed to be associated with al-Qaeda. OEF also involved actions taken domestically by the Department of Defense in support of the new homeland defense mission. One example was the formation of Joint Task Force—Olympics, the military's contribution to providing security against a possible terrorist threat to the Olympic Games held in Salt Lake City, Utah, in January 2002.

After helping establish a non-militant Islamic government in Afghanistan, the U.S. turned its sights on Iraq and its leader, Saddam Hussein. The Second Gulf War (Operation Iraqi Freedom) commenced in April 2003, but the goal this time was not simply removing Iraqi troops from Kuwait (as it was during the first Gulf War in 1990), but rather regime change and the overthrow of Hussein. The U.S. invasion of Iraq was an example of preemptive war, aimed at neutralizing Hussein's regime and its suspected ties to terrorist organizations, including as a

Figure 1-2

Operation Enduring Freedom poster (Department of Defense).

potential source of WMDs for terrorist organizations. Despite the failure of the invasion to produce any hard evidence of stockpiling of WMDs or further evidence of Iraq's ties to al-Qaeda or other terrorist organizations, the Bush administration supported the war by promoting the liberation of Iraq as a key foreign policy goal in the Middle East, which would lead to further success in the GWOT. As of March 2007, U.S. military forces remain in Iraq, continuing to combat both foreign terrorist cells as well as Iraqi insurgents.

It is unlikely that the 9/11 attacks could have been prevented. Although some clues were available, an analysis of policies and procedures indicates that government agencies were unable to share key information, despite the intentions established in the 1997 NSS. For example, considerations of legal due process and civil liberties kept the FBI and CIA from sharing information. The FBI could gather information only with proper warrants and only about domestic law-breaking, with the goal of presenting evidence in a court of law. The CIA's attention was on foreign matters, and it wanted to keep materials and the methods for getting them secret.

The Department of Homeland Security was created in response to the demands of Congress, the concerns of the American people, and the understanding emerging from the 2002 NSS. It merged 22 federal agencies with over 170,000 employees under one Cabinet-level office. The FBI and CIA remain outside of the Department of Homeland Security, but greater levels of information sharing have been established.

Maintaining American national security blends several important questions, basically asking who, why, when, and how. The "who" reflects the balance among political opinions. We can speak of this as the domestic audience: When the government develops a policy, how do people feel about it? Conservatives and liberals alike may press for peace or demand war, though for different reasons. Much depends on the "why." If a problem arises in the international system, does the response involve getting American citizens to safety, or does it demand cooperation or involvement in the affairs of other countries?

The "when" is not simply the time in history during which a problem occurs. A critical "when" issue for policy making involves whether a problem is temporary or long term. The Cold War lasted from 1946 until 1991. Was containment a good idea? When containment policy was established, it was by no means clear when the Cold War would end. Finally, the "how" reflects how the response will be managed. When America fought World War II, it was probably the largest organizational problem in our history, yet it was managed by competing government departments acting on extraordinary powers only granted to them for the duration of the crisis. It is only later that interdepartmental and interagency coordination become routine. The success of any program, however, is its capability to address the crisis at hand. Whatever the who, why, when, and how, government must adapt so as to bring appropriate organization to the problem at hand.

SELF-CHECK

1. Define asymmetric warfare.

2. One example of a U.S. government response, organizationally, after the 9/11 attacks, was the formation of the Department of National Security. True or false?

3. Which of the following countries was not identified by President Bush as part of the "axis of evil"?

   a. Iraq
   b. Libya
   c. Iran
   d. North Korea

4. The decline in economic interdependence worldwide is due to globalization. True or false?

SUMMARY

During the course of the last sixty years, America's security environment has undergone several key transformations. First, the creation of international institutions such as the United Nations has increased interdependence among nations. Second, the means of attack and defense have changed from rifles and battleships to WMDs, making even small groups potentially very dangerous. Third, new threats have arisen in the place of old threats, such as that once posed by the USSR. The circumstances of these new threats reflect long-standing concerns and analytical frameworks, such as geopolitics and power relationships. Fourth, as various threats have grown more complex, it has become necessary to develop new organizations, processes, policies, and strategies to manage the threats, as well as to increase the coordination among these elements. Of course, there are currently a number of competing perspectives within the American political system about what constitutes a threat and what the appropriate responses to these threats should be. The waxing and waning of these perspectives means managing national security will be a source of controversy for years to come.

In this chapter, you addressed all of these issues by taking a detailed look at the changing nature of national security throughout U.S. history. More specifically, you analyzed various security environments and national security policy choices during specific historical periods. You also learned to distinguish between national security policy players within and outside of government and appraised the threat situation in post-9/11 America. In addition, you examined our nation's national security policy as a response to today's changing environment and threat perceptions.

KEY TERMS

Asymmetrical warfare	The use of non-conventional warfare tactics and techniques by a less powerful force against a more powerful adversary.
Axis Powers	The alliance among Germany, Japan, and Italy during World War II.
Bipolar system	A relationship among countries in the international system in which two countries dominate and other nation-states tend to align themselves with either of the two, such as the United States and the USSR during the Cold War.
Bretton Woods Agreements	Series of post–World War II agreements that created key economic institutions intended to promote international economic stability and trade, such as the International Monetary Fund (IMF) and the International Bank for Reconstruction and Development (World Bank).
CBRNE	Abbreviation for chemical, biological, radiological, nuclear, and explosive weapons.
Central Powers	The alliance between Germany, Austria-Hungary, the Ottoman Empire, and Bulgaria in World War I.
Circular error of probability (CEP)	Term that describes the accuracy with which nuclear weapons strike their targets.
Clandestine and covert operations	Clandestine operations are secret efforts to gather information, while covert operations are intended to influence how governments behave. Covert operations could include bribes, subversion and psychological operations, and support for insurgent forces.
Collective security	An agreement among countries to unite against any aggressor.

Containment	Principal national security policy pursued during the Cold War to prevent the spread of Communism and Soviet influence.
Correlation of forces	A measure of comparative military power between the U.S. and the USSR during the Cold War, based on the combined resources of the nations that were aligned with each superpower.
Détente	Literally, a "relaxation of tensions"; refers to the efforts of the Nixon administration to promote diplomatic compromise with the USSR.
Entente Powers	The alliance between the United States, Britain, France, and Russia in World War I.
Federalist Papers	Essays authored by James Madison, Alexander Hamilton, and John Jay in 1787–1788 that argued the need for a U.S. federal government strong enough to provide for national security while also protecting states' rights and individual liberties.
Geopolitics	The political impact of geographical relationships.
Globalization	The increasing economic and social interdependence among countries.
Global War on Terrorism (GWOT)	Military campaign launched after 9/11 that targets terrorist groups in multiple countries.
Isolationism	A foreign policy based on avoiding alliances with other countries.
Marshall Plan	Plan that provided U.S. funds to help rebuild non-Communist countries after World War II.
Monroe Doctrine	A regional security policy proposed by President James Monroe in 1823 that sought to limit European influence in the Americas.
Multiple independently targeted reentry vehicle (MIRV)	Device that allows a missile to carry more than one nuclear warhead.

Multipolar system	A relationship among countries in the international system in which no country dominates, with a number of nation-states possessing military power and capable of acting independently.
National security	Protecting the United States, its citizens, and its interests through the threatened and actual use of all elements of national power.
Neutrality Acts	Laws passed by Congress in the 1930s forbidding American support for or involvement with countries at war.
Non-state actors	People or organizations that exercise political influence either domestically or internationally, such as al-Qaeda.
Operation Enduring Freedom (OEF)	Military operations in Afghanistan, the Philippines, and the Horn of Africa against terrorist groups believed to be associated with al-Qaeda.
Preemption	Taking action against a state or non-state actor before it becomes too dangerous a threat.
Prepositioning	Establishing bases and supplies in foreign countries to prepare a rapid response to future crises.
Proliferation	The supplying of other countries with the technology to build their own nuclear weapons.
Superpowers	The dominant military powers during the Cold War: the United States and USSR. After the demise of communism, the United States remained the world's lone superpower.
Unipolar system	An international system characterized by one superpower.
United Nations (UN)	International organization established after World War II to resolve disputes and stop aggression through collective security.
Weapon of mass destruction (WMD)	Device such as a chemical, biological, radiological, nuclear, or explosive weapon that can inflict widespread damage when used.

ASSESS YOUR UNDERSTANDING

Go to www.wiley.com/college/kilroy to assess your knowledge of the basics of national security.

Measure your learning by comparing pre-test and post-test results.

Summary Questions

1. During its first 150 years of existence, the United States pursued an isolationist foreign policy. True or false?

2. The United States entered World War II in 1941 as an Allied Power. True or false?

3. The international security environment that emerged after World War II can best be described as bipolar, with the United States and the USSR establishing spheres of influence over other nations. True or false?

4. After September 11, 2001, the United States returned to a policy of isolationism in foreign affairs, attempting to avoid conflict in other nations that would increase the possibility of terrorist incidents in the United States itself. True or false?

5. Which of the following was not an author of the Federalist Papers?
   (a) John Jay
   (b) Alexander Hamilton
   (c) Thomas Jefferson
   (d) James Madison

6. Which of the following countries was not part of the Entente Powers?
   (a) Germany
   (b) France
   (c) Britain
   (d) Russia

7. Which of the following countries was an original member of NATO in 1949?
   (a) Austria
   (b) Australia
   (c) Canada
   (d) Spain

8. Which of the following countries was not part of President Bush's original "axis of evil"?
   (a) Iran
   (b) Iraq
   (c) North Korea
   (d) Syria

Applying This Chapter

1. In a classroom discussion, a fellow student argues that based on James Madison's statement that security can only be measured by the "means and danger" of attack, the greatest threat the United States faces today is a terrorist obtaining a nuclear weapon. Do you agree or disagree? Why or why not?

2. With the end of the Cold War and the collapse of the former Soviet Union, the United States did not face a nation-state with a military capability equal to our own. Prior to 9/11, the military began to develop a "capability-based" force rather than a "threat-based" force, allowing it to respond to situations rather than specific threats. You've been hired as a defense analyst by a leading think tank and asked to evaluate this national security policy. As a result of 9/11, do you think this was the right approach? What type of military capability should we be developing today?

3. You are a member of the president's National Security Council. North Korea continues to defy international condemnation of its nuclear development program and has recently begun test-firing long-range missiles, which could threaten the United States. What course of action do you recommend for national security policy: containment and deterrence, preemption, or multilateral policy options? What would be some of your specific points supporting one option over the others?

4. If you were to teach a course on national security policy making, what subjects would you include? What type of model would you employ in explaining how national security decisions are made? Who would you identify as the key players?

YOU TRY IT

Asymmetrical Warfare

Analyze the topic of asymmetrical warfare. Look for specific examples in history where a weaker power has used asymmetrical means to defeat a more powerful adversary.

National Security Policies

Research national security policy under one presidential administration during the Cold War (1946 to 1989).

Analyze the security policies or "doctrines" that emerged during that administration. How did that administration attempt to "contain" Communism? What policy choices were made with regard to relations with the former Soviet Union?

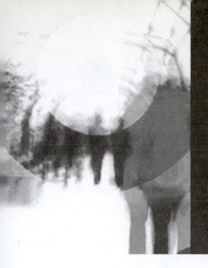

2

U.S. HOMELAND SECURITY INTERESTS

Understanding What Needs to Be Protected and How We Will Do It

Starting Point

Go to www.wiley.com/college/kilroy to assess your knowledge of U.S. homeland security interests.
Determine where you need to concentrate your effort.

What You'll Learn in This Chapter

▲ The goals of homeland security programs
▲ The actors and agencies involved in homeland security
▲ The resources that constitute critical infrastructure and assets
▲ The constitutional challenges facing homeland security

After Studying This Chapter, You'll Be Able To

▲ Assess who is served by homeland security programs
▲ Evaluate the different roles of federal, state, and local agencies
▲ Appraise the consequences of security threats and their effect on our nation's critical infrastructures and societal values
▲ Judge our nation's defensive and offensive capabilities concerning people, places, and things

INTRODUCTION

Survivors being plucked from rooftops in New Orleans after Hurricane Katrina in 2005, soot- and blood-covered faces emerging from the aftermath of the attack on the Twin Towers in 2001, illegal immigrants running across the Mexican desert at night in hopes of evading the border patrol, possible flu pandemic scenarios, and domestic wiretapping programs all are images seen in the national media. Although dramatic in their own right, these images also help explain why Americans have different opinions regarding threats to national security. To some Americans, homeland security should protect our communities against man-made threats such as terrorist attacks and biological agents. To others, homeland security is protection from natural disasters such as hurricanes and earthquakes. Homeland security does address both natural and man-made threats (as well as hurricane preparedness, response, and recovery), but the one thing all its definitions have in common is that homeland security is about protecting people and things from risks.

In this chapter, you'll taker a closer look at the various aspects of homeland security in the United States. You'll assess who is served by homeland security programs and evaluate the different roles of federal, state, and local agencies. You'll also appraise the consequences of security threats and their effect on our nation's critical infrastructures and societal values. Finally, you'll consider our nation's various defensive and offensive capabilities concerning people, places, and things.

2.1 Human Security: Protecting People

In 2002, President George W. Bush released the *National Strategy for Homeland Security*. This document serves as the foundation for current homeland security policy, and attempts to unify the wide gap in types of homeland security through the implementation of six directives assigned to the Department of Homeland Security. These directives seek to unite government agencies and protocols to ensure accountability in border and transportation security; create "smart borders;" increase the security of international shipping containers; implement the Aviation and Transportation Security Act of 2001; recapitalize the U.S. Coast Guard; and reform immigration services (Office of Homeland Security 2002, vii). The directives serve as a way to categorize the activities for planning and response to domestic threats, and define homeland security issues.

But what is homeland security? Quite simply, **homeland security** can be defined as those activities that protect people, critical infrastructure, key resources, economic activities, and our way of life. Homeland security raises a number of fundamental questions, including "What are the threats?" and "Who does homeland security protect?" Local, state, and federal homeland security policy attempt to answer these questions as well as minimize risk. Risk and the perception of risk, in turn, influence public attitudes about homeland security, and

Figure 2-1

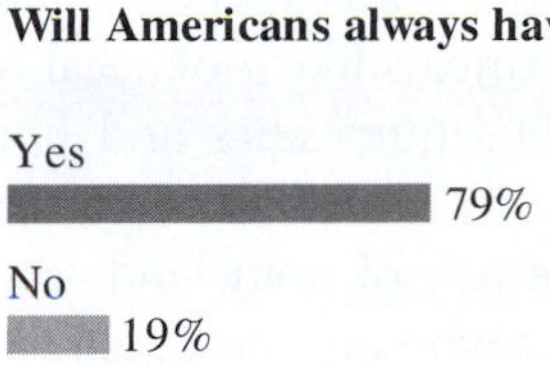

Will Americans always have to live with the threat of terrorism?

Yes
■■■■■■■■■ 79%

No
■■ 19%

Americans' views on terrorism (Source: CBS News poll, September 10, 2005).

these public attitudes consequently influence policy makers. Homeland security agencies must therefore respond to not only the threats of which they are aware, but also to the values and attitudes present among the public that they protect. For example, Figure 2-1 shows that most Americans believe the threat of terrorism is going to be a part of our lives from now on, so how we use security policy with people, things, and ideas is vitally important.

To many Americans, the concept of homeland security is relatively new, a part of the national dialogue only since the 9/11, 2001, terrorist attacks. Throughout America's existence, however, homeland security has been an integral part of our communities. From our early history onward, Americans responded to threats and disasters by offering assistance to one another, and by uniting as a whole to protect our way of life from enemy forces (Waugh 2000, 14). Long before professional fire departments and police forces, churches, civic organizations, families, and neighbors served as our first responders to natural and man-made dangers. Over time, common threats such as floods, fires, and disease required the administrative and financial capacities of government (Waugh 2000, 15). For example, as cities grew, catastrophic fires presented a real threat to life and property. Thus, during the eighteenth and early nineteenth centuries, local governments issued building codes that required residents to build with brick or stone, rather than wood, to lessen the likelihood of catastrophic fires. Public health also became a concern for policy makers during the nineteenth century. As cities became congested and little sanitation existed, diseases could spread easily. Frequent outbreaks of smallpox, cholera, yellow fever, and other diseases were not uncommon in American cities during the 1800s, and the 1918 influenza epidemic killed thousands in the U.S. In response, local officials passed public health ordinances to regulate water use and sewage treatment (Waugh 2000, 14).

Prior to the mid-twentieth century, governmental disaster activities were generally characterized as reactive, with institutions providing relief only after disasters actually occurred (Waugh 2000, 16). This method of policy making continued until 1950, when Congress passed the Civil Defense Act and the Disaster Relief Act to deal with both military-related and natural disaster events. Additional laws passed between 1950 and 2002 shifted the focus of homeland security programs from reactionary to proactive. In fact, in the beginning of the twenty-first century, the governmental definition of homeland security was expanded under the USA Patriot Act to include response to technological threats like biological weapons and terrorist activities as well as natural disasters like hurricanes and floods. Despite the growing complexity of homeland security in today's environment, the goal remains to protect people and resources. As the role of homeland security continues to expand in American society, we must ask who are the people and what are the things we are trying to protect, and who is doing the protecting?

2.1.1 Social Factors

In September 2006, the U.S. Department of the Census reported that the American population passed the 300 million mark. Considering that the population at the time of the first census in 1790 was 3.3 million, it is fair to say that some staggering changes have occurred in American society. Today, in addition to citizens born in the United States, immigration contributes over one million people to the U.S. population annually. Approximately 10 percent of American citizens (31 million people) are foreign born, and post-1990 immigrants and their children accounted for 61 percent of population growth during the last decade. Of America's 31 million immigrants, about 8 million are here illegally, and almost one-third of all immigration during the 1990s was illegal.

Regardless of where they were born, it is important to address homeland security for all U.S. residents. This can be difficult because the complex social environment which currently exists must balance how and where we live, the natural environment, technology, and the value-based world in which we make decisions regarding public safety and protection. Social factors that contribute to homeland security decision making can be defined by the following four topics:

1. **Increasing population density:** The population of the United States, like that of the entire world, increases every day. More people live in major metropolitan areas and, thus, are vulnerable to homeland security threats and disaster events. Current projections forecast that half of the world's population will live in urban areas by 2007. By contrast, in 1950, only 30 percent of the world's population lived in urban areas. By 2000, urban dwellers made up 47 percent of the total population, and this number is projected to reach 60 percent by 2030 (United Nations Population Division 2002, 1). In the United States, over 28 percent of the population lives in the ten cities with the highest population, as shown in Table 2-1 (2000 U.S. Census Data).

2. **Increased settlement in high-risk areas:** More people reside in high-risk areas, such as those prone to hurricanes and earthquakes, because of the favorable climate and availability of work in these regions. Coastal areas, for example, can be especially vulnerable because of their unique geographic characteristics and rapid population growth. Coastal counties

Table 2-1: Ten Most Populous U.S. Metropolitan Areas in 2000

Metropolitan Area	Population
New York City	20,124,377
Los Angeles	15,781,273
Chicago–Gary, IN–Kenosha, WI	8,809,846
Washington–Baltimore	7,285,206
San Francisco–Oakland–San Jose	6,816,047
Philadelphia–Wilmington–Atlantic City	5,988,348
Boston–Worcester–Lawrence, MA	5,633,060
Detroit–Ann Arbor–Flint, MI	5,457,583
Dallas–Fort Worth	4,802,463
Houston–Galveston–Brazoria, TX	4,407,579
Total population	85,105,782

(Source: U.S. Department of the Census)

constitute only 17 percent of the total land area of the United States (not including Alaska) but approximately 53 percent of the total U.S. population (Crossett, Culliton, Wiley, and Goodspeed 2004, 6). Moreover, according to the Environmental Protection Agency, "coastal population is increasing by 3,600 people per day, giving a projected total increase of 27 million people by 2015. This growth rate is faster than that of the nation as a whole" (U.S. Environmental Protection Agency 2004, 2).

3. **Increased technological risks:** The large-scale use of hazardous chemicals in production processes and the fact that airplanes carry vast numbers of passengers each day are only two of the dozens of high-risk technologies that did not exist in prior centuries. In addition, we must now contend with cyber-security and other information technology issues, biological agents (such as anthrax) found in research facilities, weaponry-like dirty bombs that can be relatively easy to make, and even information sharing among potential terrorist organizations by way of the Internet. Although this sounds overwhelming, today's increased technology also means that homeland security programs can incorporate new tools, and partner with the private sector to develop innovative solutions to security threats.

4. **Value-laden decision making:** Policy making does not exist in a vacuum. Rather, government programs come to life through a policy-making process run by people. Policy makers are guided by a complex mix of values. Five categories of values that sometimes guide decision makers are organizational

values, professional values, personal values, policy values, and ideological values (Anderson 2000, 135–137). Organizational values involve the promotion of organizational and committee interests in the decision-making process. Professional values are professional commitments that guide decision making (e.g., first responders may tend to take a public safety perspective on issues). Personal values may involve personal ambitions, reputation, and self-interest. Policy values are those that guide decision making based on a perceived public interest or when acting in accord with beliefs about what is proper, ethical, or morally correct. Finally, ideological values legitimize actions on the basis of a political ideology or belief system. Decision makers and elected officials must balance all five categories of values during the policy-making process, while setting goals for public laws and programs. This can be especially difficult when political factors enter into public debate over homeland security, especially when each person involved has a different opinion of what homeland security is and how government can best provide programs to protect society.

2.1.2 Political Factors

The United States is a constitutional republic based on **representative democracy**, a system of government in which the ultimate political authority is vested in the people, who elect their governing officials to legislate on their behalf. (There are, however, a few examples of **direct democracy** in the United States, such as New England town meetings, where people vote directly on legislative matters.) Additionally, our government embodies **pluralism** in that many groups or institutions share power in a complex system of interactions, which involves compromising and bargaining in the decision-making process. American democracy, similar to its British counterpart, is an evolutionary and organic system that has pragmatically overcome obstacles, crises, and disasters. Under this system, majority rule must be balanced with protection of minority rights to create national policy (Plano and Greenberg 1985, 8–10). This can be difficult for policy makers, however, as the need to identify which groups are protected under homeland security policies can change from one issue to the next. Illegal immigrants, for example, may have the right to work legally and may be deported if discovered, but if an immigrant family is left homeless after a flood, will government agencies ignore their survival needs? Certainly not, but it leaves policy makers and implementers in the difficult position of trying to determine to whom homeland security applies.

Further complicating homeland security issues are the horizontal fragmentations of government authority among the three major branches of the U.S. government. The **separation of powers**, through which governmental power is divided between the executive, legislative, and judicial branches of the national government, provides constitutional checks and balances that limit the individual powers of each branch. For example, the executive and legislative branches play the most important roles in homeland security, but each will be limited if the courts find laws prom-ulgated by these branches unconstitutional. In addition, the U.S. government also contains a multitude of competing agencies with overlapping jurisdictional pre-rogatives, and this can limit the effectiveness of program administration.

Adding to the horizontal fragmentation of U.S. government is the vertical division of power characteristic of our **federal system**, in which the national government shares sovereignty with state and local governments. The United States Constitution accords the states, under the Tenth Amendment, certain reserved powers not controlled by the national government. Additionally, certain powers reside exclusively in local governments. Law enforcement, health and safety codes, and emergency response are some of the programs traditionally afforded to local and state governments under the Tenth Amendment. Overall, state, county, municipal, and local governments fund and operate the emergency services that would respond in the event of a terrorist attack. The federal govern-ment comes to the assistance of a state government when it is overwhelmed by, or incapable of addressing, a disaster. The governor asks for assistance, and a presidential disaster declaration is granted (Plano and Greenberg 1985).

When policy making becomes fragmented between national, state, and local governments, it leads to difficulties in determining which level of government is actually in charge of homeland security planning and response. According to the U.S. Department of Homeland Security, every state and many cities and counties are addressing homeland security issues either through an existing office or through a newly created office. Many have established anti-terrorism task forces. Many have also published or are preparing homeland security strategies, some based on existing plans for dealing with natural disasters. This is important to the execution of homeland security programs, because "[u]ltimately, all manmade and natural disasters are local events—with local units being the first to respond and the last to leave" (Office of Homeland Security 2002, 14).

Although homeland security issues can present unanticipated demands on each level and branch of government, our federal system also provides the capacity to improvise as conditions warrant. Each level of government can coordinate with other levels to minimize redundancies in homeland security actions and ensure integration of efforts. The federal government can use knowledge from our states and communities to prioritize programs and address unique regional needs.

The Executive Branch

As previously mentioned in this chapter, the executive branch is one of the three major components of the U.S. government. As the leader of the country, the president is both the coordinator and the symbol for homeland security. The president's responsibilities for homeland security range from guiding policy initia-tives to ensuring that organizational capacities exist to ensure initiatives can be successfully executed. The direct powers of the president are set forth in Article II,

Section 2, of the U.S. Constitution, which grants the president power as the commander in chief of the armed forces, as well as in Section 3, which states in part that "he shall take care that the laws be faithfully executed." This means that the president has the power to veto bills passed by Congress and to appoint personnel to certain government offices. Additionally, the president exercises several other powers that affect homeland security policies and programs. These include formulation of the executive budget, preparation of the president's budget request for the next fiscal year, the ability to reorganize executive branch agencies, and control over the information that executive agencies supply to the Congress. This control is especially vital in the areas of national security, national defense, intelligence matters, and other areas involving restricted data. Indirect powers come from the president's own leadership style and personality. Along with the respect for the office of the chief executive and commander in chief, the president represents the strength of the United States as a political and economic force in the world. The president's ability to seize initiatives and exercise emergency powers in crises can add to the legitimacy of the institution of the presidency, and it can also help in persuading others to take some course of action.

Although no specific emergency powers are given to the president in the Constitution, the president's oath of office requires him or her to "preserve, protect, and defend" the Constitution, as well as to uphold its provisions. Presidents may claim, in times of crisis, that the Constitution permits them to exercise powers usually granted to the legislative or judicial branches of government—fusing all governmental power in the executive branch for the duration of the crisis. Overall, emergencies have helped develop the use of these otherwise dormant powers, and they have also led to the novel application of ordinary powers. Although the National Emergency Powers Act of 1976 sought to limit the emergency powers that had been granted to the president in the past via precedent, presidents still exercise vast emergency powers. Presidents retain the power to do what they want under the rubric of emergency powers until they are checked by one of the other branches of government. Checks and balances go a long way toward discouraging the president from abusing the use of the presidential emergency.

The **bureaucracy** is the sum of all federal departments, agencies, and offices that implement laws under the authority of the president. By definition, bureaucracies are hierarchical organizations that are highly specialized, and they operate with very formal rules (Plano and Greenberg 1985). Although all departments in the federal government make up the bureaucracy, some are more involved in homeland security than others. In 2002, 22 existing agencies were combined with new agencies to form the **Department of Homeland Security (DHS)**. The primary mission of the DHS is "to protect our homeland against terrorist threats" (*DHS Mission Statement* 2002, 12). As you can see in Figure 2-2, this myriad of agencies, bureaus, and offices can be confusing, but each has a unique role to play in the department The DHS is responsible for many specific homeland

Figure 2-2

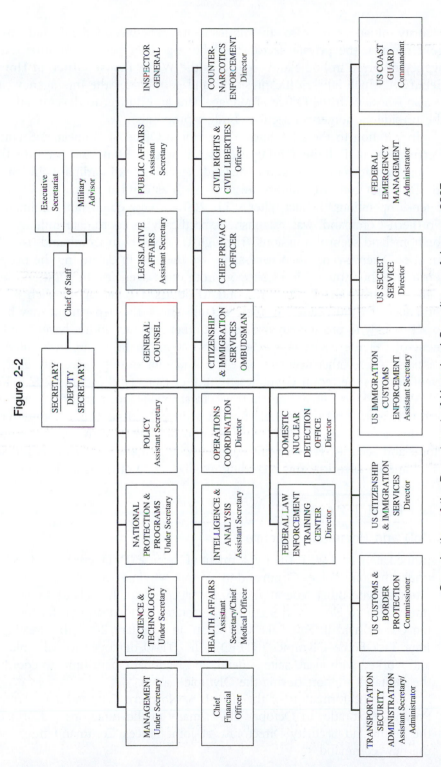

Organization of the Department of Homeland Security as of January 2007
(Source: www.dhs.gov/xabout/structure/editorial_0644.shtm).

43

security initiatives and also streamlines relations between federal, state, and local governments, the private sector, and the American people. Another executive agency involved in homeland security is the **White House Office of Homeland Security**, which advises the president and coordinates the interagency process. It also works with the Office of Management and Budget to develop and defend the president's homeland security budget proposals.

In addition to the DHS and White House Office of Homeland Security, the Department of Defense (DoD) also contributes to homeland security through military missions overseas and homeland defense. In extraordinary circumstances, the DoD can conduct military missions such as combat air patrols or maritime defense operations. In fact, after 9/11, 2001, a new combatant command, U.S. Northern Command, was established specifically to coordinate military support for homeland security missions. Through U.S. Northern Command, the Department of Defense can, when necessary, take the lead in defending the people and territory of our country, with support from other agencies. In addition, the president can order the DoD to respond to domestic catastrophes such as floods, tornadoes, and hurricanes. In these circumstances, the department may be asked to act quickly to provide capabilities that other agencies do not have. The Department of Defense also has special authorization "to take part in 'limited scope' missions where other agencies have the lead—for example, security at a special event such as the recent Olympics" (Office of Homeland Security 2002, 13).

Within the executive branch, the Central Intelligence Agency's (CIA) Counterterrorist Center and the Federal Bureau of Investigation's (FBI) Counterterrorism Division and Criminal Intelligence Section also work with the Department of Homeland Security. The two FBI agencies have primary responsibility for combating domestic terrorism and providing intelligence to other agencies and state and

---

FOR EXAMPLE

DoD and Homeland Defense

Immediately after 9/11, the Department of Defense (DoD) created a directorate under the Joint Forces Command in Norfolk, Virginia, to serve as the military's interface with other federal government agencies for homeland security support. This new Homeland Security Directorate provided support for the Olympic Games held in Salt Lake City, Utah, in February 2002, by creating the Joint Task Force–Olympics (JTF-O). The JTF-O deployed to Salt Lake City and worked with local, state, federal, and National Guard units to coordinate the military's support during the Olympic Games.

With the formation of the new U.S. Northern Command in Colorado Springs, Colorado, in October 2002, many of the functions performed by the Homeland Security Directorate at Joint Forces Command migrated to the new command.

local governments nationwide. The CIA is specifically responsible for gathering and analyzing all information regarding potential terrorist threats abroad (Office of Homeland Security 2002, 13).

Yet another federal department involved in homeland security is the U.S. Department of Justice. The attorney general, who heads the Department of Justice, is America's chief law enforcement officer and is charged with leading national enforcement efforts to detect, prevent, and investigate terrorist activity within the United States. An additional important federal department is the Department of Health and Human Services, which houses the Centers for Disease Control and Prevention and the National Institutes of Health, both of which provide critical expertise and resources related to bioterrorism.

The Legislative Branch

The legislative branch is the second major component of America's national government. This branch consists of the U.S. Congress, which is made up of the Senate and the House of Representatives. As elected representatives from their districts and states, members of Congress are affected by a number of political factors when making decisions, including constituency interests and political party affiliation. Constituency interests usually dominate the decision-making process. A constituency is made up of the voters and key interests that elected a legislator to office. Legislators can act as delegates or trustees. As a delegate, a legislator votes on issues in accord with the views of the majority of his or her constituents or with a vital block of back-home interests. As a trustee, a legislator considers interests beyond his or her constituency. He or she may think about national, environmental, humanitarian, global, or political minority interests. For example, when funding for state and local programs comes up for debate during the yearly budget process, a lawmaker behaves as a trustee when he or she considers broad national interests, such as how much federal program spending adds to the federal deficit and national debt. Thus, constituency interests are not the only consideration that members of Congress have.

With the exception of a few independents, all senators and representatives are members of a political party. Party membership can influence policy and ideological values, which in turn influence how an elected official votes. Even though party members do not always vote as a cohesive bloc, political party affiliation is still a good predictor of how most legislators will vote or act toward an issue. In addition, the political party with the majority of seats in Congress controls committee assignments and which proposed laws will be considered for passage. The more seniority lawmakers have, the greater choice they have in selecting their committee assignments. Most seek appointments to committees with jurisdiction over policies and programs in which they have a strong political interest.

Allocating federal homeland security dollars to cities across the nation can be a politically challenging task for both members of Congress and the Department of Homeland Security. In 2006, the department divvied $1.7 billion in grants, but many analysts and elected officials questioned the DHS's allocations. New York and Washington, D.C., the two cities targeted in the 9/11 attacks, lost almost half of their previous grants; mid-size cities such as Louisville, Kentucky, and Charlotte, North Carolina, received substantial increases. According to the Department of Homeland Security, this allocation of funds "was based on a detailed analysis of an area's vulnerability to threats and on peer reviews from other local and state officials." Federal officials also indicated that New York's application was flawed and did not adequately express the city's needs (Barrett 2006).

The Judicial Branch

The Supreme Court of the United States is the highest court in the nation and leads the judicial branch of the U.S. federal government. Two of the most important powers of the Supreme Court are the powers to hear cases under original and appellate jurisdiction and the power of judicial review. The Supreme Court's original jurisdiction allows it to hear all cases affecting ambassadors, public ministers, and cases in which the states are a party. The court's appellate jurisdiction allows it to hear appeals made from lower courts. This jurisdiction encompasses "all other cases" within the scope of Article III under the authority given by the Constitution.

The Constitution does not explicitly grant the Supreme Court the power of judicial review; nevertheless, the power of the Supreme Court to overturn laws and executive actions that it deems unlawful or unconstitutional is a well-established precedent. The Supreme Court first established its power to declare laws unconstitutional in the case of *Marbury v. Madison* (1803), consummating the system of checks and balances. The Court resolves conflicts under the U.S. Constitution and in accord with a body of laws through its exercise of judicial review of legislative enactments. It has the Constitutional authority to interpret laws and to declare a law "null and void" if it is found to be unconstitutional. In addition, Congress has conferred upon the Supreme Court the power to prescribe rules of procedure to be followed by the lower courts of the United States. This can be a powerful tool that dictates how homeland security programs and policies should be run in the bureaucracy, or it can set limits for procedures and statutes at all levels of government.

One example of the rule-making power of the Supreme Court can be found in the case of *Hamadan v. Rumsfeld*. The case involved a Yemeni citizen, Salim Ahme Hamadan, who was a confidant and driver for Osama bin Laden. Hamadan insisted that he was only a driver for bin Laden, although the U.S. government sought to make the case that he was actually involved in arms transfers to the Taliban. Thus, the United States wanted to try him in a military tribunal for conspiring against U.S. citizens. The Supreme Court argued in its 5–3 ruling that the proposed tribunals are in violation of both the U.S. Uniform Code of Military Justice and the Geneva Conventions, which protect the rights of detainees during wartime. The Court argued that rules regarding detainees cannot be made by the executive branch alone, and that procedures involving detainees' cases must be subject to congressional oversight (*Hamadan v. Rumsfeld,* 2006).

Non-governmental and Governmental Organizations

By definition, **a non-governmental organization (NGO)** is one that provides a service to a community free of charge or for a minimal cost that is required to defray the cost of the service(s) furnished. NGOs usually hold the special non-profit federal tax exempt status—(501)(c)(3)—and financial support for voluntary agencies is generally through donations, contracts, and grants. Many such organizations provide facilities that produce essential services for the general public. Non-governmental organizations include community service groups, church groups, and national non-profit agencies. NGO involvement in homeland security has a long history in America. The American Red Cross was established in 1905, and the Salvation Army has been providing relief assistance since 1899. NGOs can be important aids to state and local governments, providing extra help even if federal authorities are not involved. However, NGOs can also be a part of a communication program because their missions may be different than that of governmental homeland security agencies. NGOs often focus on relief, not preparedness, and they may have different definitions of disasters or emergencies.

Another important organization is the federally sponsored agency known as the Citizen Corps. The Citizen Corps began in January 2002 to encourage and enlist citizens across the country. The members of the Citizen Corps receive special training from the Federal Emergency Management Agency's (FEMA) Community Emergency Response Program to support first responders by providing immediate help to victims and by organizing volunteers at disaster sites. Citizen Corps also works with the national Neighborhood Watch Program to incorporate terrorism prevention and education into its existing crime prevention mission. The Citizen Corps additionally includes the Volunteers in Police Service, civilian volunteers trained to support police departments, and the Medical Reserve Corps, civilian volunteers who can assist health care professionals during a large-scale local emergency. Finally, Operation TIPS (Terrorism Information and Prevention System) is a nationwide program that trains truck drivers, letter carriers, train conductors, ship captains, and utility workers to report potential terrorist activity.

A growing population, diverse geography, rapid advances in technology, and decisions made in part by personal values have made homeland security a difficult goal to achieve. Despite different social and political pressures, the goal remains to protect people. As the role of homeland security continues to expand in American society, we find that homeland security is by its very nature intergovernmental and intercommunity. The American political and social system requires coordination and cooperation between and among various levels of government, as well as between the branches of government and the public as a whole to meet the challenge of protecting our citizens. Policy making in a federal democratic system can be difficult because lawmakers must balance national interests with the needs of the districts they represent, but it is this process that allows for a responsive government that can alter priorities and programs as issues and needs change over time.

SELF-CHECK

1. Which of the following is not one of the four social factors that affect policy making?

   a. Increasing population density
   b. Increased settlement in low-risk areas
   c. Value-laden decision making
   d. Increased technological risks

2. One of the key political factors influencing homeland security in the United States is the separation of powers between branches of government. True or false?

3. Define non-governmental organizations, and provide an example of one such organization with a role in homeland security.

4. Compare how each branch of government (executive, legislative, and judicial) can affect homeland security policy.

2.2 Critical Infrastructure and Key Resources

What is risk? Generally, **risk** is a combination of vulnerability and the consequence of a specified hazardous event (Department of Homeland Security 2006b, 29). In the context of homeland security, risk is the expected magnitude of loss (e.g., deaths, injuries, economic damage, loss of public confidence, or government capability) due to a terrorist attack, natural disaster, or other incident, along with the likelihood of such an event occurring and causing that loss. Everywhere, at any time, we are exposed to risks. From a homeland security standpoint, a casino in Las Vegas, a shopping mall in suburban Minneapolis, or a ride at Disney World in Orlando can pose risks to human life and critical infrastructure, such as nuclear power plants, chemical factories, or military bases. Sound unlikely? Could a mall be as risky as a chemical factory? In the article "Ten Years Later," author Richard C. Clarke envisions a country ten years after the 9/11 attacks, where terrorists strike once again on American soil, this time in places where Americans recreate and shop.

Not only is the image of an attack on a large mall a scary prospect for most of us, but it raises the question of just what, exactly, homeland security programs should protect. Most Americans recognize the need to protect facilities such as nuclear power plants, or places where goods and services meet such as airports and ports, but what about the other places we use? Should we protect the 300,000 estimated daily visitors to Disney World at the same level as passengers passing through O'Hare Airport in Chicago? Homeland securities agencies must ask what key resources are at risk and how we determine risk. In addition, they must consider who determines how to spend a finite amount of resources to protect an infinite number of places where Americans could be at risk on any given day.

Although much of the nation turned its attention to homeland security after 9/11, 2001, questions regarding the safety of infrastructure and resources have been a concern for many years. For example, in October 1997, the President's Commission on Critical Infrastructure Protection issued a report calling for a national effort to assure the security of the United States' increasingly vulnerable and interconnected infrastructures, such as telecommunications, banking and finance, energy, transportation, and essential government services. Later, on May 22, 1998, President Clinton released *Presidential Decision Directive 63* (PDD-63), which added specific policy recommendations to the 1997 report. This directive established a goal of increased security to government systems by the year 2000 and a secure information system infrastructure by the year 2003. Other initiatives in the 1998 PDD included the following:

▲ Establishing a national center to warn of and respond to attacks
▲ Ensuring the capability to protect critical infrastructures from intentional acts by 2003
▲ Addressing cyber and physical infrastructure vulnerabilities of the federal government
▲ Requiring the federal government to serve as a model to the rest of the country for how infrastructure protection is to be attained
▲ Enlisting the voluntary participation of private industry to meet common goals for protecting our critical systems through public-private partnerships

However, it was not until passage of the Uniting and Strengthening America by Providing Appropriate Tools Required to Intercept and Obstruct Terrorism (USA Patriot) Act in 2002 and the Homeland Security Act (HSA) of 2002 that many of these goals found an administrative home in the new Department of Homeland Security. Title II of the HSA outlines the requirements for the Directorate for Information Analysis and Infrastructure Protection. Among other duties, this directorate is responsible for carrying out "comprehensive assessments of the vulnerabilities of the key resources and critical infrastructure of the United States, including the performance of risk assessments to determine the risks posed by particular types of terrorist attacks within the United States (including an assessment of the probability of success of such attacks and the feasibility and potential efficacy of various countermeasures to such attacks)" (Homeland Security Act, Title II, Subtitle A, Section 201 (c)(2)).

But what is critical infrastructure? The USA Patriot Act defines **critical infrastructure** as those "systems and assets, whether physical or virtual, so vital to the United States that the incapacity or destruction of such systems and assets would have a debilitating impact on security, national economic security, national public health or safety, or any combination of those matters" (Title X, Sec. 1016(e)). Critical infrastructures are important because of the functions or services they provide to our country. Because they are complex systems, the effects of a terrorist attack on these infrastructures can spread far beyond the direct target and reverberate long after the immediate damage. For example, the information and telecommunications sector enables economic productivity and growth, and it is particularly important because it connects and helps control many other infrastructure sectors like energy, transportation, banking and finance, chemical industry, and postal and shipping. As you can see, America's critical infrastructure encompasses a large number of sectors. Other types of critical infrastructures that provide the essential goods and services Americans need to survive include agriculture, public health, and emergency services.

Key resources are "individual targets whose destruction would not endanger vital systems, but could create local disaster or profoundly damage our [n]ation's morale or confidence" (Homeland Security Act, Section 2). Key resources can be publicly or privately controlled resources essential to the minimal operations of the economy and government, and they include historical attractions or symbols, such as the Liberty Bell and other monuments that may be nationally, state, locally, or privately managed. Key resources also include individual or local facilities that deserve special protection because of their destructive potential, as well as certain high-profile events, such as the Super Bowl or the Daytona 500, where hundreds of thousands of people may gather for one event.

To protect critical infrastructure and key resources **(CI/KR)**, it is necessary to prioritize the risks to key infrastructure and assets, as well as to prioritize protection strategies. This can be difficult because assets, functions, and systems within each critical infrastructure sector are not equally important. For example, although the transportation sector is vital, not every bridge is critical to the nation as a whole. Homeland security policy makers must apply consistent methodologies to focus effort on the highest priorities, but they will need to recognize potential conflict with state and local officials trying to secure resources and help for their communities.

2.2.1 Major Initiatives

After the 9/11 attacks, the Department of Homeland Security launched a major initiative that directly focuses federal resources to protect key facilities and systems of national importance, while providing intergovernmental support to state and local officials to protect other, more regional assets. One goal of the DHS is to unify America's infrastructure protection effort by requiring a single accountable official to assess threats and vulnerabilities comprehensively across

FOR EXAMPLE

Where Will Future Attacks on America Occur?

Everyone from security policy analysts to fiction writers have weighed in on where the next attacks will occur. Will they be on a military base? A nuclear power plant? How about an amusement park or shopping mall? In the following excerpt, futurist and author Richard A. Clarke gives his vision of what could happen, demonstrating that securing the homeland means thinking beyond the obvious military or political targets:

"Two women strolling separately through Mouseworld's Showcase of the Future detonated their exploding belts in the vicinity of tour groups in the Mexican Holiday and Austrian Biergarten exhibits. Similar attacks took place at WaterWorld, in California; Seven Pennants, near Dallas; and the Rosebud Casino, in Atlantic City. By the end of the day 1,032 people were dead and more than 4,000 wounded. The victims included many children and elderly citizens. Among the dead were only eight terrorists, two each from Iraq, Indonesia, Pakistan, and the Philippines . . .

"The 4.2-million-square-foot mall, located in Minnesota, was globally recognized as the largest entertainment and retail complex in America, welcoming more than 42 million visitors each year, or 117,000 a day. On this day neither the 160 security cameras surveying the mall nor the 150 safety officers guarding it were able to detect, deter, or defend against the terrorists. Four men, disguised as private mall-security officers and armed with TEC-9 submachine guns, street-sweeper 12-gauge shotguns, and dynamite, entered the mall at two points and began executing shoppers at will. . . ."

(*Source:* "Ten Years Later" by Richard A. Clarke. Published in *Atlantic Monthy*, January/February 2005 issue.)

all infrastructure sectors to ensure we reduce the overall risk to our country, instead of inadvertently shifting risk from one potential set of targets to another. Under the president's proposal for the department, the DHS would assume responsibility for integrating and coordinating all federal infrastructure protection responsibilities. The Department of Homeland Security would consolidate and focus the activities performed previously by the Critical Infrastructure Assurance Office located under the Department of Commerce.

In June 2006, the U.S. Department of Homeland Security released the *National Infrastructure Protection Plan* (NIPP). This plan is a comprehensive risk management framework that clearly defines critical infrastructure protection roles and responsibilities for all levels of government, private industry, nongovernmental agencies, and tribal partners. The NIPP builds on the principles of the President's National Strategy for Homeland Security found in the December 17, 2003, Homeland Security Presidential Directive (HSPD 7) and companion strategies for the physical protection of critical infrastructure and key resources, as well as the strategy for securing cyberspace found in the Homeland Security Act of 2002. President Bush's HSPD 7 identified seventeen CI/KR sectors that require protective actions for a terrorist attack or other hazards, including:

▲ Agriculture and food
▲ Energy
▲ Public health and health care
▲ Banking and finance
▲ Drinking water and water treatment systems
▲ Information technology
▲ Telecommunications
▲ Postal and shipping
▲ Transportation systems including mass transit, aviation, and maritime
▲ Ground or surface and rail and pipeline systems
▲ Chemical commercial facilities
▲ Government facilities
▲ Emergency services
▲ Dams
▲ Nuclear reactors, materials, and waste
▲ The defense industrial base
▲ National monuments and icons

Because most critical infrastructure is privately owned or owned by state and local governments, the 2006 NIPP stresses intergovernmental cooperation to build integrated risk assessments for all levels of government to implement. Additionally, the NIPP incorporates an **all-hazards approach** to homeland security. It addresses "direct impacts, disruptions, and cascading effects of natural disasters (e.g., Hurricanes Katrina and Rita, the Northridge earthquake, etc.) and manmade incidents (e.g., the Three Mile Island Nuclear Power Plant accident or the Exxon Valdez oil spill)" on the nation's critical infrastructure and key assets (Department of Homeland Security 2006b, 12) Thus, the NIPP represents a public and private sector partnership that includes the following:

▲ A comprehensive approach that integrates authorities, capabilities, and resources on a national, regional, and local scale

▲ A complete and accurate assessment of the nation's critical infrastructure and key assets that not only helps inform the prioritization of protection activities, but also enables response and recovery efforts

▲ An organization and coordinating structure to enable effective partnership between and among federal, state, local, and tribal governments, regional and international entities, and the private sector

▲ An integrated approach to enhancing protection of the physical, cyber, and human elements of the nation's critical infrastructure and key assets in which individual security measures complement one another

▲ The development and use of sophisticated analytical and modeling tools to help inform effective risk-mitigation programs in an all-hazards context

With 17 possible security threat categories identified, it is difficult to determine how to protect each type of critical infrastructure and key resource and to what extent. The NIPP uses a risk management framework that combines consequence, vulnerability, and threat information to produce a comprehensive assessment of national or sector-specific risks. As shown in Figure 2-3, the risk management framework includes assessments of "dependencies, interdependencies, and cascading effects; identification of common vulnerabilities; development and sharing of common threat scenarios; development and sharing of cross-sector measures to reduce or manage risk; and identification of specific [research and development] needs" (29). This framework applies to the general threat environment, as well as to specific threats or incident situations.

2.2.2 Types of Protection

To accomplish this seemly impossible task of protecting critical infrastructure and key assets, the Department of Homeland Security has specific federal authority to

Figure 2-3

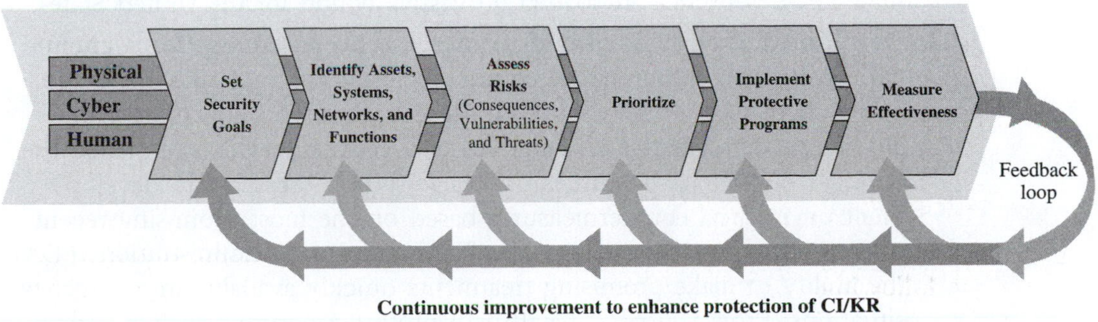

Continuous improvement to enhance protection of CI/KR

The *National Infrastructure Protection Plan* risk management framework (Source: Department of Homeland Security 2006b, 4).

carry out its mission. Among the organizational steps accomplished in the first three years of the DHS are the following:

▲ **Establishing the Domestic Nuclear Detection Office (DNDO):** The DNDO, which is located within the DHS, provides a single federal organization to develop and deploy a nuclear-detection system to thwart the importation of illegal nuclear or radiological materials.

▲ **Strengthening transportation security through screening and prevention:** Since 9/11, the Transportation Security Administration (TSA) has made significant advancements in aviation security, including the installation of hardened cockpit doors, a substantial increase in the number of federal air marshals, the training and authorization of thousands of pilots to carry firearms in the cockpit, the 100 percent screening of all passengers and baggage, and the stationing of explosives-detection canine teams at each of the nation's largest airports.

▲ **Improving border screening and security through the US-VISIT entry-exit system:** US-VISIT uses cutting-edge biometric technology to help ensure that our borders remain open to legitimate travelers but closed to terrorists. US-VISIT is in place at 115 airports, 14 seaports, and 50 land border crossings across the country. Since January 2004, more than 39 million visitors have been checked through US-VISIT.

▲ **Establishing the National Targeting Center (NTC) to screen all imported cargo:** The DHS established the NTC to examine cargo and passengers destined for the United States to identify those presenting the greatest threat. The NTC screens data on 100 percent of inbound shipping containers (9 million per year) to identify those posing a high risk. Personnel then examine 100 percent of these high-risk containers.

▲ **Expanding shipping security through the Container Security Initiative (CSI):** The CSI is currently established in over 35 major international seaports to pre-screen shipping containers for illicit or dangerous materials before they are loaded on vessels bound for the United States.

▲ **Developing Project BioShield to increase preparedness for a chemical, biological, radiological, or nuclear attack.** Project BioShield is a comprehensive effort to ensure that resources ($5.6 billion) are available to pay for "next-generation" medical countermeasures; expedite the conduct of National Institutes of Health (NIH) research and development on medical countermeasures based on the most promising recent scientific discoveries; and give the Food and Drug Administration (FDA) the ability to make promising treatments quickly available in emergency situations. Project BioShield will help protect Americans against a chemical, biological, radiological, or nuclear attack (www.whitehouse.gov/infocus/homeland/).

This list details only part of the homeland security initiatives being taken nationwide. In addition to federal programs, each state and local entity is encouraged to adopt plans to prepare for security threats. The Homeland Security Grant Program (HSGP) provides funds to states, territories, local governments, and tribal governments for preparedness planning, equipment acquisition, training, exercises, management, and administration. In 2006, over $1.7 billion was allocated to this program to help states identify and plan for possible threats to critical infrastructure and key resources (Department of Homeland Security 2006a). Overall, the emphasis on protecting critical infrastructure and key resources remains a local and state issue, with federal help available for program funding and technical assistance.

Protecting America's critical infrastructure and key resources requires more than just money, people, and materials. Cooperation between federal, state, and local governments is critical to ensuring adequate planning and protection. Critical infrastructure and key resources are the systems and assets so vital to the United States that the incapacity or destruction of such systems and assets would have a debilitating impact on security, national economic security, national public health or safety, or any combination of those matters. Destruction of these systems and individual points could create local disasters or profoundly damage national morale. The federal government must use a broad range of measures to help enable state, local, and private-sector entities to better protect the assets and infrastructures they control, and to create a more effective means of providing specific and useful threat information to non-federal entities in a timely fashion.

SELF-CHECK

1. Define critical infrastructures and key resources.

2. Which of the following is not a key federal initiative toward homeland security?

    a. Developing the *National Infrastructure Protection Plan* (NIPP)
    b. Consolidating federal responsibility for protection of critical infrastructures under the Department of Defense
    c. Identifying 17 critical infrastructures/key resources in our country
    d. Establishing a risk-management framework under the NIPP

3. One type of protection implemented by the Department of Homeland Security is improving border screening and security through the US-VISIT entry-exit system. True or false?

4. An all-hazards approach to homeland security addresses direct impacts, disruptions, and cascading effects of natural disasters and manmade incidents. True or false?

2.3 Economic Pressures and Activities

In America, the private sector provides most goods and services, so it is important to include private companies in homeland security strategies. Additionally, the private sector also owns the vast majority of America's critical infrastructure. Airlines, utilities, and agriculture production are just a few of the infrastructure and resources that are privately owned. The private sector also includes many academic, scientific, medical, engineering, and technological research facilities and institutions whose work contributes to the well-being of society as a whole. Businesses and industries have had a long relationship with the government, as both contractors for government projects and as innovators whose products help government implement programs. For example, Nexia Biotechnologies, a private biotechnology company, developed rescue therapy (post-exposure treatment) drugs for casualties of chemical weapons using biologically modified goat's milk (Nexia Biotechnologies 2004). Nexia is not a government agency, but its products are obviously of great importance to public safety and security, and its research and product development are important to government programs. Another example is the involvement of private information technology firms such as AT&T with homeland security. Companies now have entire divisions dedicated to developing homeland security initiatives, and they have worked with intelligence agencies to find new ways to monitor illegal activities in publicly accessible technologies such as the Internet. Although this close association between government and business can cause controversy, it is most often criticized when government appears to be overreaching in its control over the business community.

2.3.1 Protecting the U.S. Economy

Homeland security is not only important for business ventures, but also for community stability. Businesses depend on a steady cash flow, which can

FOR EXAMPLE

The Internet and Homeland Security

In 2006, the Internet search engine company Google refused to comply with a Department of Justice order to turn over search engine results that could be used to find and prosecute violators of the Child Online Protection Act of 1998. Google, America Online, and the other companies subpoenaed said that this ruling would hurt their businesses, which are secured by the anonymity their clients have when using the Internet (Mohammed 2006).

be disrupted if the business is forced to close by security threats. Even if the threat is short term, businesses may have difficulty remaining viable. Long-term events, such as a hurricane, may force businesses to relocate to unknown markets out of their communities. In addition, marginal businesses may not be able to survive perceived threats in their communities. The ripple effect of such difficulties will be felt throughout the community in the form of short-term and long-term unemployment and inconveniences to residents who must find needed goods and services elsewhere. In addition, when their business districts are damaged by man-made or natural disasters, communities also face a host of other long-term problems, including the following:

Oil spill

▲ Loss of property and sales tax revenues

▲ Threats to long-term business district viability

▲ The potential loss of important businesses

▲ The need to continue to find a way to attract a client and customer base

▲ The need to undertake complex reconstruction and redevelopment projects (Waugh 2000, 6–13)

2.3.2 Economic Recovery After an Incident

After a disaster or terrorist attack occurs, it's necessary to incur additional homeland security costs to address economic recovery. Thus, the *National Strategy for Homeland Security* (2002) promotes economic recovery efforts that would involve four central activities:

1. Local economic recovery
2. Restoration of financial markets
3. National economic recovery
4. Economic impact data analysis

Local economic recovery includes a federally coordinated economic recovery plan that will support state and local governments for incidents that overwhelm state, local, and private-sector resources. This approach outlines business and industry sectors that are especially vulnerable, as well as priorities for local responses. As with critical infrastructure and key resources, the emphasis is on local planning and identification of potential vulnerabilities, with fiscal and technical support coming from the federal government.

Restoration of financial markets involves the Department of Homeland Security, the Department of the Treasury, and the White House. In the aftermath of an attack or disaster, these departments would oversee efforts to "effectively monitor financial market status; identify and assess impacts on the markets from direct or indirect attacks; develop appropriate responses to such impacts; inform senior federal officials of the nature of the incident and the appropriate response options; and implement response decisions through appropriate federal, state, local, and private sector entities" (Office of Homeland Security 2002, 65).

National economic recovery further involves the Departments of Homeland Security, the Treasury, and State, as well as the White House. Because a major terrorist incident can have economic impacts beyond the immediate area, these departments would identify the policies, procedures, and participants necessary to assess economic consequences in a coordinated and effective manner. This group would develop recommendations for senior officials on the appropriate federal response and would ensure that government actions after an attack restore critical infrastructure and services as quickly as possible to minimize economic disruptions.

Analyzing economic impact data involves providing sound information about the nature and extent of the economic impact of an incident. Monitoring, assessment, and reporting protocol can provide "credible information concerning the economic status of the area before an incident, assess the direct economic impacts of the incident, and estimate the total economic consequences in a more timely and accurate manner." National efforts to develop this protocol will in turn help develop more accurate national, regional, and local economic impact data needed to assess the appropriate response to the economic consequences of an incident.

2.3.3 The Costs of Homeland Security

Similar to any government program, national homeland security funding can be a challenge to lawmakers, as funding often becomes a political issue subject to debate and influences from constituency interests. Although homeland security has direct benefits, it can also take away from spending for other programs. Sometimes money spent on homeland security can take away from resources that could be used for other types of public safety, such as cleaner water or safer highways. Funding homeland security programs involves federal, state, local, and private expenditures, all of which are subject to political and fiscal pressures.

Federal Expenditures

Figure 2-4 shows how Congress allocates federal spending across all federal agencies, and Table 2-2 shows how portions of that money have been allocated for homeland security. In fiscal year 2001 (FY 2001), before 9/11, the federal government allocated $20.7 billion to homeland security. In FY 2002, this amount increased to $33.0 billion, and by FY 2006, it was up to $49.7 billion.

Figure 2-4

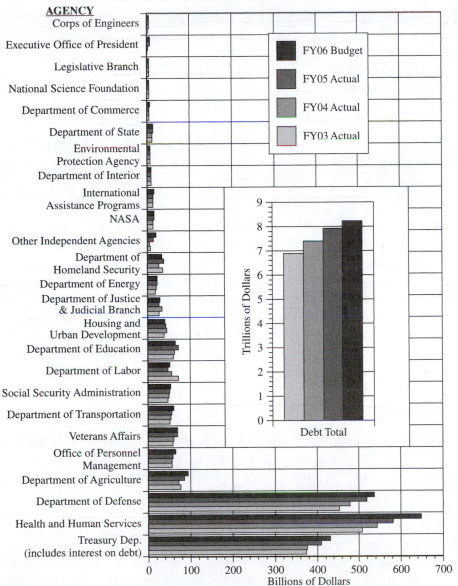

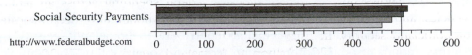

Distribution of the federal budget (Source: www.federalbudget.com).

Table 2-2: Total Federal Resources Allocated for Homeland Security, 2001–2006

(Amounts in billions of dollars)

	2001	2002	2003	2004	2005	2006
Discretionary Budget Authority						
Regular appropriations	15.0	17.1	32.2	36.5	43.0	42.2
Supplemental appropriations	3.6	12.3	5.9	0.1	0.6	0
Fee-funded activities	0.7	2.0	2.6	3.2	3.3	5.4
Mandatory Spending	1.5	1.7	1.8	1.9	2.2	2.2
Gross Budget Authority	**20.7**	**33.0**	**42.5**	**41.7**	**49.1**	**49.7**

(Sources: Congressional Budget Office; Office of Management and Budget)

The money in the federal budget is derived from federal tax revenue, so funding these increases must come from either higher taxes or cutting other programs. Included in the federal budget is funding to assist state and local governments. For example, in the FY 2007 budget request, the Bush administration proposed approximately $2.57 billion for state and local homeland security assistance (see Table 2-3). This may seem like a tremendous amount of money, but in reality, it accounts for only about 2.3 percent of the estimated $2.3 trillion federal budget for 2007.

Other Expenditures

In addition to federal money allocated, state and local governments must pay for their own homeland security efforts. Before 9/11, 2001, state and local governments spent very little money on homeland security, but by the end of 2002, states spent an estimated $6 billion and cities spent over $2.6 billion to prepare for future incidents (Office of Homeland Security 2002, 65). Fiscal pressures exist in that the tax dollars state and local governments spend defending and protecting their respective communities means a reduction in the revenues available for other programs. New costs that state and local governments must incur include protecting critical infrastructure, improving technologies for information sharing and communications, and building emergency response capacity (Reese 2005).

As state and local governments have taken on added fiscal burdens, private businesses and individuals have had to contribute to homeland security by spending money to protect property and reduce personal liability. For example, building owners have a significant stake in ensuring that their buildings are

Table 2-3: State and Local Homeland Security Assistance Programs: FY 2006 Appropriations and Budget Requests for FY 2007

(Amounts in millions of dollars)

Program	FY 2006 Appropriation	FY 2007 Request	Change from FY 2006
State Homeland Security Grant Program	$550	$633	+15.1%
Urban Area Security Initiative	$740	$838	+13.2%
Urban Area Security Initiative Infrastructure Sub-grants	$415	—	—
Port Security	$175	—	—
Rail Security	$150	—	—
Trucking Industry Security	$5	—	—
Intercity Bus Security	$10	—	—
Non-governmental Organizations Security	$25	—	—
Buffer Zone Protection	$50	—	—
Targeted Infrastructure Protection Program	—	$600	+44.6%
Law Enforcement Terrorism Prevention Program	$400	—	−100%
Assistance to Firefighters Program	$655	$293	−55.3%
Emergency Management Performance Grants	$185	$170	−8.1%
Citizen Corps Programs	$20	$35	+75%
Total	$2,965	$2,570	−13.3%

structurally sound, properly maintained, and safe for occupants. The Council of Economic Advisers estimates that private business spent approximately $55 billion per year on private security before the 9/11 attacks. As a result of the attacks, their annual costs of fighting terrorism may have increased by 50 to 100 percent; however, others argue that the overall economic cost for private industry nationwide is negligible, as increases in productivity for security-related business (e.g. security firms, fencing companies, etc.) offset specific investments businesses must take to secure individual properties or firms (Hobijin 2002, 21–33).

SELF-CHECK

1. After a disaster or terrorist incident, which of the following would not be a key economic factor?

   a. Local economic recovery
   b. Restoration of financial markets
   c. International economic recovery
   d. Economic impact data analysis

2. Since 9/11, homeland security expenditures have been incurred by local, state, and federal government agencies, but not by the private sector. True or false?

3. List some examples of how homeland security funding is allocated to state and local government agencies.

4. While federal funding for state and local homeland security assistance has increased each year since 2001, as a percentage of the federal budget, it is still less than 3 percent of total expenditures. True or false?

2.4 Societal Values: Protecting Democracy

In 2006, the *New York Times* published a story about federally approved domestic wiretapping, leading to a national debate over personal freedoms and homeland security. Under a presidential order signed in 2002, President Bush secretly authorized the National Security Agency to monitor telephone calls and e-mail messages of people inside the United States without the court-approved search warrants ordinarily required for domestic spying (Risen and Lichtblau 2005). Although government officials claimed this program was to monitor people who were possibly linked to al-Qaeda, the decision to permit some eavesdropping inside the country without court approval marked a major shift in American intelligence-gathering practices, and many have questioned whether the surveillance has stretched, if not crossed, constitutional limits on legal searches.

2.4.1 A Controversy as Old as Our Country

Limits to personal freedoms are not a new debate. The Alien and Sedition Act of 1798 was the first law passed to limit speech that was deemed hurtful to the newly established American government. Although this was a temporary law, expiring ten years after its passage, it set a precedent for legal limits to personal freedoms when a national threat is perceived by government officials. Less than a century later, during the Civil War, Abraham Lincoln suspended the **writ of habeas corpus**, the constitutional guarantee that accused persons would be brought before a judge and hear the charges against them. The Supreme Court overturned Lincoln's actions, saying he had overextended his presidential powers, but by World War I, national security was once again an issue. Thus, in 1918, Congress passed the Sedition Act. This act amended the 1917 Espionage Act and banned any language found to be "disloyal, profane, scurrilous, or abusive . . . and intended to cause contempt, scorn, contumely, or disrepute to the government." Although many portions of the Espionage Act were repealed in 1921, major sections of that act remained part of United States law, including limits to unprotected speech (see *Schenck v. United States,* 1919). Once again, America's perceived security threat diminished somewhat, so the Supreme Court relaxed some portions of laws designed to limit personal freedoms, such as the 1918 Sedition Act, but this legal stance would change again with America's entry into World War II. In 1942, for instance, the federal government authorized the forced detention of many Japanese Americans in internment camps to restrict perceived threats to national security (Dye 2005, 328). Even in 2006, the United States government holds about 400 "enemy combatants" in a special military base in Guantanamo Bay, Cuba, most of whom do not have access to lawyers, nor do they know the charges against them.

Throughout American history, the Supreme Court has upheld limits to personal freedoms such as these previous examples. Only when the perceived threat "appears to fade, do American elites again reassert their commitment to fundamental liberties" (Dye 2005, 329). However, what if the threat does not fade? As seen in the beginning of this chapter, the majority of Americans believe that homeland security threats will be a permanent part of our society. If this remains true, how will policy and programs alter how we value our civil liberties? Our pluralistic government allows many groups or institutions to share power in the policy process, which involves compromising and bargaining. As our social values change, certainly so will those influences that guide our value-laden decision making.

2.4.2 The Bill of Rights and Constitutional Issues

Critics of the Homeland Security Act often cite its limits on constitutional rights, namely the rights to freedom of speech, religion, assembly, and privacy; to counsel and due process; and to protection from unreasonable searches and seizures. Much of the debate surrounding homeland security and civil liberties stems from the passage of the USA Patriot Act in 2002, with much criticism against the act directed at the provisions for sneak-and-peek searches.

A **sneak-and-peak search** is a special search warrant that allows law enforcement officers to lawfully enter areas in which a reasonable expectation of privacy exists, to search for items of evidence or contraband and leave without making any seizures or giving concurrent notice of the search. Law enforcement has used sneak-and-peek searches for investigations involving contraband material like drugs or weapons, but the USA Patriot Act extends this authority to investigations involving terrorist suspects. In addition, under this act, some warrants may come from the **Foreign Intelligence Surveillance Court (FISC)** instead of a common federal or state court. FISC warrants are not public record and, therefore, are not required to be released. Other warrants must be released, especially to the person under investigation.

Another controversy involving the USA Patriot Act surrounds the use of **National Security Letters (NSLs)**. FBI field supervisors can issue NSLs without a prosecutor, grand jury, or judge. They receive no review after the fact by the Department of Justice or by Congress. Federal laws expanded by the USA Patriot Act give anti-terrorism and counter-intelligence investigators access to an array of consumer information through National Security Letters. Consumers seldom learn that their records have been reviewed unless they are prosecuted. Some examples of records accessible to investigators include driver's licenses, hotel bills, storage rental agreements, apartment leases and other commercial records, cash deposits, wire and digital money transfers, and even patient business records and personal health information (Gellman 2005).

After passage of the USA Patriot Act, the Department of Homeland Security established the Office for Civil Rights and Civil Liberties in 2003. This agency is charged with providing legal and policy advice to the Department of Homeland Security's leadership on a wide range of civil rights and civil liberties issues. Additionally, public outcry over the extended powers of law enforcement led to revisions in sneak-and-peak rules during the 2005 reauthorization process.

It is important to recognize that homeland security programs may limit constitutional protections in the Bill of Rights, including protections of personal freedoms such as the freedoms of speech and assembly and the rights of the accused. The federal government's position is that laws such as the USA Patriot Act do not hinder personal freedoms (as stated in the Bill of Rights; see sidebar) when used for peaceful debate. According to the language of the act, "[p]eaceful political discourse and dissent is one of America's most cherished freedoms, and is not subject to investigation as domestic terrorism. Under the USA Patriot Act,

THE BILL OF RIGHTS

The first ten amendments to the U.S. Constitution are collectively known as the Bill of Rights. Some of the amendments in the Bill of Rights that have the most direct impact of personal freedoms include the following:

✔ **Amendment I:** "Congress shall make no law respecting an establishment of religion, or prohibiting the free exercise thereof; or abridging the freedom of speech, or of the press; or the right of the people peaceably to assemble, and to petition the government for a redress of grievances."

✔ **Amendment II:** "A well regulated militia, being necessary to the security of a free state, the right of the people to keep and bear arms, shall not be infringed."

✔ **Amendment IV:** "The right of the people to be secure in their persons, houses, papers, and effects, against unreasonable searches and seizures, shall not be violated, and no warrants shall issue, but upon probable cause, supported by oath or affirmation, and particularly describing the place to be searched, and the persons or things to be seized."

✔ **Amendment V:** "No person shall be held to answer for a capital, or otherwise infamous crime, unless on presentment or indictment of a grand jury, except in cases arising in the land or naval forces, or in the militia, when in actual service in time of war or public danger; nor shall any person be subject for the same offense to be twice put in jeopardy of life or limb; nor shall be compelled in any criminal case to be a witness against himself, nor be deprived of life, liberty, or property, without due process of law; nor shall private property be taken for public use, without just compensation."

✔ **Amendment VI:** "In all criminal prosecutions, the accused shall enjoy the right to a speedy and public trial, by an impartial jury of the state and district wherein the crime shall have been committed, which district shall have been previously ascertained by law, and to be informed of the nature and cause of the accusation; to be confronted with the witnesses against him; to have compulsory process for obtaining witnesses in his favor, and to have the assistance of counsel for his defense."

the definition of 'domestic terrorism' is limited to conduct that (1) violates federal or state criminal law and (2) is dangerous to human life. Therefore, peaceful political organizations engaging in political advocacy will obviously not come under this definition" (USA Patriot Act, Section 802). The question remains, however, as to who determines what is peaceful political discourse and what is not.

FOR EXAMPLE

"Radical Militant Librarians" Take on Reauthorization of the USA Patriot Act

In winter 2005, Congress was debating the reauthorization of the USA Patriot Act when internal e-mails from the FBI surfaced, in which FBI agents complained about "radical militant librarians" while criticizing the reluctance of FBI management to use the secret warrants authorized under Section 215 of the USA Patriot Act. "While radical militant librarians kick us around, true terrorists benefit from Office of Intelligence Policy and Review's failure to let us use the tools given to us," the e-mail stated, and it went on to criticize administration policy that did not use records searching to the fullest extent possible. Section 215 of the USA Patriot Act allows for court orders to acquire "the production of any tangible things (including books, records, papers, documents, and other items) for an investigation." This means that library records are subject to court orders, and like medical records or bank accounts, a library patron's book usage is treated as confidential information.

Incensed by these e-mails, the American Library Association argued that it is because of "radical militant librarians" arguing on behalf of library users that Americans have the right to read freely, without government interference or surveillance.

Where do we draw the line between privacy and protection? Libraries have become places to get information from a variety of media. Public Internet access, for example, is available at most libraries. Should this type of access be monitored? On the other hand, should we restrict investigators from accessing private information? Are library records as critical as medical information or financial accounts?

Americans value their personal freedoms, and we can argue that our society's basic foundations include the civil liberties and rights established in the Constitution. Even though protecting the nation from threats at the expense of personal freedoms is not a new debate, the general public's views on matters of homeland security sometimes dramatically differs. This can affect politics and program implementation. Homeland security presents a new challenge to protecting personal liberties, as we have found through the use of intelligence gathering and expanded federal authority under the USA Patriot Act, and many legal questions remain unanswered. The American public must continue to debate the tradeoffs between personal freedoms and homeland security as federal policies and programs continue to evolve.

SELF-CHECK

1. Identify the key personal freedoms established in the Bill of Rights.

2. A sneak-and-peak search is a special search warrant that allows law enforcement officers to lawfully enter areas where a reasonable expectation of privacy exists, to search for items of evidence or contraband and leave without making any seizures or giving concurrent notice of the search. True or false?

3. The writ of habeas corpus was suspended in the United States during which of the following conflicts?
   a. War of 1812
   b. Civil War
   c. World War I
   d. First Gulf War

4. National Security Letters require judicial review after issuance. True or false?

SUMMARY

Homeland security is the combination of activities that protect people, key infrastructure and assets, economic activities, and our way of life. This chapter explored the fundamental questions regarding homeland security: who and what it protects, and how the structure of our government affects decision making and national initiatives. More specifically, in this chapter, you assessed who is served by homeland security programs; evaluated the different roles of federal, state, and local agencies; appraised the consequences of security threats and their effect on our nation's critical infrastructures and societal values; and judged our nation's defensive and offensive capabilities concerning people, places, and things. You also explored how the concept and perception of risk influences public attitudes, which in turn influence policy makers. Finally, you learned about the role of homeland security and the social value of our personal freedoms.

KEY TERMS

All-hazards approach	An approach to homeland security that addresses impacts, disruptions, and cascading effects of both natural disasters and manmade incidents.

Bureaucracy	The sum of all federal departments, agencies, and offices that implement laws under the authority of the president. By definition, bureaucracies are hierarchical organizations that are highly specialized, and they operate with very formal rules.
CI/KR	Abbreviation for critical infrastructure and key resources.
Critical infrastructure	Systems and assets, whether physical or virtual, so vital to the United States that the incapacity or destruction of such systems and assets would have a debilitating impact on security, national economic security, national public health or safety, or any combination of those matters.
Department of Homeland Security (DHS)	Federal department created in 2002 with the primary mission of protecting the United States against terrorist threats.
Direct democracy	A system of government in which people represent themselves and vote directly on legislative matters.
Federal system	A vertical division of power found in the United States in which the national government has some exclusive powers, state and local governments have some exclusive powers, other powers are shared by all levels of government, and some powers are reserved to state and local governments.
Foreign Intelligence Surveillance Court (FISC)	Court that can issue search warrants that are not public record and therefore not required to be released.
Homeland security	Those activities that protect people, critical infrastructure, key resources, economic activities, and our way of life.
Key resources	Individual targets whose destruction would not endanger vital systems,

but could create local disaster or profoundly damage our nation's morale or confidence. Key resources can be publicly or privately controlled resources essential to the minimal operations of the economy and government.

National Security Letter (NSL)

Letter issued by an FBI field supervisor without a prosecutor, grand jury, or judge. An NSL receives no review after the fact by the Department of Justice or by Congress. Federal laws expanded by the USA Patriot Act give anti-terrorism and counter-intelligence investigators access to an array of consumer information through NSLs.

Non-governmental organization (NGO)

An organization that provides a service to a community free of charge or for a minimal cost that is required to defray the cost of the service furnished. NGOs usually hold special non-profit federal tax-exempt status and receive financial support through donations, contracts, and grants.

Pluralism

A system of government in which many groups or institutions share power in a complex system of interactions, which involves compromising and bargaining in the decision-making process.

Representative democracy

A system of government in which the ultimate political authority is vested in the people, who elect their governing officials to legislate on their behalf.

Risk

The combination of vulnerability and the consequence of a specified hazardous event.

Separation of powers

System through which governmental power is divided between the executive, legislative, and judicial branches of the national government.

Sneak-and-peek search

A special search warrant that allows law enforcement officers to lawfully enter areas in which a reasonable expectation of privacy exists, to search for items of evidence or contraband and leave without making any seizures or giving concurrent notice of the search.

White House Office of Homeland Security

An executive agency that advises the president on homeland security issues and works with the Office of Management and Budget to develop and defend the president's homeland security budget proposals.

Writ of habeas corpus

The constitutional guarantee that accused persons will be brought before a judge to hear charges against them.

ASSESS YOUR UNDERSTANDING

Go to www.wiley.com/college/kilroy to assess your knowledge of the basics of U.S. homeland security interests.
Measure your learning by comparing pre-test and post-test results.

Summary Questions

1. Homeland security only protects people. True or false?
2. Laws restricting personal freedoms date back to the 1790s. True or false?
3. Sneak-and-peak searches are illegal. True or false?
4. Homeland security involves local, state, tribal, and federal agencies. True or false?
5. Coastal counties constitute only 17 percent of the total land area of the United States (not including Alaska), but account for 53 percent of the country's total population. True or false?
6. Which of the following is **not** a national key resource?
   (a) Washington Monument
   (b) The Corn Palace in Mitchell, South Dakota
   (c) The Liberty Bell
   (d) The Pentagon
7. Which of the following has raised a controversy regarding civil liberties under the USA Patriot Act?
   (a) FBI access to library records
   (b) Posting socialist ideas on a personal blog
   (c) Media coverage of the war in Iraq
   (d) Banning anti-war books from schools
8. Which of the following agencies was **not** involved in homeland security prior to 9/11?
   (a) Department of Homeland Security
   (b) Department of Defense
   (c) Department of Health and Human Services
   (d) Department of Transportation
9. The portion of Section 215 of the Patriot Act that caused a large public outcry involved the search of which type of records?
   (a) Voting records
   (b) Driver's license tests
   (c) School attendance records
   (d) Library records

10. Which of the following statements is true with regard to sneak-and-peek searches?
    (a) They have been used in drug enforcement, weapons searches, and homeland security enforcement.
    (b) They require notice of inspection to the occupants.
    (c) They require confiscation of evidence.
    (d) They can be issued by law enforcement agencies without any judicial approval.

Applying This Chapter

1. You are asked to join a local discussion group that focuses on issues related to the Internet and the First Amendment. How does the Internet help or hurt the freedom of expression in this country? Should blogs, webpages, and other online journals be considered private expression or public information? Should Internet content be regulated?

2. If you were in the FBI and needed a search warrant to "look around" a suspected terrorist's apartment, what type of warrant would you need? Where would you go to secure this warrant?

3. You are the mayor of a small town and need to determine the critical infrastructure and key resources for your community. Where would you go for help? What would be some topics for your plan, and what topics or issues do you see as being in your jurisdiction? What would be some recommendations for spending priorities?

4. You are the librarian in a county library. You have noticed four men coming in daily for many weeks using the library's computers. They spend most of the day in front of the computers. One night, after hours, you pull up the history files in the computer and notice they have been visiting websites for groups advocating terrorist activities. What do you do? What do you do if you receive inquiries from law enforcement asking for any information on suspicious activities? Do you forward the information you have regarding your patrons, or do you protect the patrons' privacy rights?

Security v. Civil Liberties?

Analyze the original provisions of the USA Patriot Act. Write a paper on whether you believe the act has enhanced security at the expense of freedom or has been a reasonable response to the threat the United States faces today.

Forum Discuss?

Policy Recommendations

Evaluate the *National Infrastructure Protection Plan* (NIPP). Assess its strong points, as well as where it comes up short. Make a policy recommendation to the Secretary of Homeland Security for a future revision of the NIPP.

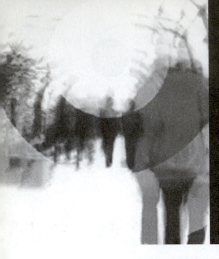

3

THE ALL-HAZARDS PERSPECTIVE
Understanding the Nature of Threats Due to Natural, Accidental, and Man-made Disasters

Starting Point

Go to www.wiley.com/college/kilroy to assess your knowledge of the basics of the all-hazards perspective.
Determine where you need to concentrate your effort.

What You'll Learn in This Chapter

▲ The difference between natural, accidental, and man-made disasters
▲ The history of the types and sources of disasters in the United States
▲ The consequences and management of natural, accidental, and man-made disasters in a post-9/11 world

After Studying This Chapter, You'll Be Able To

▲ Evaluate the types of natural, accidental, and man-made disasters that can and do occur in the United States today
▲ Assess the nature of our response to natural, accidental, and man-made disasters in the United States
▲ Judge how disasters can have catastrophic effects on and implications for our nation's response in the war on terrorism

INTRODUCTION

After the terrorist attacks against America on 9/11, the national response was to elevate terrorism to the highest category of current and potential threats to the U.S. homeland. In other words, the attitude toward homeland security was to take an "exclusive" view, focused only on terrorist threats, rather than an "inclusive" view that assessed all potential hazards as threats to the homeland.

In this chapter, you will evaluate the types of natural, accidental, and man-made disasters that can and do occur in the United States, as well as assess the nature of our response to these disasters. You will also judge how today's disasters can have catastrophic effects and implications for our nation's response in the war on terrorism. Similar to an act of terrorism, a disaster of any type can have devastating consequences for our nation's critical infrastructures, as well as effects on commerce and our way of life. How the United States has responded to such occurrences in the past, both organizationally and operationally, has been impacted by the events of 9/11.

3.1 Natural Disasters: Things We Can Expect to Happen

Prior to 9/11, terrorism was a relatively rare occurrence within the United States. Most of the nation's response capability at the local, state, and federal levels was focused on threats of nature, or **natural disasters**, such as hurricanes, tornados, floods, and forest fires. Although there was concern for attacks in the form of a potential nuclear exchange with the former Soviet Union during the Cold War, most of the emphasis on **civil defense**, or the protection of the nation against threats within the United States, was focused on our nation's capability to respond to acts of nature. Various government agencies charged with civil defense and response missions, such as the **Federal Emergency Management Agency (FEMA)** and the National Guard, were primarily organized to respond to the consequences of natural disasters, such as occurred in New Orleans in September 2005 with Hurricane Katrina.

It seems that regardless of where you live in the United States, you are bound to be subject to the extremes of nature. On the East and Gulf Coasts, you can experience the effects of hurricanes, which occur seasonally from June to November. On the West Coast, you are more likely to be subject to earthquakes and devastating forest fires. In the heartland of America, you tend to be prone to experience the consequences of tornados, floods, and severe winter storms. Lest we forget about Alaska and Hawaii, they too have unique environmental problems due to hazards such as tidal waves and volcanoes.

Given the certainty that natural disasters will occur, our nation has a long history of preparation for such disasters and the capability to respond in a crisis. Local communities have developed emergency response capabilities, often tailored to the threats their communities face. For example in Greenville, North Carolina, there is not a robust supply of road salt and sand to respond to winter storms. Thus, when such storms hit in 2004, the community was not prepared and quickly exhausted local resources. However, due to the flooding experienced in eastern North Carolina during Hurricane Floyd in 1999, the local community is much better prepared for the threat of a hurricane and has a well-rehearsed community response plan in place to deal with such a disaster.

3.1.1 The History of Natural Disasters in the United States

One of the earliest disasters recorded in history was the "Great Fire of London" in September 1666, which destroyed much of the city and caused over £10 million (British pounds sterling) in damage. Yet, ironically, there was little loss of life. In the United States, the best-known fire occurred in Chicago in 1872, destroying over 17,000 buildings and killing over 250 people. However, the most devastating fire in our nation's history occurred in Peshtigo, Wisconsin, in October 1871, where over 3.8 billion acres were destroyed and 1,500 lives were lost (Infoplease n.d.).

Despite these examples, the most devastating natural disaster in our nation's history remains the hurricane that hit Galveston, Texas, in September 1900, destroying over 3,500 buildings and killing over 6,000 inhabitants of the island. The hurricane was estimated to have winds clocking 140 miles per hour, making it a Category 5 storm by today's standards. Most of the damage, however, was not caused by winds but by the tidal surge, estimated at over 15 feet, which swamped the island, destroying a town of 37,000 people. Estimated damage was placed at $20 million dollars ($700 million in today's dollars) (1900 Storm n.d.).

When people think of earthquakes, they naturally think of California, the San Andreas Fault, and the April 1906 San Francisco earthquake. This event was the worst earthquake recorded in American history, killing over 3,000 people (Epic Disasters n.d.). Although California has the most deadly recorded earthquakes in the United States, major earthquakes have also hit Alaska, Hawaii, and South Carolina. Furthermore, the most deadly earthquakes ever in the U.S. could yet occur in the nation's midsection, impacting major population centers along the Mississippi Valley. For this reason, FEMA continues to consider this region, located along the New Madrid Fault Line, as one of a number of potential disaster areas due to the scale of the damage that could occur, the breadth of area impacted (eight states, four FEMA regions), and the potential for significant secondary effects due to extreme weather and climate conditions depending on the time of year such an event might occur (Lowder 2006).

FOR EXAMPLE

The New Madrid Fault Line

In 1811 and 1812, three major earthquakes occurred in the midsection of the United States along the New Madrid Fault Line (see Figure 3-1). The earthquakes were huge, believed to be of a magnitude of 8.0 on the Richter scale, and were felt even along the East Coast. New lakes were formed, and the Mississippi River was reported to have flowed backward. However, harm to buildings and people was limited due to the sparse populations that existed around the quakes' epicenters at that time. If such an event were to occur today, the major population centers of St. Louis, Missouri; Cairo, Illinois; and Memphis, Tennessee would be severely impacted. According to the U.S. Geological Survey, "[e]ven today, this region has more earthquakes than any other part of the United States east of the Rocky Mountains. Government agencies, universities, and private organizations are working to increase awareness of the earthquake threat and to reduce loss of life and property in future shocks" (United States Geological Survey n.d.).

Figure 3-1

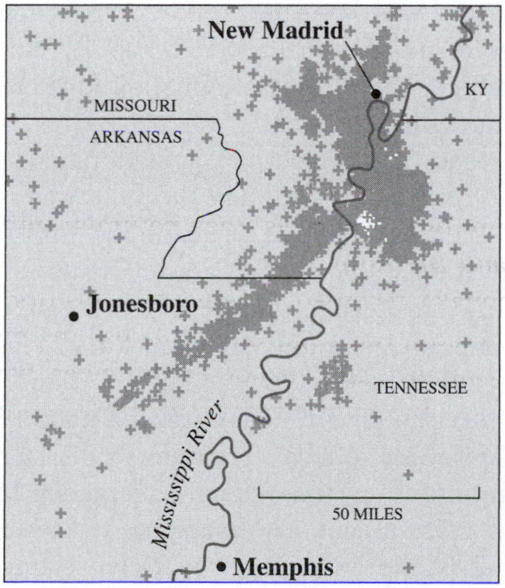

New Madrid Fault Line and major population centers
(FEMA, by permission).

3.1.2 Natural Disaster Response

The United States has a long history of preparing for and responding to natural disasters. For instance, Benjamin Franklin helped form the Union Fire Company in Philadelphia, Pennsylvania, in 1736 as a voluntary firefighting society in which members pledged their support to protect each others' property. Later, Franklin went on to organize the nation's first fire insurance company in 1752, based on the economic threat from a fire disaster.

For most of our nation's history, response to natural disasters was dependent on grass-roots, citizen-based volunteer organizations, where members of the community came together to meet the needs of others when a disaster struck. There was little expectation that the federal government would provide relief other than financial recourse, as occurred in 1803, when Congress authorized funds to support a New Hampshire town devastated by fire. Even then, and for the next 100 years, federal assistance was limited to public infrastructure, mostly roads, bridges, and so on (Federal Emergency Management Agency n.d.).

In the 1930s, during the presidency of Franklin D. Roosevelt, increased federalization impacted disaster relief through organizations such as the Reconstruction Finance Corporation and Bureau of Public Roads. The federal government also made more federal support available to local communities through the assistance of organizations such as the Army Corps of Engineers, which performed much of the work on the nation's transportation infrastructure, including roads, bridges, dams, and waterways for flood control projects. It wasn't until 1968 and the passage of the National Flood Insurance Act, however, that the federal government made a commitment to provide financial support to private property damaged in a natural disaster.

Throughout this time, the primary organizational response to a disaster remained at the local community level, and the state was only impacted when local remedies were exhausted by the scale of the disaster. Furthermore, it wasn't until 1974 and the passage of the Disaster Relief Act that the president established the authority to declare a **state of emergency** due to a disaster, making the affected area of the country eligible for increased federal support and funding.

Finally, in 1979, the U.S. government created a national agency to provide a coordinated federal response to local community's disaster needs. Established under the Carter administration, the Federal Emergency Management Agency (FEMA) consolidated most of nation's fragmented disaster response mechanisms, including those of the Department of Defense under its civil defense responsibilities, into one federal agency. The first director of FEMA, John Macy, "emphasized the similarities between natural hazards preparedness and the civil defense activities. FEMA began development of an Integrated Emergency Management System with an all-hazards approach that included 'direction, control, and warning systems which are common to the full range of emergencies from small isolated events to the ultimate emergency—war'" (Federal Emergency Management Agency n.d.).

Later, under the leadership of James Lee Witt during the Clinton administration, FEMA became a Cabinet-level agency, recognized as the **lead federal agency** for coordinating the efforts of all other federal agencies in disaster response. However, FEMA was still under the auspices of the Robert T. Stafford Disaster Relief and Emergency Assistance Act **(Stafford Act)**, originally passed by Congress in 1985, providing the means by which the president can declare a state of emergency and thus authorize federal funds for disaster relief to both public agencies and private persons. Since its passage, the Stafford Act has been amended a number of times, with the most comprehensive changes occurring in 2000. The Stafford Act designated state governors as the lead officials for determining the need for federal assistance based on the scope of the disaster and the exhaustion of local remedies. Under the original intent of this act, the president was limited to a reactionary role, responding to a stated need rather then being proactive in anticipating a need. FEMA also operated primarily in a response mode, only showing up at the scene of a disaster once local authorities determined the need for federal assistance (Miskel 2006, 103).

During the late 1980s and early 1990s, however, FEMA came under sharp rebuke by the public and state and local governments for its slow response to disasters, even though the Stafford Act remained in effect. Also, changes to legislation during the 1980s expanded the categories of eligibility for federal disaster assistance to both individuals and organizations. Thus, between 1984 and 1988, there were only 26 disaster declarations, yet from 1989 through 1993, that number jumped to 42, and from 1994 to 1997, it rose to 97 (England-Joseph 1998).

To get a better idea of some of the events precipitating the changes to federal disaster response during this period, consider the example of Hurricane Andrew. In 1992, this devastating storm slammed into South Florida, with winds in excess of 170 miles per hour. Over 23 people were killed in the storm, and the region suffered over $26 billion in property damage. The Florida National Guard was quickly overwhelmed with the state of the disaster, prompting the president to send in active duty service members from the Tenth Mountain Division, stationed in Ft. Drum, New York. FEMA was the lead federal agency for organizing the federal response effort. However, due to the slow response and lack of coordinated effort, FEMA was heavily criticized, prompting President Clinton to fire its director, replacing him with James Lee Witt in 1993, the first professional emergency manager to serve in this position (Glasser and White 2005; National Oceanic and Atmospheric Administration 2002).

3.1.3 Natural Disasters in a Post-9/11 World

After the terrorist attacks on the U.S. homeland on 9/11, 2001, the federal government established the Department of Homeland Security (DHS) to respond to the threat of terrorism on American soil. As part of the reorganization of the federal government, FEMA was brought under the control of the new DHS structure, losing its status as an independent federal agency. The initial proposal, in theory, to consolidate all federal agencies with responsibility for responding to domestic threats (whether from terrorism or natural disasters) appeared to make sense operationally. Because terrorist incidents involved the potential for catastrophic events on par with natural disasters or with even greater consequences, FEMA would be a key player in coordinating the federal response to any incident of this scale.

One of the first significant tests of the DHS structure came in August 2005, when Hurricane Katrina, a Category 3 storm, hit the Gulf Coast city of New Orleans head-on with winds in excess of 125 miles per hour. Initially, the damage to the city and neighboring community of Gulfport, Mississippi, was extensive, but not catastrophic. Three days later, however, the levees broke in New Orleans, causing extensive flooding. The failure of the city government or state to exercise an effective evacuation plan left people stranded on rooftops or sheltered in places such as the Superdome. The city devolved into chaos as law enforcement officers failed to show up for work and lawlessness ensued. The federal government eventually called in active-duty military forces to patrol the streets and restore order and basic services. In the aftermath, there was much finger pointing by city, state, and federal officials as to whose fault it was for the poor response. FEMA's director, Michael Brown, was fired, but he later appeared somewhat vindicated on the talk show circuit, offering evidence as to how FEMA was neglected and how his advice was ignored by senior Bush administration officials. In the end, over 1,300 people died in Katrina's aftermath, and more than 1 million people were evacuated to other locations, such as Houston, Texas, where many remain to this day. In addition, over $44 billion in property damage occurred to New Orleans and the coastal towns of Mississippi (Lowder 2006; Gannon 2005).

Unfortunately, within 30 days after Katrina, a second barrel blast occurred with Hurricane Rita hitting the coast of Texas. Although the human tragedy of this storm was much less, the economic impact was great, with major oil refineries in Port Arthur, Texas, extensively damaged. It took months for these facilities to recover, causing fuel shortages all along the East Coast and spikes in gas prices.

After 9/11, the primary threat focus of the federal government was (and still is) terrorism. Although DHS leaders, such as Michael Chertoff, stated publicly that the DHS maintained an all-hazard perspective, even before these catastrophic hurricanes hit, it was evident that with regard to funding and organizational status under the DHS, FEMA was being marginalized and its leadership ignored. On the organizational chart, the director of FEMA at the time of Hurricanes Katrina and Rita, Michael Brown, was considered Under Secretary for Emergency Response, a position that afforded him direct access to the Director of DHS. Yet, operationally, it made the director of FEMA one of five under secretaries in the organization. As for resources, FEMA saw its operational budget reduced in the years prior to 2005 as well, further indicating its loss of status within the DHS hierarchy (Glasser and White 2005).

What made the situation in the Gulf States particularly egregious was the public perception that the federal government did not care. The lack of initial concern, and slow response in the aftermath of the devastating floods, led to charges of racism against the Bush administration because most of the victims were African American and poor, despite that fact that most of the violence and human misery was caused by victims taking advantage of other victims. Television images of looting, homeless people massed in the squalor of the Superdome, and even reports of murders and rapes made New Orleans look like a city in war-torn Somalia rather than Louisiana. U.S. Coast Guard and National Guard helicopters rescuing victims off rooftops further lent to charges of government incompetence at best and dereliction of duty at worst. The Bush administration did its best at damage control, trying to deflect criticism on the poor performance of New Orleans Mayor Ray Nagin and Louisiana Governor Kathleen Blanco for not doing what they should have done at the local and state level. Such attempts only proved counterproductive, however, as the public communicated their belief that in a post-9/11 world, they expected the federal government to be more proactive, whether the threat be a natural disaster or a terrorist incident.

Responding to such criticism, President Bush took proactive measures prior to Hurricane Rita, appointing the current U.S. Coast Guard (USCG) Commandant, Admiral Thad Allen (then Vice Admiral and USCG Chief of Staff), as the **Principal Federal Official (PFO)** and **Federal Coordinating Officer (FCO)** in charge of coordinating all post-Katrina federal agency support on behalf of the U.S. government. President Bush also gave the active-duty military a more prominent role in preparation for Hurricane Rita by positioning himself in the command center at the U.S. Northern Command headquarters in Colorado Springs, Colorado, as the hurricane made landfall. These actions were intended to communicate to the American public that the federal government was engaged and would no longer react to natural disasters in the same way again.

As a result of Hurricanes Katrina and Rita, there was some discussion by members of Congress and others that FEMA should be restored to its status as an independent federal agency, out from under DHS control. Secretary of Homeland Security Michael Chertoff argued the need to keep FEMA under DHS control in order to maintain a unified federal response to any catastrophic event, whether a terrorist incident or a natural disaster. Secretary Chertoff did make some organizational changes within FEMA, however, replacing political appointee Michael Brown with a professional emergency responder, R. David Paulison. FEMA also underwent significant internal leadership changes to deal with other post-Katrina failings with regard to the lack of accountability over federal payouts to victims and charges of waste, fraud, and abuse of the compensation programs.

In October 2006, President Bush signed the DHS appropriations bill for 2007, which made changes to the Stafford Act under Title VI, the "Post-Katrina Emergency Management Reform Act of 2006." The act gave FEMA a quasi-independent status but kept it under DHS, restoring some of its original authorities and correcting some of the weaknesses that Congress perceived in the Stafford Act. The end result of all these changes will likely be an expanding federal mandate, at the expense of local and state authorities, when it comes to homeland security policies.

SELF-CHECK

1. Since 9/11, FEMA has been returned to its status as an independent federal agency, out from under control of the Department of Homeland Security. True or false?

2. According to the Stafford Act, which official has responsibility for recognizing the need for a federal declaration of a state of emergency and requesting federal support?

   a. The president
   b. The Secretary of the DHS
   c. The local mayor
   d. The state governor

3. Define PFO.

4. James Lee Witt was the first professional emergency manager to lead FEMA. True or false?

3.2 Accidental Hazards: Things We Can Try to Prevent

When considering security from an all-hazards perspective, one area of concern that is often neglected is protection from accidental hazards. Many times, after a personal accident occurs, we ask ourselves, "What could I have done to prevent this?" The same holds true for public and private organizations, which can suffer catastrophic losses from accidental hazards. For this reason, most businesses and individuals carry accident protection insurance for both natural and accidental hazards, such as broken water pipes in our homes or traffic accidents while driving our cars.

But what is the difference between a disaster and an accident? A **disaster** that is not natural can best be understood as "an unintentional event that causes extensive damage, injury, and loss of life" (Pocock n.d.). The difference between a disaster and an **accident** is based on the scale of the accident and the impact.

From a national security perspective, what may first appear to be an accident may also be intentional and not accidental, such as the reports of the first plane crash into the World Trade Center on 9/11. The second, third, and fourth crash, of course, dispelled the belief that the first was an accident. In a post-9/11 world, with the heightened threat of terrorism occurring in the United States, any incident that may at first appear accidental requires local, state, and federal officials to conduct full investigations to determine probable cause.

3.2.1 History of Accidental Hazards in the United States

The previous section discussed natural disasters, highlighting some of the most significant incidents in our nation's history. Most accidental disasters, by comparison, are often much smaller in scope, but not necessarily less deadly. Accidents involving hazardous materials, such as toxic chemicals, fuels, and explosives, can have devastating effects on local population groups. For example, the worst industrial accident in the world occurred in Bhopal, India, in 1984, when a faulty vault caused a leak of methyl isocyanate (MIC) gas, eventually leading to an explosion that sent toxic cyanide gas into the atmosphere. Over 3,800 people died in the immediate blast and from toxic effects of the gas. It is also estimated that as many as 20,000 people have died since as a result of health issues caused by breathing the toxic fumes (Broughton 2005).

In the United States, one of the greatest concerns has been the potential damage caused by an accident involving a nuclear weapon. There have been numerous "incidents" since the advent of nuclear weapon technology, but to date, there is no documented nuclear "accident" that has resulted in catastrophic loss of life or property due to a nuclear explosion or emission of radiological material. Examples of nuclear weapons incidents typically include improper storage or movement of weapons, or crashes of vehicles, mostly aircraft, carrying such weapons. Most of these incidents occurred during the height of the Cold War in the 1950s and 1960s, when operational deployments involving nuclear weapons were at their highest levels. For example, the U.S. Air Force experienced a number of incidents of jettisoned nuclear weapons, or crashes of airplanes carrying these weapons. The U.S. Navy also experienced

FOR EXAMPLE

January 24, 1961; Goldsboro, North Carolina

A near catastrophe occurred in eastern North Carolina in 1961, when a B-52 bomber experienced a midair implosion, causing two nuclear weapons to be jettisoned in flight. Although one of the bombs deployed safety, the other did not, breaking apart as it made ground contact. Fortunately, one of six failsafe mechanisms survived the impact, preventing the nuclear warhead from detonating. Yet, the bomb's uranium core was never found. President John F. Kennedy was informed of the accident, only to find out that there had been "more than 60 accidents involving nuclear weapons" to include "two cases in which nuclear-tipped anti-aircraft missiles were actually launched by inadvertence." The Goldsboro incident led the United States to increase the safety devices on its nuclear weapons. The Soviets were also encouraged to take similar precautions to prevent a nuclear accident (Tiwari and Gray n.d.).

incidents involving nuclear weapons. As late as 1984, the Navy was involved in an accident at sea between the USS Kitty Hawk (an aircraft carrier) and a Soviet Victor-class nuclear submarine. The Kitty Hawk was carrying nuclear weapons, and it can be assumed that the Soviet sub was also carrying nuclear torpedoes (Tiwari and Gray n.d.).

3.2.2 Accidental Hazard Prevention and Response

The key to accidental hazard mitigation is to take precautionary steps intended to keep an accident from happening in the first place, and if it does occur, to keep the accident from becoming a disaster. For example, building codes today require commercial properties to have smoke detectors, alarm systems, and in some cases, sprinkler systems. In new residential construction, homes are required to have smoke detectors pre-wired into the electrical system (with battery back-ups). Even though these codes may not be able to prevent property damage from occurring, they can help people escape a fire and thus prevent an accident from becoming a personal disaster. In other words, such measures can't stop accidents from happening, but they do intend to lessen the impact once an accident occurs.

In the United States, accidents involving hazardous wastes and chemicals have also occurred, promoting the federal government to develop strict safety and security guidelines for industries involving chemicals and other hazardous materials. The **Environmental Protect Agency (EPA)** is the lead U.S. government agency for assuring compliance with U.S. codes and statutes related to industrial plant safety and security.

The United States also belongs to the **Organization for Economic Cooperation and Development (OECD)**. The OECD's Chemical Accidents Program helps member countries in "developing common principles and policy guidance on prevention of, preparedness for, and response to chemical accidents; analyzing issues of concern and making recommendations concerning best practices; and facilitating the sharing of information and experience between both OECD and non-member countries. It is carried out in co-operation with other international organizations" (Organization for Economic Cooperation and Development n.d.).

Chemical engineers in the United States also belong to organizations that share information and educational resources on chemical safety. For example, the American Institute for Chemical Engineers (AIChE) runs the Center for Chemical Process Safety, whose goal is to "identify and addresses process safety needs within the chemical, pharmaceutical, and petroleum industries. CCPS brings together manufacturers, government agencies, consultants, academia, and insurers to lead the way in improving industrial process safety" (Center for Chemical Process Safety n.d.).

Techniques routinely employed today to prevent accidents from happening include the use of technology, particularly sensors, to monitor storage facilities, transportation conditions of hazardous material, and other dangerous areas in the production of those chemicals or materials. Examples include pressure values, closed-circuit television monitors, automated switching centers, and so on, but the key is always the "human monitor" who has to observe and respond to the technological warning signs.

However, such mechanisms are by no means foolproof. For instance, in the case of an industrial accident in Apex, North Carolina, in October 2006, a series of safety inspections that noted unsafe storage procedures went unheeded by company officials until it was too late. The facility routinely contained a number of hazardous materials, including paints, solvents, and pesticides, although exactly what was in the warehouse the night of the explosion will never be known as the company did not keep records outside of the plant. The company had been cited for numerous storage violations due to improper storage of combustible materials. There had also been concern over the location of the warehouse near residential units, churches, and schools. Although no one was killed in the explosion, 30 people did seek medical help due to inhalation of toxic fumes. In addition, some 17,000 residents, over half the town's population, were required to evacuate the area until hazardous materials **(HAZMAT)** teams could assess the damage and determine it was safe for residents to return. The explosion was a reminder of the dangers of toxic materials being handled and stored in close proximity to populated areas (CNN 2006).

When an accident occurs involving hazardous materials, most local communities have the services of trained HAZMAT teams, who are equipped to respond to accidents involving such materials. Fire departments or emergency medical service providers are most likely to have this capability. With the creation of the Army National Guard **Weapons of Mass Destruction Civil Support Teams (WMD-CSTs)** in most states within the United States, these units also have personnel trained to operate in contaminated areas due to potential terrorist acts involving hazardous materials. The creation of WMD-CSTs was authorized by President Clinton in 1988. These teams began to operate in 2000, and as of September 2006, there were 42 certified teams, with the goal of eventually fielding 55 units. Thus, every state and territory will eventually have a dedicated team. The teams are normally located in a part of the state near an airport, which allows them access to the most vulnerable areas and enables them to deploy rapidly in a crisis. The mission of the WMD-CSTs is to "support local and state authorities at domestic [WMD] incident sites by identifying agents and substances, assessing current and projected consequences, advising on response measures, and assisting with requests for additional military support" (Global Security n.d.). Figure 3-2 shows the Forty-second Civil Support Team in Greenville, North Carolina, conducting HAZMAT training.

Figure 3-2

Forty-second Civil Support Team conducting HAZMAT training
(Courtesy of Major Scot Peeke).

3.2.3 Accidental Hazards in a Post-9/11 World

Because accidental hazards can be understood as those events caused by technological mishap, in a post-9/11 world, the concern is that when such events occur, it may not be immediately known whether they are, in fact, accidental and not caused by deliberate, malevolent tactics by terrorists, or even simple human error. A potential train derailment carrying chemicals such as molten sulfur, benzene, or other toxic materials near a school or football stadium, where there is a large concentration of people on any given day, could give local security officials and emergency managers ulcers as they try to think through all the possible "what if" scenarios in their communities and whether such events are truly accidental or not.

For that reason, the focus today in security education with regard to all-hazard threats is on **risk management**, defined as "a process involved in the anticipation, recognition, and appraisal of a risk and the initiation of action to eliminate entirely or reduce the threat or harm to an acceptable level" (Ortmeier 2005). Chapter 4 explains this process in much greater detail, but an example is the insurance industry, which applies risk management strategies in its attempts to understand an individual's or corporation's tolerance for risk and loss. These companies base their cost estimates on the location of the home or business, as well as the threats (or dangers) associated with either location or type of business based primarily on three factors: vulnerability, probability, and criticality.

▲ **Vulnerability** means exposure to risk, such as by living or working in or near a high-crime area.

▲ **Probability** refers to the likelihood of a home or business suffering loss due to an all-hazard assessment; for example, an oceanfront vacation home in Miami, as opposed to a brick ranch house outside of Cincinnati, has greater likelihood to suffer loss due to the history of hurricanes in South Florida.

▲ **Criticality** relates to the impact of loss on an individual or company; for instance, there would be a high degree of criticality if you had all your corporate assets in one location, rather than dispersed, and this location was destroyed.

The method used in the process for identifying and evaluating risks is called **risk assessment**, "an objective analysis of an organization's entire protective system" (Ortmeier 2005).

In December 2006, the DHS issued new guidelines for the "high-risk" chemical industries, in particular requiring them to perform comprehensive risk assessments that documented measures taken to prevent or mitigate the effects of a terrorist attack or other hazards. The new guidelines require these chemical plants to make their assessments and subsequent security plans to address those areas of vulnerability available to the DHS, which will then audit compliance through their own surveys and audits. Companies failing to implement required changes to their security posture will be subject to heavy fines, up to $25,000 per day for non-compliance (Department of Homeland Security 2006).

Due to the potential damage from a terrorist attack against any production, storage, or transfer facility involved with hazardous materials, there is increased sensitivity and awareness on the part of security managers and corporate leaders to the nature of the threats they face and the consequences of such actions. This increased terrorist threat awareness to inherent vulnerabilities that could be exploited by terrorist groups also has the effect of making those facilities safer from accidental hazards, through increased vigilance and awareness. Reducing vulnerability to terrorist threats also can reduce vulnerability to accidental hazards through the implementation of better control and accountability practices, better physical and personnel security procedures, and better technical control procedures. Thus, a potential byproduct of living in a post-9/11 world may be a decrease in both the frequency and severity of all-hazard accidents, preventing them from escalating into potential disasters.

SELF-CHECK

1. Risk management involves which of the following areas of analysis?
   a. Criticality
   b. Vulnerability
   c. Probability
   d. All of the above

2. What is HAZMAT?   *Hazardous Materials Team*

3. Although there have been incidents involving nuclear weapons, to date there has not been an accident whereby a nuclear weapon has detonated, causing a nuclear explosion. True or false?

4. Army National Guard Civil Support Teams came into existence after 9/11. True or false?

3.3 Man-made Hazards: Things We Hope Don't Happen

As part of the responsibilities of any security manager or emergency planner, one must look across the full spectrum of hazards to include those that are either intentional, malevolent acts, such as a terrorism, as well as those that are created as a result of unintended consequences, such as human error. In other words, although a hazard may not exist initially, through a series of actions (or inactions), an accident or even a disaster may occur by virtue of man-made efforts, done without foresight of the consequences of those actions. Sometimes it can be a simple design flaw in a construction project, which later causes destruction, or it can be the result of demographic changes in a community that place citizens at risk, based on planning decisions made years or even decades earlier. Such scenarios tend to play out only after the fact, after an accident or disaster occurs. But in today's post-9/11 world, serious thought needs to be placed in recognizing potential hazards based on man-made actions, both now and in the future. As other chapters in the text focus specifically on terrorist acts, this section focuses on those man-made disasters caused by human error.

3.3.1 History of Man-made Disasters Caused by Human Error in the United States

There may be a fine line drawn between many accidental disasters and man-made disasters caused by human error. In other words, an accidental disaster may be exacerbated by environmental conditions created by man, often as a process of development and modernization. This is true for natural disasters as well. One of our nation's greatest disasters caused by flooding was an example of both.

In 1889, the town of Johnstown, Pennsylvania, was destroyed in a devastating flood, which occurred after a dam broke upriver. Over 2,200 people perished in the flood. Although it was natural weather conditions that triggered the high water levels and placed stress on the dam structure holding back the man-made reservoir, it was a known problem at the time due to the increased development of the area and growth of vacation homes and recreational facilities up river. Warnings to shore up the dam went unheeded. Only after the disaster occurred were engineers brought in to repair the dam to specifications that would prevent another catastrophe (National Park Service n.d.).

To a certain extent, the destruction caused by the collapse of the Twin Towers in New York City on 9/11 is believed to have been a result of the unique structural design that did not allow the buildings to withstand the damage caused by the high heat and stress created by the impact of the jetliners. The engineers, to their credit, did not foresee a scenario such as large passenger planes crashing into these buildings, and therefore they did not plan for such a threat to the structural integrity of the Towers. However, in one of his tapes released after the attacks, Osama bin Laden is credited with stating that he knew such an event would occur based on his knowledge of the building's design. If that is true, the potential for future terrorist attacks against targets in America, exploiting known potential man-made disasters, is extremely great and worrisome.

On the flip side, the terrorist attack on the Pentagon on 9/11, although significant in loss of life and damage, could have been much worse if not for new construction that had occurred to the building in recent years. The renovations to the Pentagon were done in "slices," meaning portions of the building were evacuated and offices relocated to other sites around Washington, until the construction had been completed. Also, the way the building collapsed around the impact site served to isolate other parts of the building from damage and physical harm to its occupants.

The most recent example of a natural disaster exacerbated by man-made engineering problems was the collapse of the levee system in New Orleans during Hurricane Katrina. Part of the failure of the federal government to respond quickly was due to the initial report that the levees had held and widespread flooding had been averted. Yet that scenario quickly ended as the levees were breached and flood waters engulfed the city, trapping people on rooftops and devastating entire neighborhoods. The levee system in New Orleans was created by the Army Corps of Engineers in 1889, and was later shored up in 1927 after flooding of the Mississippi River. Yet, as New Orleans grew and more residential housing went into areas below sea level, the risk of a catastrophic disaster increased. The levees were believed to have been designed to withstand a Category 3 hurricane, although there was some doubt at that evaluation due to uneven repairs, primarily those areas that were supposed to have been repaired by the City of New Orleans and not the Corps of Engineers (Carrns and McKay 2005).

Hurricane Katrina made landfall in Louisiana on August 29, 2005, rated as a Category 3 hurricane with sustained winds of 125 miles per hour. FEMA had placed such a scenario as one of its "worst-case" disasters, although their planning scenario in this case was South Florida and floodwaters coming from Lake Okeechobee as a result of a hurricane (the other "worst-case" planning scenarios were a terrorist attack on New York City and the New Madrid earthquakes) (Lowder 2006). However, even with the expectation that the there would be major damage and destruction and loss of life, most planners thought the levees would hold (or at least, hoped they would).

3.3.2 Man-made Disaster Mitigation and Response

It is virtually impossible to anticipate all potential man-made disasters that could occur on any given day. Only after the event, many times, will we learn of structural faults in construction design, or poor maintenance records, or any other combination of factors that could contribute to unintended consequences. In other words, who would have known that a disaster could result?

For this reason, the adage that "an ounce of prevention is worth a pound of cure" holds true when considering the potential for man-made disasters and the focus on mitigation over response. For example, homes can now be built with special construction techniques that enable them to better withstand the effects of high-winds associated with hurricanes. High-rise buildings in

earthquake-prone areas are designed with "flexible" foundations capable of withstanding the stress of ground tremors. Beachfront areas of the East Coast require elevated or "stilt housing" to raise them above coastal floodwaters. Yet, despite these known hazards, developers continue to build in floodplains or along coastlines, and homeowners continue to accept risk due to their desire to live in such areas.

To mitigate the potential damage from future man-made disasters, the EPA requires new businesses or other developers to file **environmental impact statements**, noting the hazards posed by such building projects to local communities. For the most part, these tend to focus on issues such as toxic wastes and damage to local water supplies, watersheds, and/or natural habitats from potential problems such as chemical effluents or sewage. Yet, the EPA also considers the broader impact of locating new residential construction or schools near sites that could pose potential disasters, such as chemical storage facilities or transit sites. This is due to the fact that as communities grow, what used to be located on the "outskirts" of town, such as an oil refinery or commercial railroad switching center, is now located in town and could pose potential dangers to local communities.

The responses to man-made disasters caused by human error are much the same as for other disasters, but with a focus on identifying the causes and effects of the accidents. A good example is that of the Federal Aviation Administration (FAA) and its investigation process after an airline accident occurs. The investigators seek to identify the cause of the accident, whether technological mishap,

---

FOR EXAMPLE

EPA-Sponsored Drill to Test Emergency Responders

In September 2006, the EPA and Marathon Petroleum Company LLC co-sponsored a drill to test local, state, and federal emergency response agencies' plans for managing a gasoline spill along the Kanawha River in Charleston, West Virginia. In addition to Marathon, other participants included West Virginia's Department of Environmental Protection, the City of Charleston, emergency responders from two surrounding counties, and the U.S. Coast Guard.

No actual oil spill occurred. Rather, the exercise focused on what would happen if a storage tank were to collapse and oil was spilled into the river. Participants also rehearsed how they would conduct residential evacuations, as well as road closures and other required procedures necessary to test their local emergency response plans (United States Environmental Protection Agency 2006).

human error, or terrorist attack. For instance, the crash of Egypt Air Flight 990 off the coast of Massachusetts in October 1999 is one example where, to this day, the FAA does not know what caused the crash. There appeared to be no mechanical failure, no explosion, and no other suspected terrorist incident. The result of the investigation was inconclusive, not knowing whether the crash was caused by pilot error or an intentional act to crash the plane by one or more of the flight crew.

If an investigation determines that human errors caused a disaster, such as an airline crash or the meltdown of a nuclear reactor (similar to what occurred at Chernobyl, Ukraine, in 1986), the remediation is to offer better training or education. If the disaster is caused by design flaws or failure to follow procedures (if there were even procedures to be followed), the response is usually organizational, with the intent to correct the error and prevent such a situation from arising in the future. However, due to the shear volume of potential disasters caused by human error, mitigation still remains the best "response."

3.3.3 Man-made Disasters in a Post-9/11 World

As a result of 9/11 and the attacks on buildings in New York and Washington with large concentrations of workers, new designs for buildings with high occupancy are being considered, including the replacement building planned for the World Trade Center. Structural changes in building design can lessen the impact of a potential terrorist attack in the future. Simple changes include new locations for air filtration systems and return vents, keeping them from street-level access where they could become contaminated by chemical or biological agents. Also, collective protection systems, such as those designed into military vehicles, can be helpful in reducing the impact of a dirty bomb and preventing the spread of radiological contamination. Water treatment plants, food processing centers, and other potential terrorist targets can also be "hardened" against the effects of a terrorist attack by reducing the vulnerabilities inherent in these types of facilities due to man-made errors in both handling procedures and technological shortcomings of current systems.

Furthermore, recognizing the potential for **secondary and tertiary effects**, or consequences that are compounded during a natural or accidental disaster due to man-made errors, will only help emergency planners and security managers better prepare their communities for future disasters. Preventing accidents and deterring attacks is obviously the best course of action, but mitigating the effects of an accident or terrorist attack due to measures taken to correct or counter man-made hazards is equally important.

SELF-CHECK

1. The threat of man-made hazards today is not as significant as it was in the past due to required design changes in the construction industry, an example being the levees in New Orleans, which stood up to Hurricane Katrina. True or false?

2. What is an environmental impact statement?

3. Which of the following would be a secondary or tertiary effect due to a man-made hazard?

   a. A farm destroyed by flooding due to a river overflowing its banks
   b. A fire in a warehouse caused by lightning
   c. A 12-car accident on an interstate due to an ice storm
   d. A bridge collapsing during a hurricane due to structural faults during construction

4. Man-made disasters can be caused by either a malevolent act (such as terrorism) or by human error. True or false?

SUMMARY

In this chapter, you learned about threats to homeland security from an all-hazards perspective, focusing on natural disasters, accidental disasters, and man-made disasters. The intent of this chapter was to remind you that even in a post-9/11 world, the most prevalent scenarios we face as a nation will continue to be threats from natural, accidental, and man-made hazards. As Chapter 9 notes, throughout history, incidents of domestic terrorism within the United States have been rare, yet they have had potentially catastrophic effects. On the other hand, natural, accidental, and man-made hazards may be more of the norm, but their effects are rarely catastrophic (except, of course, for those people whose lives are directly impacted by such events).

Yet, as this chapter points out, as a result of the events of 9/11, the implications for managing risks and assessing consequences from non-terrorist threats can have far-reaching implications for how well the nation is prepared to respond to a catastrophic terrorist event. Lessons learned from Hurricane Katrina alone have caused a shake-up in the Department of Homeland Security and contributed to further discussions at all levels of government on whether the new models of federal response are adequate to the task. If anything, the implication is for an ever-increasing federal mandate to deal with all kinds of threats at all levels, whether states want assistance or not. An example of the tensions that can occur with such a broadened federal response happened in Florida in October 2005, when Governor Jeb Bush did not want federal help to respond to Hurricane Wilma. Due to the poor federal response to Hurricane Katrina, the U.S. military sought to be "proactive" by pre-positioning forces in Florida under the authority of the U.S. Northern Command. However, the head of the Florida National Guard responded that the state did not need active-duty military assistance and that the local "incident commander" would be Governor Bush rather than a uniformed federal official (Sylves 2006).

Understanding the nature of threats today from an all-hazards perspective requires security managers at all levels of government, as well as the private and non-profit sectors, to have a thorough knowledge and understanding of the capabilities of each others' organizations to know what each brings to the fight. A common saying today among homeland security officials is that during a crisis, whether caused by a natural hazard, accidental hazard, man-made hazard, or terrorist event, it is no time to be exchanging business cards!

In this chapter, you evaluated the types of natural, accidental, and man-made disasters that can and do occur today. You also assessed the nature of our response to natural, accidental, and man-made disasters in the United States. As a result of reading this chapter, you can now judge how disasters today can have catastrophic effects and implications for our nation's response in the war on terrorism.

KEY TERMS

Accident	An unintentional incident that causes damage, injury, or loss of life, but on a lower scale than a disaster.
Civil defense	The protection of the nation against threats within the United States.
Criticality	The impact of loss on an individual or company.
Disaster	An unintentional event that causes extensive damage, injury, and loss of life.
Environmental impact statement	Statement of the hazards posed by a building project to the local community. Such statements are required under the National Environmental Protection Act for all major building projects or legislation that will impact the environment both positively and negatively.
Environmental Protection Agency (EPA)	The lead federal agency for assuring compliance with U.S. codes and statutes related to industrial plant safety and security.

Federal Coordinating Officer (FCO)	The single individual, usually the head of the lead federal agency, designated to work under the PFO for coordinating the federal response to a domestic situation.
Federal Emergency Management Agency (FEMA)	Agency created in 1979 to provide a coordinated federal response to local communities' disaster needs.
HAZMAT	Abbreviation for hazardous materials.
Lead federal agency	A single federal agency designated as having overall responsibility for coordinating federal response to a domestic situation, such as a natural disaster or terrorist incident.
Natural disaster	The effect of a naturally occurring phenomenon, usually referred to by the insurance industry as an "act of God." Examples of natural disasters include hurricanes, tornados, floods, and forest fires due to natural causes.
Organization for Economic Cooperation and Development (OECD)	International economic organization whose goals include developing common principles and policy guidance on prevention of, preparedness for, and response to chemical accidents.
Principal Federal Official (PFO)	The single lead federal representative with overall responsibility for the federal response to a domestic situation, such as a natural disaster or terrorist incident. This individual may or may not be the head of the lead federal agency.
Probability	The likelihood of suffering loss due to potential risks.
Risk assessment	Identifying and evaluating risks based on an objective analysis of an organization's entire protective system.
Risk management	A process involved in the anticipation, recognition, and appraisal of a risk and the initiation of action to eliminate entirely or reduce the threat or harm to an acceptable level.
Secondary and tertiary effects	Consequences that are compounded during a natural or accidental disaster due to man-made errors.
Stafford Act	Originally passed by Congress in 1985 as the Robert T. Stafford Disaster Relief and Emergency Assistance Act, this act provides the means by which the president can declare a state of emergency, authorizing federal funds for disaster relief to both public agencies and private persons.

State of emergency	A declaration by the president in response to a disaster, making the affected area of the country eligible for increased federal support and funding.
Vulnerability	Exposure to risk in general.
Weapons of Mass Destruction Civil Support Teams (WMD-CSTs)	Teams within the Army National Guard that have personnel trained to operate in contaminated areas due to potential terrorist attacks involving hazardous materials.

ASSESS YOUR UNDERSTANDING

Go to www.wiley.com/college/kilroy to assess your knowledge of the basics of the all-hazards perspective.
Measure your learning by comparing pre-test and post-test results.

Summary Questions

1. An "inclusive" view toward homeland security would take an all-hazards perspective to threat assessments, looking beyond just terrorism. True or false?

2. As a result of 9/11 and the creation of the Department of Homeland Security, FEMA was elevated to a stand-alone Cabinet-level agency, focused only on non-terrorist threats. True or false?

3. To date, in the United States, there has been no documented nuclear "accident" that resulted in catastrophic loss of life or property due to a nuclear explosion or emission of radiological material. True or false?

4. North Carolina is the only state without a dedicated Army National Guard WMD-CST. True or false?

5. Man-made disasters can be caused by malevolent acts (such as terrorism) and by human error. True or false?

6. Since 1979, the lead federal agency for disaster response has been which of the following?
   (a) FEMA
   (b) DHS
   (c) U.S. Coast Guard
   (d) EPA

7. Which federal agency is responsible for evaluating environmental impact statements?
   (a) FBI
   (b) Department of the Interior
   (c) DHS
   (d) EPA

8. Which of the following organizations possesses special teams called WMD-CSTs, trained in providing civil support through the ability to operate in contaminated environments?
   (a) Army National Guard
   (b) FEMA
   (c) EPA
   (d) OECD

9. FEMA was established under which U.S. president's administration?
   (a) Gerald Ford
   (b) Jimmy Carter
   (c) Bill Clinton
   (d) George H.W. Bush

Applying This Chapter

1. You are serving as a local emergency manager responsible for coordinating your community's response to an accidental hazard, such as a train derailment with toxic chemicals involved. What resources would you have available at your disposal? What could you count upon from the state and federal levels? What other resources can you think about tapping into to respond to a natural disaster?

2. You are an urban planner in a large metropolitan area and are considering building designs and construction. What factors would you consider in new buildings to prevent man-made disasters or secondary or tertiary effects of terrorist attacks from occurring?

3. Your local community is planning a training exercise to prepare for a possible natural disaster, such as a hurricane. What planning considerations would you recommend including in such an exercise? What local agencies and individuals would you involve in the exercise? Why?

All Hazards Assessment

Provide a study of accidents that have occurred in your state and/or local community. Determine the cause of each. Identify, if possible, whether any of these accidents could be attributed to either natural or man-made hazards. Analyze any secondary or tertiary effects that could have been caused by man-made hazards. Evaluate the remediation efforts put into place after the accident occurred.

Natural Disaster Case Study

Write a case study of the federal response to a natural disaster, such as a hurricane or flooding. Determine the roles played by local, state, and federal agencies. Assess the type of assistance provided by FEMA and evaluate the appropriateness of the aid, based on the situation. Explain what might have been different if that disaster had occurred in a post-9/11 world.

4

A CONCEPTUAL FRAMEWORK—ASSESSING THREATS AND INTERESTS

A Risk Management Approach to All-Hazards Assessments

Starting Point

What You'll Learn in This Chapter

▲ The concept of risk management and its role in homeland security programs
▲ The different types of risk models
▲ The role of models in risk assessment
▲ The application of models in real-life situations

After Studying This Chapter, You'll Be Able To

▲ Evaluate why risk assessment is important for homeland security programs
▲ Appraise different risk assessment models to program evaluation
▲ Assess threats to communities using risk matrices
▲ Judge the usefulness of the Emergency Management Planning Model

INTRODUCTION

In a televised address to the nation on the fifth anniversary of the 9/11 attacks, President George W. Bush said that the United States was fighting an ongoing war on terror that required changes in homeland security programs to address the threats to the country.

> *We've created the Department of Homeland Security. We have torn down the wall that kept law enforcement and intelligence from sharing information. We've tightened security at our airports and seaports and borders, and we've created new programs to monitor enemy bank records and phone calls . . . We have broken up terrorist cells in our midst and saved American lives . . .*

While increased communications resulting from the passage of the USA Patriot Act (discussed in Chapter 2) have helped expose potential terrorists and terror attacks, some critics argue that homeland security initiatives have not made the country safer. In fact, Americans as a whole are split on the success of homeland security programs. In an ABC News Poll published the day before the president spoke to the nation on prime-time television, 38 percent of Americans surveyed said that the government is doing all it can to prevent further terrorist attacks, and only 52 percent said the war on terrorism is going well. If half of Americans do not think homeland security is making the country safer and half believe the country is on the right track, which perspective is correct? Before we can even ask if programs are successful, we must first decide what the risks to our security are and what interests we need to protect. This highlights the importance of the assessment process in which we identify threats and interests in our communities. This process is necessary to implement homeland security programs more effectively.

In this chapter, you will evaluate why risk assessment is important for homeland security programs. You'll also appraise different risk assessment models and learn how to assess threats to communities using risk matrices. Finally, you'll judge the usefulness of a specific tool known as the Emergency Management Planning Model.

4.1 A General Framework of Analysis—What to Assess

Hazard assessment is the process by which we identify new and existing threats and assess the level of risk to a population. As an example, since 9/11, the most visible program requiring hazard assessment in the United States is airline and airport security. In 2006, an estimated 658 million people entered or left the United States by air. Additionally, the number of airline travelers leaving the United States for other countries increased from about 8 million travelers in 1975 to over 55 million travelers in 2000 (U.S. Bureau of Statistics, October 2006). Because each traveler must go through airport security, for many Americans, the airport is the one place where federal homeland security programs may affect their lives. Consider, for example, what happened in August 2006, when American and British airports banned liquids and gels in carry-on luggage after British authorities announced an alleged terrorist plot to create explosives on board aircraft that were capable of destroying planes. After the ban, travelers endured long security lines and dumped thousands of bottles of liquids into airport trash cans. By the end of September 2006, the Transportation Security Administration relaxed the rules somewhat, but not before hearing complaints from angered passengers who threw away drinks, shampoos, baby formula, medicines, and even holy water (Pitchford 2006). When security rules create long lines and restrict people's ability to travel freely, homeland security can become a hotly debated topic with people asking who or what is really a threat.

4.1.1 The Disaster Impact Process

When conducting any hazard assessment, you must first determine what factors to assess. At the most basic level, what you'll need to assess can be viewed in terms of interest and threats.

▲ **Interests** are the human (individual or group), environmental, political, or economic components of society we seek to protect through homeland security programs.

▲ **Threats** are events that can destroy or damage human, environmental, political, or economic interests. Potential threats can be natural or man-made.

Interests and threats intersect in program implementation, so it is important to understand how disasters affect daily life. The **disaster impact process** is the way we can consider the effects a disaster will have on a community by examining the conditions before, during, and after the disaster. This process includes the following three phases:

1. The first phase of the disaster impact process is the pre-impact phase, which includes planning and mitigation efforts. Identifying pre-impact conditions can help define the characteristics and issues that make communities vulnerable to disasters. It can also identify how specific segments within a community may be affected.

2. The second phase is the actual disaster event, which includes specific hazard conditions and community response. Information about the

disaster impact process can be used to identify event-specific conditions that determine the level of disaster impact within the community.

3. The third phase is the emergency management intervention phase, which includes response, recovery, and program evaluations. Understanding this phase of the disaster impact process allows planners to develop suitable emergency management responses and to determine whether their efforts are working to minimize potential threats. Whereas the first two steps of the disaster impact process are discussed next, this third phase is examined in a later section of the chapter.

4.1.2 Pre-Impact Conditions

As previously mentioned, the first phase of the disaster impact process is the pre-impact phase, which includes planning and mitigation efforts. Identifying pre-impact conditions can help define the characteristics and issues that make communities vulnerable to disasters. It can also identify how specific segments within a community may be affected. Pre-impact conditions are defined as hazard exposure or physical and social vulnerabilities.

Pre-impact interventions and hazard vulnerabilities will affect post-impact response and disaster effects. Additionally, individual hazards must be addressed as both individual events and multiple events. For example, hurricanes may produce tornados, flooding, and heavy winds and rain, each with different potential impacts that can also increase when they happen in combination.

Communities and states must determine to what level each type of threat may affect their population. This process involves the use of mapping, data analysis, and modeling. Models can help define the process by which disasters produce community impacts. For instance, Lindell and Prater's model, as depicted in Figure 4-1, illustrates how three pre-impact conditions—hazard exposure, physical vulnerability, and social vulnerability—interact with emergency management interventions and event-specific conditions. Before we look at the model, however, let's define these three types of pre-impact conditions.

▲ **Hazard exposure** is the probability of occurrence of a given event magnitude. Hazard exposure assessment defines specific types of events, both natural and man-made, that threaten lives or property. These threats can vary in intensity and occurrence across the country. Hazard assessment can be difficult if historical data are insufficient, if the hazard is newly discovered, or if the physical and social vulnerabilities are not fully understood. Natural hazard exposure risks can be simply living in a floodplain or living on a hillside subject to landslides. Man-made hazard

Figure 4-1

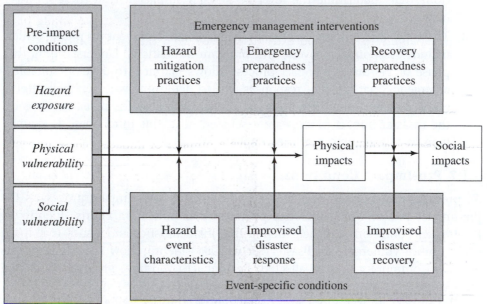

The disaster impact process (Source: Adapted from Lindell and Prater [2003]).

exposure risks can be living near places such as nuclear power plants or chemical factories.

▲ **Physical vulnerability** includes three specific categories of vulnerabilities: human, agricultural, and structural.

- **Human vulnerability** refers to individual vulnerabilities to environmental extremes. Extreme environments include those influenced by temperature, wind, radiation, and chemical exposure. Human vulnerabilities vary, so even when populations are exposed to a disaster, we can assume that some people will die, others will be severely injured, still others slightly injured, and the rest will survive unscathed. Typically, the people most susceptible to any environmental stressor will be the very young, the very old, and those with weakened immune systems.

- **Agricultural vulnerability** is agricultural plant and animal vulnerability to environmental extremes. Similar to humans, there are differences among individuals within each plant and animal population. Risk assessment for plants and animals is more complex than human vulnerability assessment because of the large number of species in the plant and animal kingdoms.

- **Structural vulnerability** describes structural limits to a building's capability to withstand extreme stresses (e.g., high wind, hydraulic pressures of water, seismic shaking) or features that allow hazardous materials to infiltrate the building.

▲ Finally, **social vulnerability** is a person's or group's ability to anticipate, prepare for, and cope with disasters.

After a disaster actually occurs, it can have a number of impacts. These impacts may be physical, social, or both. Physical impacts include casualties (direct and indirect deaths), as well as damage (losses of structures, animals, and crops). Social impacts, on the other hand, are less visible than physical impacts, and they can develop over a long period of time. It is important that risk assessment include and even model social impacts because they can cause significant problems in the long term for individuals and communities. Types of social impacts include the following:

▲ **Psychosocial impacts** are impacts on mental health and the ability to get treatment after a disaster.

▲ **Demographic impacts** are impacts on a community's population following a disaster. One way to assess population changes after a disaster is to use the demographic balancing equation, defined as $P_a - P_b = B - D + IM - OM$, where P_a is the population size after the disaster, P_b is the population size before the disaster, B is the number of births, D is the number of deaths, IM is the number of immigrants, and OM is the number of emigrants. The magnitude of the disaster impact, $P_a - P_b$, is for the population of a specific geographical area and two specific points in time. Ideally, the geographical area would correspond to the disaster impact area, P_b would be immediately before disaster impact, and P_a would be immediately after disaster impact (Smith, Tayman, and Swanson 2001).

▲ **Economic impacts** refers to the property damage caused by disaster impact, which creates losses in asset values that can be measured by the cost of repair or replacement. Disaster losses in the United States are initially borne by the affected households, businesses, and local government agencies whose property is damaged or destroyed, but some of these losses are redistributed during the disaster recovery process.

▲ **Political impacts** are changes in the political structure of a community after a disaster. There is substantial evidence that disaster impacts can cause social activism resulting in political disruption, especially during the seemingly interminable period of disaster recovery. The disaster recovery period is a source of many victim grievances, and this creates many opportunities for community conflict, both in the United States (Bolin 1982, 1993) and abroad (Bates and Peacock 1993).

The physical impacts of a disaster combine with improvised disaster recovery to produce the disaster's social impacts (Committee on Disaster Research in the Social Sciences 2006). Thus, as you can see from Figure 4-1, it is apparent that communities should engage in two types of assessment to best plan for emergencies. First, physical impact assessment can form the basis for hazard mitigation and emergency preparedness. Second, risk assessment can direct recovery preparedness practices to reduce social impacts.

4.1.3 Event-Specific Conditions

The second phase of the disaster impact process is the actual disaster event, which includes specific hazard conditions and community response (planned and improvised). Information about the disaster impact process can be used to identify the event-specific conditions that determine the level of disaster impact within a community. However, risk assessment is difficult because of the inherent complexity of natural and man-made disasters. For example, coastal communities face a number of risks from hurricanes, including flooding, wind damage, storm surge, and rain. Thus, it can be difficult to separate the types of threats, but it is possible to characterize them in terms of six significant characteristics. These are as follows:

▲ **Onset speed:** How fast the event begins
▲ **Perceptual cues:** What types of cues indicate the onset of the threat, such as wind, rain, or ground movement
▲ **Intensity:** How strong the threat is
▲ **Scope:** The size of the area that the threat impacts
▲ **Duration:** How much time the event lasts
▲ **Probability:** How often the event may occur

The first two characteristics—onset speed and perceptual cues—can help determine the amount of forewarning that affected populations will have to complete emergency response actions.

We can also categorize hazard events such as storms or terrorist attacks by examining the potential losses (property and lives) they may cause. For example, a tornado may cause more concentrated damage than a hurricane. Yet another way of categorizing hazard events is to examine how a hazard may expose physical, social, or structural vulnerabilities in communities. For example, floods may affect

---

FOR EXAMPLE

Risk Assessment and Hurricane Katrina

Hurricane Katrina struck the Gulf Coast of the United States in August 2005, killing over 1,300 people in Louisiana and Mississippi. This hurricane was a major natural disaster, exceeding the economic costs of Hurricane Andrew in August 1992, which had a price tag of $25 billion in storm-related damage. Although models can predict the physical damage from a hurricane or even the potential flooding from failed levees, it is hard to estimate the other social impacts of a disaster like Hurricane Katrina, such as the psychological and demographic impact on New Orleans residents in particular. The entire demographic of New Orleans has changed since the storm, with over 200,000 residents, mostly African American, relocating to other states (mainly Texas), the majority of whom will not return. Also, during the reconstruction of New Orleans, a large number of Hispanics moved into the city, not only leading to a social impact, but also to a political impact on future elections and power shifts between minority constituencies (Miskel 2006).

---

certain low-elevation neighborhoods in a community, but they may not affect neighborhoods on higher ground. Knowing the type of hazard and how it will affect an exposed community is also helpful in modeling disaster responses. For instance, a chemical attack would evoke a community response much different than a forest fire. An event's characteristics will affect response, recovery, and mitigation efforts as well. Thus, a community will not respond to a hurricane in the same way that it would respond to an event such as the 9/11 attacks.

4.1.4 Final Thoughts on What to Assess

To be successful in national hazard assessment, it is important that all levels of government cooperate to monitor issues and events that could lead to man-made or natural disasters. Today, the USA Patriot Act strengthens intergovernmental partnerships among local jurisdictions and higher governmental authorities with greater available resources. The Department of Homeland Security coordinates resources for sharing information with intermediate and local jurisdictions, in part to improve risk assessment. As Hurricane Katrina has shown, however, even with new organizations and legislative initiatives, the best models and risk assessments don't always help us truly understand the long-term impact of disasters on a community or a nation. This makes the risk assessment process much more dynamic and not simply a matter of running algorithms through a computer program.

SELF-CHECK

1. Which of the following is not a phase of the disaster impact process?

   a. Pre-impact phase
   b. Recovery
   c. The actual disaster event
   d. Emergency management interventions

2. Hazard assessment is the process by which we identify new and existing threats and assess the level of risk to a population. True or false?

3. $P_a - P_b = B - D + IM - OM$ is an example of a(n):

   a. risk matrix.
   b. impact analysis.
   c. demographic balancing equation.
   d. recovery balancing equation.

4. Which phase of the disaster impact process includes planning and mitigation efforts?

   a. Recovery phase
   b. Event phase
   c. Mitigation phase
   d. Pre-impact phase

4.2 A Matrix Approach—How to Assess

In June 2006, the United States Department of Homeland Security released the *National Infrastructure Protection Plan* (NIPP). This is a comprehensive risk management framework that clearly defines critical infrastructure protection roles and responsibilities for all levels of government, private industry, nongovernmental agencies, and tribal partners. Risk management is a systematic and analytical process to consider the likelihood that a threat will endanger an asset (e.g., a structure, individual, or function) and to identify actions that reduce the risk and mitigate the consequences.

An effective risk management approach includes the following types of assessments:

▲ A **threat assessment** identifies and evaluates threats based on various factors, including capability and intentions as well as the potential impact of an event. Even when such an assessment exists, however, we will never know whether we have identified every threat or event, and we may not have complete information about the threats that we have identified. Consequently, two other elements—vulnerability assessments and criticality assessments—are essential to better prepare against threats.

▲ A **vulnerability assessment** identifies weaknesses that may be exploited and suggests options to eliminate or mitigate those weaknesses.

▲ A **criticality assessment** systematically identifies and evaluates an organization's assets based on a variety of factors, including the importance of its mission or function, whether people are at risk, and/or the significance of a structure or system. Criticality assessments provide a basis for prioritizing which assets require higher or special protection.

A good risk management approach is adaptable to all levels of government and across the public and private sectors. The 2006 *National Infrastructure Protection Plan* (NIPP) uses a risk management framework that combines consequence, vulnerability, and threat information to produce a comprehensive assessment of national or sector-specific risks. The risk management framework includes assessments of "dependencies, interdependencies, and cascading effects; identification of common vulnerabilities; development and sharing of common threat scenarios; development and sharing of cross-sector measures to reduce or manage risk; and identification of specific [research and development] needs" (29). The framework applies to the general threat environment, as well as to specific threats or incident situations. Further, because most critical infrastructure is privately owned or owned by local or state agencies, the 2006 NIPP stresses intergovernmental cooperation to build an integrated risk assessment that all levels of government can implement.

The NIPP incorporates an all-hazards approach to homeland security that addresses the direct effects of natural and man-made incidents on the nation's critical infrastructure and key assets. It is a public and private sector partnership that includes a risk assessment of America's threats and assets. The goal of risk assessment in the NIPP is to help prioritize protection activities and enable disaster responses and recovery efforts. Additionally, the NIPP requires the development and use of sophisticated analytical and modeling tools to help inform effective risk-mitigation programs in an all-hazards context.

Risk assessment can help determine the nature and extent of risk by analyzing potential hazards and evaluating existing conditions of vulnerability that could pose a potential threat to people, property, livelihoods, and the environment on which they depend (United Nations Office for the Coordination of Human Affairs 2005). Risk assessment for homeland security has two main objectives: risk reduction and hazard assessment. **Risk reduction** is an examination of the actions necessary to decrease detected or projected levels of danger and to identify the resources required for implementing those actions (Dynes 1972). In other words, hazard identification and assessment are the procedures through which we can monitor environmental threats; risk reduction is the development and implementation of activities aimed at mitigation, preparedness, response, and recovery (Mileti 1999).

4.2.1 Risk Matrices

Risk assessment is an effective tool to identify safety risks from various sources and to determine the most cost-effective means to reduce risk. One method of risk assessment is to use a matrix. A **matrix** is a tool for decision making that uses a grid design to weigh the frequency of an event against its severity to rank potential costs or damage. As shown in Figure 4-2, FEMA incorporated the risk matrix approach developed by Arthur D. Little into its practices for hazard planning and management. Construction of a risk matrix starts by first establishing how the matrix is intended to be used. Little's risk matrix approach requires the following steps (Federal Emergency Management Agency 1997, 314):

1. **Identify and characterize hazards:** Define and describe hazards, measures of magnitude and severity, causative factors, and interrelations with other hazards.
2. **Screen risk:** Rank or order the identified hazards as a function of the relative degree of risk.
3. **Estimate risk:** Apply the process or methodology to evaluate risk.
4. **Assess acceptability:** Determine whether the risks that have been identified and estimated in the previous steps can be tolerated.
5. **Develop alternatives to reduce risk:** Select cost-effective actions to reduce or mitigate unacceptable risks, including technological and management controls.

Figure 4-2

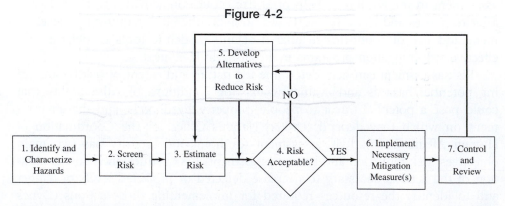

The risk matrix process (Source: Federal Emergency Management Agency 1997, 315).

6. **Implement:** Implement mitigation measures to control risks to acceptable levels.

7. **Control and review:** Periodically monitor and review risks.

The risk matrix approach assigns qualitative measures to prioritize risk by weighing the frequency of an event to its severity. For example, severity may range from minor to catastrophic impacts on lives, property, the economy, and the environment. Frequency can range from low (less than once every 1,000 years) to high (more than once in 10 years). After establishing categories, a matrix can be constructed. A risk matrix can be very simple, such as a two-by-two grid, or very complex, with ten or more categories for each factor. Different criteria for categorizing the severity and frequency of an event will vary, so using a risk matrix without clear definitions of the categories can lead to inaccurate assessments. Figure 4-3 employs categories and definitions found in the FEMA publication *Multi-Hazard Identification and Risk Assessment: A Cornerstone of the National Strategy* (1997).

As you can see, the matrix in Figure 4-3 uses the qualitative measures A, B, C, and D to prioritize action for specific hazards based on their frequency and severity. These classes are as defined follows:

▲ **Class A:** Hazards in this class are high risk and have the highest priority for mitigation and contingency planning (immediate action). Examples of potential losses include death, complete shutdown of key assets and critical infrastructure for more than one month, and severe damage to more than 50 percent of the property located in the affected area.

Figure 4-3

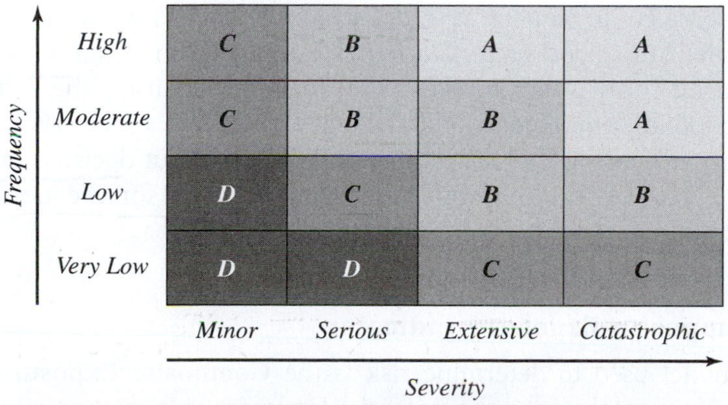

A risk matrix (Adapted from Federal Emergency Management Agency 1997).

▲ **Class B:** Class B hazards are moderate to high-risk conditions that are addressed by mitigation and contingency planning (prompt action). Examples of potential losses include permanent disability or severe injury or illness, complete shutdown of key assets and critical infrastructure for more than two weeks, and severe damage to more than 25 percent of the property in the affected area.

▲ **Class C:** These are risk conditions sufficiently high to give consideration to further mitigation and planning (planned action). Examples of potential losses include injury or illness not resulting in disability, complete shutdown of key assets and critical infrastructure for more than one week, and severe damage to more than 10 percent of the property in the affected area.

▲ **Class D:** Class D hazards are low-risk conditions that may be addressed by additional mitigation contingency planning (advisory in nature). Examples of potential losses include treatable first aid injury, complete shutdown of facilities and critical services for more than 24 hours, and severe damage to no more than 1 percent of the property located in the affected area.

Risk matrices are effective for assessing both natural and man-made disasters. The scenarios and consequences can be adapted for any disaster, as long as they are simple to use and understand. Additionally, a good matrix design will include clear guidance on applicability and likelihood ranges that cover the full spectrum of potential scenarios and descriptions of the consequences of concern for each consequence range. A good risk matrix will also have clearly defined tolerable and intolerable risk levels and show how scenarios that are at an intolerable risk level can be mitigated to a tolerable risk level on the matrix. Finally, a good risk matrix should provide clear guidance on what action is necessary to mitigate scenarios with intolerable risk levels. For example, a risk matrix analysis could be helpful in determining the risks associated with building a hospital in a flood zone. During Hurricane Katrina, many hospitals and medical facilities in New Orleans were flooded, requiring the evacuation of patients, supplies, equipment, and staff. It would thus appear risky to rebuild community services such as hospitals in a flood zone, but decision makers must balance the risk of flooding with convenient location for the population the facility serves.

Can be made tolerable. How?

4.2.2 Composite Exposure Indicator

Another model used to determine risk is the **Composite Exposure Indicator (CEI)**. This approach ranks the potential for losses in a given region for single or multiple hazards by assigning a numeric value to the exposure potential for

Figure 4-4

Variable	Unit of Measure	Mean	Standard Deviation	Minimum	Maximum
Hospitals	$\#/mi^2$	0.005	0.028	0	1.297
Population	# persons/mi^2	213.767	1,519.663	0.053	62,245.000
Nuclear Power Plants	# plants/mi^2	0.000	0.001	0	0.010
Toxic Release Inventory	# sites/mi^2	0.059	0.228	0	4.913
Public Water Supplies	$\#/mi^2$	0.005	0.077	0	4.276
Superfund Sites	# sites/mi^2	0.001	0.003	0	0.056
Sewage Treatment Sites	# sites/mi^2	0.014	0.056	0	2.460
Utility Lines	Ft/mi^2	647.161	404.752	0	2,756.591
Airports	$\#/mi^2$	0.002	0.003	0	0.100
Roads	Ft/mi^2	665.084	443.725	0	11,633.116
Railroads	Ft/mi^2	420.221	361.616	0	4,624.799
Pipelines	Ft/mi^2	300.052	726.723	0	32,188.936
Dams	$\#/mi^2$	0.012	0.031	0	1.246
Bridges	$\#/mi^2$	0.270	0.591	0	13.767

A CEI analysis (Source: Federal Emergency Management Agency 1997).

communities (Federal Emergency Management Agency 1997). Although this method was originally designed for natural or technological disasters, it can be adapted for homeland security issues very easily.

FEMA has used this approach to quantify 14 variables in 3,100 U.S. counties, with rankings based on the amount of each variable present. This method implies that the larger a county's CEI is, the higher the county's exposure is to potential damages from natural or man-made hazards (see Figure 4-4). FEMA uses these variables to plan response levels for different regions. Based on these variables, FEMA has also drawn several conclusions about the nation's counties:

▲ The number of hospitals and the population within a county are highly correlated.

▲ Hospitals and population are moderately correlated with a county's number of bridges.

▲ The number of public water supply systems and sewage treatment sites are strongly correlated.

▲ Public water supply systems and sewage treatment plants are moderately correlated with the length of pipelines and the number of dams.

▲ The length of roads is moderately correlated with sewage treatment sites.

4.2.3 HAZUS

Since 1997, another model used for risk assessment is HAZUS. HAZUS stands for **HAZ**ards **U**nited **S**tates and is a natural hazard loss estimation software package developed by the Federal Emergency Management Agency (FEMA) in 1997. The most recent version of the software is HAZUS-MH MR2. (MH stands for "multi-hazards.") It is available free of charge to public and private agencies and organizations. HAZUS uses a geographic information system (GIS) software package that analyzes potential losses from floods, hurricane winds, and earthquakes before or after a disaster occurs. The model estimates risk in three steps. It calculates the exposure for a selected area; characterizes the level of intensity of the hazard affecting the exposed area; and it uses the exposed area and the hazard to calculate the potential losses in terms of economic losses, structural damage, or other factors determined by the user. Potential loss estimates analyzed in HAZUS-MH include the following:

▲ Physical damage to residential and commercial buildings, schools, critical facilities, and infrastructure

▲ Economic loss, including lost jobs, business interruptions, and repair and reconstruction costs

▲ Social impacts, including estimates of shelter requirements, displaced households, and population exposed to scenario floods, earthquakes, and hurricanes

HAZUS uses flexible programming that frames assessments as a series of modules. Thus, new modules, improvements, and data may be added without reworking the entire methodology. This allows for a rapid transfer of information so that decision makers have the most up-to-date data available at all times, and it saves upgrade and maintenance costs for users (Federal Emergency Management Agency 1997). The modules incorporated in HAZUS include earth science hazards, data inventories, director damage, induces damage, direct economic/social losses, and indirect losses.

Figure 4-5

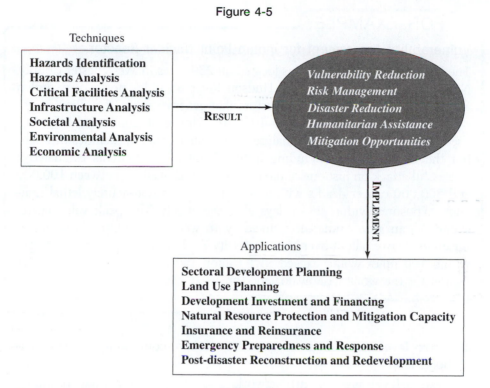

The vulnerability assessment process (Source: National Oceanic and Atmospheric Administration 2006).

4.2.4 Vulnerability Assessments

Vulnerability assessment is a technique developed by the Coastal Services Center (CSC) of the National Oceanic and Atmospheric Administration (NOAA) for coastal communities facing the threat of natural hazards such as flooding and hurricanes. As depicted in Figure 4-5, vulnerability analyses include critical facilities analyses, societal analyses, environmental analyses, and economic analyses (National Oceanic and Atmospheric Administration 2006).

Vulnerability assessment techniques can determine the vulnerability of infrastructure networks and individual structures, as well as the economic, environmental, and societal vulnerabilities posed by natural hazards. Vulnerability assessment can be used to determine the effects of single hazards or multiple hazards, and it can address impacts on both public infrastructure and private sector interests (such as tourism). These assessments can be on the macro, micro, and system levels.

▲ **Macro level assessment:** Multinational, regional, national, or subnational level

> ## FOR EXAMPLE
>
> ### Vulnerability Assessment for Indian Point Nuclear Reactor
>
> The Indian Point power plant is located on 239 acres in Westchester County, New York, on the banks of the Hudson River 35 miles north of midtown Manhattan. The plant has two reactors that generate over 16 million megawatts of electricity every year. In 1994, the Union of Concerned Scientists used vulnerability analysis to analyze the threats to nuclear facilities throughout the United States, including Indian Point. The scientists estimated a successful attack on just one of the reactors would result in between 100,000 and 500,000 cancer deaths within 50 miles, due to non-acutely lethal radiation exposures within seven days after the attack. The peak value corresponds to an attack timed to coincide with weather conditions that maximize radioactive fallout over New York City. Additionally, economic damages within 100 miles would exceed $1.1 trillion and could be as great as $2.1 trillion for the worst case evaluated (Lyman 2004).

▲ **Micro level assessment:** Metropolitan, urban, community, or neighborhood level

▲ **System level assessment:** Network, grid, area, or individual structure level (National Oceanic and Atmospheric Administration 2006)

4.2.5 Final Thoughts on How to Assess

Risk management is a systematic and analytical process to consider the likelihood that a threat will endanger an asset and to identify actions that reduce the risk and mitigate the consequences of an attack. An effective risk management approach includes a threat assessment, a vulnerability assessment, and a criticality assessment. Hazard assessment is the process by which we identify new and existing threats and assess the level of risk to a population. Risk reduction involves an examination of the actions necessary to decrease the detected or projected levels of danger and to identify the resources required for implementing those actions. Because the available resources are rarely equal to the threat, this process implicitly defines the remaining level of danger considered to be acceptable. One method is to use a matrix. A matrix is a tool for decision making that uses a grid design to weigh the frequency of an event against its severity to rank potential costs or damage. FEMA incorporated the risk matrix approach, developed by Arthur D. Little, into hazard planning and management. Other tools include the Composite Exposure Indicator, HAZUS, and vulnerability assessments.

SELF-CHECK

1. An effective risk management approach includes a threat assessment, a vulnerability assessment, and a criticality assessment. True or false?

2. What does HAZUS stand for?

   a. Hazard Assessment Zoning Under States
   b. Hazards Under Susceptibility
   c. Hazard Zones in the United States
   d. Hazards United States

3. A micro-level vulnerability assessment includes multinational, regional, national, or subnational structures. True or false?

4. The Composite Exposure Indicator (CEI) ranks the potential for losses in a given region for single or multiple hazards by assigning a numeric value to the exposure potential for communities. True or false?

4.3 The Emergency Management Planning Model

When it comes to emergencies, there is a need to have an ongoing cycle that keeps planning in the forefront. The six "phases" of the disaster life cycle—mitigation, risk reduction, prevention, preparedness, response, and recovery—also describe a model for emergency management planning. In reality, these phases might better be called functions, since they are neither discrete nor temporally sequential (Federal Emergency Management Agency 2006c).

For each step of the disaster life cycle, as shown in Figure 4-6, modeling risks can be an effective tool for decision making, but it is important to understand how a model will be used. Models can give insight into predicting damages from disasters, but decision makers need to use data appropriate to each phase. For example, if a risk assessment is used when determining the best site for critical infrastructure such as a new power plant, a model similar to a risk matrix would be appropriate to assess risk for different locations during the prevention phase. However, if a risk assessment is to be used for state budgets, a CEI model would be helpful in determining fiscal considerations like rebuilding costs versus mitigation costs for different areas of the state. Thus, understanding each phase of the disaster life cycle is critical to making good decisions.

4.3.1 Mitigation

Hazard mitigation is sustained action to alleviate or eliminate risks to life and property from natural or man-made hazard events (United Nations Office for the

Figure 4-6

FEMA's disaster life cycle (Source: FEMA 2006).

Coordination of Human Affairs 2005). Mitigation activities include land use planning, adoption of building codes, elevating structures, property acquisition, and relocation outside floodplains. Mitigation decreases the need for post-disaster response and expenditures across all levels of government and for property owners.

Mitigation is a separate phase of the disaster life cycle, but it can also take place during the planning, response, and recovery phases. In the planning phase, mitigation can include building public awareness of mitigation techniques, creating state and local hazard mitigation plans (under the Disaster Management Act of 2000), integrating hazard mitigation criteria into local comprehensive plans, and engineering public facilities to withstand the effects of an event. Mitigation during the response and recovery phase includes locating emergency equipment and supplies out of high-risk areas and permanent relocation or retrofitting.

An example of federal mitigation policy is the **National Flood Insurance Program (NFIP)** administered by FEMA. The three components of the NFIP are flood insurance, floodplain management, and flood hazard mapping. Communities participate in the NFIP by adopting and enforcing floodplain management ordinances to reduce future flood damage. In exchange, the NFIP makes federally backed flood insurance available to homeowners, renters, and business owners in these communities. Community participation in the NFIP is voluntary, but nearly 20,000 communities across the United States and its territories participate. Since the NFIP began, participating communities have saved almost $1 billion per year through implementing sound floodplain management requirements and property owners purchasing flood insurance. Additionally, buildings constructed in compliance with NFIP building standards suffer approximately 80 percent less damage annually than those not built in compliance (Federal Emergency Management Agency 2006b).

Another federal mitigation tool is the Disaster Mitigation Act of 2000 (also referred to as DMA 2000). This law requires state, tribal, and local governments to conduct risk assessment through mitigation planning. DMA 2000 amended the Robert T. Stafford Disaster Relief and Emergency Assistance Act by repealing its previous mitigation planning provisions (Section 409) and replacing them with a new set of requirements. This new section emphasizes the need for state, tribal, and local entities to closely coordinate mitigation planning and implementation efforts by identifying natural and man-made threats to communities nationwide (Section 322). DMA 2000 also requires state mitigation plans as a condition of disaster assistance, and federally approved state plans can increase the amount of funding available to states and local governments through the Hazard Mitigation Grant Program (HMGP). Since the passage of DMA 2000, all 50 states have enacted laws that enforce disaster planning requirements for local governments. Under the act, local governments and states must address the following types of hazards for their plans to be approved:

▲ Dam failure   ▲ Nuclear explosion
▲ Earthquake   ▲ Terrorism
▲ Fire or wildfire   ▲ Thunderstorm
▲ Flood   ▲ Tornado
▲ Hazardous materials   ▲ Tsunami
▲ Heat   ▲ Volcano
▲ Hurricane   ▲ Wildfire
▲ Landslide   ▲ Winter storm

4.3.2 Risk Reduction

Risk reduction is the application of appropriate techniques and management principles to reduce the likelihood of an occurrence or its consequences, or both (United Nations Office for the Coordination of Human Affairs 2005). Examples of risk reduction include regulations that limit construction in areas that are susceptible to hazard impacts and building construction practices that make individual structures less vulnerable to natural hazards. For example, building construction in floodplains is regulated at the federal level through the NFIP, and communities participating in the NFIP must adopt minimum building standards set forth by FEMA for residents to be eligible for subsidized federal flood insurance. These codes set standards for various aspects of construction to protect general health and safety, including appropriate building construction practices for hazardous locations by establishing code provisions to require hazard-resistant building designs and materials. In the United States, local building codes may be based on a model code or a state code. Currently 17 states have established statewide building codes that prohibit further local amendment without state approval. Building codes are enforced by local governments as an exercise of police power (Federal Emergency Management Agency 2006b).

Another example of risk reduction is the Department of Homeland Security (DHS) grant program to reduce risk from terrorist attacks on rail systems. The majority of mass transit systems in this country are owned and operated by state and local government and private industry, but securing these systems is a shared responsibility between federal, state, and local partners. Thus, the DHS provides grants to railways to be used for planning, training, equipment, and other security enhancements. One project funded by this program is the National Capital Region Rail Security Corridor Pilot Project. This project includes numerous components, including a virtual security fence that will detect moving objects, perimeter breaches, left objects, removed objects, and loitering activity. The seven-mile stretch of track will be monitored continuously, and the data that is gathered will transmit simultaneously to multiple locations, such as U.S. Capitol Police, U.S. Secret Service, CSX, and other applicable federal or local agencies (Department of Homeland Security 2006d).

4.3.3 Preparedness

Preparedness actions are pre-impact actions that provide the human and material resources needed to support active responses at the time of hazard impact. Assessing threats and risks in a hazard analysis is the first step in emergency preparedness, and a hazard analysis should consist of four parts: emergency assessment, hazard operations, population protection, and incident management. Emergency assessment consists of the actions that define the potential scope of disaster impacts, such as staffing plans for first responders. Hazard operations consist of short-term actions to protect property, such as boarding up windows. Population protection actions protect people from impact; an example would be an evacuation order. Incident management actions activate and coordinate the emergency response. Incident management can be seen in communication between responders, agencies, and affected communities.

Another step in preparedness is to determine responsibilities and procedures for community organizations. Organizations must acquire personnel, facilities, and equipment resources to implement their plans and to remain prepared through ongoing training (Federal Emergency Management Agency 2006c).

4.3.4 Response

Disaster response is the reaction individuals have when faced with the onset of a disaster. Response can be very quick, as was the case during the 9/11 attacks in New York City, or it can be delayed, as was seen after Hurricane Katrina in 2005. Disaster response delays can occur because people have limited information, or they may be in denial that the disaster is actually happening to them. Disaster victims often devote considerable effort to helping their neighbors, contrary to the stereotype of selfish protection of one's self and one's property (Lindell and Prater, 2003). Additionally, people in nearby areas move in to offer assistance, and when existing organizations seem incapable of meeting the needs of the emergency response, they evolve to take on new members and new tasks, or new organizations may emerge.

The National Response Plan establishes a comprehensive all-hazards approach to enhance the capability of the United States to manage domestic incidents. The plan incorporates best practices and procedures from incident management disciplines—homeland security, emergency management, law enforcement, fire-fighting, public works, public health, responder and recovery worker health and safety, emergency medical services, and the private sector—and integrates them into a unified structure. It forms the basis of how the federal government coordinates with state, local, and tribal governments and the private sector during incidents. It establishes protocols to help do the following:

▲ Save lives and protect the health and safety of the public, responders, and recovery workers

▲ Ensure security of the homeland

▲ Prevent an imminent incident, including acts of terrorism, from occurring

▲ Protect and restore critical infrastructure and key resources

▲ Conduct law enforcement investigations to resolve the incident, apprehend the perpetrators, and collect and preserve evidence for prosecution and/or attribution

▲ Protect property and mitigate damages and impacts to individuals, communities, and the environment

▲ Facilitate recovery of individuals, families, businesses, governments, and the environment (Department of Homeland Security 2006c)

The NRP is built on the template of the National Incident Management System (NIMS), which provides a consistent doctrinal framework for incident management at all jurisdictional levels, regardless of the cause, size, or complexity of the incident. The purpose of the NRP is to provide an all-hazards approach to domestic incident management. The NRP provides the framework for federal interaction with state, local, and tribal governments; the private sector; and NGOs for domestic incident prevention, preparedness, response, and recovery activities. It serves as the foundation for the development of detailed supplemental plans and procedures to effectively and efficiently implement federal incident management activities and assistance in the context of specific types of incidents.

Figure 4-7

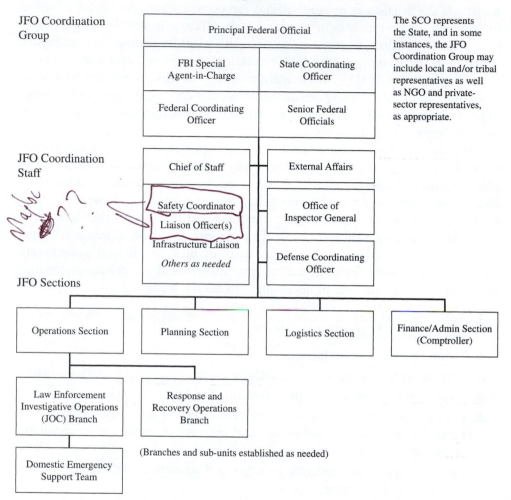

JFO structure for terrorist attacks (Source: FEMA).

One component of the NRP is the establishment of <u>Joint Field Offices (JFOs)</u>. As shown in Figure 4-7, the JFOs coordinate national response from a centralized location close to the incident. Their primary responsibility is to assist with local threat response and provide incident support to state, local, tribal, and governments and the private sector. The JFO system enables the effective and efficient coordination of federal incident-related prevention by providing "in the field" support for on-scene efforts and conducting broader operations that may extend beyond the incident site.

4.3.5 Recovery

Recovery is the period of time after a disaster. It can be of immediate, short-term, or protracted duration. During a disaster or immediately following, recovery often consists of providing assistance for preserving life and basic subsistence to affected populations. The recovery phase also includes damage assessment, debris clearance, and reconstruction of infrastructure and build-ings. Beyond physical reconstruction, recovery should also address the social, economic, and political needs of the community. Community reconstruction can take a very long time, and after large-scale disasters, some communities never fully recover. For example, before Hurricane Katrina devastated New Orleans, the city had a population of approximately 485,000. One year later, population estimates range from approximately 155,000 to 198,000. It is pro-jected that by 2008, about 198,000 people will live in New Orleans, about half of the pre-storm population, and the city may never regain all of its lost residents. When a portion of the population is missing, businesses lose reve-nue, schools lose students, and cities lose tax money. City services cannot function at optimum levels, and governments must provide services with fewer funds. Removing debris and rebuilding the physical elements of a city may be the easy part. It can be far more complex and difficult to repair the social fabric that makes a community function.

Effective recovery programs are possible only with good planning during the pre-impact phase. Communities should plan for the inevitable disaster, and pre-impact actions should include recovery planning. It is important for communities to develop the financial and material resources needed to support a prompt and effective disaster recovery. Plans should include responsibilities and assignments for impact assessment, debris management, infrastructure restoration, housing recovery, economic recovery, and linkage to hazard mitigation. Successful recov-ery plans should contain six components:

1. Communities should establish a recovery organization and chain of command.

2. Recovery planning should identify temporary housing for potential evacuees.

3. The plan should indicate how to accomplish the essential tasks of clean up (e.g., damage assessment, debris removal and disposal, infrastructure restoration, and permit processing). This is an important step because clean up must be underway before the reconstruction can begin.

4. Along with reconstruction, recovery plans should include methods to mon-itor contractors and retail pricing so that the population is not exploited.

5. Plans also need to address historic sites that may be affected.

6. Recovery plans should recognize that recovery period is a good time to enact policies for hazard mitigation projects in the community.

FOR EXAMPLE

How Much Does It Cost to Rebuild?

On August 29, 2005, Hurricane Katrina struck the Gulf Coast, causing flooding to over 80 percent of the city of New Orleans, an area seven times the size of Manhattan. According to the Department of Homeland Security, Katrina affected more than 1.5 million people and forced more than 800,000 citizens from their homes—the largest displacement of people since the great Dust Bowl migrations of the 1930s. Since the storms hit, government, private, and voluntary organizations have worked in concert to help rebuild the region. Congress authorized over $110.6 billion in aid for relief, recovery, and rebuilding efforts.

One year after Hurricane Katrina struck the Gulf Coast, the Department of Homeland Security issued a report that provided a status of the federal government's activities to help with recovery. Among the findings are the following facts about reconstruction in New Orleans. The figures are for federal aid only, and they do not include state, local, NGO, and private sector contributions.

▲ Funds allocated for rebuilding infrastructure (e.g., streets, bridges, airports, utilities) = $70.1 billion
▲ Funds allocated for housing and related structures (e.g., homes and farms) = $21.9 billion
▲ Funds allocated for other rebuilding efforts (e.g., businesses, parks, schools) = $18.6 Billion

This equals about $368 for every man, woman, and child in the United States. (Department of Homeland Security 2006a)

SELF-CHECK

1. Which of the following is not one of the phases of the disaster life cycle?
   a. Response   c. Prevention
   b. Matrices   d. Recovery
2. Which of the following is an example of a federal mitigation program?
   a. FEMA   c. NFIP
   b. NRP   d. FHA
3. The National Response Plan establishes a comprehensive all-hazards approach to enhance the ability of the United States to manage domestic incidents. True or false?
4. The Joint Field Office system enables the effective and efficient coordination of state-run incident-related prevention only by providing "in the field" support to state and local on-scene efforts. True or false?

SUMMARY

In this chapter, you evaluated why risk assessment is important for homeland security programs; appraised different risk assessment models to program evaluation; assessed threats to communities using risk matrices; and judged the usefulness of the Emergency Management Planning Model.

Potential threats can be natural or man-made, and they can affect personal, economic, political, or environmental interests. Interests and threats intersect in program implementation, so it is important that we understand the "disaster impact process." Only through an assessment of threats and interests can we understand the impact disasters will have on the physical, social, economic, and political characteristics of our communities. Risk assessment aids the decision-making process, and it can be helpful in reducing costs to communities by allowing emergency managers to focus mitigation, risk reduction, and preparedness programs on those areas that need the most protection.

KEY TERMS

Agricultural vulnerability	Agricultural plant and animal vulnerability to environmental extremes; the ability of livestock and crops to withstand disasters.
Composite Exposure Indicator (CEI)	A hazard assessment model that ranks potential for losses in a given region for single or multiple hazards by assigning a numeric value to the exposure potential for communities. FEMA has used this approach to quantify 14 variables in 3,100 U.S. counties, with rankings based on the amount of each variable present.
Criticality assessment	Process that identifies and evaluates an organization's assets based on a variety of criteria.
Demographic impacts	Effects on a community's population after a disaster.
Disaster impact process	The way to examine the effects a disaster will have on a community. The first step of the disaster impact process is the pre-impact phase, which includes planning and mitigation efforts. The second phase is the actual disaster event, which includes specific hazard conditions and community response. The third phase is the emergency management intervention phase, which includes response, recovery, and program evaluation.

Disaster response	The reaction individuals have when faced with the onset of a disaster.
Economic impacts	Changes in asset values after a disaster that are measured by the cost of repair or replacement.
Hazard assessment	The process by which we identify new and existing threats and assess the level of risk to a population.
Hazard exposure	The likelihood that specific disasters will occur; the probability of occurrence of a given event magnitude.
Hazard mitigation	Sustained action to alleviate or eliminate risks to life and property from natural or man-made hazard events.
Human vulnerability	Individual vulnerability to environmental extremes.
Interests	The human (individual or group), environmental, political, or economic components of society that we seek to protect through homeland security programs.
Matrix	A tool for decision making that uses a grid design to weigh the frequency of an event against its severity to rank potential costs or damage.
National Flood Insurance Program (NFIP)	FEMA-administered program that features three major components: flood insurance, floodplain management, and flood hazard mapping.
Physical vulnerability	The ability to prepare for, cope with, and withstand disasters; includes human vulnerability, agricultural ability, and structural vulnerability.
Political impacts	Changes in the political structure of a community after a disaster.
Preparedness actions	Pre-impact actions that provide the human and material resources needed to support active responses at the time of hazard impact.
Psychosocial impacts	Effects on mental health and the ability to get treatment after a disaster.
Recovery	The period of time after a disaster. It can be of immediate, short term, or protracted duration.
Risk reduction	An examination of the actions necessary to decrease detected or projected levels of danger

	and to identify the resources required for implementing those actions.
Social vulnerability	A person's or group's ability to anticipate, prepare for, or cope with disasters.
Structural vulnerability	A building's ability to withstand extreme stresses or features that allow hazardous materials to infiltrate the building.
Threat	Natural or man-made event that can destroy or damage human, environmental, political, or economic components of society.
Threat assessment	Process that identifies and evaluates threats based on various criteria.
Vulnerability assessment	Process that identifies weaknesses in a structure, individual, or function.

ASSESS YOUR UNDERSTANDING

Go to www.wiley.com/college/kilroy to assess your knowledge of the basics of threat assessment.

Measure your learning by comparing pre-test and post-test results.

Summary Questions

1. Hazards only occur naturally. True or false?
2. The disaster impact process includes event-specific conditions. True or false?
3. A CEI is a program that uses geographic information systems. True or false?
4. Effective recovery programs benefit from planning during the pre-impact phase. True or false?
5. Which of the following is **not** a part of the disaster life cycle?
   (a) Mitigation
   (b) Response
   (c) Recovery
   (d) Vulnerability
6. Which of the following is **not** a social characteristic that can be impacted by natural disasters that affect homeland security?
   (a) Demographic
   (b) Economic
   (c) Psychosocial
   (d) Ecological
7. Which of the following is **not** an assessment method?
   (a) Homeland Security Index
   (b) HAZUS
   (c) Composite Exposure Index
   (d) Vulnerability assessment
8. Which of the following security agencies does **not** conduct risk assessments?
   (a) Department of Homeland Security
   (b) NOAA
   (c) FEMA
   (d) Department of State

Applying This Chapter

1. Your boss asks you to explain the phases of the disaster life cycle. How would you do this? Why is it more appropriate to call these phases "functions"?

2. During a meeting of community leaders, someone asks how vulnerable your community is to terrorist attacks. Your initial planning assessment was that this type of threat was low, but new information at the meeting indicates the need for a new risk assessment. Develop a risk matrix that includes terrorist threats. Explain some techniques that a community can employ to reduce the risk of this type of threat.

3. You are an analyst for an energy company that is expanding its nuclear power generation capabilities by building new nuclear power plants. You are responsible for providing a recommendation for possible sites for the new plant. Which hazard assessment method(s) would be most helpful in your analysis? What are some community characteristics you would consider when planning a new plant?

4. You are a town planner in a small coastal town. You are responsible for making recommendations to the town council for policies that will help reduce risks from hurricanes and flooding. What types of mitigation policies would you recommend? What types of activities could the town regulate to reduce risks?

Risk Management Models

Models are analytical tools. They are not authoritative, meaning they can help assess possible outcomes in planning efforts, but they may not be deterministic in predicition outcomes. Based on the models described in this chapter, design your own risk management model, looking at one particular man-made or natural hazard.

Vulnerability Assessment

Within your local community, perform a vulnerability assessment for various hazards, whether natural or man-made. Determine implications of your micro analysis at the macro and system analysis levels.

5

STATE ACTORS AND TERRORISM
The Contemporary State System and State Sponsors of Terrorism

Starting Point

Go to www.wiley.com/college/kilroy to assess your knowledge of the basics of state actors and terrorism.
Determine where you need to concentrate your effort.

What You'll Learn in This Chapter

- ▲ The international system of states and their use of force
- ▲ The responses available to the inter-state system to deal with states that violate international norms about the use of force
- ▲ The definition of terrorism and the role played by states in using terror
- ▲ How the international community of states regulates the use of force between states
- ▲ The U.S. response in the wider global security environment
- ▲ The countries listed by the United States as state sponsors of terrorism

After Studying This Chapter, You'll Be Able To

- ▲ Assess the relationship between the international system of states and the use of terror as a weapon
- ▲ Evaluate the different forms of state terrorism (internal and external)
- ▲ Argue the differences between internal and external state terrorism
- ▲ Appraise the options open to the inter-state community to regulate the use of force
- ▲ Appraise the U.S. response to state sponsorship of international terrorism
- ▲ Judge the various U.S. responses to state-sponsored terrorism

INTRODUCTION

Today, we face different security challenges than those presented in the twentieth century by the superpower rivalry of the Cold War. With increasing processes of globalization, we have not only become more aware of the threats that challenge human security on a day-to-day level, we have also come to realize that many threats can no longer be dealt with purely on a state-to-state basis (if indeed they ever could). The global security environment in the twenty-first century is characterized by a multitude of interconnected factors that make it a more difficult environment within which states formulate their foreign policy objectives. Security used to be seen under the ultimate purview of the sovereign state; however, globalization has demonstrated that security challenges do not come exclusively from the aggressive behavior of other states. They also find expression in complex economic and social relations, as well as in actors other than the state (non-state actors). A potent example of this is, of course, the terrorist attack on 9/11, in which a transnational terrorist organization attacked the world's strongest military power, the United States. With this increasing threat of non-state actors using terrorism to force their views on the world, security experts realize that a sole focus on states is not sufficient in protecting us from contemporary security threats.

In this chapter, you will assess the complex relationship between the international system of states and the use of terror as a weapon. You will also evaluate the different forms of state terrorism (internal and external), argue the differences between these forms of terrorism, and appraise the options open to the inter-state community to regulate the use of force. Finally, you'll take a closer look at the various U.S. responses to state-sponsored terrorism.

5.1 Defining Terrorism

Terrorism is often defined as a form of political violence. However, this is simultaneously too simplistic and too broad a statement to offer a comprehensive understanding of terrorism. Political violence can be found in many variations in the relations between states, as well as in the relations between different groups within states. Thus, equating every form of political violence with terrorism would not help distinguish terrorism from other events, especially inter-state and civil war.

▲ **Inter-state war** is war between two or more states.
▲ **Civil war** is war that occurs within one state.

Nonetheless, we need to emphasize that terrorism takes place within the overall context of **political violence**, or the use of force in the pursuit of political objectives. The overriding political motivation behind terrorism is important because it distinguishes terrorism from criminal activity. Although victims can be terrorized during a crime, a criminal act is only terrorist if the purpose of the act is to further a particular political goal rather than, as is the case with most crime, to achieve personal and material goals, such as greed, anger, or jealousy (Cunningham 2003; Nacos 2006).

To distinguish terrorism from other forms of political violence, scholars and security experts alike have tried (and are still trying) to come up with clear conditions under which it can be argued that a particular form of political violence actually constitutes terrorism. In trying to uncover these conditions, however, we have to realize that the definitional process in itself is filled with political ambiguities. Many writers point out that the definition of terrorism very much depends on the definer's own perceptions (Cunningham 2003) or on the context within which specific actions take place, as well as the context within and the purpose for which the definition is constructed (White 2003).

Knowing that it is difficult to come by a comprehensive definition of terrorism shouldn't stop us from trying to define that which we would like to combat. In formulating our own understanding of this global problem, however, we should always realize that the mere act of defining holds specific biases that can clearly come up against other interpretations. In other words, we should be aware of the possibility that, depending on circumstances and context, our own definition can change. For the purpose of examining state actors in relation to terrorism, in this chapter we will use the following definition of **terrorism:**

> *Use or threat of use of seemingly random violence against nontraditional targets to instill a climate of fear so that the fear will induce political acquiescence and/or a political change in favor of those instigating the violence.*

There are several issues in this definition that need to be explained, including the following:

▲ By specifying the seemingly random aspect of violence, we allude to the psychological power of terrorism. The apparent randomness leaves the target audience with the impression that terrorists can "attack anything, anywhere, anytime" (Jenkins 1986, 777). At the same time, however, it needs to be understood that when planning a terrorist attack, much careful organization goes into the selection of targets so that the highest psychological effect can be achieved (Hoffman 1998).

▲ Although many terrorist attacks have focused on military installations, military personnel, and other representatives of the military institutions of the target state, an important part of terrorism is its use of civilians as immediate targets. This is important because terrorism functions as a **force multiplier** (it gives the appearance of strength when there is none or only very little), and the civilian nature of targets carries more psychological weight.

▲ The climate of fear is crucial to understanding the power of terrorism as a strategy. Motor vehicle accidents kill many more people worldwide than do terrorist attacks, but they do not create a climate of fear that could potentially change the political environment. As Glover explains, "[t]he violence or the threats have to be of the kind that can strike *terror* into people" (Glover 1991, 256; emphasis in original). The fear element is important because it is both a goal and a tactic. It amplifies a terrorist actor's strength, and serves to work toward affecting a larger audience so as to coerce the audience to influence state policy (Badey 1998). Furthermore, the goal is often not to kill the immediate victims, but to use their deaths to further a specific set of political goals. In other words, the death of the immediate victims is a "mere" means towards a greater end of achieving political change.

5.1.1 The Historical Context of Terrorism

Terrorism as the use of violence for political purposes has a long and ancient history (Kegley, Sturgeon, and Wittkopf 1988, 24). Consider the assassination of Julius Caesar in 44 B.C. as an historical example of a terrorist attack, especially when one thinks about the fact that political assassination is today considered an expression of terrorism (Combs 2000, 18). The term *terrorism,* however, is generally traced back to eighteenth-century France, and its first use refers specifically to the "régime de la terreur" (1793–1794) headed by Maximilien Robespierre and his Jacobin Party. The revolutionary state used purposeful, fear-inspiring, and seemingly random yet carefully orchestrated violence "designed to consolidate the new government's power by intimidating counter-revolutionaries, subversives, and all other dissidents whom the new regime regarded as 'enemies of the people'" (Hoffman 1998, 15). Thus, in eighteenth-century France, terrorism was associated with the abuses of power by the revolutionary state to both quell political opposition and subdue the general population into enforced endorsement of the politics of the revolutionary régime (until of course, Robespierre's favored tool of execution, the guillotine, was used against Robespierre himself).

This, in some form, is similar to our current understanding of terrorism as the use of violence for political objectives through the use of seemingly random acts of violence designed to instill fear into a large audience to compel them to affect a political change in line with the desires of those carrying out the terrorist act(s). However, a clear difference between Robespierre's reign of terror and our general understanding of terrorism today is the level of existing political control in the hands of terrorists. Under Robespierre, terrorist violence was carried out by those in control of the state apparatus; today, we generally perceive terrorist violence as carried out by those fighting the state and/or from a position of relative weakness (Hoffman 1998, 44; Nacos 2006, 11).

The realization that our concept of terrorism has changed over time tells us that we have to be careful about understanding the context within which we want to study terrorism, because depending on the time period under consideration, we can associate terrorism with different actors. By the same token, historical examples take us into the specific role played by states (and by groups using terrorism as a mean to become a state) in utilizing terror as a specific means of social control.

5.1.2 Terrorism and Political Violence

Political violence used under the label of terrorism is designed to create an atmosphere of fear. This fear, rather than the actual level of violence, is intended to influence an audience larger than the immediate victims so as to force them

---

FOR EXAMPLE

The Irgun and the Creation of the Israeli State in 1948

Prior to Israeli independence, Jewish terrorist organizations (Irgun, Haganah, and Lehi—also known as the Stern Gang) mounted a strategy of surprise attacks against unsuspected targets that, in combination, struck at the psychological ability of the British colonizers to maintain their position of power. With these attacks, the terrorist organizations attempted not only to militarily weaken the British forces, but to inflict psychological terror to undermine overall British support for maintaining forces in Palestine. The objective was to make Britain's stay in Palestine untenable. In Menachem Begin's own words (leader of Irgun, and later Israel's prime minister from 1977–1983):

> The very existence of an underground must, in the end, undermine the prestige of a colonial regime that lives by the legend of its omnipotence. Every attack which it fails to prevent is a blow at its standing. Even if the attack does not succeed, it makes a dent in that prestige, and that dent widens into a crack which is extended with every succeeding attack (Begin 1977, as quoted in Hoffman 1998, 53).

The success of the terror strategy became clear in May 1948 when British rule over Palestine formally ended, and Israel proclaimed itself an independent state. Today, the nation of Israel opposes terrorism as a tactic being used by Palestinian groups seeking to establish a Palestinian state by arguing that in the current context, the targeting of civilians is an illegitimate form of political violence. Yet Lehi, one of the groups that used terror tactics when fighting for Israel's independence from Britain, took that name because it stood for "Fighters for the Freedom of Israel."

to change their behavior. Ultimately, the purpose of the fear created through terrorism is to immobilize the target audience into inaction and/or to get them to acquiesce to policies in line with the terrorists' goals.

To achieve this, it is not always necessary to kill a large number of people, as long as the immediate victims relate to a larger audience in such a way that the larger audience identifies with the victims and sees itself as a potential future target. The seeming randomness of terrorist attacks, as well as the often non-military nature of victims, serves to enhance the level of fear experienced by the larger audience. So far we know that terrorism is politically motivated violence. It is often (but not exclusively) carried out by those without the ability to exercise direct control over their target audience and, therefore, fear is used as a weapon to force acquiescence. Furthermore, context matters. Depending on one's ideological or historical context, one's view of terrorism can change.

In the next section, we will look at states to examine how they are involved in the use of terrorism as a strategy to further their goals and to assess what the inter-state community can do about it. First, however, we need to determine what we mean by the terms "state" and "inter-state system."

SELF-CHECK

1. Terrorism has a universally agreed-upon definition. True or false?

2. Inter-state war can be defined as:
   a. war within a state.
   b. war between two or more states.
   c. civil war.
   d. none of the above.

3. Historical examples show that our perception of terrorism always stays the same. True or false?

4. Terrorism can function as a force multiplier, creating the appearance of strength when there is none or only very little, by:
   a. targeting strong states.
   b. targeting civilians.
   c. targeting the economic infrastructure of a state.
   d. targeting other terrorist organizations.

5.2 States and the Use of Force in the Inter-State System

Historically speaking, the state is a relatively recent form of political organization. The state as political entity emerged from the economic and technological changes that replaced the feudal system (Cusimano Love 2003, 12).

As the state's defining characteristic, we refer to the notion of **sovereignty**, a concept that goes back to the Treaty of Westphalia (1648) where the seeds of our modern state system were sown. The **state** denotes a distinct political community that spans a definable geographical territory, acknowledges one form of authority over that territory and population, and is recognized by other sovereign states (Cusimano Love, 2003). Sovereignty confers this authority to the state and recognizes "that there is a final and absolute authority in the political community" (Hinsley 1986, 1, as cited in Held 1993, 215). In other words, there is no other authority above the level of the state with the ability to make decisions affecting the population and/or territory represented by the state. A combination of states then relate to each other, knowing that each is assumed to be the final arbiter of its internal affairs. When we describe this collection of sovereign states with no higher authority above them, we use the term **anarchy**. This is not the same as chaos, but simply refers to an absence of a central government or overarching authority regulating the behavior of states.

This anarchic environment (where sovereign states relate to each other without a higher authority telling them what to do) results in each state acting in pursuit of its own interests. Moreover, the fact that there is no central world government also explains "why force can be considered within the bounds of acceptable behavior in cases of extreme international conflict, but unacceptable in domestic political contexts" (Kelleher and Klein 1999, 147). In this environment, states are considered the main actors on the world stage and the sole legitimate users of force within and between states. **Self-help** (the idea that each state has to rely on its own strength and that it cannot wait for others to help it in a situation of crisis) is considered to be the main behavioral characteristic, and, in the absence of an overarching authority, states act out of positions of distrust against other states and thus reserve the right to defend themselves against outside threats with the possible use of force.

5.2.1 The State and the Use of Force

"State" is primarily a legal/political term that represents a distinct political authority both with respect to what happens inside the state as well as what happens in the relations between states. Nowhere is the notion of state sovereignty more obvious and important than in the use of force. As Bushnell et al. explain, "the essential distinguishing feature of all states, as sets of institutions, is their monopoly or pretense of monopoly over legitimate acts of violence" (1991, 5). With respect to the political community inside state borders, the sovereign state is considered the sole authority to employ force so as to provide order and stability for its population (e.g. police force, legal system, etc.). With regard to relations between states, the lack of an overarching central authority regulating inter-state relations means that the state as a politico-legal and territorial entity is also the only arbiter (referee) in relations between states. This means that the state has recourse to the use of force to defend itself against outside aggression (e.g., establishment of armed forces). Indeed, "the role of force and the threat of the use of force [is] a major component of international relations" (Stohl 1984, 43).

We can therefore say that the state is a political entity imbued with the capability to employ coercive force to provide liberty and security to its citizens by upholding order internally and by protecting against outside aggression.

> "In the international context, the theory of sovereignty has implied that states should be regarded as independent in all matters of internal politics, and should in principle be free to determine their own fate within this framework. External sovereignty is an attribute which political societies possess in relationship to one another; it is associated with the aspiration of a community to determine its own direction and policies, without undue interference from other powers (Held 1993, 216).

5.2.2 The State and Intervention

Although internally there are many different forms of political organization that order the running of a state, in relation to other states, sovereignty denotes a relative equality between state actors. In other words, how states are organized internally can take many different forms such as democracies (each with their different variations), authoritarian regimes, theocracies, monarchies, and so on. Yet, despite these internal differences, sovereignty between state actors implies a mutual recognition that the government of a state is the sole authority over that state. Moreover, sovereignty implies the related concept of **non-intervention**. Because a state is considered the only legitimate representative of the population within a specific territory, no outside interference is allowed. This leads to the assumption that what happens inside a state should be of no concern to the relations between states. Of course, it should be noted right away that in this idealized form, sovereignty has never truly existed. States have many ways through which they engage in the internal affairs of other states to fulfill their interests. What is important here is that, as a legal concept, sovereignty orders the relations between states. Despite internal differences, material capabilities, access to resources, and size, sovereignty also implies equality between actors; only states have "legal standing in international agreements" (Cusimano Love 2003, 13). With this in mind, it becomes clear that the structure of anarchy serves as an environment where use of force is reserved to state actors and is considered a legitimate course of action for states to follow if their security is at stake.

Where, then, does this leave us with respect to terrorism? If states have legitimate recourse to violence and act out of the political necessity of self-help, can their use of violence ever be called terrorism? Many authors (e.g., Jenkins 1986, Hoffman 1998) say that we should only focus on non-state actors when it comes to understanding terrorism. These authors argue that terrorism constitutes illegitimate use of force, and non-state actors (based on our definition of the state as the legitimate exerciser of force) never have legitimacy using force. Moreover, even in instances of internally directed terrorism (abuses of power by a state against its own population), Laqueur (1987) argues that enough terms exist to describe abusive actions by states against their citizens that the application of the label "terrorism" is not useful (as cited in White 2003, 9). Nonetheless, even Wilkinson, who generally favors a focus on non-state actors, has pointed to the need for keeping an eye on state actors because "one cannot adequately understand terrorist movements [non-state actors] without paying some attention to the effects of the use of force and violence by states" (Wilkinson 1981, 467). Moreover, the state's capability to use force has created an inherent tension that makes the use and the abuse of force more likely to be employed by states rather than by non-state actors. Stohl (1984), for example, has argued that the state is a more likely user of terrorism, even if most scholars would prefer to call the state's use of force "coercive diplomacy" rather than terrorism (43).

To work through some of these contradictory assessments, the next section examines the concept of state terrorism. Similar to the term "terrorism" itself, state terrorism is a highly disputed field of study, and we should remember that different perceptions are also influenced by the context within which the definitions are made (remember, for example, the section on the need to understand historical context earlier in this chapter). Or, in the words of UN Ambassador Charles Yost:

> The fact is, of course, that there is a vast amount of hypocrisy on the subject of political terrorism. We all righteously condemn it—except when we ourselves or friends of ours are engaging in it. Then we ignore it or gloss over it or attach to it tags like "liberation" or "defense of the free world" or "national honor" to make it seem like something other than what it is (1972; as cited in Stohl and Lopez 1984, 5).

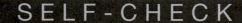

SELF-CHECK

1. Which of the following does not officially define a state?

   a. Distinct geographical territory
   b. One recognized political authority
   c. Recognition by other sovereign states
   d. One ethnic or religious population group

2. What does the term "anarchy" refer to in international relations?

   a. A sense of chaos
   b. The lack of an overarching authority regulating the behavior between states
   c. The fact that states must always use force in their relations with other states
   d. State abuse directed against its own population

3. In today's international system, states can no longer employ force on their own, even in matters of self defense. True or false?

4. Self-help is a term that describes the idea that each state has to rely on its own strength and that it cannot wait for others to help it in a situation of crisis. True or false?

5.3 State Actors: What Is State Terrorism?

As the earlier discussion on the state illustrated, states derive their legitimacy from internal composition and external recognition. Internally, theories of the state postulate that legitimacy is conferred by the state's capability to provide security for the population. Citizens give their sovereignty to the state so as to provide them with order, security, and well-being. External recognition, however, is not contingent on internal politics but is derived from the practice of adhering to sovereignty. The state is imbued with the power to use force within and between states (Held 1984, 48–49). In other words, there are two directions in which state power is employed: internally, to provide order; and externally, to protect against outside aggression. When either is abused, we can talk of **state terrorism**. This distinction then results in separate discussions on internal and external terrorism.

5.3.1 Internal State Terrorism

When examining **internally directed state terrorism**, we are talking about the use of force by the state apparatus against its own population. In line with our working definition of terrorism, we're referring to the systematic terrorizing of segments of or the entire population through the seemingly random use of violence to instill fear and coerce acquiescence of the population with state policies.

Because states by definition have power, they have the capability to terrorize their populations more effectively than those without control over state institutions (Combs 2000, 66). In this vein, Edward Hermann (1983) has argued that more attention should be focused on internal terrorism because more misery has been inflicted on populations by repressive policies than from "any other form of state-sponsored terror" (cited in White 2003, 9). Glover goes even further by stating "even a casual study of state terrorism shows that it totally dwarfs unofficial terrorism in its contribution to human misery" (Glover 1991, 273). The state-directed terror of the Jacobin Party under Robespierre shows, for example, how through control of the state apparatus, high numbers of people can be subdued first by random executions directed by the Committee of Public Safety and second by the terror instilled in the overall population.

The twentieth century has seen many instances of internal state terrorism. Examples include Hitler's Germany, Mussolini's Italy, Stalin's USSR, or Pol Pot's Cambodia, to name but a few, whose actions led to the deaths of tens of millions of people. Through systematic repression and persecution, people were deprived of liberty and life to support particular regimes. In each instance, the state apparatus was used to impose a particular kind of political order and ideology. Large segments of the population were killed, and others were held in check by the fear of being killed themselves.

> [S]tate terrorism can be seen as a method of rule whereby some groups of people are victimized with great brutality, and more or less arbitrarily by the state or state supported actors, so that others who have reason to identify with those murdered, will despair, obey or comply (Schmid 1991, 31).

These forms of state-imposed or state-directed violence are not limited to the totalitarian regimes of Nazi Germany, fascist Italy, or Stalin's Soviet Union. Since the end of World War II, we have seen many governments use terror against their populations. Among other instruments of terror, states have used death squads, blatant human rights violations, arbitrary arrests, disappearances, and more to intimidate any form of actual and/or perceived opposition. Some examples of this type of state behavior occurred in Argentina, Chile, and Greece during the 1970s and El Salvador, Guatemala, Colombia, and Peru in the 1980s. In each of these cases, state power was abused by those in government to oppress the population through horrendous human rights abuses. A more recent example can of course be seen in the genocide that is currently being perpetrated in Sudan, where hundreds of thousands of people have been killed since the internal conflict in the Sudanese region of Darfur started in 2003 (BBC News 2004).

Rummel's (2006) research offers the conclusion that this type of state terror is linked to the level of power that a state possesses. The more state power that is concentrated in a few hands, the more likely it is that this power will be abused. He argues that "the less freedom people have, the greater the violence; the more freedom, the less the violence." This is called **Rummel's power principle**, where "power kills and absolute power kills absolutely" (2006, xvi). Bushnell et al. (1991) describe this as a "phenomenon in which the relationship between the apparatus and power of the state and the rights of citizens has become severely distorted and one-sided" (9). Rummel's solution is the development of democratic principles and practices so that people are able to exercise control over the state apparatus. Bushnell et al. (1991) also seem to support this notion, as they state that "most cases of state terror are closely associated with the concentration of power in a single leader such as Stalin, Hitler, Pol Pot, Jim Jones, Khomeini, Pinochet, etc." (12). It thus stands to reason that when the institutions of government are decentralized and under democratic control, it is more difficult to abuse the state's power either internally or externally.

However, despite statistical evidence that democracies kill fewer people than non-democracies (Rummel 2006), for the purposes of our discussion on state terrorism, we need to point out that the distinctions between internal and external terrorism are not always clear. Sometimes, internal state terrorism is connected to state-supported terrorism, where another state aids the state terrorist through provisions of weapons, training, and funding, which are then used internally against the state's population. Wilkinson states, "Western democracies have often been guilty of backing regimes and groups which have been involved in committing terrorist attacks on the civilian population" (2000, 67). During the Cold War, for example, the U.S. government funded, provided training, and generally assisted many client states, especially in Latin America (Wilkinson 2000, but also see, e.g., Menjívar and Rodríguez 2005). These client states then used their U.S.-backed power to violently subdue their own populations. Whether it was necessary for the United States' national security to support repressive regimes and help overthrow democratically elected governments (e.g., Iran in 1953 and Chile in the early 1970s) is less important than the realization that democracies, too, have a tenuous relationship to the support of violence as an extension of foreign policy. Although Wilkinson uses Israel as his example of "clear cut and comprehensive evidence of a democratic government employing ruthless acts of counter-terror against terrorist opponents" (Wilkinson 2000, 68), it is clear that these are not isolated instances. It appears, then, that states have generally engaged in this type of behavior as a way to enhance their perceived national interests (see, e.g., Perdue 1989). This observation takes us into the use of state violence in the external realm, where terror is directed against other states.

5.3.2 External State Terrorism

If internally directed state terrorism consists of the abuse of state power against the state's own citizenry, **externally directed state terrorism** is the abuse of state power against citizens/governments from other states to motivate the target state to make policy changes in line with the political objectives of the "aggressor" state.

The biggest difficulty encountered when examining state terrorism as an extension of foreign policy is that in the inter-state environment, states are often seen as relating to other states out of a self-interested and at the same time distrustful manner. This means that states generally use a variety of methods short of outright warfare to "persuade" other states to act in a manner consistent with their own interests. For instance, states use diplomatic, economic, social, and political means to maximize their interests, and throughout history, we have seen that states also use violence (both overt and covert) as a means to achieve their objectives. The most obvious example of overt violence would be warfare.

Jenkins (1986), however, comments on how the total destructiveness of war has resulted in "self-imposed and externally imposed constraints" (775), meaning that overt warfare is used less because it could potentially be too destructive. Nonetheless, Jenkins continues by explaining that these constraints have led to an increase in non-regular warfare, in which states often resort to covert warfare to achieve their perceived interests (see also Cline and Alexander 1986). Thus, we can see that to avoid total war, states rely more and more on covert means to affect political objectives through other states. The main difference between internal and external terrorism (other than the obvious difference of where the violence is directed) is that "[u]nlike the internal coercive diplomacy (which may be obvious to all observers, whether or not they are willing to label it as such), clandestine operations are, by their very nature, conducted in secrecy and consequently are very difficult to discern" (Combs 2000, 73).

Per our working definition, terrorism is the purposeful pursuit of political change through violent means by attacking non-traditional targets to inflict psychological terror into a larger audience so that political change can be affected. State sponsorship then implies the assistance of one (or more) state(s) in terrorist activities so as to affect the politics of another state. While this seems relatively self-evident, the nature of the inter-state security environment and the secrecy involved in forms of state sponsorship, as well as the overall political nature of terrorism itself, make it difficult to assess precisely whether and in what form a particular state is engaged in support of international terrorist activities. Because foreign policy already includes a substantial amount of coercion with respect to other states (Schelling 1966, cited in Stohl and Lopez 1988, 1), it is increasingly difficult to ascertain what level of coercive activity constitutes terrorism and what is mere "state business as usual."

Cline and Alexander (1986) point out a range of activities that can be counted as a form of state sponsorship of terrorism. These activities "range from simple diplomacy and propaganda designed to encourage a climate of discontent in another country, to direct logistic and financial support of terrorist acts" (Cline and Alexander 1986, 5–6). Combs (2000) distinguishes between two levels at which states engage in externally directed terrorism: state-sponsored and state-supported terrorism. The difference between these two categories rests with the level of direct involvement between a state and the terrorist activity. In state sponsorship, "there is more involvement by the state" (e.g. direct control of particular groups and decision-making); in state-supported terrorism, "the state usually aids or abets existing terrorist groups that have varying degrees of independence" (Combs 2000, 73). In both instances, however, it is important for the state involved to be able to hide its activities.

States try to minimize their culpability, especially when the likelihood of military retaliation by the target state is quite high. When a state uses overt military aggression against another state, the target state has two options to respond. It can use its own military capabilities to defend itself. It can also mobilize the collective security arrangements of groups such as the United Nations to use collective self-defense against the aggressor state. To avoid this action, state-sponsored and state-supported terrorism can become very attractive because a state can use "terrorist acts to enhance state goals in other countries" (Combs 2000, 73) and thus aim to avoid outright war. Whereas terrorist non-state organizations are known for claiming responsibility for their attacks, states are extremely careful to distance themselves from their support of terrorism for the very purpose of avoiding being held accountable.

Although "governments have long engaged in various types of illicit, clandestine activities" (Hoffman 1998, 185), we have in recent years come to associate state-sponsored terrorism with the deliberate use of terrorist means by a state as an extension of that state's foreign policy. Cline and Alexander (1986) explain that the nature of state support for irregular forms of violence is linked to their perceived and actual power position in the international system. As such, state-supported warfare can be seen as an extension of foreign policy when the state in question wants to have deniability of responsibility. It is important to note, however, that state terrorism of this kind is not contingent on a state's relative weakness or indeed its non-democratic character, but rather should be seen as a reflection of the state's security interests (see, e.g., Badey 1998).

The secret nature of externally directed state terrorism presents us with a double problem. On the one hand, its secrecy makes it difficult for outsiders to determine with accuracy that terrorism has been used. On the other hand, this difficulty is exactly what makes the use of this kind of state terrorism an extremely attractive option to states who don't want their interests, let alone their involvement in another state's affairs, known to the rest of the inter-state community. With this in mind, what can be done about these states? If any state can resort to this covert extension of foreign policy, how does the inter-state system respond to this use of force? The next section briefly examines how the international community of states attempts to regulate the use of force. This is followed by an assessment of how the United States in particular has tried to deal with state-sponsors of terrorism.

SELF-CHECK

1. Externally directed terrorism is the abuse of state power against citizens/governments from other states to motivate the target state to make policy changes in line with the political objectives of the "aggressor" state. True or false?

2. Which of the following is not a characteristic of internally directed state terrorism?
   a. Use of force by the state against its own population
   b. Oppression of one's own population to force policy change on another state
   c. Systematic terrorizing of segments of or the entire population through seemingly random use of violence
   d. Creating an atmosphere of fear to get the population to comply with state policies

3. Describe Rummel's power principle.

4. State-sponsored and state-supported terrorism are the same thing. True or false?

5.4 The Global Response

The state is considered the legitimate exerciser of force both internally and externally. Based on the concepts of sovereignty and anarchy, states are assumed to act in a self-interested and distrustful manner toward one another, and the use of force is considered legitimate in the realm of inter-state relations. Over time, however, states have established practices to settle actual and potential disputes peacefully. Through customary practice as well as formal institutions, states have developed a large body of norms and standards to regulate the relationship between one another.

5.4.1 The United Nations and Collective Security

As a global security organization, the United Nations (UN) has established in its charter specific guidelines designed to curb the use or even the threat of use of force in the relations between states. As such, the charter states the basic rule when it comes to the use of force: It is forbidden. More specifically, Article 2(4) of the United Nations Charter states:

> *All members shall refrain in their international relations from the threat or use of force against the territorial integrity or political independence of any state, or in any other manner inconsistent with the purposes of the United Nations.*

One exception to this basic rule is limited to situations of individual or collective self-defense if an armed attack occurs against a member state (UN Charter, Article 51). A further exception occurs when a United Nations Security Council resolution has authorized the use of force to reverse a situation that challenges international peace and security. However, the primary function of the United Nations is to ensure that all peaceful means are exhausted before a state has to resort to the use of force. For this purpose, member states have devised many mechanisms and instruments to bind themselves together closer and to discuss potential problems in international forums before they escalate into violent conflict.

Moreover, when war does break out between states, the inter-state community has developed further standards by which it can be waged so as to curb the worst excesses of warfare.

> *The rules of war grant civilian combatants [sic] who are not associated with "valid" targets at least theoretical immunity from deliberate attack. They prohibit taking hostages. They prohibit violence against those held captive. They define belligerents. They define neutral territory. These rules are sometimes violated—and those responsible for the violations become war criminals. But violations in no way diminish the validity of the rules* (Jenkins 1986, 779).

In other words, although many assume that certain levels of violence are part and parcel of the inter-state system (in as much as states are constantly prepared to defend themselves against outside aggression), how violence is used is at least somewhat regulated through established practice and treaty-based norms.

When states violate these standards, the international community of states has recourse to verbal, economic, and military sanctions to make the state refrain from continuing to use force. States come together to protect themselves from aggression through what is known as collective security arrangements. Collective security refers to cooperative arrangements between states set up to avoid war. The purpose is for all states in the arrangement to work together if one state behaves aggressively towards the other state(s).

Clearly, there are means through which states combine their resources to deal with threats to international peace and security. However, in the case of state terrorism, especially when terrorism constitutes a strategy of covert warfare or the

> ### FOR EXAMPLE
>
> **The United Nations, Collective Security, and the 1991 Gulf War**
>
> After Saddam Hussein's Iraq invaded the neighboring state of Kuwait on August 2, 1990, the United Nations passed a series of resolutions calling on Iraq to withdraw. When Iraq didn't comply, it passed economic sanctions against Iraq. Finally, with Iraq in continuing defiance of the United Nations mandate, a military coalition (led by U.S. forces) forced Iraq out of Kuwait. "Operation Desert Storm" lasted from January 16, 1991, until February 28, 1991, and is often portrayed as a revival of the UN's concept of collective security, where, in the case of an aggressor state, all other states band together to restore international peace and security. In other words, even though the UN says that force should never be used, it nonetheless has provisions for how to deal with states (even by use of force) that violate this rule.

extension of foreign policy, these guidelines are less able to deal with states because their reason for using terrorist tactics is for precisely the purpose of defeating existing norms and standards. Because of the existing limitations placed on the use of force, states will try to circumvent any potential regulation of their use of force by employing tactics that are less traceable and have a high level of deniability. So, then, how do states deal with the threat posed by state-sponsored terrorism?

5.4.2 The United Nations' Response to Terrorism

The United Nations has a range of anti-terrorism conventions, but many authors have argued that these conventions only focus on specific acts rather than on state actors (Joyner 2004). Although these conventions are important in coordinating inter-state cooperation, it should nonetheless be emphasized that without the political will of all member states, it is unlikely that these conventions on their own can tackle the problem of terrorism, especially when it is used as a state strategy of its covert foreign policy. Moreover, the majority of UN anti-terrorism conventions treat the problem as a crime rather than as a form of armed force. Indeed, Joyner (2004) reports that so far "[n]o specific international agreement has yet been adopted in the UN (by either the Security Council, or General Assembly, or International Law Commission, or the Sixth (Legal) Committee) that outlaws 'terrorism,' much less provides for a satisfactory, universally agreed upon definition of the concept" (242).

Under the United Nations Charter, all conflicts, including the threat of terrorism, need to be resolved by peaceful means, and only when peaceful means have been exhausted is it possible to consider the use of force to deal with the maintenance of international peace and security. When force is applied, states need to follow the accepted rules of engagement, and even in the case of individual or collective use of force, the defending state is still bound to abide by accepted limitations on the use of force (e.g., use of force must be proportional to the initial act of aggression; civilians need to be protected; etc.). Before the application of force however, the United Nations emphasizes the peaceful resolution of conflict. With respect to terrorism, it has devised several treaties and conventions to limit the threat of terrorist attacks. More specifically, the United Nations has tried to enhance the international community's ability to deal with terrorism by outlawing the following acts:

▲ Hijacking of aircraft (1963, 1970)
▲ Attacking airports (1971, 1973)
▲ Posing threats to international maritime navigation (1988)
▲ Taking hostages (1979)
▲ Harming diplomatic agents (1973)
▲ Bombing civilians (1991)
▲ Protecting nuclear materials (1980)
▲ Terrorist bombings (1997)
▲ Financing of terrorist activities (1999)

In identifying specific terrorist acts, the UN has started the difficult process (difficult because member states often interpret security threats differently) of creating a body of instruments designed to define, prohibit and punish acts of transnational terrorism as international crime (Joyner 2004). However, without a clear definition of terrorism itself, without specific global rules as to what to do with state sponsors, and with the ultimate intent of state sponsors to "escape identification, and hence international military response and economic sanction" (Hoffman 1998, 195–196), it becomes increasingly difficult for individual states with their own interpretations of what constitutes state terrorism to see the United Nations as a suitable environment within which their security interests can be met. Moreover, because of the problem in linking specific actors to terrorist acts, the United Nations to this day has been stifled by disagreements over whether states should even be included as terrorist actors (see, e.g., Hoffman 1998, Joyner 2004). Furthermore, because states still see their interests best served by their own actions, states have devised their own security mechanisms to deal with specific state threats both within and outside the context of the United Nations. Joyner (2004) argues that rather than looking to the UN in the fight against terrorism, "genuine international cooperation between the governments of individual states remains the key ingredient to coordinating efforts to combat a common enemy" (242). Therefore, states as part of their security mandate have come up with their own strategies for protecting themselves against the threat of state-sponsored terrorism.

SELF-CHECK

1. Article 2(4) of the United Nations Charter states: "All members shall refrain in their international relations from the threat or use of force against the territorial integrity or political independence of any state." True or false?

2. What are the two exceptions to the UN's ban on the use of force?

3. Define collective security.

4. Which of the following is a limitation on the United Nation's response to terrorism when it comes to dealing with state actors?

   a. Lack of a common agreement on a definition of terrorism
   b. Lack of a collective security agreement in the U.N. Charter
   c. Insufficient voting membership in the General Assembly
   d. Opposition by member states to join the Security Council

5.5 The United States and State Sponsors of Terrorism

Despite the fact that this chapter has argued that there are two main variants of state terrorism (internal and external), we will move away from the internal dimension and concentrate solely on the use of terrorism as an extension of foreign policy. To understand this, we will look at the state terrorism threats confronting American security. How does the United States, one particular state actor, frame its security policies with respect to other states, especially those it sees as engaging in this form of terrorism?

Although the United States has a vast arsenal to deal with international terrorism (see, e.g., the *2006 National Strategy for Combating Terrorism,* where the U.S. outlines how it plans to deal with transnational terrorism), it has created a very specific foreign policy tool to deal with state actors. In 1979, the Export Administration Act established a list of state sponsors of international terrorism. This act called on the secretary of state to designate states that have repeatedly provided support for acts of international terrorism (Pillar 2003, 158), and inclusion on the list is based on the following criteria outlined in the Anti-Terrorism and Arms Export Amendments Act of 1989:

▲ Allowing territory to be used as a sanctuary
▲ Furnishing lethal substances to individuals/groups with the likelihood that they will be used for terrorism
▲ Providing logistical support to terrorists/groups
▲ Providing safe haven or headquarters for terrorists/organizations

▲ Planning, directing, training, or assisting in the execution of terrorist activities

▲ Providing direct or indirect financial support for terrorist activities

▲ Providing diplomatic facilities, such as support or documentation, to aid or abet terrorist activities

As a counter-terrorism tool, the state sponsors list was designed to put an economic burden on the states listed so as to get them to change their behavior and thus to improve U.S. security interests. Being placed on the Department of State's designated state sponsor list results not only in the stigma of being labeled a state sponsor of terrorism, but also carries serious economic implications. Inclusion on the list results in the automatic attachment of sanctions against the state in question. The sanctions include being barred from receiving both various forms of U.S. assistance and U.S. support for loans from multilateral lending institutions (e.g., the World Bank and IMF), and it generally puts stringent import and export controls on such a country (O'Sullivan 2003). Moreover, recent additions to the sanctions regimes against these countries include making it a crime for "individuals to engage in financial transactions with countries on the list;" withholding foreign assistance even from "countries that give foreign aid, loans or subsidies to countries on the list;" and allowing U.S. citizens to sue countries on the terrorism list for "acts of torture, extrajudicial killing, and terrorism" (Peed 2005, 1327–1328).

As of 2006, the U.S. list of state sponsors of terrorism includes Cuba, Iran, Libya, North Korea, Sudan, and Syria (listed in alphabetical order). You can see the geographic location of Iran, Syria, and Sudan in Figure 5-1. The following section gives brief overviews of each country before offering a discussion on the efficacy of the list in combating state sponsors of terrorism. The chapter concludes by examining suggestions for how state sponsorship in particular and state terrorism in general can be combated.

5.5.1 Cuba

Cuba has been on the State Department's list of designated state sponsors of terrorism since 1982. Its inclusion was warranted primarily due to its political system and its function as a client state of the former Soviet Union. Cuba was described as "a base for exporting revolution to Nicaragua and throughout Central America and the Caribbean, the vital seaway constituting much of the southern frontier of the United States" (Cline and Alexander 1986, 12). Sullivan (2005) states that "while the [then] [a]dministration provided no explanation in the *Federal Register* notice as to why Cuba was added to the terrorism list, various U.S. government reports and statements under the Reagan [a]dministration in 1981 and 1982 alleged Cuba's ties to international terrorism" (3). Cline and Alexander (1986), for

Figure 5-1

Map depicting the location of three state sponsors
of terrorism—Iran, Syria, and Sudan.

example, have linked Cuba to active support of revolutionary forces in Colombia, Peru, and Nicaragua, especially through the provision of training and funds. However, since the end of the Cold War, most authors assert that Cuba no longer engages in active state support of terrorist organizations (e.g., Hoffman 1998; Nacos 2006). Pillar (2003) states that the "Castro regime's post-cold war retrenchment has been so extensive that it is doing nothing either in terrorism or other military or external activities that would appear to qualify it for its pariah status." As to why Cuba remains on the list, is in Pillar's view "a function of internal politics—those of Cuba as well as of the United States" (161).

In other words, whatever is left of Cuba's former state support of terrorism (such as provision of safe haven for ETA members and tangential assistance to members of Colombia's terrorist groups, such as the FARC and ELN) is in itself not enough to warrant Cuba's continued inclusion on the list. If it was, other countries would by default also have to be listed (such as Pakistan or Saudi Arabia). Nacos (2006) likewise notes the fact that even though "there was no evidence that [Cuba] provided support to terrorist groups," it remained on the State Department's list. She, however, links this to the fact that Cuba failed to cooperate with the United States in its post-9/11 global war on terror (107–108). Indeed, the State Department's 2005 Country Reports on Terrorism begins its assessment of Cuba's continuing role as state sponsor by noting, "Cuba actively continued to oppose the U.S.-led Coalition prosecuting the global war on terror and has publicly condemned various U.S. policies and actions" (2006, 172). This adds an interesting component to the discussion of state sponsorship, at least to the extent that in view of U.S. security politics, the level of cooperation in the U.S. war on terrorism can have serious repercussions as to how a country is perceived by the United States. (This also foreshadows a later discussion on the efficacy of the list in as much as it is less designed to deal with state-sponsored terrorism and is instead an overall reflection of the U.S. view of security concerns more broadly.)

5.5.2 Iran

Iran has been on the State Department's list since 1984. Iran was placed on the list after it was determined that the country supported Hezbollah, a militant Islamic group that in 1983 used suicide truck bombs against the U.S. Marine barracks in Beirut, Lebanon, killing 241 service members (O'Sullivan 2003, 49). In fact, an earlier event, the American embassy takeover in 1979 by Iranian students, is seen as the beginning of a new type of state-sponsored terrorism. Although purportedly the hostage taking was instigated and maintained by Iranian students, the fact that the Iranian revolutionary government not only didn't condemn the acts but moved to show active support for this attack against American security interests indicated a change in how state sponsorship was perceived. Until then, governments in similar situations were sometimes seen as "caught somewhere in the middle," neither "quite a hostage" nor "quite a go-between." However, the Khomeini government's "endorsement in late November [1979] of the embassy takeover . . . changed the nature of the discussion of terrorism for this case and perhaps for the international system in general" (Stohl and Lopez 1984, 5). Up until the embassy takeover, states had been seen as distinct from terrorist organizations operating on their territory. The Iranian situation changed this perception:

> *The Iranian situation had "joined" (in a legal sense) all of the issues. What was originally a nongovernment act became a government act. What was first terrorism became surrogate warfare* (Stohl and Lopez 1984, 6).

Hoffman (1988) states that this "pivotal event" inaugurated an "increasingly serious and extensive state-sponsored terrorist campaign directed by the Khomeini regime in Iran against the United States as well as other Western countries" (186) and turned Iran into "the most significant source of state-sponsored terrorism" (Wilkinson 2000, 63). Iran's support of terrorism is considered so extensive that Pillar (2003) distinguishes three ways through which Iran supports international terrorism. It engages in the "extraterritorial assassination of Iranian oppositionists." Also, Iran provides "money, training, weapons, and other assistance to terrorist groups that oppose Israel, the Arab-Israeli peace process, or the established order in a number of countries in the Middle East, North Africa, and Asia." Finally, Iran engages in "regular . . . surveillance of U.S. installations and personnel overseas" (159). Although this third point on its own doesn't constitute terrorist activity, Pillar explains that it nonetheless is important to consider because it would make it easier to carry out future Iranian terrorist attacks against these potential targets.

Although Iran is the "premier state sponsor of terrorism" (Hoffman 1998, 193), we need to recognize that Iran's sponsorship isn't the only security concern. As Pillar (2003) describes, Iran's nuclear program, "overall opposition to the Middle East process, and policies toward moderate regimes in its own neighborhood" constitute similar and sometimes even more serious security concerns (159). Wilkinson (2006) also notes how the Iranian regime played "the key part in encouraging its ally in Sudan, the National Islamic Front, to turn Sudan into a useful platform for training, safe-haven and assistance to a variety of extremist factions such as Islamic Group, Hamas, Hezbollah, PIJ and others" (65).

It is thus not surprising that the State Department's *Country Reports on Terrorism 2005* states that "Iran remained the most active state sponsor of terrorism" (2006, 173). Iran's strong opposition to Israel has led it to support both Shiite groups (e.g., Hezbollah) and Sunni groups (e.g., Hamas, and Palestinian Jihad), as well as secular groups (e.g., PFLP-GC) because they all share a common motivation, that of violent opposition to Israel (Nacos 2006, 110–111). This makes Iran an influential actor, and getting Iran to cooperate in the war on terrorism would require an acknowledgement on its part of Israel's right to exist. This, however, has become increasingly less likely, especially considering Iranian President Ahmadinejad's inflammatory language against Israel. The most poignant example of this was heard in October 2005, when he called for Israel to be "wiped off the map" (BBC News 2005). In other words, Iran constitutes a very serious security threat, not just because it sponsors terrorist organizations to achieve its own state goals, but also because it opposes U.S. interests in the region and poses a threat as a potential developer of nuclear weapons.

5.5.3 Libya

Libya has been on the State Department's designated state sponsor list since 1979. Especially during the 1970s and 1980s, Libya was known for its active support of international terrorism by "providing training camps, safe-havens and cash and weapons for certain favoured groups" as well as "using terrorism as a weapon against Libyan dissidents abroad" (Wilkinson 2000, 63). It supplied weapons to the Irish Republican Army (IRA) and provided support to Palestinian terrorist organizations opposed to the Israeli-Palestinian peace process, such as the Abu Nidal Organization, Palestine Islamic Jihad, and Ahmed Jibril's Popular Front for the Liberation of Palestine (PLFP-GC). Libya was conclusively linked to at least 15 state-sponsored terrorist incidents in 1987 and 8 in 1988. Moreover, the bombing of Pan Am Flight 103 over Lockerbie, Scotland, in 1988 led to the "indictment of two Libyan employees of that country's national airline who are alleged to have been agents of Qaddafi's intelligence service" (Hoffman 1998, 192–193). Even though the Qaddafi government admitted culpability, handed over the agents involved to a Scottish court, started paying reparations to the victims' families, has now "broken completely with its former client Abu Nidal, implemented procedures to prevent terrorists from entering Libya or using its territory, cooperated on counterterrorism with moderate Arab states, acted in accordance with an Arab League agreement to extradite suspected terrorists, and transferred support from Palestinian rejectionists to Arafat's Palestinian Authority," it remains on the list "because of unfinished business related to prior terrorism and because of a lack of other pressing concerns" (Pillar 2003, 160).

This assessment mirrors the points made in the State Department's reporting, where Libya is described as having "continued to cooperate with the United States and the international community in the fight against terrorism" (2006, 174). Nonetheless, Levitt (2002), for example, still maintains that the steps toward cooperation are limited and that "Libya maintains 'residual ties' to terrorist groups" (45–46). Clearly, residual ties to past alliances and different interpretations over levels of cooperation make it difficult to assess the extent of Libya's change. However, Libya's renouncement of support for terrorism and more importantly its steps toward dismantling its weapons of mass destruction program have ensured that U.S.-Libyan relations have drastically improved. Indeed, Libya's removal from the state terrorism list is forthcoming. The U.S. started restoring diplomatic relations with Libya in 2004 (Nacos 2006, 113), and Secretary of State Condoleezza Rice announced in May 2006 that the U.S. will open an embassy in Tripoli and take Libya off the designated state sponsors list (St. John 2006). These positive steps have resulted in calls for Libya to function as a model for other states currently on the state sponsor list, most notably North Korea and Iran (Achin 2006, St. John 2006).

5.5.4 North Korea

Not unlike Cuba, evidence of North Korea's current active support for terrorism is thin. On the list since 1988, a year after Pyongyang agents were implicated in the mid-air bombing of a South Korean passenger jet over the sea near Myanmar, North Korea is listed also because its actions against South Korea (e.g., using a powerful bomb at the Martyr's Mausoleum in Rangoon, Burma, killing 17 South Koreans officials in 1983) and its practice of assassinating North Korean dissidents. However, North Korea has not exhibited any of its previous acts that would warrant its continued inclusion on the list.

Indeed, the State Department's listing of North Korea begins with the following assessment: "The Democratic People's Republic of Korea (DPRK) is not known to have sponsored any terrorist acts since the bombing of a Korean Airlines flight in 1987" (2006, 175). Furthermore, North Korea is noted for having returned Japanese abductees in 2003 and for continuing negotiations about other abductees suspected to be in North Korea since the end of the Korean War. Thus, to understand the presence of North Korea on the list, we have to recognize the importance of North Korea's nuclear program (see, e.g., Peed 2005) as well as its intransigence towards the global war on terror that warrants, according to the State Department, North Korea's continued position on the designator list. In other words, North Korea presents itself as another relic of the Cold War, and because it provides serious security concerns especially in the field of nuclear technology, these facts explain its continuing presence on the list much more than any actual support for terrorism. Pillar (2003) describes that although North Korea might continue to give shelter to "Japanese extremists [members of the Japanese Red Army] and in recent years has tried to kidnap (and perhaps assassinate) a defector or two, and possibly to assassinate a South Korean official" (161), what is more important to current U.S. security concerns is North Korea's nuclear program.

5.5.5 Sudan

Sudan's inclusion on the State Department's list is more recent than any of the other countries and only goes back to 1993. Hoffman noted in 1998 that Sudan may not be among the "current active sponsors of international terrorism," but it is nonetheless considered to "play [a] critical role in abetting and facilitating terrorist operations" (194–195). More recently, it has been noted that similar to Libya, Sudan has taken some positive steps toward cooperation in the United States' global war on terror, but as Levitt (2002) describes, "Sudan continues to provide groups like al-Qaeda, Egyptian Islamic Jihad, Hamas and Palestinian Islamic Jihad with safe haven for logistical and support activities" (46). After the installation of an Islamic government in 1989, "Sudan provided a host of mostly Islamist terrorist groups with training camps and other resources" (Nacos 2006, 113), and it provided safe haven to Osama bin Laden in 1991. Sudan tried to improve its international standing by offering to extradite bin Laden to either the United States or Saudi Arabia in 1996 (a move that was supposed to change its image in line with what had happened when it extradited Venezuelan Carlos Ramirez Santos—better known as the international terrorist Carlos the Jackal—to France in 1994). Neither Saudi Arabia nor the United States accepted the offer of extradition, however.

After Sudan's cooperation in the post-9/11 global war on terror (e.g., Sudan arrested dozens of suspected al-Qaeda affiliated terrorists), the United Nations lifted its sanctions against Sudan (imposed in 1995). Nonetheless, it still remains on the State Department's list, primarily because of its continuing internal conflicts and the tenuous regional security situation. The State Department's report thus states:

> While there remains significant concern in the international commu-
> nity over Sudan's handling of internal rebel movements, specifically
> in western Sudan, there is no current data indicating that interna-
> tional terrorists operate in Darfur. The flow of weapons and person-
> nel between Sudan and most of its western, southern, and eastern
> neighbors, however, has weakened international efforts to stabilize the
> region. Many of Sudan's borders, particularly those along the Red
> Sea coast, remain porous and easily penetrable. This fact very likely
> allowed subversive elements and smuggled humans to enter Sudan
> without knowledge of any government security units and compounds
> problems in securing the region (2006, 175).

Nonetheless, it should also be noted that although the State Department is concerned about Sudan's internal conflict (the United States was the first to term the conflict in Darfur a genocide), it is also mindful of the opportunities Sudan can provide in the global war on terror. There have been reports of increased intelligence sharing between the Central Intelligence Agency and Sudanese governmental officials, as well as cooperation in other areas. Silverstein (2005) thus states that "Sudan's intelligence service presents an opportunity to gather information on suspected extremist groups in countries where United States agents are unable to operate effectively." Whether this will lead to Sudan's eventual removal from the state sponsor list remains to be seen. Sudan's human rights record as well as its history with extremist organizations certainly indicates that it still has a long way to go.

5.5.6 Syria

Syria has been listed as a state sponsor by the State Department since 1979. It is known for providing safe havens for Hezbollah and other radical Palestinian groups as well as the PKK. Wilkinson (2000) states, however, that Syria is also known to exercise "some restraint over the activities of these groups because the late President Assad wished to retain the option of diplomatic negotiations with Israel for the return of the Golan Heights" (63). In recent years, it has been described both as a no longer very active state supporter of terrorism (Hoffman 1998) and as a master at disguising its support for terrorism "beneath a cloak of state secrecy" (Combs 2000, 78). The overriding concern for the United States, however, rests with convincing Syria of the need for peace with Israel (Levitt 2002; Pillar 2003). Due to this overriding regional security concern, Syria's support for terrorist organizations is considered a bargaining chip in its negotiations with Israel. Pillar (2003) asserts that if "Syria and Israel succeed in reaching a peace agreement, Syria's support to the terrorist groups will be dealt with—because the Israelis would settle for nothing less" (161).

Since the global war on terror, Syria has shown some efforts at cooperation with the United States (e.g., arrest of alleged Syrian affiliates with al-Qaeda; the slowing of weapons transfers from Syria to Hezbollah; sharing of intelligence with U.S. agencies), but Levitt (2002) still considers its actions "business as usual" (49), especially because the groups known to have been supported by Syria in the past have continued to use terrorism (e.g., Hamas, PIJ, PFLP, DFLP, and Hezbollah). Moreover, Levitt cites Israeli news reports that have stated that "Syria has reportedly allowed 150–200 al-Qaeda operatives to travel through Damascus and settle in Ayn al-Hilweh and other Palestinian refugee camps in Syrian-controlled Lebanon" (52). Nacos, on the other hand, states that there is no evidence of Syrian support for al-Qaeda. Indeed, she cites the 2003 State Department's *Patterns of Global Terrorism* report that notes the Syrian government "cooperated significantly with the United States and other foreign governments against al-Qaeda, the Taliban, and other terrorist organizations and individuals. It has also discouraged any signs of public support for al-Qaeda, including in the media and at mosques" (Nacos 2006, 114).

The State Department's *Country Reports on Terrorism 2005* publication makes more critical observations. Although it notes that the "Syrian Government has not been implicated directly in an act of terrorism since 1986" and that Syria has cooperated in the past, the report also states that in "May [2005], the Syrian Government ended intelligence cooperation, citing continued U.S. public complaints about the inadequate level of Syria's assistance to end the flow of fighters and money to Iraq." Moreover, although Syria has publicly condemned international terrorism, it still reserves the right to make a "distinction between terrorism and what they consider to be 'legitimate armed resistance' by Palestinians in the Occupied Territories and by Lebanese Hezbollah" (2006, 176).

5.6 Implications of the U.S. Response to State-Sponsored Terrorism

Even a cursory glance at all six countries on the State Department list shows the diverse nature of these countries, and Pillar (2003) warns us of the problematic nature of applying a single label for such a variety of states.

SELF-CHECK

1. Which of the following countries is not included on the State Department list of state-sponsors of terrorism?

   a. Iran

   b. North Korea

   c. Syria

   d. Lebanon

2. The Anti-Terrorism and Arms Export Amendments Act of 1989 defines conditions that will lead to classification of a state-sponsor of terrorism, such as allowing its territory to be used by terrorists as a sanctuary. True or false?

3. Why is Iran labeled the "the premier state sponsor of terrorism"?

4. What is the internal problem in Sudan that is of concern to the United States? Has this stopped the United States from keeping Sudan as a strategic partner in the global war on terrorism?

Membership on the list implies some level of uniformity; however, even our brief discussions (especially of Cuba, North Korea, and Libya) indicate that the level of actual support for terrorism is often less a concern than other security interests that have warranted these countries' continued inclusion on the list. For this reason, many authors limit their discussions to Iran and Syria (and to a lesser extent Sudan) because Cuba and North Korea, are seen as no longer actively supporting international terrorism (Wilkinson 2000; Nacos 2006), and because Libya is actually in the process of being taken off the list due to its compliance with international conditions. We included them here, however, because they are still present on the designated state sponsor list, and their presence on the list says as much about the list itself as it does about these countries' continued security threat.

The following section takes a look at some of the criticisms brought against the list to examine how the list specifically and U.S. counter-terrorism policy toward state sponsors generally might be improved.

5.6.1 Criticisms of the State-Sponsored List

The fact that other issues "have hijacked counter-terrorism with regard to certain states on the list, as well as certain ones not on it" (Pillar 2003, 162) presents a major stumbling block to the list's capability to function effectively. North Korea's inclusion is a reflection of its nuclear ambitions and the threat this poses to U.S. security interests. Cuba's inclusion "reveals [more] about the U.S. domestic interplay surrounding Cuba than any objective reality concerning Cuba's foment of terrorism." Syria has less restrictive sanctions imposed against it because of its important role as regional player in the Middle East process (O'Sullivan 2003, 9). Sudan is on the list because of its internal conflicts while also engaged in intelligence cooperation with the United States. Iran is suspected of supporting terrorists in neighboring Iraq, but its current security threat is measured more by its potential nuclear programs than its support for terrorism. Libya, for all intents and purposes, should be off the list already. This alone indicates that there are specific U.S. concerns that are reflected in the list, rather than any objective measure of a state's engagement with support for terrorism. How else could we understand the absence of other countries from the list, such as Pakistan and Saudi Arabia?

Pillar (2003) describes how "Pakistan has stayed off the list not because it is doing less than any of the listed states to foster terrorism (untrue) but because imposing this additional penalty would have drawbacks in light of other U.S. interests in Pakistan and the U.S. stake in maintaining an even-handed approach toward South Asia as a whole" (162). Saudi Arabia has a tenuous relationship to Islamic fundamentalism, and "especially because of its long-standing habit of funding Islamist groups has been described as playing a unique role in financing a global network of terrorist breeding grounds" (Nacos 2006, 115). Yet, Saudi Arabia is not on the list. It is not merely a large supplier of energy resources, but more importantly plays too important a role in allowing U.S. military access to the region for its relationship with America to be jeopardized by being placed on the state sponsor list.

Clearly, "state sponsors of terrorism are only part of the story about the connections between states and terrorists" (Nacos 2006, 118). State-sponsorship is an important element in global security affairs, but it is just that—only one variable in the calculations a state makes about how to keep itself and its security interests safe. It should thus not be surprising that there are varied reasons for why countries are on the list and stay on the list. Nonetheless, despite the fact that we can understand the thinking behind the U.S. reasoning for placing or not placing certain countries on the list, we should still note that in applying these varying standards, these actions can "reduce the credibility of U.S. counterterrorist policy" overall (Pillar 2003, 163).

The state terrorism list is often described as a tool of political jockeying: "Its history is replete with moves of questionable sincerity, creating classifications that are out of step with countries' practices" (Peed 2005, 1329). In addition to the political nature of the list, however, the list also raises the question of the utility of a sanctions regime, at least one that is as rigid as the automatic imposition of highly restrictive sanctions as the state sponsor list. Even though we already discussed that sanctions can vary considerably between the countries listed, it should not be forgotten that the ultimate impact of being branded a state sponsor is "a major impediment to business" (Pillar 2003, 162). Yet, how effective is this impediment to inducing behavioral change in the targeted state? Has inclusion on the list led to changed behavior?

FOR EXAMPLE

Do Sanctions Work?

In the 1980s, Libya was linked to the bombing of a discotheque in Berlin, Germany (1986), and two of its agents were found to have planted a bomb on Pan Am Flight 103, which exploded over Lockerbie, Scotland, in 1988. The Qaddafi regime was also accused of links to terrorist attacks by the Abu Nidal Organization. More recently, and especially since the global war on terror, Libya has tried to extricate itself from international isolation, and as described earlier, it is en route to re-establishing full diplomatic relations with the United States.

How much, however, can this change be attributed to being listed on the state sponsor list and thus having an extensive sanctions regime imposed against it? O'Sullivan (2003) argues that while the United States imposed sanctions against Libya have had some discernable effect, sanctions generally and U.S. unilateral sanctions in particular are not enough for us to fully understand Libya's change. She has argued that when sanctions had some effect in furthering the broad U.S. goal of containing Libya, it was only in conjunction with the wider United Nations effort of isolating Libya. Furthermore, although Libya's positive change can be in part attributed to a combination of U.S. and UN sanctions, these sanctions "cannot on their own claim all the success. Rather, sanctions complemented domestic challenges and international changes to inspire a significant reorientation of Libya's external behavior" (O'Sullivan 2003, 210).

Overall, we can conclude that economic sanctions are not entirely successful in "effecting positive changes to these countries' policies on terrorism" (Hoffman 1998, 191). Moreover, if perceived globally as too inflexible, they can have the opposite effect of isolating not the state sponsor but the credibility of the state imposing sanctions. This proves to influence not only the relationship between the United States and Libya, but also more broadly the overall counter-terrorism strategy upheld by the United States. What then can be done to improve the U.S. approach to state sponsors of terrorism?

5.6.2 How Can the State Sponsor List Be Improved?

Because of the varied range of states included in the state sponsor list, some authors (Pillar 2003; Peed 2005; Sullivan 2005) have argued that more leeway needs to be built into the system to allow the United States more flexibility in dealing with the wide range of states engaged in behavior that uses terror as a covert strategy of foreign policy. This kind of flexibility could be built into the system at different points:

1. It is necessary to create a more accurate list. This will give more credibility to this tool and make its impact more effective. Accuracy, by following

more objective (less politically influenced) criteria, will "abate international cynicism over the list's political motives, ultimately strengthening the list as the legal and diplomatic tool it was designed to be" (Peed 2005, 1323).

2. To create a more accurate terrorism list, it will be necessary to make it easier to add and remove countries. This would also make it easier to bring about behavioral change (Sullivan 2005). The current difficulty both in adding and removing states from the list leads to the result that those not on the list can see value in utilizing terrorism, especially when they know that they fulfill a wider overall security need of the United States. By the same token, those already on the list, knowing that to be removed is near impossible, have no real incentive toward improving their status as state sponsor.

3. A tiered approach toward sanctions could more adequately reflect the actual level of state support for terrorism and could reward behavior that is moving towards the desired result. In line with the second point, a tiered approach would work for incentives as well as punishment. The automatic imposition of sanctions makes customization of policies toward a particular state more difficult (Pillar 2003). The graduated sanctions approach, on the other hand, could function as a warning to those not yet fully deemed a state sponsor but on their way. Likewise, those wanting to be removed from the list could show positive steps and be rewarded by a gradual loosening of the sanctions.

4. With changes to the State Department's list, it would also be easier to integrate the U.S. approach more closely to a global response. This would add credibility to the U.S. approach and also link the fight against state sponsorship into a global system of regulating the use of force.

It is this last point that we will now turn to as a way to conclude this chapter on state terrorism.

If states are sovereign actors in the world and have the capability to frame their security policies according to their perceived interests, why is it important to stress the global response angle? Why not go with the accepted maxim that despite the equalizing concept of sovereignty, strong states have the capability to frame their policies more forcefully than weak states? It doesn't need much explanation to say that strong states have a natural tendency to see their views, wishes, and interests prevail. Nonetheless, even states as powerful as the United States (with economic wealth, higher military spending than all other countries combined, highly advanced technology, and high levels of soft power) need to take account of the power of reputation and credibility as intangible but valuable assets for long-term U.S. security interests. The United States has a long history of exporting ideas of justice, equality, and freedom to the rest of the world, and through this has created lasting friendships and alliances. To jeopardize these for the sake of political wrangling over the state terrorism list would be counterproductive. It should be noted that the 2003 *National Strategy for Combating Terrorism* recognizes the need for international cooperation and states the following:

> *We will use UNSCR 1373 and the international counter-terrorism conventions and protocols to galvanize international cooperation and to rally support for holding accountable those states that do not meet their international responsibilities (19).*

For this to happen, it will be necessary to actually strengthen those institutions that could make cooperation easier. To this effect, Mahbubani (2003) argues:

> *The key challenge of the twenty-first century will be to manage this shrinking globe as the forces of globalization generate growing interdependence day after day after day. The need for multilateral institutions and processes will grow in tandem. But multilateralism will succeed only if the great powers, and especially the United States, support it (139).*

In other words, although there are many limitations to how the inter-state system regulates the use of force, and the secret nature of terrorism as an extension of a state's foreign policy poses specific problems to the international community of states, the global response is still better suited than a focus on unilateral interpretation of the threat as well as the solution to state sponsorship. The continuing difficulty, however, rests with the problem of convincing especially strong states to recognize the benefit of cooperation.

SELF-CHECK

1. Sanctions are entirely successful in effecting positive changes to a country's policies on terrorism. True or false?

2. One recommendation for improving the state-sponsor list is to go with a tiered approach, classifying states by level of support and then designing policies commensurate to the nature of the support. True or false?

3. What does Pillar say about why Pakistan isn't on the state-sponsor list?

4. Which one of the following is not one of the points through which the state sponsor list could be improved?
   a. Create a more accurate list
   b. Make inclusion on the list a permanent condition
   c. Make it easier to be added to or removed from the list
   d. Integrate the U.S. approach to state sponsorship with a global system of regulating use of force

SUMMARY

In this chapter, you assessed the relationship between the international system of states and the use of terror as a weapon; evaluated the different forms of state terrorism (internal and external); argued the differences between internal and external state terrorism; assessed the options open to the inter-state community to regulate the use of force; appraised the U.S. response to state sponsorship of international terrorism; and judged the various U.S. responses to state sponsored terrorism

Despite the fact that the definition of the state lends itself to the distinction between internally- and externally-directed state violence we concluded that more often than not internal and external terrorism are linked by the fact that some states lend assistance (financial, technical, military, etc.) to other states, which then use this support to terrorize their own populations. At the inter-state level, however, attention is focused less on how states treat their own populations and more on how states behave toward each other. Here we found that focusing on the concept of state terrorism as covert warfare or the extension of a state's foreign policy helps us better understand how the United States can respond to the threat of state-sponsored terrorism now and in the future.

KEY TERMS

Anarchy	Absence of a central government or overarching authority regulating the relations between states.
Civil war	War that occurs within a state.
Externally directed state terrorism	The abuse of state power against citizens/governments from other states in order to motivate the target state to make policy changes in line with the political objectives of the "aggressor" state.
Force multiplier	That which increases the appearance of strength.
Internally directed state terrorism	The use of force by the state apparatus against its own population.
Inter-state war	War between two or more states.
Non-intervention	The principle that no one outside of a state can interfere in the internal affairs of that state.
Political violence	The use of force in the pursuit of political objectives.
Rummel's power principle	"Power kills and absolute power kills absolutely"; in other words, the more power that is concentrated in a few hands, the more likely it is that this power will be abused.

Self-help	The idea that each state has to rely on its own strength and that it cannot wait for others to help it in a situation of crisis; assumed to be the key behavioral characteristic of sovereign states and explains how in international relations the use of force is sometimes considered acceptable (as in the case of self-defense).
Sovereignty	The idea that there is a final and absolute authority in the political community.
State	A distinct political community that spans a definable geographical territory, acknowledges one form of authority over that territory and population, and is recognized by other sovereign states.
State terrorism	When state's legitimate use of force/power is abused.
Terrorism	Use or threat of use of seemingly random violence against non-traditional targets in order to instill a climate of fear so that the fear will induce political acquiescence and/or a political change in favor of those instigating the violence.

ASSESS YOUR UNDERSTANDING

Go to www.wiley.com/college/kilroy to assess your knowledge of the state actors and terrorism.

Measure your learning by comparing pre-test and post-test results.

Summary Questions

1. There is one commonly held definition of terrorism in the international community today. True or false?

2. Inter-state war involves conflict between two or more states. True or false?

3. Terrorism can function as a force multiplier (giving the appearance of strength when there is none or only very little) because the civilian nature of targets carries more psychological weight. True or false?

4. Anarchy is the presence of a central government or overarching authority regulating the relations between states. True or false?

5. Sovereignty implies the principle of non-intervention, in which states are constrained in their reaction to events taking place within another sovereign state's borders. True or false?

6. Economic sanctions are usually successful in getting a state to moderate its policies on terrorism. True or false?

7. The majority of UN anti-terrorism conventions treat the problem as a crime rather than as a form of armed force. True or false?

8. North Korea's inclusion on the list of state sponsors of terrorism is primarily due to development of its nuclear program. True or false?

9. Which of the following is **not** an example of terrorist acts that would provoke a UN response?

    (a) Taking hostages

    (b) Posing threats to international maritime navigation

    (c) Harming diplomatic agents

    (d) Participating legitimately in the political process of a country

10. Which of the following is **not** on the current U.S. list of state sponsors of terrorism?

    (a) Cuba

    (b) Saudi Arabia

    (c) Syria

    (d) Iran

11. Which country recently renounced its support for terrorism and will likely be removed from the U.S. list of state sponsors of terrorism?

(a) Libya

(b) Sudan

(c) North Korea

(d) Pakistan

12. Which country has been on the State Department list of state sponsors of terrorism since 1982 and remains on the list primarily due to domestic U.S. politics?

(a) Syria

(b) Cuba

(c) Iran

(d) Libya

Applying This Chapter

1. If you were the Jordanian ambassador to Israel, how would you argue your nation's support for terrorist groups, such as Hamas or Islamic Jihad, against Israel?

2. During a visit to France on a student exchange program, you encounter European students who argue that the U.S. threat of war against Iran or North Korea (e.g., threatening to use nuclear weapons if necessary) constitutes a form of state terrorism. Do you agree or disagree? Why or why not?

3. A Palestinian student makes a case in class that one man's freedom fighter is another man's terrorist. Do you agree or disagree? Why or why not?

4. Israel has made official statements that it would never allow Iran to acquire nuclear weapons and would "do what was necessary" to protect itself, including acting preemptively against Iran. Do you think Israel is justified in taking unilateral action against Iran, a state it considers to be a sponsor of terrorism?

YOU TRY IT

Removing a State from the List

You work in the State Department and are charged with determining whether a country should be taken off the designated state sponsor list. Present the case for why one country (your choice) should be removed from the list. Develop a policy proposal outlining reasons for removal.

Adding a State to the List

In the same scenario, decide on one country that should be added to the state sponsor list. Develop a policy proposal outlining your reasons for the inclusion of this country on the list.

6

NON-STATE ACTORS AND TERRORISM

Understanding the Threat from Non-State Terrorist Actors

Starting Point

Go to www.wiley.com/college/kilroy to assess your knowledge of the basics of non-state actors and terrorism.
Determine where you need to concentrate your effort.

What You'll Learn in This Chapter

▲ The definition of non-state terrorism
▲ The history of terrorism and how it affects terrorist organizations' underlying rationale and continuing belief in the efficacy of violence
▲ The different types of terrorist organizations and examples of each type
▲ The methods employed by terrorist organizations
▲ What can be done to fight non-state terrorism

After Studying This Chapter, You'll Be Able To

▲ Assess the historical development of twentieth-century terrorism
▲ Evaluate the interrelated nature of all terrorism while taking note of the socio-historical specificity of each type of terrorism
▲ Critique different types of terrorist organizations and recognize the different aims and goals they seek to achieve
▲ Manage tools for combating international terrorism

INTRODUCTION

In the previous chapter, the role of states in the commission of terrorism was examined. We looked at how the inter-state system is organized and how states, by their capability to employ force, also have the capability to abuse their power. When they do so (either against their own populations or against the populations and/or governments of other states), it could be considered a form of terrorism.

In this chapter, we turn our focus to terrorism conducted by non-state actors. Thus, you will learn the definition of non-state terrorism and assess the historical development of this form of terrorism throughout the twentieth century. You'll evaluate the interrelated nature of all terrorism while taking note of the socio-historical specificity of each type of terrorist act or organization. Finally, you'll critique different types of terrorist organizations and recognize the different aims and goals they seek to achieve, as well as develop an understanding of the various tools used to combat international terrorism.

6.1 Non–State Terrorism and Its Impact on the Inter-State System

This chapter examines a different type of actor: the non-state actor. Quite simply, a non-state actor is an entity that operates below the level of the state. We apply the label "non-state actor" to varied entities, including (but not limited to) the following:

▲ Transnational corporations, or private corporations that operate in more than one state (e.g., IBM)
▲ Non-governmental organizations, such as the International Red Cross
▲ Terrorist organizations, including the Irish Republican Army (IRA), Sendero-Luminoso (Shining Path), and of course, al-Qaeda

Clearly, we are not assuming that these three categories of non-state actors are the same. Of course, they have entirely different sets of goals, methods, and impacts on the world. What they do have in common, however, is that they are all operating without the element of power associated with the state. Our focus will thus be on the **non-state terrorist actor**, a term that applies to a variety of groups with different aims and identities but that all share two elements: they don't have access to state power, and they believe that they can achieve their goals only through violence.

This chapter uses the working definition of terrorism set forth in Chapter 5, which is the use or threat of use of seemingly random violence against non-traditional targets to instill a climate of fear so that the fear will induce political acquiescence and/or a political change in favor of those instigating the violence. This definition speaks to the kind of political violence that is linked to terrorism and also emphasizes the importance of fear as a weapon to achieve change. However, because this chapter is specifically concerned with the threat of terrorism posed by non-state actors, it is important to include these actors in our definition. Those authors who specifically include non-state actors as part of their definition of terrorism (e.g., Badey 1998; Hoffman 1998) do so because they locate the threat posed by terrorism in the realm of the inter-state system. In international relations, legitimate use of force is reserved to states, and any use of force outside the state paradigm poses a particular threat not only to the targeted state(s), but also to the entire inter-state system. Terrorism is often thought of as a strategy of the weak, and in a system where legitimate power is

FOR EXAMPLE

Non-State Terrorism as a Threat to the Inter-State System

Despite the fact that the United Nations (UN) explicitly forbids the use or threat of force in inter-state relations, it nonetheless allows a state to use force when it has been attacked by another state. In other words, when one state is attacked by another state, that state has the capability to strike back to defend itself from outside aggression. To be able to defend itself, however, the state needs to know against whom it is retaliating. Thus, when a non-state entity attacks a state, the question of self-defense becomes extremely difficult, especially when it is unclear where the attacking group is located and whether or not it speaks to and for another state.

In the case of the attacks by al-Qaeda against the United States on 9/11, the United States was targeted by a non-state terrorist organization. If the organization does not speak for a particular state, then against whom does the United States defend itself? In the case of al-Qaeda, the United States was able to show the links between this non-state actor and a specific state, Afghanistan. The relationship between the Taliban regime in Afghanistan and al-Qaeda allowed the United States to focus its military actions on Afghanistan to deal with the threat posed by al-Qaeda.

How would the United States have dealt with al-Qaeda if it had not been able to link it to a specific state? You might say that if people who carry out the attacks come from a particular state, the United States could retaliate against that country. However, just because individuals in a particular country carry out attacks against another state does not mean that the entire state is responsible for those actions. In these instances, another state would be deemed the aggressor if that state were to attack the other state. You can see that the situation therefore becomes extremely difficult when a state opts to defend itself against non-state terrorist organizations.

by definition given to the state, any non-state group taking up terrorism invariably does so to challenge and change existing power structures either by taking over the locus of state power or by radically transforming it.

6.1.1 The Threat of Non-State Terrorism to a State

Another way of looking at the dangers posed by non-state actors when they employ terrorism is that they challenge the fabric of the entire state itself. Non-state terrorist organizations take up terrorism in order to achieve a particular political goal. In using force against the state and groups of the population that represent the state, they are actively challenging state power, and they do so in order to replace the state with a system that, according to their underlying motivations, reflects a "better" model of political organization. In fact, non-state terrorist organizations almost always start off as domestic terrorist movements that challenge their respective states to replace the state institutions with ones that reflect the terrorists' underlying motivations. In so doing, however, these movements often challenge the territorial integrity of the existing state by either subverting its capability to exercise control over its population and institutions or by leading to a break up of the state and the subsequent establishment of a separate state (secession). In either case, the state's capability to exercise sovereignty in its relations with other states can be severely compromised. In most cases, this can also draw other states into the conflict, so what started as a domestic affair can take on international dimensions. For these reasons, non-state terrorist entities are extremely dangerous to international security and therefore need special attention by those studying the phenomenon of terrorism.

A state's use of terrorism as a strategy (whether internally or externally directed) is shrouded behind a veil of secrecy. In fact, an important difference between state terrorism and non-state terrorism centers on two complementary notions:

1. The level of power available to achieve political goals (by definition, the state has power, whereas non-state actors do not)
2. Their status in the inter-state system and how it reflects the ways in which they go about the business of terrorism

States recognize the limitations placed on them by the inter-state system when it comes to abusing state power; therefore, they hide their use of terrorism. Non-state actors, on the other hand, do not feel part of the inter-state system and therefore use terrorism to force their way onto the international stage. In other words, whereas the state wants deniability and thus tries to hide its activities, the non-state organization relies on the terrorist acts to tell the world who the organization is and what it wants.

Hoffman (1998, 183–184) gives a very good overview of the different stages that terrorist organizations go through to propel themselves onto the international stage, where they feel they can get a level of power that will help them achieve their political objectives. His five stages of terrorism are as follows:

1. **Attention:** Violence is a tool that allows the terrorists to bring attention to their cause. The emphasis here is placed on shock value to project the terrorists into the media agenda so that their objectives can be aired.

2. **Acknowledgement:** After the terrorists have achieved attention, this next step tries to gain them some level of support. Here, it is not enough that people know about the terrorists' objectives; it is also necessary that they understand where the terrorists are coming from and that this understanding translates into a modicum of support for the cause. Violence at this stage has two purposes: to indicate that there is strength behind the action (remember, violence is a strength amplifier; it projects power where there is none or only little); and to show that the cause must be worthy, not only because people believe in it, but because they are willing to inflict violence for it.

3. **Recognition:** The goal of acknowledgement is to bring attention to a cause, but recognition implies that once a cause has been acknowledged, it is viewed as a right and/or just cause deserving of international recognition. This stage also implies that those who have put the cause to the attention of the state or the international community are the legitimate representatives of the cause.

4. **Authority:** With attention, acknowledgement, and recognition, terrorists have achieved part of their political objective, but this is not enough to be truly able to institute their desired political outcomes. For this, they must be recognized as the legitimate authority. Thus, the fourth stage requires that the terrorists are able to translate their goals into direct outcomes, such as "changes in government and/or society that lie at the heart of their movement's struggle. This may involve a change in government or in the entire state structure, or the redistribution of wealth, re-adjustment of geographical boundaries, assertion of minority rights, etc." (Hoffman, 1998, 184).

5. **Governance:** The final stage of the process is completed when the terrorist organization has been able to institute its policies (authority) and thus is able to exercise "complete control over the state, their homeland, and/or their people" (Hoffman, 1998, 184).

We can gain a better understanding of these stages by looking at the development of terrorist movements over time. This will allow us to see how ideas have shaped terrorists' underlying rationale for taking up violence (because history shows that it works) while also explaining that in response to different socio-historic environments, terrorist organizations undergo change to increase their chances of achieving their political objectives. In other words, the following section looks at the recent history of some terrorist movements to show how terrorism is a "learning" process while also emphasizing the inherent adaptability of terrorist organizations to their specific environments.

6.1.2 History of Ideas Underpinning Terrorist Movements

The nineteenth century saw the emergence of a number of anarchist and socialist movements across the world that attempted to change societies toward what they saw as more equitable forms of democracy (ones that included the democratic distribution of wealth). These movements were frustrated with the slow development of political change and resorted to the use of violence to bring about the overthrow of oppressive forms of government. Based on a variety of interpretations of the writings of Karl Marx, as well as those of violent anarchists such as Mikhail Bakunin, Sergey Nechaev, and Peter Kropotkin, social theories developed that premised themselves on the need for drastic social and political change to bring about a new political order. In this environment, two distinct groups emerged:

▲ **Anarchists** believed that governments act against the interests and rights of people to behave as they want, and they thus attempted to rid politics of the corrupting influence of all forms of government.

▲ **Socialists,** on the other hand, wanted to control the machinations of the state so as to allow the state to redistribute wealth and ensure the rights of people.

These two ideas spread across Europe and resulted in many capitals being engulfed by revolutionary violence alongside calls for direct democracy. However, the established governments and their armies soon managed to repress these revolutionary tendencies. In an ironic twist, the repression of anarchist and socialist ideas by established governments had the effect of confirming the anarchist and socialist notion that government is a tool to oppress the people. As a direct response, more violence against institutions of the state ensued. Jensen (2004, 128) describes this relationship between anarchist violence and the government response in the following words:

> Police brutality ignited chain reactions of violence in which the anarchists met acts of police brutality with bloody responses. Massive government crackdowns followed, but only provoked even more spectacular assassinations and terrorist bombings.

Although terrorists operating in nineteenth-century Russia, Europe, or even the United States weren't identical, they did have one thing in common: a lack of legitimate access to force. Because they were non-state actors, they didn't have access to state power, so they had to fight the state by unconventional means. The violence associated with anarchism and socialist movements was thus also associated with covert violence and assassinations, as described by White (2003, 68):

> Though they [revolutionaries of the mid-nineteenth century] could not successfully confront armies and police forces in Paris, Vienna, or Berlin, they could plant bombs and set factories aflame. A campaign of subversive revolutionary violence followed. The term terrorism was increasingly used to describe this violence.

At the same time that ideas about anarchism and socialism influenced various movements across the world, so did ideas about nationalism. **Nationalism** refers to the belief that political communities share common characteristics such as language, religion, or ethnicity, and that the state only gains legitimacy by representing these shared characteristics (Abercrombie, Hill, and Turner 1988). This infers that self-government by the members of the national group allows the fullest expression of political community. Especially in places of foreign occupation and imperialism, nationalism proved a powerful tool to challenge foreign influence and to strengthen calls for national self-determination. Despite popular notions to the contrary, anarchists' violence consisted of isolated incidents and was mainly carried out by individuals who felt that they could instigate a wider revolution through sporadic but dramatic acts of violence. On the other hand, acts carried out under a nationalist banner had the effect that they could mobilize entire groups of people, so forms of terrorism soon took on a wider following.

At the end of the nineteenth century, a growing number of ideas combined notions of individual liberties with principles of social justice and a need for political change. Although the individuals and organizations that espoused these ideas had different views on the desired outcome, over time, those ideas that rested on the assumption that violence would speed up the desired goal certainly gained the upper hand. The sporadic successes of anarchist violence (e.g., the assassinations of President William McKinley in the United States and Czar Alexander II in Russia) further fuelled the belief that violence (whether organized or not) could yield results. After a belief in the efficacy of violence was combined with ideas of national self-determination, terrorist violence increased exponentially.

This combination of anarchist violence, ideas about social justice, and mobilization under the banner of national self-determination can be seen very strongly in the example of the early twentieth-century Irish revolt against British rule and the development of one of the world's oldest terrorist organizations, the Irish Republican Army (IRA). We clearly cannot give a comprehensive account of the history of conflict in Northern Ireland, but we can stress that the development of the IRA represents a growing convergence between ideas of anarchist/terrorist violence and the pursuit of nationalist goals. The notion of using anarchist violence in pursuit of a nationalist goal had worked to create the republic of Ireland. The successful use of terrorism by the Irish meant that nineteenth-century ideas about violence continued to affect people in the twentieth century and, more importantly, also influenced subsequent nationalist movements to try the same tactics. The successful application of terrorist violence in pursuit of nationalist goals by the Irish was widely regarded as a success for terrorism as a strategy for national self-determination. The IRA's accomplishment in achieving statehood reinforced the belief in the efficacy of extra-normal violence (in the sense of being directed against an established state) against foreign rule, particularly when carried out under the banner of nationalist aspirations.

We can see from the development of terrorism how ideas take hold and influence different people over different time periods and in different regions. For example, just as the Irish nationalists had resorted to the propaganda of violence espoused by the nineteenth-century anarchists (especially those in Russia), their own success influenced the decision of Jewish terrorist organizations operating in Palestine in the 1930s and 1940s to employ terrorism against outside (specifically British) interference and in support of national independence. The success of Jewish terrorist operations against the militarily much stronger British forces resulted in the creation of the Israeli state in 1948 and in turn influenced subsequent terrorist operations. These groups were now further strengthened in their belief that terrorism as a strategy worked and, moreover, that terrorism under a nationalist mantle would unite the population and lead to the creation of independent homelands. The rise of nationalism, as well as the use of terrorism as part of a revolutionary struggle for national independence, spread to many colonized countries.

In the case of Israel's fight for independence in 1948, the Irgun's achievements influenced other anti-colonial struggles, and the process of decolonization saw the use of terrorism under the banner of national self-determination as a specific strategy to remove a foreign occupying force. Hoffman (1998) describes that "successful" applications of terrorism could be seen in both the Algerian anti-colonial struggle against France (1954–1962) and in Cyprus' struggle against British colonial rule (1955–1959). Both resulted in success for those employing terrorism against a militarily stronger opponent. In these cases, terrorism was but one approach among a range of strategies (ranging from individual instances of terrorist violence to outright guerilla tactics and revolutionary war), but the overall successful outcome of the Algerian and Cypriot struggles nonetheless symbolized success for terrorism and, as such, explains why so many subsequent ethno-nationalist movements also "reserved the right" to resort to terrorism.

Indeed, these successes shouldn't just be seen in terms of individual nationalist struggles, but should also be viewed in the wider context of terrorism itself. Hoffman (1998) thus states that for terrorism, the "tactical successes and political victories won through violence by groups like the Irgun, EOKA, and the FLN clearly demonstrated that despite the repeated denials of the governments they confronted, terrorism does 'work'"(65).

6.1.3 The Internationalization of Terrorism

Because of the successes of a number of anti-colonial, nationalist struggles, the use of this form of political violence became even more widespread for a number of ethno-nationalist/separatist groups. As decolonization proceeded, however, other groups (notably those with less of an emphasis on ethno-nationalist aspirations) also saw terrorism as a way to further their particular political aspirations. The 1960s through the 1980s saw a surge in terrorist violence expressed by **ideological terrorist groups**, particularly in Western Europe. These groups wanted to challenge the fabric of the existing liberal democratic state either from a left-wing or a right-wing political framework. This "explosion" of terrorism was influenced by the earlier successes of ethno-nationalist struggles, which had reaffirmed the notion that political objectives could be achieved through violence.

At first, a great deal of this ideological terrorism was **domestic terrorism**, meaning that the groups directed their violence against the specific states in which they resided. However, this did not yield the expected results. One reason for this outcome (or lack thereof) was that many ideological terrorist groups were too small to effect change. As a result, they increasingly built and relied on ties to other terrorist organizations across state borders to more effectively learn from each other and to combine resources, which increased the possibility of attaining attention and recognition. To put it another way, when these terrorist organizations realized that the domestic realm of their political goals was no longer enough to guarantee the success of their strategy, terrorism became internationalized. **International terrorism** is terrorism that relies on an increasing link between groups from different states as well as an increasing internationalization of the targets (in other words, people are targeted even though they are not from the immediate target state) to speak to a wider audience. The main motivation behind this export of primarily domestic political goals to the international scene was to increase the effectiveness of terrorism as a political strategy and to increase the likelihood of gaining international attention (Hoffman 1998).

The terrorist organization most often cited as having internationalized terrorism is the Palestinian Liberation Organization (PLO). With the creation of the Israeli state in 1948, the Palestinians had been widely displaced, and those that had been incorporated into the Israeli state were often living under conditions of second-rate citizenship. Many Palestinians had not accepted the creation of the Israeli state because they felt that the territory upon which they resided was "rightfully" theirs (see United Nations n.d. for the history of this long-standing and entrenched conflict; see also Rotberg 2006 for how history is perceived differently by the different sides in the conflict). Thus, violence was an oft-used tool to oppose the new situation, and the PLO emerged as a strong force against the Israeli state. Acting as the representative of the Palestinian cause, the PLO had long attempted to use terrorism as a strategy to "undo" the creation of the Israeli state and to allow the Palestinians a rightful state of their own. However, despite decades of terrorist attacks against Israel, as well as attempts by Arab states to wage war against that country (unsuccessful on four separate occasions), the Palestinians were for several decades unable to bring their situation to the attention of the international community, at least not to the point that their efforts were being addressed. (At this point, we need to remember Hoffman's five stages of the terrorism strategy. If the first stage, attention, is not achieved, it is extremely unlikely that the entire strategy will ever pay off.)

This situation changed in 1972. On September 5 of that year, a Palestinian terrorist group (the Black September organization) operating under the umbrella of the PLO took nine Israeli athletes hostage at the Munich Olympic Games after having killed two at the start of their operations. The events that unfolded shocked the world, not just because the spirit of the Olympics had been perverted, but also because through modern communications tools, people across the world were able to follow the events on their television screens and were thus intimately involved in the tragedy. A failed rescue attempt by the German police led to the violent deaths of all nine hostages as well as one German police officer and all but three of the hostage takers.

6.1.4 The Meaning Behind the Internationalization of Terrorism

How was the Munich event different from previous acts of terrorism? Clearly, the attackers targeted symbolic victims that would represent a weak spot for the wider target audience. Because they were not strong enough to take on the Israeli state apparatus, the terrorists concentrated on soft targets in order to instill fear in the wider target audience. So far, then, this attack follows the overall logic of terrorism and doesn't represent a clear break. However, the fact that the Israeli targets were attacked at an international event in Germany in front of a global audience, combined with the fact that the hostage takers demanded the release not just of Palestinians in Israeli prisons but also of members of a German terrorist organization (the Red Army Faction) in German prisons, symbolized a qualitative break with the terrorist incidents of the past. Terrorist organizations were now reaching out to other terrorist organizations in order to combine their resources to strike terror and to increase their ability to reach an audience that might have the capacity to grant them attention and recognition. Because the Munich hostage takers had a global audience, they generated much debate about why this had happened and thus also created much disagreement about whether there was a legitimate cause for which Palestinians in general were fighting. As Hoffman (1998, 75) states:

> [E]ighteen months after Munich, the PLO's leader, Yassir Arafat, was invited to address the UN General Assembly and shortly afterwards the PLO was granted special observer status in that international body. Indeed, by the end of the 1970s, the PLO, a non-state actor, had formal diplomatic relations with more countries (eighty-six) than the actual established nation-state of Israel (seventy-two). It is doubtful whether the PLO could ever have achieved this success had it not resorted to international terrorism.

In other words, by internationalizing their terrorist strategy, the PLO had managed to get global attention, receive acknowledgement of the plight of Palestinians, and be recognized the legitimate representative of the Palestinian cause. In one "failed" terrorist attempt (most of the terrorists died and did not have their immediate objectives realized), the Palestinian terrorist organization had reached three of Hoffman's five stages of terrorism. The message to other terrorist organizations was clear: If you want to bring your cause to the attention of the international community, it is not enough that you target your own state; you must draw in the wider international community by using dramatic acts of violence against unsuspecting targets. As we might imagine, the use of international terrorist attacks has been the favorite tool of terrorist organizations since then.

What can we learn from this rather simplified historical overview? To understand non-state terrorism, we must understand the history of how violence for political ends has been used in the past by those without the elements of power associated with the state. We must also recognize that there is a historical learning process through which terrorist organizations adapt to changing environments. Indeed, although it is clear that terrorists learn from each other, it is just as important to recognize that terrorists learn from history. As White (2006) says, understanding the historical context is important because terrorists are themselves products of the past and they "study the past to learn their trade" (27). Moreover, because of past successes (no matter how limited), newer terrorist organizations are strengthened in their beliefs that violence works and that all they need to do is find novel ways to get the world's attention. We will keep this brief historical overview in mind as we move into a discussion of the different types of terrorist organizations.

SELF-CHECK

1. Which of the following is not a non-state actor?

   a. International Red Cross
   b. IBM
   c. Sendero Luminoso
   d. USAID

2. "Non-state terrorist actor" is a term that applies to a variety of groups with different aims and identities but that all share two elements: they don't have access to state power, and they believe that they can achieve their goals only through violence. True or false?

3. Nationalism refers to the belief that political communities share common characteristics such as language, religion, or ethnicity and that the state only gains legitimacy by representing these shared characteristics. True or false?

4. The terrorist organization most often cited as having internationalized terrorism is the Palestinian Liberation Organization (PLO). True or false?

6.2 Different Types of Terrorist Organizations

The Memorial Institute for the Prevention of Terrorism (MIPT) database lists more than 850 terrorist organizations for the time period from 1968 until present time. Of course, we should note that many of those organizations are no longer in existence. Some have been destroyed by successful counter-terrorism operations, and many have just collapsed under their own weight or the fact that they could not achieve the goals they had set for themselves. But even if we limit the time period to the year 2005, we are still confronted with the fact that over 150 terrorist organizations were active during those 12 months. Confronted with this many organizations, we need to ask ourselves, how can we make comparisons or talk comprehensively about organizations as varied as the Tamil Tigers in Sri Lanka, Hezbollah in Lebanon, and al-Qaeda? How do we make sense not just of these three examples, but also of the many different organizations in their entirety as non-state threats to state security?

Some authors differentiate between different tactics or targets to assess terrorist organizations. However, because there is not much tactical variation between terrorist organizations (Jenkins 1982, 1987), and because the targets can vary according to their symbolic value (and this depends on the motivation behind the terrorist organizations), Cunningham (2003) states that it might be more useful to concentrate on motivation to differentiate between different organizations. We will follow this form of typology to understand how and why non-state terrorism manifests itself around the world and what the international community and individual states might be able to do about it. Because we cannot give a detailed account of every single terrorist organization that exists today, we will only use a select number of "case studies" to further illustrate a particular point made about specific types of organizations. (Again, for information on more terrorist organizations, see the MIPT database.)

Cunningham's differentiation rests on three types of primary motivation underlying all terrorist organizations: political ideology, ethno-nationalism, or religious extremism (2003). Before we start looking at these different types of motivations, however, we should emphasize that "any classification of terrorist groups is bound to simplify a complex reality" (Laquer 1987, 205). Indeed, Cunningham, too, explains the following:

> This is not to say that all groups are singular in focus. Some groups may have competing motivations, while individual members may have their own reasons for joining terrorist groups. What concerns us here is finding the primary reason for why a group as a whole chooses to conduct terrorist operations. Underlying the primary reasons are complex interactions of psychological, environmental, political, cultural and socio-economic variables (Cunningham, 2003, 27).

In the following subsections, we will go through each type of terrorism to see what its goals and motives are, and we'll also look at some examples of groups in each category. This will allow us to examine the question of why different groups employ terrorism and how they might be stopped. We will then look at the methods terrorist organizations employ (in other words, the "how" of terrorism) before going into what can be done about these methods.

6.2.1 Ethno-Nationalist/Separatist Terrorism

Even though terrorism can be traced back to the beginnings of recorded history (Kegley, Sturgeon, and Wittkopf 1988, 24), and even though the roots for much ethno-nationalist/separatist terrorism come from the power struggles left after the collapse of the Ottoman and Hapsburg Empires before World War I, "it was only after 1945 that this phenomenon became a more pervasive global force" (Hoffman 1998, 45). **Ethno-nationalist/separatist terrorism** refers to the use of terrorism by a sub-state, ethnic, or national group to change its access to state power. Here, ethnicity is used to "forge a national identity" (White 2006, 179). This can mean that a group sees itself as in the minority in a state where governmental power is controlled by members of a different ethnic group and where, because of this, the group is, or perceives itself to be, in a politically inferior position. To change its actual or perceived politically marginalized position, the group resorts to the use of violence to either take over the state apparatus or to gain rights of secession and form its own independent state. There are many examples of groups through-out the twentieth century that fall under this category, such as the previously discussed Irish Republican Army (IRA), the Tamil Tigers of Sri Lanka (LTTE), the Basque Nation and Liberty (ETA), and also Hamas in the Palestinian territories.

While operating from a position of relative weakness vis-à-vis the state, ethno-nationalist groups have a built-in benefit over terrorist groups with other underlying motivations by having wider "populist appeal within their ethnic populations" (Cunningham 2003, 31). This means that these types of terrorist organizations have a relatively guaranteed support base because they can appeal to shared his-tory, common culture, and ethnic heritage. When the terrorist organization can demonstrate to the wider ethnic/nationalist group that they are being marginalized or oppressed by another group, by the state, or by an outside force, they will find it easier to mobilize their constituents into continuing their support for drastic and violent measures to change this situation. This could certainly be seen in the nationalist struggles against colonialism. The decolonization that swept the globe following World War II was influenced by the nationalist aspirations of different groups, and, to expel foreign occupiers, many groups sought to achieve victory against an often-overwhelming military force by resorting to terrorism. As we saw earlier in the chapter, the Irgun were a very good example of this.

More recent variants of the ethno-nationalist/separatist terrorism variety are found in the actions of the Tamil Tigers in Sri Lanka, the Kurdish PKK in Turkey, and the Chechen rebels in Russia to name just a few. What these groups have in common is a historical connection between their group members that is intensified over time through the continuation of the "armed struggle" against their oppressors. Ethnicity serves as a mobilizing device around which a group can become more cohesive and can more easily combine its resources to fight a common "enemy."

The Effectiveness of Ethno-Nationalist Terrorism

Ethno-nationalist/separatist terrorism has been described as the most long-lasting of all types of terrorism (Wilkinson 1986; Hoffman 1998). Although not all ethno-nationalist terrorist organizations are successful, they can certainly keep their struggle alive by the sheer fact that they have an automatic audience, a ready-made popula-tion within which to hide from the authorities, and a large support base from which to draw more recruits for their attacks. Moreover, the relatively high success rate of this type of terrorism is another element that distinguishes it from other types (espe-cially ideological terrorism). The mobilization of an ethnic identity around the con-cept of statehood allows this type of terrorist organization to exercise a much greater level of control over what type of resolution is acceptable. The reasons for this have been ascribed to the notion that there is a supposedly natural link between a national grouping and statehood and that in cases where the state wants to avoid and/or cease violence, existing states might have to concede power and at times territory to other groups in order to allow them to fully participate in the inter-state system.

Terrorism as a strategy to pursue ethno-nationalist goals has a long history and many examples; however, not all terrorist organizations appeal to a wider ethnic community for their support. Others appeal to shared ideologies in order to measure their strength and to use that support as justification for the use of violence against the existing state. It is these groups that we will turn to next.

6.2.2 Ideological Terrorism

Ideological terrorism refers to those organizations that are "driven by ideology" (Cunningham 2003, 30). **Ideology** is most commonly understood as a "tightly knit body of beliefs organized around a few central values" (Abercrombie, Hill, and Turner 1988, 118); examples include communism, fascism, and variations of nationalism. From this perspective, we can subdivide "ideological terrorism" into left-wing and right-wing terror groups, depending on whether these groups identify with communist or fascist ideological concepts (Hoffman 1998). Many of the right-wing and left-wing terrorist organizations have as their basic motivation the strong belief that their ideological outlook is the correct and thus only way for tackling what they perceive as the problems confronting their group and the wider society within which their group operates. The explicit exclusion of liberalism from the definition of ideology already indicates that groups defined by their ideology see as their main target system that of the liberal democratic state. They are motivated by the conviction that "the social structures imposed by a modern industrial society" need to be replaced (White 2003, 172). What the structures should be replaced with depends on the ideological direction espoused by the terrorist organization. For left-wing terrorists, Marxist/Leninist inspired revolutionary change of the capitalist state is the answer, whereas for right-wing terrorists, the goal is the "destruction of the liberal-democratic state to clear the way for a renascent National Socialist ('Nazi') or fascist one" (Hoffman 1998, 165).

The preoccupation with this type of terrorism stems primarily from the experiences of left-wing terrorists in Western Europe in the 1960s and 1970s and right-wing terrorists in the 1980s and 1990s. This is not to say that this type of terrorism was (or is) not found in other regions of the world (one need only look at the occurrence of terrorism in Latin America to know that this is not true); it is the fact that these types of terrorism occurred overwhelmingly in ostensibly stable liberal democratic states that lies at the base of scholarly interest in ideological terrorism. The nature of liberal democratic states is that they are founded on the notion of representation and an acceptance of pluralistic viewpoints. In other words, it is assumed that under liberal democracies, people have the ability to express their opinions and have those opinions reflected through the accepted political process rather than through resorting to violence. What concerned scholars during the 1960s and 1970s was the question of why European countries in particular experienced a wave of left-wing terrorism when their liberal democratic nature should have allowed expression of different opinions without violence.

Wilkinson (1986) explains that the ideological nature of many terrorist organizations was such that they knew that their opinion was held by only a minority within the overall population and therefore could never reflect the majority's will. In a political system where power is allocated according to majority representation, they could never see their aims and goals translated into any concrete level of political power. It is for this reason that we need to understand why ideological terrorists find themselves adopting terrorism to force their opinion on others. In Wilkinson's words:

> Whatever their ideological colouring, terrorists in democratic societies are desperate people bitterly opposed to the prevailing regime, alienated from all liberal democratic values. Yet, by definition, liberal societies contain overwhelming majorities in favour of liberal institutions and values. Knowing as he does that the liberal democratic government enjoys such universal support and legitimacy, the fanatical dissident may give up all hope of gaining influence of political power by peaceful and legitimate means such as electoral struggle—if ever, indeed, he had such hopes—and may consider instead various violent alternative roads to power, including political terrorism. Hence the paradox that a growing popular consensus on the legitimacy of liberal democratic government renders a desperate internal challenge by minorities most fanatically opposed to it more probable (1986, 94).

Whereas ethno-nationalist/separatist terrorist movements can claim some wider popular support based on ethnicity and the struggle for full representation, the ideological terrorist is described to be driven by the sheer knowledge that he or she is in the minority and can never hope to achieve political power through non-violent means. Indeed, as Cunningham states:

> The common thread of ideologically motivated terrorist groups is that they all espouse extremist views that fail to motivate large audiences of followers. They remain isolated from the political mainstream (2003, 31).

The claim to holding absolute truth, however, leads the ideological terrorist group to pursue its political agenda through violent means. The historical context of ideological terrorism can be found in theories of revolution, and strong ties exist to models of guerilla warfare (White 2006, 208). The experiences and writings influencing and coming from the decolonization movements also show much reference for the need to use violence to overthrow repressive structures, be these elite governmental institutions or remnants of former colonial masters. Despite the similarities between many ideological terrorists and guerilla warfare, however, it is important to note that unlike guerilla fighters, who are after territory and in most cases exhibit elements of resembling armed forces, ideological terrorists make no

FOR EXAMPLE

The Ideological Terrorism of the Red Army Faction

The ideological terrorist organization known as the Red Army Faction (RAF) or Baader-Meinhoff Gang operated in Western Germany primarily during the 1970s and early 1980s, but it didn't officially disband until after the end of the Cold War. It was an organization that had emerged from the student revolts of the late 1960s that shook much of Western Europe. This "counter-culture" reflected an increasing concern by Europe's youth about the growing disparities between the developed and the less developed world, as well as increasing concern with rising militarism and visions of Western imperialism (evidenced most strongly by first French and then American actions in Indochina/Vietnam). In response to these concerns, the RAF took it upon itself to help bring about the violent overthrow of the capitalist system that it perceived to be at the root of global inequality. Because the group did not have the wider support of German society (something it attributed to the numbing effects of capitalism on the national psyche), members were convinced that only through violence could they show the inner oppressive workings of the supposed liberal state and awaken the German population to rise to revolution.

Composed of a hard-core center of 10 to 20 operatives, with maybe several hundred more as their wider support base, this left-wing terrorist organization attacked military installations, diplomats, and industrialists in order to gain attention and ultimately destroy the foundation of the liberal state. The group hoped to force the state's hand into adopting ever-more repressive tactics, and in so doing, they felt the state would show its true colors to the overall population. This, so it was assumed by the terrorist group, would then lead to a violent revolution. The first generation of this organization, however, was ultimately captured by German security forces and imprisoned, where in 1977 they committed suicide. Subsequent generations continued in their struggle but were just as ineffective in reaching a larger support base. Instead of bringing about revolutionary change, they were actually "responsible for the massive internal security apparatus that dominates Germany today, and they managed to keep the extreme left from being effective on the political spectrum" (White 2003, 178).

In 1992, after the Cold War ended and the support it received from communist states dried up, the RAF issued a peace proclamation indicating that the end of this organization was near. Although some sporadic incidents occurred following the peace proclamation, it was clear that the Red Army Faction had not been able to influence the German population or even come close to having its views affect political change. In 1998, the RAF "issued a communiqué stating that it was ceasing operations" (White 2003, 178).

such pretensions (Hoffman 1998; White 2006). Their idea is based on belief in the cleansing power of violence as well as of terrorism as a unique strategy that can benefit those in positions of weakness. From this perspective, any violence can be beneficial because it "contribute[s] to a general feeling of panic and frustration among the ruling classes and their protectors" (White 2006, 213).

The Effectiveness of Ideological Terrorism

It is often said that "[u]nlike ideological terrorists, ethnic terrorist organizations tend to be long-lasting" (White 2006, 180). The "proof" of the short-lived nature of ideological terrorists is seen in the demise of the classic left-wing terror organizations of the 1960s and 1970s in Western Europe (and to a lesser degree, in the United States). The sheer fact that they were either captured and/or destroyed by the state (e.g., the Italian Red Brigade and the Weathermen in the United States in the early 1980s) or that they out of their own accord dismantled their organization (as with the remnants of the German Red Army Faction following the end of the Cold War) seems to indicate that this type of ideological terrorism has no staying power. Indeed, although liberal democracies are portrayed as being most vulnerable to ideological terrorism (Wilkinson 1986), liberal democracies also provide the greatest defenses against this type of terrorism, in as much as they provide pluralistic outlets that inhibit the majority of a population from being enticed into joining ideological terror organizations or even from being convinced by their ideas. As for right-wing terrorist organizations, many have tried to emulate the successful type of organization found among many of their left-wing counterparts (Hoffman 1998), and although an upsurge in right-wing violence marked much of the 1990s in European liberal democracies and the United States, the fact that no coherent platform could or would prevail seems to further strengthen the notion that ideological terrorism is not a successful strategy. Whereas ethnic loyalties can override allegiance to the existing state because groups can play on ethnic histories, ties, and ethnic responsibilities, ideologies seem to be too restrictive to "convince" large numbers of people over a long period of time that violence under an ideological banner is acceptable and sustainable.

Other regions around the world have seen (and some still are seeing) long-lasting ideological terror campaigns. Indeed, in some states it is even possible to have several terrorist organizations from both sides of the ideological spectrum operate at the same time, leading to long-lasting and seemingly intractable conflicts that cannot easily be confronted by specific counter-terrorism measures alone.

An example of ideological terrorism that does not neatly fit into the previous description can be found in the various terrorist organizations that exist in Colombia. In response to vast social inequalities that existed between urban and rural communities and the perceived role of the Colombian government in this situation (especially due to the effects of governmental policies on rural, agrarian, and urban working class populations), the Colombian National Liberation Army

(Ejercito de Liberacion Nacional, or ELN) formed to bring socialism to Colombia. This group was strengthened in its left-wing ideology by the success of the Cuban revolution in 1959, and its purported goal was to wrestle power from the government and replace it with a form of popular democracy, one that could lead to egalitarian distribution of wealth across the regions and across classes.

As a left-wing ideological terrorist organization, the ELN was not alone in its struggle against the Colombian state as well as against foreign influence, especially foreign capital over strategic resources. It was soon joined in its struggle by the Revolutionary Armed Forces of Colombia (Fuerzas Armadas Revolucionarias de Colombia, or FARC), a terrorist organization that grew out of Colombia's Communist party. However, the fact that Colombia saw the emergence of two left-wing terrorist organizations does not imply that these two actively joined forces. Instead, their different versions of what the future Colombian state should look like as well as their different (even though at times overlapping) support bases meant that they would often not just fight the government, but also each other. Moreover, in their attempts at gaining influence, they established vast expertise in kidnappings, extortions, and hijackings, and also extensively relied on proceeds from the drug trade in their respective territories in order to finance their operations. Although the ELN primarily relies on ransoms from extortion (especially of foreign oil company employees), the FARC has concentrated more directly on controlling the drug trade.

What we can see in Colombia is a deadly combination of what Hoffman (1998) has described as the cycle of violence, where the instrumental use of violence for political ends turns into an end in itself. In other words, although the use of violence might have originated with specific political objectives, it has over time become what is often referred to as **narcoterrorism**, violence often used merely to guarantee continued profit from the drug trade, as well as to hold on to territory to ensure the continuation of drug production. Left-wing violence in Colombia is expressed in Marxist inspired rhetoric, but it primarily serves the interests of the drug industry. However, violence is also carried out in opposition to rightist paramilitary groups. Counter-terrorist measures used by the Colombian state have resulted in the formation of a separate terrorist organization, the United Self-Defense Forces of Colombia (Autodefensas Unidas de Colombia, or AUC).

The formation of the AUC, an umbrella organization of various nationalist paramilitary groups was encouraged by the Colombian government to protect the government and the economic interests of wealthy citizens. Because the FARC in particular had secured sizeable territorial control over areas of Colombia, the struggle of the paramilitary groups was aimed at turning the population against the influence of FARC and the ELN. However, the Colombian government had to officially withdraw its support from the AUC, especially when the group's terrorist methods came to light. Moreover, the AUC's own reliance on drug cartels and other criminal activities to finance its operations made it increasingly difficult for the Colombian government to maintain its links (especially when, as part of internationally sponsored peace talks, the United States took a more active role in combating the international drug trade and thus demanded the Colombian government go after FARC and AUC members with ties to organized crime). Despite many efforts at a peace process, Colombian society is still divided on ideological grounds, and it continues to suffer from terrorist incidents even though these are often carried out in furtherance of a purely economic interest (that of the drug trade) rather than a political concern.

What can we learn from the Colombian example? Hoffman (1998) states that the increasing links between terrorism and criminal activity (especially of the transnational kind) have made it even harder to find ways to combat terrorism. It might be true that the purely ideological terrorism that occurs in established liberal democracies has no staying power (as was seen in the case of Italian and German left-wing terrorist organizations), yet the continued relevance of ideological world views when coupled with purely criminal organizations (those motivated solely by economic interests) can lead to an even more intractable conflict situation that makes the state more vulnerable and that makes resolution increasingly unlikely.

6.2.3 Religious Terrorism

At a conference on future terrorism in early 2001, Brian Jenkins, a leading writer on the topic of terrorism, made the following observation:

> The motives driving terrorism have changed from ideology to ethnic conflict and religious fanaticism. This has produced a new breed of terrorists, people less constrained by the fear of alienating perceived constituents or angering the public. Some of the notions that I once offered about self-imposed constraints on terrorist behavior appear to be eroding as terrorists move away from political agendas and into realms where they are convinced that they have the mandate of God. Large-scale, indiscriminate violence is the reality of today's terrorism (Jenkins, 2001, 324).

Religious terrorism is terrorism with the primary motivation of furthering a particular religious set of ideas. Or, as Juergensmeyer states, religious terrorism refers to "public acts of violence for which religion has provided the motivation, the justification, the organization, and the world view" (2003, 7). Some people have argued that religion provides a similar framework for terrorists as that found under the heading of ideology, but most terrorism experts emphasize that religion can add a specific element to terrorism that makes it even more difficult to deal with than political ideology alone. Indeed, Hoffman explains that:

> Terrorism motivated either in whole or in part by a religious imperative, where violence is regarded by its practitioners as a divine duty or sacramental act, embraces markedly different means of legitimization

and justification than that committed by secular terrorists; and these distinguishing features lead, in turn, to yet greater bloodshed and destruction (Hoffman 1998, 88).

Juergensmeyer (2001) elaborates on this by showing how violence can take on an otherworldly function in as much as it takes on the appearance not only of furthering a particular political goal for the greater good of humanity (as ideologues might assume), but also of furthering the objectives of a divine entity.

By identifying a temporal social struggle with the cosmic struggle of order and disorder, truth and evil, political actors are able to avail themselves of a way of thinking that justifies the use of violent means" (183).

Thus, the main difference between secular and religious terror organizations comes from their approach to their constituency and to violence. All types of terrorism believe in the efficacy of violence (Hoffman 1998), and all types also have a relationship with the community they and their actions seek to represent. But, whereas for the secular terrorist organization (whether ethno-nationalist or ideological) this communal bond held elements of constraints on the amount of violence inflicted, the fact that for the religious terrorist organization the "community" has moved from an earthly constituency to a divine, or otherworldly, community has also meant that constraints against levels of violence are now removed. Thus, according to Hoffman, terrorists of the past (with their emphasis on goals rooted in the political aspects of this world) would select symbolic targets and would engage in "highly selective and mostly discriminate acts of violence" (1998, 197). In contrast, religious terrorism "has often led to more intense acts of violence that have produced considerably higher levels of fatalities than the relatively more discriminating and less lethal incidents of violence perpetrated by secular terrorist organizations" (Hoffman 1998, 93).

What is it about religion that allows the terrorists who operate under its cloak to inflict greater numbers of casualties? Hoffman provides an answer by pointing to "the radically different value systems, mechanisms of legitimization and justification, concepts of morality, and world-view embraced by the religious terrorist compared with his secular counterpart" (1998, 94). By being carried out in the name of a higher transcendental dimension, violence moves from the instrumental realm of operating for a communal purpose (freedom from ethnic/ideological oppression) to a divinely inspired act (carrying out God's will). Moreover, in acting in the name of a deity, religious terrorists are not bound by earthly constraints. Morals regulate the behavior of mortals, and acting in God's name is the highest moral act there is. We thus see that religious terrorism can kill more people in more spectacular ways and might not be limited by any moral constraints, at least not ones located in the earthly realm.

Although in the United States in particular the fear of international terrorism concentrates on the threat of religious terrorism based on readings of Islam, it is important to note that "violent ideas and images are not the monopoly of any single religion. Virtually every major religious tradition—Christian, Jewish, Muslim, Hindu, Sikh and Buddhist—has served as a resource for violent actors" (Juergensmeyer 2003, xii). Indeed, Hoffman (1998) and Juergensmeyer (2001, 2003) are but two scholars who have given detailed information on how different religions have served as justificatory models for violence and how it was only relatively recently that terrorism moved from the religious into the secular realm. In fact, Rapoport tells us that "virtually all instances of terrorist activity, prior to the French Revolution, which were justified *had to be* justified in religious terms" (2001, 7; emphasis added). Thus, with the advent of the modern era, the religious dimension was relegated to a status of lesser importance than the principal motivations of ethnicity and nationalism on the one hand and ideology on the other. It thus appears that our current preoccupation with religion is actually an age-old connection that was obscured for the last 200 years or so by notions of nationhood, self-determination, and revolutionary struggle.

Historical Examples of Religious Terrorism

The following are a few examples of the religious terrorist groups that have existed throughout history:

▲ **Zealots and Sicarii:** These are Jewish sects that operated during the first century against the Roman Empire. The groups' preferred method was assassination by dagger (*sica*), mostly in an open, public space, using the public as means of escape. Their purpose was to incite the wider Jewish population to revolt by attacking the Romans so that the Romans would use increasingly more repressive tactics against the Jewish population. The Zealots and Sicarii did generate two Jewish uprisings resulting in the Jewish War of AD 66, but the desired outcome of defeating the Romans did not materialize; instead, faced with submission to Roman rule, the groups chose to commit group suicide (Pape 2005).

▲ **Thugs:** This was an eleventh-century religious cult/group of bandits that terrorized India. They engaged in ritual murder of random travelers on specified holy days throughout the year; the group's victims were strangled with silk ties before being robbed. These murders were designed to serve the Hindu goddess of terror and destruction (Kali), but it is unclear whether this was the primary motivation or whether indeed (as current usage of the term "thug" implies) these were common murderers out for material gain (see Nacos 2006, 37). The Thugs were suppressed by the British during the middle of the nineteenth century.

▲ **Assassins:** This group operated between the eleventh and thirteenth centuries in Persia (now Iran) and Syria. They were an offshoot of the Muslim Shi'a Ismaili sect. The group's preferred methods were assassinations by dagger and the use of suicide attacks; members were known for not attempting to escape after their mission had been accomplished (see Nacos 2006, 36). Their purpose was to defeat Sunni rulers in an attempt to conquer present-day Syria and Iran and establish their own rulers, which they perceived to be more true to Islam. Many attacks resulted in the targeted sultans in Persia entering into negotiations with the Ismaili assassins. Thus, the threat of a dagger often resulted in political negotiations, but ultimately the entire Ismaili population was almost entirely exterminated by Mongol invasion of Iran in 1258 (Pape 2005).

Old and New Terrorism

Is the world seeing a resurgence of religious terrorism? We already know that secular terrorist organizations are supposed to exhibit greater constraints on their ability to exercise indiscriminate killings. But, are there other differences that indicate that we have seen a qualitative difference between the terrorism of old and that of today? Martha Crenshaw (2000, 411) gives a good overview of how scholars have tried to portray the differences between the old and the new terrorism, as depicted in Table 6-1.

From the distinctions set forth in Table 6-1, it seems apparent that old counterterrorism measures no longer apply (Hoffman 1998). Indeed, from this distinction between "old" and "new" terrorism, we can see how attempts at negotiations would fall on deaf ears because the all-or-nothing framework espoused by religious terrorists precludes them from being able to enter into negotiations with those who have to be eliminated in order to serve a higher power. But it isn't merely the religious aspect that poses problems for countermeasures. Scholars also point to, for example, the more decentralized nature of terrorist movements that adds to our difficulties in trying to deal with them. The fact that many of the new terrorist organizations have no historical pattern of behavior (because they are new, we don't know what they are likely to do), lack a centralized structure that could be damaged and possibly destroyed by targeting the leadership, and operate under new methods of social organization that makes infiltration extremely difficult means that we might have to completely rethink our traditional counterterrorism approaches. But, before we do so, it is worth examining these apparent new features of terrorism in a more detailed manner.

Crenshaw (2000) herself points out that although these distinctions create neat categories, they also oversimplify and possibly lead us to the wrong conclusions. Thus, the evidence that is used to explain the "new" category comes almost exclusively from event-driven research, where generalizations are often inferred from single events. We should be cautious in our assumptions that the new, religious kind of terrorism is the only one engaged in particularly catastrophic terrorism. The use of suicide terrorism has increased and this certainly implies a greater

Table 6-1: Old vs. New Terrorism

	"Old" Terrorism	*"New" Terrorism*
Goal	To achieve political power through revolution, national liberation, or secession	To transform the world
Limits on violence	Groups want popular support and therefore will show some restraint	Groups' religious motivation implies lack of earthly constraints because support is divinely inspired (conventional left-right ideological distinctions aren't applicable)
Purpose of violence	Violence is a method through which groups communicate to their audience, with results expected in the here and now	Groups seek to destroy an impure world and bring about apocalypse; they are inclined to use more lethal methods to bring about this end
Level of results	Measured destruction	Higher number of deaths and easy use of suicide missions
Group structure	Participants are linked in tight, structured conspiracies	Participants are in decentralized, diffuse organizations united by common experience rather personal interaction with other members

lethality, but we should not assume that this has happened primarily as a result of religion. Indeed, Crenshaw already noted in 2000 that the "Liberation Tigers of Tamil Eelam (LTTE), a resolutely secular nationalist group, has practiced the human bomb technique for more than 20 years" (Crenshaw 2000, 414).

What this indicates is that our neat categorization might lead to predictions about one particular kind of underlying motivation that doesn't hold true and that detracts from a larger understanding that causes groups to take up any kind of terrorism in the first place. Moreover, Tucker (2001) explains that many of the features associated with the new terrorism are actually not so new. Thus, the "new" networked structure associated with recent terrorism can be seen in the workings of the PLO and even the RAF and is not necessarily a recent development. Instead, Tucker suggests that a less hierarchical form of organization is actually a return to more traditional forms of organization that have reemerged as "the distorting effect of an alien pattern of thought (Marxism-Leninism) dissipates" (Tucker 2001, 4). Even the notion of whether new terrorism is automatically more lethal is unclear according to Tucker, and he certainly warns against a quick assumption of equating increased lethality and even the possible use of WMDs with religious terrorism. He thus explains that although religious inspired terrorists might eschew politics:

> . . . politics will not leave them alone. Whether or not they had political objectives or thought about them, Islamic fundamentalists in Egypt and Algeria were undone in part by the political problems that arose from their extreme violence. Their own supporters and sympathizers turned against them. Over time, even militant Islamist groups will learn a lesson about the use of extreme violence—there are good reasons to avoid it—or suffer a decline in life expectancy (Tucker 2001, 7).

These are important points to consider because it does mean that we shouldn't let our focus with one particular kind of terrorism detract from our ability to deal with the other types of terrorism. Nonetheless, the focus on a new terrorism is still convincing in the sense that an increased use of particular methods still indicates the possibility of increased lethality even if it does not mean that one particular kind of terrorism is more likely to employ it. Thus, after we've given a brief overview of what can be done to counter religious terrorism, we will turn to the methods employed by terrorists in order to see whether there are particular methods that make it harder to formulate concrete counter-terrorism measures.

SELF-CHECK

1. Ethno-nationalist/separatist terrorism refers to the use of terrorism by a sub-state, ethnic, or national group to change its access to state power. True or false?

2. Examples of ethno-nationalist/separatist terrorist groups include all of the following except:

   a. the Tamil Tigers.
   b. the Irish Republican Army.
   c. the Basque Nation and Liberty.
   d. al-Qaeda.

3. The assassins were Jewish sects that operated in the first century against the Roman Empire. True or false?

4. The goal of old terrorism was to gain political power through revolution, national liberation, or secession, whereas the goal of new terrorism is to transform the world. True or false?

6.3 Terrorist Methods

Just as it's important to understand the underlying motivations that propel terrorist organizations into using violence for political ends, we also need to examine what types of violence are being used. This section examines the methods and tactics employed by terrorist groups. What this section shows is that on one hand, there is not much variation in terms of what kind of tactics terrorist organizations will resort to. On the other hand, there are certainly "phases" of what tactic is "in" and what is "out," and that these phases lead to intra-tactic variation and innovation. Terrorist organizations copy each other and will use those methods that they perceive to be working. Just as over time, terrorist organizations spawn other terrorist organizations by promulgating the belief that violence works, we can also see that organizations with opposing underlying motivations will employ the same tactics because they perceive them to work (White 2006). Moreover, terrorist organizations are also in competition with other terrorist organizations for support from the wider community, and although their tactics are primarily designed to strike fear in the opposing target audience, we have to acknowledge that some forms of violence are employed as a message to a terrorist organization's own constituency. In other words, terrorist tactics also serve as a symbol of the terrorist organization's commitment to the "cause."

6.3.1 Primary Tactics of Terrorism

What, then, are those methods that terrorist organizations employ? Jenkins (1982) asserts that there are six primary tactics employed by all terrorist groups. These are bombings, assassinations, armed assaults, kidnappings, hijackings, and barricade and hostage incidents. Indeed, Jenkins asserts that terrorists employ "a limited tactical repertoire" with bombings taking up almost half of all tactics employed (14). Moreover, this limited tactical repertoire doesn't change much over time. Instead, different periods might exhibit a greater emphasis of one tactic over any of the others (e.g., embassy takeovers in the 1970s, airline hijackings in the 1980s, etc.), but beyond these basic tactics, terrorists show little variation. Instead, as Jenkins states:

> Terrorists appear more imitative than innovative. New tactics, once they are introduced, are likely to be widely imitated (15).

Part of why terrorists have such a limited repertoire of tactics lies in the fact that they make do with what they've got and what is perceived to be working. Terrorists, by definition of their non-state nature, do not have recourse to vast military arsenals. This fact alone explains why they resort to apparent surprise attacks to generate a psychological impact that creates the impression of greater strength than exists in reality. Terrorist organizations look for moments of opportunity and employ the most straightforward method until that method no longer carries the notion of succeeding in the overall strategy. It is in response to security forces' improved detection methods that terrorists will respond with modification and/or innovation (Hoffman 1998), but otherwise their tactics remain rather conservative (see, e.g., Carlton 1979, 209).

Jenkins (1987) explains that when there is innovation, it is often in response to the changed security environment, as well as in response to technological changes in warfare. He thus locates the developmental aspect of increased numbers of terrorist incidents as well as the increased number of fatalities associated with terrorist incidents in the wider realm of global developments. As security forces improve in their counter-terrorist operations, terrorist organizations adapt to avoid infiltration, detection, and destruction and to be able to continue with their form of violence in pursuit of their political objectives. As technological capacities improve the capability of states to engage in ever more destructive warfare, so will terrorist organizations' capabilities to use the same technological advances to their advantage. For example, the invention of gunpowder and, of course, the use of dynamite drastically changed the terrorist's ability to inflict violence in past centuries (see, e.g., Jensen 2004). The cloak-and-dagger tactics of the zealots have been relegated to the sidelines by the powerful impact that can be made in terms of both numbers of victims and dramatic effect. What cannot be clearly determined, however, is whether the impact of numbers outweighs and thus encourages the use of bombs over their impact in terms of dramatic effect. In other words, it is not clear whether specific methods are being used because they're readily available (as Jenkins suggests) or because the underlying motivation of killing large numbers of people encourages the search for ever more destructive techniques (as many scholars suggest when looking at religious terrorism). We should probably discount neither and instead concentrate on limiting the availability of more destructive weaponry to terrorists, as well as examine ways to incorporate marginal, isolated, and alienated groups into mainstream society before they turn to religious violence as their answer (Hoffman 1998, 128). Moreover, we should keep in mind that the development of available technologies certainly allows terrorists to "communicate" their political agenda even more effectively than in the past.

6.3.2 Use of Weapons of Mass Destruction

In this sense, we can understand how Nacos (2006) adds missile attacks and weapons of mass disruption/mass destruction (described in Chapter 8) to the basic list of terrorist tactics. Clearly, terrorist organizations will use any tool that they can obtain relatively easily that makes an impact concomitant with their cause. The danger to people and states, of course, resides in the ever-greater destructiveness of the methods used, as well as the possibility that the mere threat of use of these weapons already leads to changes in policies. These changes could be interpreted by terrorist organizations as successful outcomes for their strategy, further reinforcing the notion that violence works. However, although it might seem logical that terrorists would use ever more destructive weapons to carry out their objectives, we must also take into consideration that terrorists are operationally rather conservative (Carlton 1979; Jenkins 1982) and that they will obtain weapons as long as the act of obtaining them doesn't jeopardize their organizational existence. Thus, if it were to present too great a threat of detection, terrorists would rather use lower-tech weapons, especially if they can make the same impact by applying these weapons in nontraditional manners. In other words, the way in which weapons are used matters as much as the choice of weapon or tactic in the first place.

From this perspective, Jenkins (1987) assessed the likelihood of terrorist organizations obtaining and using nuclear devices, such as that depicted in Figure 6-1, as "neither imminent nor inevitable" (5). Referring to the internally directed symbolism of terrorist attacks, Jenkins based this assessment on the fact that methods are used to frighten the target but also to strengthen the internal cohesion of the terrorist organization. Because the indiscriminate killing of large numbers of people by nuclear devices could pose threats to internal group cohesion, Jenkins feels that the use of nuclear devices by terrorist organizations is unlikely to happen in the future. But, we of course must take into account the time when Jenkins was making this assessment (the 1980s) and look at the qualifiers that he himself already listed at the time of writing. Indeed, he explained that the threshold of constraints that inhibit terrorist organizations from using nuclear devices could be overcome if the global environment itself makes the use of such devices more likely. In other words, Jenkins warns of the dangers of states making the use of nuclear devices more likely and how this could have a spill-over effect for terrorist organizations also contemplating the use of nuclear technologies. In our current climate of increased possibilities for nuclear proliferation (e.g., the break-up of the Soviet Union has led to lax security measures for nuclear and other weapons facilities), this is certainly a danger that we must tackle carefully to avoid the possibility of spill-over. The fact, however, that these weapons have not yet been used (with the notable exception of the sarin gas attack by the Japanese cult Aum Shinrikyo in 1995) also indicates that there might still be a level of moral constraint to terrorist organizations that would dissuade them from using weapons of mass destruction with such a high moral threshold as to prove counterproductive to the organization.

We also still need to ask ourselves, what if those moral and political constraints have disappeared? This of course is the major concern when we examine the increasing impact of religious terrorist organizations that are presumed to no

Figure 6-1

Nuclear weapon launch.

longer have a sufficient link to earthly constituencies but act in the name of a higher authority, one that is beyond human notions of authority and constraint. Moreover, as terrorist organizations increasingly rely on a global constituency, it is certainly thinkable that the "increased deaths of one country's citizens may not reduce sympathy, support, and recruitment for the group in other countries" (Crenshaw and Cusimano Love 2007, 123). Nonetheless, it is worth recalling Tucker's (2001) point that we should not assume that because of religion, terrorist organizations are more likely to use more lethal methods. Instead, Tucker argues that any group's use of WMDs depends on the external environment within which the organizations operate. Moreover, according to Tucker:

> . . . *mass-casualty attacks, like another unusual form of terrorism, suicide attacks, are not exclusively a religious phenomenon. Indeed, most terrorist groups with religious motivations today conduct their operations with methods and results (in numbers wounded) that do not differ from those of their secular predecessors* (8).

This potential impact of globalization's influence on increased terrorist lethality also brings up the potential that it is not necessarily the religious aspect of terrorist organizations but rather their relationship to global processes that might explain their greater danger to the inter-state system. This is certainly a question that is examined when we turn to the most recent terrorist "innovation," suicide bombing. This is a tactic that has received much media attention in the last couple of decades (especially since this tactic was employed against the United States). The next section thus looks at the concept of suicide terrorism.

6.3.3 Suicide Terrorism

Over the last 25 years, we have seen an apparent rise in suicide terrorism, and with this trend have emerged questions as to whether we're witnessing a qualitative change in terrorism. The late 1960s saw the internationalization of terrorism. Due to newer telecommunications technologies and the growing need to reach larger audiences, terrorist organizations expanded their targets and shared their "expertise" with each other, leading to even greater cross-learning and adaptation. More people from more countries were now vulnerable to terrorist attacks. Today, due to a combination of religious fanaticism and the availability of more sophisticated technologies (a result of the process of globalization), we ask ourselves whether we are witnessing yet another qualitative shift and whether this also indicates that terrorists will become more and more lethal in their attempts to influence political decision-making processes. What, then, is **suicide terrorism**, and what, if anything, can we learn from it in terms of our ability to understand how terrorism changes? As Pape (2005) explains:

> *What distinguishes the suicide terrorist is that the attacker does not expect to survive the mission and often employs a method of attack (such as a car bomb, suicide vest, or ramming an airplane into a building) that requires his or her death in order to succeed. In essence, suicide terrorists kill others at the same time that they kill themselves (10).*

The intent and knowledge of the imminent death of the perpetrator distinguishes this form from any other terrorist method. Terrorists can be captured and/or killed during and after any terrorist operation, yet their death is a requirement for the method of suicide terrorism to be successful. What makes this tactic so shocking is its apparent incongruous nature. At first glance, it seems incomprehensible that a terrorist could use his or her own death as a tool through which to achieve political objectives. How does the terrorist believe that his or her death could lead to the success of a wider political agenda when he or she is no longer alive to ensure that these political changes will take place?

Many have started associating this form of terrorism with a rise in religious terrorism, in which the terrorist organization's audience is no longer situated in the earthly realm but is found in the otherworldly realm to which the perpetrator will gain access only through his or her death. Following the 9/11 attacks, we started hearing that the perpetrators were Islamic fundamentalists who held beliefs of being rewarded in the afterlife for their violent acts. This certainly engendered a sense that this seemingly irrational act of violence was associated with religion and moreover with the otherworldly aspect of the constituency in whose name the terrorists carried out the attacks. However, as we will see from a discussion of the literature around this particular method of terrorism, suicide terrorism is not limited to the religious realm, and it is better understood from the group's perspective rather than from the individual motivations that lead men and women to expect their own death in their terrorist acts. Therefore, we cannot fully answer the question of why it is carried out by focusing on the possible rewards achieved by an individual suicide terrorist in the afterlife. Instead, we have to look at the organization's underlying rationale for choosing one terrorist method over another.

Hoffman and McCormick (2004) explain the phenomenon of suicide terrorism by looking at the overall terrorist strategy and examining where suicide terrorism operates. They apply a functional analysis to this particular tactic by placing it in the overall context of various strategies applied over time. As such, they argue that suicide terrorism is a particular signaling device that operates in two directions. It signals to the target audience that the perpetrators are willing to engage in ever more violent tactics unless their demands are met. Also, they signal to their own constituents that their cause is particularly important and the organization is particularly suited to defending the cause because they are willing to lay down their lives for the benefit of the wider group. Just as with any other terrorist tactic, this dual dimension of violence is important. Under the first function, suicide terrorism implies an increase in costs to the target audience because with suicide bombs comes possibly higher numbers of victims and the fact that traditional means of deterrence might no longer be effective (it is difficult to threaten to lock someone up or to shoot them if they are already prepared to die). Under the second function, suicide terrorism represents a powerful mobilization device inasmuch as it shows resolve (commitment to die for the cause or group) and strength (if some members are "expendable," the group must be strong enough to compensate for the loss of those members). Although all terrorism methods have this dual function of signaling both to the target and to the group's own constituency, Hoffman and McCormick (2004) identify a number of advantages that suicide terrorism specifically brings to the terrorist organization, as discussed next.

Advantages of Suicide Terrorism

The following are examples of reasons why terrorist groups might resort to using suicide terrorism as a tactic:

▲ **It is a reliable means to inflict large number of casualties.** Bombs placed in strategic locations can be detected and disarmed, but "human bombs" are easier to hide because they can blend into a group of people. They also have the ability to walk up to a target and detonate themselves at the last minute.

▲ **Suicide terrorism produces an "echo effect."** This form of attack leads to greater headlines, greater shock, greater fear, and therefore a greater impact.

▲ **It demonstrates the "rationality of irrational agents."** In other words, "human bombs" can't be deterred by death or incarceration because they are already willing to die.

▲ **It solidifies social norms.** The suicide bomber's death is used to celebrate the collective act of resistance, and through this collective act, the wider support base is bonded more strongly to the organization.

▲ **It is a form of auto-propaganda that reinforces the group's sense of purpose.** Suicide attackers represent the "purest" relationship to the overall goal, and as such, these attacks symbolize the underlying reasons for which the group is fighting and thus serve as a way to increase group cohesion.

▲ **Suicide attacks avoid moral backlash because self-sacrifice offers atonement for soft targets.** To put it in other terms, because the suicide terrorist "sacrifices" his or her own life, it can be shown as a level of atonement for having to inflict civilian casualties for the greater good of society. The self-sacrificial act can strengthen support for an act that would otherwise have repulsed most of the wider support base.

▲ **It is inexpensive.** It is much less costly for an organization to employ a suicide bomber than to think and carry out extensive bombing campaigns that rely on hidden or even remote control bombs.

By focusing on such a rational approach to the use of suicide terrorism, Hoffman and McCormick (2004) can separate between the organization's choice of this tactic and the individual terrorist's own rationale for laying down his or her life. These findings seem to confirm Dale's (1988) research into religious suicide in Islamic Asia, where in a historical study of three Asian-Muslim communities employing suicide tactics against successive colonial regimes, he found that what seemed purely irrational on the part of the victim could actually be seen as a rational tactic for the terrorist organization, and that from this perspective, suicide terrorism "merely" constitutes one tactic among several others. Thus, it might be more important to examine when and how a group makes the decision to utilize suicide terrorism rather than to focus on what type of individual can be used to carry out these missions:

> The fact that some Muslims may have been influenced to participate in attacks because they were young or old or poor is psychologically interesting but ultimately irrelevant to an understanding that the jihads were a byproduct of the prolonged confrontation between Western powers and Asian Muslim communities (Dale 1988, 56).

Moreover, Dale also notes that the rational decision by a group to commit suicide attacks can also be seen in the fact that the attacks took place during specific moments of crisis when all other tactics seemed to fail. Indeed, he notes that "the cessation of attacks may be attributed to significant changes in the political environment of the Muslim communities, which offered Muslims alternative means of realizing their goals" (54). This indicates that we might be wrong in assuming that there is nothing that can be done to stop suicide terrorism. If looked at from a group perspective, it is certainly possible to foresee how a group might revert back to non-suicide tactics if they perceive these tactics to no longer lead them to their desired outcomes. Moreover, Dale's research also shows that in times of outside occupation (in the form of colonialism), especially when it is coupled with alien concepts of social organization (e.g., different culture, different religion, different concept of politics), it becomes more likely that the group will consider resorting to suicide terrorism.

This notion of suicide terrorism in response to foreign occupation is certainly a point made by Robert A. Pape (2003, 2005), who studied 315 incidents of suicide terrorism that occurred between 1980 and 2003. He found that not only is suicide terrorism not reserved to Islamic terrorists (the majority of terrorist suicide attacks are actually carried out by the Tamil Tigers in Sri Lanka, a secular, Marxist-Leninist group), they are also not random expressions of simply personal frustration and belief in rewards in the afterlife (95 percent of all suicide attacks are part of strategically organized campaigns). These attacks are all carried out to achieve a secular, political goal: to gain "control of what the terrorists see as their national homeland, and specifically at ejecting foreign forces from that territory" (Pape 2005, 39). Pape's primary finding is that suicide attacks are not irrational. Instead, we should recognize the highly organized and planned nature of these attacks to see at what point the rationale for the attacks is developed and what aims are being pursued by this strategic choice:

> If suicide terrorism were mainly irrational or even disorganized, we would expect a much different pattern: political goals would not be articulated (for example, we would see references in news reports to "rogue" attacks), or the stated goals would vary considerably even within the same conflict. We would also expect the timing to be either random, or perhaps event-driven in response to particularly provocative or infuriating actions by the other side, but little if at all related to the progress of negotiations over issues in dispute that the terrorists want to influence (Pape 2005, 41).

Why would it be important to understand suicide terrorism as a rational choice? Why do we make this distinction between group strategies and individual suicide bombers? If it is indeed crazy individuals who carry out these attacks guided only by their belief that they are acting in the name of a divine entity, there isn't much we can do about this. We could try to stop all public gatherings and/or increase our technical abilities to detect explosives through clothing, but even if we could do these things, we wouldn't be any safer. If, however, we can uncover when an organization decides the moment is ripe for using suicide terrorism, and if we uncover what it is these organizations aim to achieve with this tactic, we will be able to think about means to counter this tactic. We might be able to find ways to dissuade organizations from making that first calculation that suicide bombing gets them closer to their objective. Pape's research certainly allows us to think in these terms. Even the most religiously fervent terrorist organizations had a specific political goal in mind when they made the decision to start a suicide bombing campaign. Pape shows that in most cases, the purpose was to influence ongoing negotiations. This, then, means that there is an objective important to terrorist organizations that is located in the earthly realm, even if a group's outward rhetoric (and often the mobilization of its foot soldiers) depends on its interpretations of the divine will. The purpose of locating suicide terrorism among a variety of terrorist choices actually allows us to examine when suicide terrorism is chosen, when it is not chosen, and when an organization might move back from its strategy of employing such a tactic. Recognizing that suicide terrorism is a strategic choice allows us to find moments of opportunity for engaging the organization in negotiations to stem their use of this tactic.

SELF-CHECK

1. According to Jenkins (1982), there are six primary tactics employed by all terrorist groups. These tactics include all of the following except:
   a. bombings.
   b. assassinations.
   c. drug trafficking.
   d. kidnappings.

2. One reason that a terrorist group might consider using suicide bombing is that it is inexpensive. It is much less costly to an organization to employ a suicide bomber than to think and carry out extensive bombing campaigns that rely on hidden or even remote control bombs. True or false?

3. Suicide bombings are only carried out by Islamic terrorist organizations. True or false?

4. The use of missile attacks or WMDs by terrorist groups cannot be ruled out as potential method of attack. True or false?

6.4 Counter-terrorism Efforts

Cunningham (2003) explains that focusing on underlying motivation allows us to think about how we might stop or at least reduce the threat of terrorism:

> *If groups are motivated to carry out violence in the name of an oppressed and victimized minority group with whom they have significant popular support, the approach will be very different than if facing religiously motivated fanatics who are isolated from the mainstream and are willing to kill and die for their cause. One can negotiate with ethno-national groups and attempt to eliminate the underlying structural causes that give rise to terrorism. One cannot negotiate with people who make no demands other than their enemies' destruction (28).*

For our distinction between ethno-nationalist/separatist terrorism on one hand and ideological terrorism on the other, it becomes clear that, albeit difficult, demands from ethno-nationalist groups who speak for a larger and relatively cohesive group can be incorporated into the attempts of the state to deal with the threat of terrorism. Ideological groups, however (and as we will see in our next section, also specifically religious-inspired terrorist organizations), make it extremely difficult for the state to constructively engage in negotiations. Because these terrorists envision the destruction of the state, there seems to be no alternative that could lead to the coexistence of the state's and the group's aims. It is for this reason that Cunningham (2003) explains "it is difficult for governments to negotiate with ideological extremists unless they [the ideological organizations] make an effort to give up their political violence in favor of non-violent political engagement" (31). The logical conclusion from this is that the only option to the state is elimination of the group. Thus, for the state, it becomes important to further isolate an already marginal group and to convince the wider population that the group does not represent their aims and needs.

6.4.1 Counter-terrorism against Ethno-Nationalist/Separatist and Ideological Terrorism

The process of elimination can work on reducing any support for a terrorist group in the community so that it can no longer hide among supporters and can ultimately be captured by the state. Hoffman (1998) supports this notion when he states that "both left- and right-wing terrorist organizations must actively proselytize among the politically aware and radical, though often uncommitted, for recruits and support, thus rendering themselves vulnerable to penetration and compromise" (171).

How this might be done can be seen in the example of how the Italian government dealt with the ideological terrorist group the Red Brigades, an ideological, left-wing terrorist group that operated in Italy especially in the 1970s and 1980s. The Italian government focused on the contradiction between the Red Brigades' outward pretensions of wanting to achieve a Communist-inspired revolution that favored the working classes and their own elitist and bourgeois backgrounds. An extensive public diplomacy campaign by the Italian government (alongside other counter-terrorism measures, such as promises of amnesty and increased infiltration methods) worked on demonstrating that the underlying motives of the organization were not those of the overall population. Instead, this group was shown to be merely using indiscriminate violence for no other reason than their own personal gratification. A population that had long suffered from the violence of the Red Brigades was further disillusioned by realizing that the aims of the group had no grounding in their own experiences. This was certainly a contributing factor that made it easier for the government's security forces to infiltrate and ultimately capture the main figures of this organization, which then led to the group's demise. This strategy of elimination can work because the group does not have a strong foothold in a wider support base.

In cases of ethno-nationalist terrorism, however, the terrorist group can claim allegiance to a wider society by the sheer fact of shared history and ethnicity. Even when the overall population does not hold the same extremist views that espouse the use of violence, they are nonetheless often persuaded by the group's commitment to the overall nationalist goal. As Cunningham (2003) explains, "the source of authority and legitimacy of an ethno-nationalist terrorist group comes from its members' identity as association with a perceived victimized minority" (32). The strength of popular support then also implies that the government's response to this type of terrorism cannot be one of "elimination." The group's overall aims are not necessarily the destruction of the state, but a change of the state to reflect their aspirations of gaining political power. White (2003) explains that governments in the end "might have to open the doors to political participation" (187) unless they want to see themselves embroiled in never-ending conflict or their potential destruction. From this realization comes the fact that a "government must convince the leaders of the ethnic group in question that it has a vested interest in maintaining the social structure and it can achieve its goals by working within the current system" (188). Although clearly this policy is not without its limitations, governments that have instituted policies of power-sharing coupled with appeals to moderates from within the ethnic communities have seen a drastic reduction in ethno-nationalist violence (as has been the case with the ongoing peace processes in Northern Ireland, Turkey, Spain, and Sri Lanka).

Functions of Violence

The relationship between a terrorist organization and wider support structures is instrumental in showing the possibilities for counter-terrorism. This relationship also influences the degree to which violence is employed by the terrorist organization. Nonetheless, the **dual function of violence** (and by extension, the tactics employed by terrorist organizations) should be noted here. On the surface, violence is always directed against a specific target (the externally directed dimension of violence), yet we must also recognize that there is an internally directed dimension of violence that reflects the position of the terrorist organization within the overall social and political structures within which or against which it manifests itself.

On one hand, violence indicates the struggle against the perceived inequalities perpetrated by the target state(s). On the other hand, however, violence also serves to demonstrate to the wider population for which the organization claims to speak that here is an organization that represents the true needs of the community. Violence thus serves the instrumental purpose of demonstrating commitment to the cause and to the organization's constituency. Because of this internally-directed dimension of violence, both ethno-nationalist/separatist and ideological terrorist organizations are constrained in their use of violence. In other words, although both types of terrorist organizations clearly adopt the view that violence serves their purpose, they are nonetheless constrained by how much violence will further that goal. Too much violence can actually backfire because the community for which the terrorists claim to speak can end up being repulsed by the levels of death committed in their name. As Stern (2003) says, "terrorists . . . depend on the broader population for support" (39), and violence can result in that support being taken away. It is for this reason that many terrorists limit how much death and destruction they cause because they are rooted in the moral frameworks of their wider communities (e.g., Jenkins 1986; Hoffman 1998). Killing is thus not carried out for the sake of killing but for the sake of carrying a specific message both to the target and to the organization's wider support structure. We will see in our next section, however, that because this constraining element seems to disappear with religiously motivated terrorism, methods to counter this specific threat face new challenges.

6.4.2 Counter-terrorism Against Religious Terrorism

When looking at religiously motivated terrorism, we are confronted with the fact that religious terrorism seems to combine the strength of the ethno-nationalist terrorism with the intractability of ideological terrorism. In other words, because religion and identity are often inseparable, large groups of the world's populations identify strongly with particular religions and thus form "natural" constituents for any group claiming to use violence on behalf of a specific religion. This means that similar to ethnicity, religion offers a rather natural support base. Although adherents to the same religion do not by default support the strategy of terrorism, they can nonetheless share a feeling of marginalization that crosses state-boundaries and is not limited to ethnicity. As was seen with ethno-nationalist terrorists, this large support group offers ways to address some of the underlying grievances so as to find a resolution that is acceptable to both the target state and the organization's support base. However, in religious terrorist organizations, this cross-over to ethno-nationalist terror groups is countered by similarities to ideological terrorist groups that make the possibility of negotiations extremely difficult to even contemplate.

Because many religious terrorist organizations operate on the assumption that they have the only truth and that to carry out God's will they have to annihilate the enemy, they hold views similar to those espoused by ideological terrorists. Any public diplomacy effort that would attempt to make a religious group see "the errors of its religion" or that would prove that the organization was acting contrary to its professed beliefs (as was done with the Red Brigades, for example) would ultimately fail. In fact, it might actually backfire, especially when put forward by a target state or a number of states that hold different religious views from the religion under which the terrorist campaign is waged. For ideological terror groups, elimination (e.g., capture and destruction of the organization as well as a public diplomacy campaign to erode the last remnants of an already weak support base) was suggested as a counter-terrorism method. This is impossible to contemplate for a religious terrorist organization because its support base is potentially endless. Moreover, as we can see from past terrorist movements, overreactions on the part of governments can actually lead to an increase in public support for the organization. Because the organization may have a seemingly endless number of potential recruits, it does not appear advisable to engage in an elimination process.

What then can be done? It might be possible to examine the relationship between religion and politics. Our recent emphasis on religious terrorist groups has emphasized the other-worldly orientation of this type of terrorism; however, it might be necessary to uncover the secular political goals of the overall support base and in addressing these needs, it might be possible to erode the support for extremist justifications for violence in God's name. Tucker (2001) already alluded

FOR EXAMPLE

Hamas: Religion, Nationalism, and Constructing a Social Support Base

Hamas is a religious, nationalist terrorist organization that operates in the Palestinian territories, the West Bank and the Gaza Strip. Hamas can be traced back to the nonviolent activities of the Muslim Brotherhood, but since 1987, Hamas has been the military wing of Muslim Brotherhood activities.

The underlying goals of this organization are to create an Islamic Palestinian state, one that would include the Palestinian territories and all of what is now the state of Israel. Despite instances of cooperation, Hamas has been in constant conflict with the Palestinian Authority/PLO, primarily because of its emphasis on creating an Islamic state rather than a secular one as envisioned by the Palestinian Authority. Hamas has been vehemently opposed to the peace process because it sees any compromise solutions to the Israeli-Palestinian conflict as a tacit acceptance of the Israeli state. In its opposition to Israel, Hamas has engaged in extensive suicide campaigns.

Because of its Islamist ideology that places a great deal of emphasis on preaching, education, and charity work, Hamas has created "an active network of social services within the Palestinian Territories" (Memorial Institute for the Prevention of Terrorism n.d.). With these, Hamas provides essential services to Palestinians, such as education and health care. Thus, although some elements of Hamas continue to violently oppose the Israeli state and be in conflict with the Palestinian Authority/PLO, a large number of Hamas activities consist of carrying out services that the Palestinian Authority is unable to provide. This has resulted in political support being drawn away from the Palestinian Authority toward Hamas, and it has been argued that as a consequence, "Hamas has been able to leverage its popular support into increased support for its terrorist activities" (Memorial Institute for the Prevention of Terrorism n.d.).

to the political context within which religious terrorist organizations operate, even if they don't willingly acknowledge this political element. Re-assessing the political structures will prove to be fertile ground upon which to engage the support base while simultaneously employing standard counter-terrorism measures to seek and apprehend those that would carry out violent attacks. By separating the support base from the extremist violent organization, it may be possible to contemplate negotiations of underlying needs, even if, as Cunningham (2003) suggests, this is extremely difficult, especially in groups such as Hamas, where the social and political base are so interconnected with the religious ideology of the movement.

Hamas' social activities, more than its terrorist activities, explain how in January 2006, Hamas won a landslide victory in Palestinian parliamentary elections (winning 74 out of a possible 132 seats). This posed a problem for the Palestinian Authority, Israel, and the international community because it placed into positions of the governing authority members of an organization characterized by many states as a terrorist organization. Yet, although many states were appalled that a terrorist organization could be voted into government, it might be important to remember that as Hoffman wrote in 1998, increased political participation might actually result in less militancy. Indeed, many observers hope that access to political power might moderate Hamas' goals and objectives.

It remains to be seen whether Hamas will moderate its views as a result of having to govern, but Hamas does prove an interesting test case for why a terrorist organization can garner so much support. Per our discussion on religious terrorist organizations, the sheer fact that the organization appeals to a particular religion might mean that it has automatic followers based purely on shared religion. However, as the case of Hamas indicates, what is more important to understanding Hamas' popularity is not its holding to Islamic precepts alone, but the fact that the organization has integrated itself into the fabric of Palestinian life through the provision of services that the authorities had not been able to provide. Where the PLO was unable (or unwilling due to its many corrupt institutions) to provide for Palestinians, Hamas emphasized community over official politics and thus proved itself to be part of and for the people.

How to Counter Religiously Motivated Terrorism

As we said earlier in this chapter, it might be useful to re-examine our belief that religious terrorist organizations can never be negotiated with. Although not necessarily implying that we should give concessions to those that employ violence in order to instigate political change, it might nonetheless be important to reconsider our thinking about religious terrorism. Are religious terrorist organizations completely taken over by some zeal that makes it impossible to examine which of their needs could be realistically met? Juergensmeyer offers some insights when he explains the relationship between violence and religion. In his 2003 book *Terror in the Mind of God*, Juergensmeyer discusses the long-standing and often ambivalent relationship between religion and violence. He observes that although religion lends a powerful justificatory model for the use of violence, when violence is carried out in the name of religion, it is mostly by marginal groups within that religion and not by the majority moderates. This means that although violence has catapulted marginal groups to center stage, it also leaves much scope for the moderate majority to oppose the use of violence and whittle away at the support base for the extremists. In other words, we might have to combine the approaches for ethno-nationalist and ideological terrorist groups to find an approach that can work on eliminating a support base for religiously motivated terrorists while at the same time giving a more powerful expression to those moderate voices that often are relegated to the sidelines by religious extremists.

6.4.3 Counter-terrorism Against Suicide Terrorism

As we discussed in the previous section, the importance of recognizing the rational decision-making process that leads organizations to take up a suicide campaign comes from the fact that it allows us to see specific options for how this method can be stopped. After we understand the political context within which or against which suicide campaigns are waged, we can start looking to the changing political environment to see what caused these same campaigns to stop. In this vein, Dale's (1988) historical examination of suicide campaigns fought by Islamic communities against outside colonizers found that suicide campaigns were abandoned "when new political opportunities made suicidal attacks irrelevant anachronisms" (56). In other words, because suicide campaigns were expressions of political choice rather than representations of particular religious world views, after the needs of the community could be expressed in other political forums, the use for suicide campaigns abated. This observation allows Dale to suggest that a logical solution to the use of suicide campaigns could be to "make fundamental changes in prevailing social-economic relationship or political structures if terrorism is to be brought to an end" (57). Of course, getting to the required political and structural changes is not an easy or short-term undertaking. What we should learn from Dale's findings is that we need to look for ways of allowing the opening up of political space that could take over the space currently occupied by suicide terrorism today.

Before we can reconsider how political space is occupied, however, we should heed Sprinzak's recommendations that rest on the need for re-examining whether suicide terrorism is the expression of irrational fanatics or a politically calculated decision by terrorist planners. His research had shown that one of the strengths associated with suicide terrorism comes not from the act alone, but also from the perception it creates among the target audience that suicide bombers are "irrational fanatics." Thus, Sprinzak (2000) suggests that to counter suicide terrorism:

> It is important not to succumb to the idea that they are ready to do anything and lose everything . . . . The perception that terrorists are unde-

terrable fanatics who are willing to kill millions indiscriminately just to sow fear and chaos belies the reality that they are cold, rational killers who employ violence to achieve specific political objectives (73).

Sprinzak explains that suicide campaigns can be eradicated through the application of complementary political and operational strategies. Under the political strategy, Sprinzak considers political and economic sanctions that should be used against the terrorist's community, as well as the use of coercive diplomacy against foreign states that are supporting the terrorists' campaigns. Because the political strategy will require a certain amount of time before it pays off, however, Sprinzak outlines operational tactics that could achieve the more short-term goals of the overall strategy. As such, the operational campaign should consist of counter measures that do the following:

▲ Target the organizational structure
▲ Provide physical deterrence to make suicide bombing harder
▲ Carry out a public reassurance effort to inoculate the target audience against the psychological warfare waged against them by the terrorists

Pape's (2003, 2005) research into the strategic decision to employ suicide terrorism mirrors Sprinzak's finding that it is not the irrationality we should focus on, but rather the political context within which suicide terrorism occurs. Sprinzak focuses on the need to undo the myth of the irrational act, but he also emphasizes the need for greater protection of likely targets. This is a finding that is similar to Pape's notion that the United States' strategies in the war against terrorism should concentrate less on offensive military action and more on strengthening homeland security to thwart future attacks against the United States. Pape's research has shown that suicide campaigns, whether carried out by religious or secular terrorist organizations, occur mainly as a result of foreign occupation rather than Islamic fundamentalism. The logical solution then would be to withdraw foreign forces, specifically American forces from the Middle East. However, recognizing the impracticability of this solution, Pape calls for an alternative strategy to "reduce the likelihood of suicide terrorism without compromising our core national security interests" (2005, 237). This strategy would need to be based on the realization that neither offensive military action nor limited concessions could reduce the threat of terrorism and that instead improved homeland security and defensive measures need to be explored (2003, 14). In fact, as a direct recommendation to the current U.S.-led war on terrorism, Pape (2005, 237) argues that two goals need to be accomplished: The current pool of terrorists needs to be defeated, and a new generation of terrorists needs to be prevented from arising in the future. For this strategy to work, we must make the connection between the politics of suicide terrorism and foreign occupation rather than the concentrating on some relationship between a particular religion and violence. If we don't make this connection, we are likely to employ tactics under the first goal that make it impossible for us to achieve the second goal. In Pape's words:

> An attempt to transform Muslim societies through regime change is likely to dramatically increase the threat we face. The root cause of suicide terrorism is foreign occupation and the threat that foreign military presence poses to the local community's way of life. Hence, any policy that seeks to conquer Muslim societies in order, deliberately, to transform their culture is folly. Even if our intentions are good, anti-American terrorism would likely grow, and grow rapidly (2005, 245).

What, then, does this discussion of suicide terrorism tell us about how terrorism in general can be defeated? Sprinzak, Dale, and Pape certainly recognize and even highlight the important role played by military action in defeating terrorism, yet they nonetheless emphasize that an over-reliance on military action can actually prove counterproductive. Instead, it is important to consider the context within which non-state organizations use violence to achieve their political objectives. We have seen that different organizations all see violence as the legitimate tool to further their goals and that despite different underlying motivations, all terrorist organizations learn from past attempts to challenge the inter-state system through violence.

Thus, to counter terrorism, we too must learn from past efforts to see that there is a relationship between terrorism and the measures used to fight it. As Pape made clear, if we only rely on offensive military force try to achieve the objective of defeating the current pool of terrorists, we are making it impossible to achieve the goal of deterring future terrorists because our current actions are creating more not fewer terrorists. Jensen's (2004) research into nineteenth-century anarchist violence had made the same connection. An over-reliance on physical suppression resulted not in the elimination but rather in an increase in anarchist violence against the state. And of course Dale's historical case studies also showed that suicide attacks were not prevented by "more sophisticated police techniques or undertaking punitive military action" (1988: 57).

Moreover, although it is important to look at underlying motivations and how they can lead to the need for different counter-terrorism methods, our discussion on religious terrorism in general and the use of suicide terrorism in particular has certainly shown that a reliance on simplistic understandings can have serious repercussions for counter terrorism. If counter-terrorism operations rest on faulty assumptions, their strategies can inadvertently result in the opposite of what they were supposed to achieve. Pape (2005) showed that if we assume suicide terrorism is only carried out by Islamic fundamentalists, and because of that, we employ a strategy of changing Muslim societies, we're actually engaging in practices that make future terrorism more likely. Likewise, if we treat religious terrorism as a type of terrorism that is incompatible with any kind of political engagement, we leave elimination as the only strategy (as suggested by Cunningham 2003). Perpetuating the assumption that all religious violence is without any political framework further marginalizes those communities that because of their marginalization took up violence in the first place. We thus continue to encourage even further violence.

SELF-CHECK

1. Violence has a dual nature: an internally directed dimension and an externally directed dimension. True or false?

2. In countering terrorism, it is not important to recognize the type of terrorism being employed because there are few differences between ethno-nationalist, ideological, and religious terrorism. True or false?

3. Pape (2005) argues that an effective counter-terrorism strategy needs to be based on the realization that neither offensive military action nor limited concessions could reduce the threat of terrorism, and that improved homeland security and defensive measures instead need to be explored. True or false?

4. The Italian government was successful in its efforts to defeat the Red Brigades by emphasizing which counter-terrorism method?

   a. Public diplomacy aimed at reducing public support
   b. Extensive use of military campaigns
   c. Soliciting UN support
   d. Ignoring the Red Brigades

SUMMARY

Non-state terrorism is terrorism perpetrated by those who do not have access to state power. Terrorism is therefore a "popular" strategy for those who see themselves as oppressed by the current (inter-related) systems of local, regional, and global power relations. Yet, despite the fact that a majority of people around the globe suffer from global inequalities, this has not resulted in every disadvantaged group taking up terrorism as a strategy to advance its political position. It is thus important to recognize the underlying motivations that propel a group to change its current position through violent means.

In this chapter, you assessed the historical development of twentieth-century terrorism. You also evaluated the inter-related nature of all terrorism while taking note of the socio-historical specificity of each type of terrorism. Finally, you critiqued different types of terrorist organizations and the different aims and goals they seek to achieve, as well as learned about some of the tools for combating international terrorism.

KEY TERMS

Anarchists	People or groups who seek to abolish all governments because they believe that governments act against the interests and rights of people to behave as they wish.
Domestic terrorism	Terrorism directed by a group against the specific state within which they reside.
Dual function of violence	Refers to the fact that terrorist violence is both externally directed (directed against a specific target) and internally directed (intended to solidify a support base).
Ethno-nationalist/ separatist terrorism	Use of terrorism by a sub-state, ethnic, or national group in order to change its access to power either by taking over the state or by forcing secession to form its own independent state.
Ideological terrorist groups	Groups that challenge the fabric of existing liberal democratic states from either a left-wing or a right-wing political framework.
Ideology	A tightly knit body of beliefs organized around a few central values; examples include communism, fascism, and variations of nationalism.
International terrorism	Terrorism that relies on an increasing link between groups from different states as well as an increasing internationalization of targets in order to speak to a wider audience.
Narcoterrorism	Terrorist violence used to guarantee continued profit from the drug trade.
Nationalism	The belief that political communities share common characteristics such as language, religion, or ethnicity, and that a state only gains legitimacy by representing these shared characteristics.

Non-state terrorist actor	Term that applies to a variety of groups with different aims and identities but that all share two elements: (1) they don't have access to state power, and (2) they believe that they can achieve their goals only through violence.
Religious terrorism	Terrorism with the primary motivation of furthering a particular religious set of ideas.
Socialists	People or groups who want to control the state apparatus so as to redistribute wealth and ensure the rights of the people.
Suicide terrorism	Method of attack in which the attacker does not expect to survive.

ASSESS YOUR UNDERSTANDING

Go to www.wiley.com/college/kilroy to assess your knowledge of the basics of non-state actors and terrorism.
Measure your learning by comparing pre-test and post-test results.

Summary Questions

1. A non-state actor is an entity that operates below the level of the state. True or false?

2. Which of the following is not one of Hoffman's five stages of terrorism?
   (a) Attention
   (b) Acknowledgment
   (c) Recognition
   (d) Political participation

3. Anarchists want to control the machinations of the state so as to allow the state to redistribute wealth and ensure the rights of the people. True or false?

4. Cunningham's differentiation rests on three types of primary motivation underlying all terrorist organizations, including which of the following?
   (a) Political ideology
   (b) Ethno-nationalism
   (c) Religious extremism
   (d) All of the above

5. International terrorism relies on links between groups from different states and uses targets that are not necessarily from the immediate target state. True or false?

6. Narcoterrorism refers to the use of terrorist violence to overthrow a state. True or false?

7. One reason terrorist organizations employ suicide as a method is because it is considered a cheap alternative to other more sophisticated methods, such as remote-controlled bombs. True or false?

8. Which of the following is a characteristic of new terrorism, as opposed to old terrorism?
   (a) Its goal is to transform the world.
   (b) Participants want popular support, so they therefore show some restraint.
   (c) Groups participating in this form of terrorism seek measured destruction.
   (d) None of the above

9. Hamas is a religious, nationalist terrorist organization that operates in the Palestinian territories, the West Bank and the Gaza Strip. True or false?

10. The dual function of violence includes which of the following dimensions?

(a) Internal

(b) External

(c) Neither a or b

(d) Both a and b

Applying This Chapter

1. If you were the U.S. ambassador to Israel, how would you argue your nation's condemnation of Palestinian groups such as Hamas and their use of terrorism in support of their goal of a Palestinian state, in light of Israel's use of similar tactics to gain its independence?

2. Explain to another student in your class the differences between the three types of terrorist groups described in this chapter. Ask him or her to then provide examples of each type of group.

3. A newspaper headline describes a suicide terrorism attack in Lebanon. A classmate comments that it really should be called a "homicide terrorism attack" because the goal of the bomber was to kill as many people as possible, along with himself. Do you agree or disagree? Why or why not?

4. Describe various recourses to counter ethno-nationalist and ideological terrorism. How do these differ from methods to counter religious terrorism?

Analyzing Terrorist Organizations

You work in the State Department and are charged with researching foreign terrorist organizations and determining how to classify them based on the three primary motivations of political ideology, ethno-nationalism, and religious extremism. Analyze the following organizations and determine their primary motivational factor. Choose one group and decide how best to craft a policy to counter its goals and objectives.

   a. MRTA (Peru)
   b. Basque Separatists (Spain)
   c. Tamil Tigers (Sri Lanka)

Classifying Narcoterrorism

The FARC in Colombia has been identified by the State Department as a narcoterrorist organization, due to its links to narcotics trafficking as a means to finance its operations. Research the FARC and its links to narcotics trafficking. Determine whether the FARC's involvement in drug trafficking makes it more of a criminal organization or a terrorist organization. Propose means to counter the FARC's influence in Colombia based on your assessment.

7

CYBER-TERRORISM AND CYBER-WARFARE
Understanding the Threat to Information and Information Systems

Starting Point

Go to www.wiley.com/college/kilroy to assess your knowledge of the basics of cyber-terrorism and cyber-warfare.
Determine where you need to concentrate your effort.

What You'll Learn in This Chapter

▲ The definitions of cyber-terrorism and cyber-warfare
▲ The capability and intent of national and non-state actors with regard to the threat they pose in cyberspace
▲ The consequences of a cyber-attack
▲ The defenses against cyber-terrorism and offensive cyber-warfare capabilities of the United States

After Studying This Chapter, You'll Be Able To

▲ Assess information-based threats to our nation's critical infrastructures
▲ Evaluate the difference between capability and intent with regard to cyber-terrorism threats
▲ Appraise the consequences of cyber-terrorism and its effect on our nation's critical infrastructures
▲ Judge our nation's defensive and offensive capabilities concerning cyber-warfare

INTRODUCTION

The information age brought both blessings and curses as we became more enamored with technology. Nearly everyone has gone to the grocery store or bank and heard the dreaded words, "Our computer system is down. I can't help you right now." Or, much worse, imagine taking a child to the hospital for an emergency, only to find out important medical information needed to treat the child—such as blood bank data or drug interaction information—is not available due to a computer glitch. Whether we like it or not, we are citizens of a new world called **cyberspace**—the notional environment in which digitized information is communicated over computer networks—and the ability to collect, store, retrieve, and process information is critical to our lives, as well as our nation's survival.

In this chapter, you will assess information-based threats to our nation's critical infrastructures. You will learn what cyber-terrorism is, as well as evaluate the difference between capability and intent with regard to cyber-terrorism. Next, you'll appraise the consequences of cyber-terrorism and its effect on our nation's infrastructure. Finally, you'll learn about our nation's defensive and offensive capabilities concerning cyber-warfare.

7.1 The Cyber-Terrorism Threat

In the 1992 Hollywood movie *Sneakers,* the antagonist, Cosmo (played by Ben Kingsley) made the comment that power and future conflict would all be about information—who controls it also controls what we see, think, hear, and do. In the past, such information control remained in the hands of gatekeepers such as the media, government, and educational institutions. Today, information is more diffused, and the means to use it, both positively and negatively, have grown considerably in the last couple decades. As one example, think about computers and how they are now nearly as common as television sets in American homes. Today's schools require classes to teach computer literacy. Businesses require basic computer skills for practically any conceivable job. For example, auto mechanics depend on a computer chip in a car to diagnose a problem; wait staff and merchants use computers to read credit cards, process orders, and manage inventories; soldiers use sophisticated weapons-guidance programs to conduct fire-control missions; and scientists depend on high-speed computers to process mathematical formulas and determine complex algorithms in their experiments. At the end of the day, there are very few of us who can claim not to have had some interaction with computers at school, home, and/or work.

On a larger scale, consider all of the things we take for granted each day: electricity, potable water, indoor plumbing, telephones, televisions, airlines, etc. All of these comprise elements of our nation's critical infrastructures—systems and assets, whether physical or virtual, that are so vital to the United States that the incapacity or destruction of such systems and assets would have a debilitating impact on physical security, national economic security, national public health or safety, or any combination of these matters. These systems supply power generation, communications, transportation, and many other elements of daily life, and they provide us the standard of living we've come to enjoy (and expect) in this country.

Yet, all of our nation's critical infrastructures ride on information systems that are vulnerable to disruption, whether that disruption comes from natural or man-made sources. We all know the effects of a thunderstorm on television reception during the Super Bowl, or a programming error on a cell-phone satellite. Most times, such disruptions are a minor inconvenience, and they are fixed rather quickly. Sometimes, however, the outage lasts much longer, such as during a hurricane, when we may not be able to restore power or communications for days or weeks on end.

Unfortunately, our understanding of how to manage information and protect our critical infrastructures from both accidental and intentional damage is limited at best. It usually takes some type of catastrophic failure before we realize how interconnected our world is and how complex those linkages can be. For many, it took the threat of a global computer shutdown on January 1, 2000. Called the Y2K bug (a programming technique used to save computer memory space by using two digits instead of four for the year portion of dates), it caused global panic from both government and the private sector, as millions of dollars were spent correcting the error. Many feared that major industries would be impacted by computer systems that were not "Y2K compliant," causing them to shut down. In the end, much of the concern appeared to have been for naught, as the year 2000 began with few disruptions to any of our critical infrastructures. Yet, Y2K did wake us up to the fact that we are an information-dependent society and that a major disruption, such as the one predicted for Y2K, would have catastrophic consequences for the United States and for commerce in a globalized world. If anything, the preparations for Y2K caused our leaders in government, business, the military, and law enforcement to seriously consider the consequences of such a disruption.

For this reason, the potential for a cyber-attack by a terrorist organization or a nation-state using cyber-warfare has the capability to create a similar effect psychologically on our society as would the use of a weapon of mass destruction (WMD). In other words, if a terrorist is able to demonstrate an ability to attack one of more of our nation's critical infrastructures, it would be considered akin to use of a weapon of mass disruption in that it would cause more than a simple inconvenience to our everyday lives. Rather, it would evince the government's inability to protect us from future attacks, leading to a loss of trust or confidence in our nation's leadership. Such an attack could also have the effect of rendering

FOR EXAMPLE

Y2K Preparations

In the city of Chesapeake, Virginia, government leaders were so concerned about the potential impact of the Y2K bug on traffic that they took the precautionary step of installing stop signs at major intersections of the city, in anticipation that if all the traffic lights were to stop functioning at once, there would be gridlock.

our nation financially bankrupt and our law enforcement authorities helpless to deal with the consequences and the potential for widespread panic. For example, if such an attack on the power grid were able to effectively disable major sections of our country in winter, people's lives could be threatened directly. In fact, just such a scenario was envisioned for Y2K by the Canadian military as it prepared for the worst in its remote northern provinces.

7.1.1 Defining Cyber-Terrorism Attacks and Cyber-Warfare

To understand the threat posed by cyber-terrorism and cyber-warfare, we must first define what they are. Dorothy Denning, an expert on information warfare and computer security at the Naval Post Graduate School in Monterey, California, defines **cyber-terrorism** as the use of computer-based operations by terrorist organizations conducting cyber-attacks that "compromise, damage, degrade, disrupt, deny and destroy information stored on computer networks or that target network infrastructures" (Denning 2004, 91). Because computer technology has become inexpensive and the tools (basically, a computer and a modem) are readily available, practically anyone has the ability to become a cyber-terrorist today. A teenager's attempt to "hack" into a Department of Defense web site may seem innocent enough at first, but the shortcomings or "holes" in the computer system's defenses exposed by these hacks could be exploited by terrorist organizations. These organizations could then utilize cyber-espionage to steal information from the computer systems while remaining undetected to the authorized users.

What makes cyber-terrorist acts difficult to detect is that, for the most part, computer attacks are anonymous, making it hard to determine the source of an attack. Most computer intrusions thus far have been attributed to self-proclaimed computer hackers or possible criminal elements, but there is a possibility that some of these intrusions have been probing actions—cyber-reconnaissance conducted by terrorist organizations to detect our defenses and responses. Such actions would likely be performed before a full-scale cyber-assault on our banking system, for example. Because the volume of cyber-incidents grows each year, determining which could be terrorist-related becomes more problematic. For example, the Department of Defense (DoD) Joint Task Force for Computer Network Operations (JTF-CNO) reported that there were 780 cyber-incidents against DoD information systems in 1997, rising to over 28,000 incidents in 2000 (Denning 2004, 92). Much of that increase has to do with better detection and awareness, but the implications are still enormous.

As compared to cyber-terrorism, **cyber-warfare** connotes conflict between nation-states using cyber-based weapons. For example, during both the First and Second Gulf Wars, the United States military conducted cyber-warfare against the Iraqi military, using conventional electronic warfare tools (radar jamming, etc.), as well as computer-based tools to attack Iraqi communications and command and control infrastructure, such as air defense systems. Cyber-warfare can be used to target both military and civilian infrastructure during a military conflict, or as part of operations prior to actual hostilities. In other words, following the "Art of War" teachings of ancient Chinese philosopher Sun Tzu, it is better to win wars without having to fight, by convincing your adversaries of the futility of their efforts. For this reason, cyber-warfare can have its greatest impact before conventional military operations because it attempts to influence the decision making of key adversary leaders. An example of this application of cyber-warfare occurred during the NATO air campaign against Serbian forces in Kosovo in 1999. Although NATO air forces used the hard power of military air strikes to destroy the Serb military, cyber-warfare efforts used "soft power" to target Serb leader Slobodan Milosevic's inner circle of advisors, business contacts, and family in an attempt to get him to capitulate to NATO's terms.

Based on these experiences in previous conflicts, the United States recognizes that as much as we can use cyber-warfare to our advantage in a conflict, our adversaries can also utilize it against us. In most cases, we are more vulnerable to cyber-attacks, given our military's dependency on a robust **C4I** (command, control, communications, computers, and intelligence) architecture. For this reason, the military response to cyber-warfare will be addressed in detail in a later section of this chapter.

7.1.2 What Can Cyber-Terrorism and Cyber-Warfare Do?

Cyber-terrorism and cyber-warfare are both focused on information systems and using the many means available (electronic, human, and otherwise) to cause both physical effects and psychological influence. As discussed earlier in this chapter, our society is a networked society, completely dependent on information systems for processing and storing data related to practically every aspect of our daily lives. Even minor disruptions can have major consequences. When a homeowner in Indiana recently received a tax bill for $8 million dollars on a house worth $122,000, the "glitch" also impacted the state tax budget, reflecting a $3.1 million dollar shortfall for the year (Astahost 2006). Such glitches can also have life and death consequences, such as when one such error left five Pacific Island nations off of a tsunami warning list (Song 2006).

One key sector of our economy that depends on information technology is the banking and finance industry. Most everyone has a bank account, and many of us struggle to balance our checkbooks each month. Imagine the global impact if a computer glitch (intentional or not) suddenly caused a "bank error in your favor" and every account holder suddenly had an additional $5,000 in his or her account. Hopefully, if it were your account, you would call the bank before spending it. Many people would not, however, leading to multiple financial problems for the bank, consumers, and merchants when those checks bounced. On a larger scale, banks and businesses do report losses every year due to computer glitches or computer hacking, and these losses have broad economic impact. Dorothy Denning notes that in 2000 alone, computer viruses and hackers were responsible for the loss of $1.6 trillion dollars in the global economy, about $266 billion in the U.S. economy alone (Denning 2004, 93).

Could terrorists or other nations target our banking system with a cyber-attack aimed at crippling our economy and destroying public confidence in our financial institutions? The federal government thinks so, as well as the banking sector. As a result of such concerns, the Clinton administration established a system of **Information Sharing and Advisory Councils (ISACs)** in 1998 in an attempt to foster public-private partnerships in all sectors of our nation's critical infrastructures, including banking and financing. The ISACs were just one recommendation that emerged from a study of our nation's vulnerability to cyber-based threats.

For instance, in 1997, the President's Commission on Critical Infrastructure Protection (PCCIP) published its findings on the vulnerability of our nation's critical infrastructure to terrorism, primarily on using cyber-weapons. In the report, the Commission reported that our nation was ill-prepared for cyber-terrorism or cyber-warfare, identifying the eight critical infrastructures listed below. In the follow-up implementation plan, Presidential Decision Directive (PDD) 63: Critical Infrastructure Protection (May 1998), the Clinton administration assigned each infrastructure to a federal agency for oversight and coordination with the private sector through the ISACs. The eight critical infrastructures and the agencies to which they were assigned are as follows:

▲ Information and communications: Department of Commerce
▲ Banking and finance: Department of Treasury
▲ Water supply: Environmental Protection Agency (EPA)
▲ Aviation, highways (including trucking and intelligent transportation systems), mass transit, pipelines, rail, and waterborne commerce: Department of Transportation
▲ Emergency law enforcement services: Department of Justice

▲ Emergency fire service and continuity of government services: Federal Emergency Management Agency (FEMA)

▲ Public health services, including prevention, surveillance, laboratory, and personal health services: Department of Health and Human Services

▲ Electric power, oil, and gas production and storage: Department of Energy (White House 1998)

The Commission Report also led to the formation of the **Critical Infrastructure Assurance Office (CIAO)** under the Department of Commerce, as well as the National Information Protection Center (NIPC) under the Department of Justice. The CIAO became the center for coordinating the ISAC process and encouraging the private sector to cooperate with the federal government in ensuring it was protecting itself against threats from cyber-terrorism, as well as other threats from both man-made and natural disasters. In other words, cyber-terrorist threats were one of many threats to these critical infrastructures, ranging from insiders, such as disgruntled employees, to cyber-warfare by nation-states, to environmental disasters, such as floods.

The CIAO played a crucial role in coordinating the government response to the Y2K scare. Because it was located in the Department of Commerce, it provided accessibility to government agencies (local, state, and federal) as well as private sector corporations responsible for running our nation's power industries, financial centers, telecommunications systems, and transportation systems—all of which were concerned with a possible cyber-shutdown due to a computer programming error. After the "end of the world as we know it" did not occur on January 1, 2000, most people returned to business as usual in both the public and private sector. Much of the work of the CIAO, which was located within the Department of Commerce to respond specifically to the Y2K problem, was then transferred to the new **National Infrastructure Protection Center (NIPC)**, which was housed in the J. Edgar Hoover FBI Headquarters building in Washington, D.C. Rather than simply addressing the implications of a computer programming error, the NIPC became the operations center for tracking cyber-attacks on the nation's critical infrastructures, utilizing people from the FBI, Department of Defense, intelligence community, Department of the Treasury, and Department of Energy. The component that was missing was the private sector, because most corporations in America, due to the use of proprietary information, did not want to be as open with their company's operations and possible vulnerabilities with military, law enforcement, or intelligence agencies as they were with their Department of Commerce colleagues.

Today, one of the areas of greatest concern with regard to cyber-threats and critical infrastructure is the software and hardware interface referred to as **Supervisory Control and Data Acquisition (SCADA)**. Since 1998, most of the computerized management and switching that occurs in industry, transportation, telecommunications, and so on, has been done by the use of SCADA systems. For instance, to keep trains from colliding, computers are programmed to automatically switch tracks through the use of SCADA systems. Another example of such a system would be a filtration unit on a water treatment plant. If a computer detected a filter had not been changed when it was programmed to do so, the SCADA system would automatically shut the plant down to prevent nonpotable water from entering a city's water supply. If a cyber-attack targeted a SCADA system and changed programming data, you can imagine the potential consequences.

SELF-CHECK

1. Define cyber-warfare.

2. Which of the following is not one of our nation's critical infrastructures vulnerable to a cyber-attack?

   a. Water supply systems
   b. Information and communication systems
   c. Public health services
   d. National park services

3. One of the areas of greatest concern with regard to cyber-threats and critical infrastructure is the software and hardware interface referred to as Supervisory Control and Data Acquisition. True or false?

4. The functions of the CIAO, after the Y2K scare, were initially transferred to the NIPC, which was run by the Department of Defense alone. True or false?

7.2 Assessing Capability and Intent

The intelligence community determines whether a nation-state or non-state actor poses a threat to the United States based on a combination of two variables: capability and intent. Capability refers to the means to inflict harm; intent relates to the broader political goals and objectives of a nation vis-à-vis the United States. For example, Great Britain possesses nuclear weapons (capability), but it does not show the political will (intent) to use them against us; thus, it is not a threat. Similarly, if a nation does not possess capability to do us harm, even though their rhetoric indicates a desire to do so, it is not a threat. During the Cold War, the U.S. intelligence community categorized countries by level of threat (Tier 1, Tier 2, etc.) based on these two criteria of capability and intent.

With the end of the Cold War and the demise of the former Soviet Union and its satellite states, the new threat of global terrorism emerged, to include state-sponsors of terrorism and non-state actors, such as al-Qaeda. Intelligence analysts continue to use a similar spectrum in assessing the level of threat based on the criteria of capability plus intent. This model also pertains to cyber-terrorism and cyber-warfare, with the greatest threat still being a nation-state that has both cyber-warfare capability and the intent to use it against the United States and its allies. Figure 7-1 displays the types of cyber-threats that exist today, based on capability and intent. Here, threats are classified as ranging from hackers to professional information warriors.

7.2.1 Who Can Conduct Cyber-Terrorism and Cyber-Warfare?

Figure 7-1 also shows the range of threats to information systems. The common threat portrayed in this image is the damage that can be done by insiders, or trusted individuals who work at a plant, facility, organization, etc., who have access to critical information architecture such as an information technology expert or systems administrator. Such individuals, if they are bent on causing damage or destruction (intent), clearly possess the capability to do so. However,

Figure 7-1

National Security Threats	Information Warrior	Reduce U.S. Strategic Advantage; Create Chaos and Target Damage; Destroy Critical Infrastructure
	National Intelligence	Gain Information for Political, Military, and Economic Advantage
Shared Threats	Terrorist	Visibility; Publicity; Chaos; Political Change
	Industrial Espionage	Competitive Advantage; Intimidation
	Organized Crime	Revenge; Retribution; Financial Gain; Institutional Change
Local Threats	Institutional Hacker	Monetary Gain; Thrill; Challenge; Prestige
	Recreational Hacker	Thrill; Challenge

INSIDERS

Types of cyber-threats.

the level of threat can vary depending on the motivation. Most insider threats are considered lower-tier threats because they are motivated by revenge due to being fired, demoted, and so on—typically not the same threat posed by an apocalyptic terrorist with insider access, bent on greater destruction or disruption.

Terrorist Groups

To date, the threat from terrorist groups, such as al-Qaeda, using cyber-based weapons has yet to materialize, although evidence exists that they are aware of the capability. We suspect that terrorist groups use the Internet for communication and cyber-reconnaissance of suspected targets. We also suspect they are familiar with the use of standard hacking tools and believe they have been probing our nation's cyber-defenses, looking for weaknesses that could be exploited. For example, in fall 2001, an FBI investigation of cyber-activity turned up significant probing of critical infrastructures in the United States, such as emergency telephone systems, electrical power generation systems, water facilities, nuclear power plants, and so forth (Gellman 2002). Also, captured computers from al-Qaeda training sites in Afghanistan showed an increased level of interest by terrorists in the feasibility of conducting cyber-terrorism, possibly in conjunction with a physical WMD attack. This is one reason that Y2K caused so much concern—it did expose many weaknesses in the information systems involved in operating our nation's critical infrastructures. In addition, recreational and institutional hackers can also expose vulnerabilities, and terrorist organizations can learn from these actions and possibly exploit the weaknesses they expose.

Criminals

In the banking and finance industries, there is more concern over institutional hackers linked to criminal activities than over terrorists. Criminals using identity theft and other cyber-means to gain personal information are routinely robbing banks of millions of dollars each year. Knowing that federal law enforcement officials are not concerned with small dollar amounts (less than $50,000), these criminals go for less conspicuous activity. They also rely on the terrorist threat to gain information, using social engineering tricks (such as impersonating FBI agents) to gain access to financial records (Sullivan 2005). The link to terrorists became clear after the post-9/11 investigations, which showed that fraudulent accounts were used by the terrorists for transferring funds to support the attacks. Bank officials also believe that terrorists are gaining financial support through criminal activity—using the vulnerabilities in the information system, rather than attacking the system—but an actual attack could be only be a matter of time.

Nation-States

The greatest concern at the national level has been (and remains) the threat of cyber-warfare conducted by a nation-state against the United States, either as a act of war, in conjunction with military action, or conducted asymmetrically, attempting to negate America's military superiority by preventing the United States from even being able to deploy its forces overseas. By attacking our critical infrastructures using both conventional acts of sabotage and cyber-warfare, an adversary could do such harm to our nation that our military and economic power could be negated. One such series of incidents that raised these concerns occurred as the United States prepared for Operation Desert Fox in Iraq. Just prior to initiating combat operations, the DoD noticed increased cyber-activity targeting DoD information systems, which appeared to be coming from a Middle Eastern country, possibly Iraq.

The incidents, termed Solar Sunrise, occurred in February 1998, indicating a pattern of behavior that could be considered a threat to DoD information systems. Probing actions by an unknown source caused the DoD to take a number of precautions to protect critical information related to the planning and execution of Desert Fox. The probing incidents were widespread against Air Force, Navy, and Marine Corps information systems throughout the world. After a series of investigations, the "attackers" ended up being two teenagers living in California, who were being mentored by an Israeli, Ehud Tannenbaum, who was only suspected of being a recreational hacker (Global Security, n.d.).

Despite the results of the Solar Sunrise investigation, the cyber-threat from nation-states is real. Beginning in the mid-1980s, foreign intelligence agencies such as the former Soviet KGB and East German STASI were conducting cyber-espionage using third parties. The first documented case occurred in 1986, when a group in West Germany, know as the Hanover Hackers, and their ring leader, Markus Hess, were arrested and charged with espionage. They had hacked into a number of DoD computer systems, stealing classified information and selling it to the KGB and STASI. They were only discovered when a University of California employee, Cliff Stoll, noticed a 75-cent billing error on the university's computer accounts and decided to investigate. He tracked the error to an unauthorized account accessing the Lawrence Berkeley National Laboratories, which was conducing classified work for the DoD. Stoll's pioneering work in computer security and the resulting arrest of Hess were documented in a book, *The Cuckoo's Egg: Tracking a Spy Through the Maze of Computer Espionage.*

Later, an unclassified Defense Science Board report issued in 1996 identified ten countries that were developing capabilities related to information warfare, which included the use of information and computer security. These countries were Russia, China, India, Iran, Iraq, North Korea, Cuba, Libya, Syria, and Egypt. Although it mentioned varying degrees of sophistication, the study concluded that each nation recognized its own vulnerability to cyber-warfare, thus demanding an increase in defensive capabilities, as well as an interest in developing offensive capabilities (Office of the Undersecretary for Defense Acquisition and Technology 1996).

Today, intelligence estimates indicate more than 120 nations are suspected of having some form of offensive cyber-warfare capability (Bayles 2001). Termed **Computer Network Attack (CNA)**, the offensive component of Computer Network Operations (CNO), it is often a simple turning of a switch or a keystroke, which changes the intelligence and espionage function, called Computer Network Exploitation (CNE), into a hostile action. CNE is considered a passive activity because the cyber-sleuth's goal is to remain anonymous and undetected. By going offensive, the "cover" is blown, and a known vulnerability in a computer system used to gain intelligence and information now becomes the same means by which an offensive cyber-attack takes place.

In the future, countries will develop more complex and sophisticated CNA capabilities as a means to offset the overwhelming military superiority of the United States. Seen as a "cheap fix," nations such as China will employ asymmetric tactics to defeat the United States by crippling our nation's capability to even wage war. In a book published in 1999, two Chinese colonels advocated employing such an approach, using cyber-warfare and other means to attack the United States in a future conflict (Liang and Xiangsui 1999). The tactics they advocated to undermine our support networks and digitally destroy critical infrastructure were very much in line with Eastern military philosophy as seen in Sun Tzu's classic *The Art of War,* where the ultimate military goal is to defeat an adversary's will to fight without having to actually enter into military combat (Armistead 2004). What is interesting in the Chinese colonels' text is the assertion that it is not a matter of *if* China goes to war with the United States, but simply *when*.

7.2.2 Tools of Cyber-Terrorism

What makes Computer Network Attacks (CNAs) so pernicious is the universality of the required weapons—in this case, simply a computer and a modem (capability). If an individual or nation-state has the intent, becoming a threat in cyberspace is a relatively easy proposition. The question is the severity of the action and the ability to, in fact, detect where a cyber-attack comes from and how someone is doing it. Current laws do not allow federal government agencies, such as the DoD, from "hacking back" on Internet Service Providers (ISPs) because computer attacks are still initially considered criminal activity, putting them under the purview of law enforcement agencies, such as the FBI, for investigation. In other words, if a system administrator detects a CNA occurring against his or her information system, he or she can only determine the immediate source of the intrusion (ISP), which may or may not be where the attack is originating from. In the case of the Solar Sunrise incidents mentioned earlier in this chapter, the attacks against DoD computer systems appeared to be coming from university computers, such as those at Harvard and Texas A&M, because the Israeli student organizing the attacks knew that security protocols on most university computer systems were lax and easy to manipulate. Only through a thorough investigation of related ISPs did FBI investigators determine the sources of the attacks.

Denial of Service (DOS) Attacks

The most typical CNA is a **Denial of Service (DOS) attack**, which renders a user's computer useless or targets an entire network. These can be done by computer viruses, such as the I LOVE YOU virus detected in 2000, which possibly affected over 45 million users worldwide. This virus caused over $10 billion in damage due to lost revenue, remediation, and so on (Times of India 2000). What made the I LOVE YOU virus so sinister is that it occurred shortly after the MELISSA virus was detected the previous year, which also caused major disruptions worldwide. It appeared that the hacker, in this case, used lessons learned from the MELISSA virus to create a more deadly virus with broader consequences. In other words, instead of just sending an email with an infected file, which when opened could damage other computer files, the newer virus created self-extracting files that proliferated through an affected computer's email address book, sending infected files to one's contacts—which they, in turn, thought were coming from a trusted source. If a terrorist organization or nation-state wanted to use a CNA, they would not have far to go to study the effects of and responses to such incidents to develop an ever deadlier "strain" of computer viruses.

Hacking Tools

Another means of CNA is the use of computer hacking tools that can be used to deface web sites and insert false information. For example, stock market data could be manipulated to show either a loss or gain that did not occur, causing panic selling or buying. Given the current volatility of oil futures and other petroleum markets, you can image what the global consequences of such an attack would be. For this reason, the Securities and Exchange Commission (SEC) is particularly watchful of unusual investor activity and market vulnerability. Another example of this sort of attack would be manipulating data or generating false activity, such as fictitious email, unbeknownst to the user. Can you imagine the reaction on Wall Street if false information on interest rates appeared to be coming from the Federal Reserve?

Synchronized Cyber- and Physical Attacks

Returning to our previous discussion on the use of SCADA and related Digital Control Systems (DCS), one scenario that worries cyber-defenders in the United States is the possibility of terrorists being able to conduct cyber-attacks that are synchronized with physical attacks. In other words, it's not just "digital bullets" that authorities are concerned about, but rather the potential for real physical destruction that could occur from cyber-terrorism due to the linkages between information systems and physical infrastructure. An example would be manipulating a DCS that controls the floodgates for a hydroelectric dam. The fact that one al-Qaeda laptop seized in Afghanistan showed multiple visits to a website known as "the Anonymous Society," with a link to a sabotage handbook that explained how to conduct just such an attack, makes such a scenario plausible (Gellman 2002).

SELF-CHECK

1. The two variables used to assess threats to our nation include capability and access. True or false?

2. Which type of person can do the most damage across all threat levels?

   a. Cyber-terrorist
   b. Trusted insider
   c. Computer hacker
   d. Organized criminal

3. Define Computer Network Attack (CNA).

4. The most common CNA is a Denial of Service (DOS) attack, which renders a user's computer useless or targets an entire network. True or false?

7.3 Assessing Consequences

On March 23, 1996, the RAND Corporation ran an exercise in Washington, D.C. with over 60 participants, using a scenario developed by David Ronfeldt and John Arquilla called "The Day After . . . in Cyberspace." The purpose of the exercise was to assess how our national decision makers would respond to a series of acts related to cyber-warfare coming from an unknown source. In the exercise, what began as cyber-reconnaissance soon developed into cyber-attacks on the nation's banking and financial infrastructure, leading to more targeted attacks on our defense and intelligence communities. The exercise ended with the United States launching a pre-emptive nuclear strike on China, the supposed source of the cyber-attacks, only to realize after that the source wasn't China at all, but rather cyber-terrorists whose goal was to precipitate a global conflict (Anderson 1996).

This could be considered a worst-case scenario of what cyber-warfare or cyber-terrorism could lead to, given the difficulty in actually determining the source of any cyber-attack. Computer forensics is a new and growing discipline, leading to some intelligence agencies coining the phrase **COMPINT,** or computer intelligence—what we can lean from analyzing computer traffic, email, website hits, hard drives, etc. Yet, even though we are learning more about the technology involved, it appears the "bad guys" are also becoming more sophisticated at covering their tracks and using commercial off-the-shelf hacking tools that are readily available (one such tool is called an "anonymizer," which allows you to remain anonymous), leaving less of a signature to follow.

For example, an on-going cyber-sleuth investigation continues under the codename Moonlight Maze. This investigation began in March 1998, after the accidental detection of a series of intrusions into computer databases at the Department of Defense, Department of Energy, NASA, and private universities and research labs doing classified government work. Documents accessed included military installation maps, military organizational information, and military-related research. Although Department of Defense investigators eventually traced the activity back to the former Soviet Union, as of this date, the investigation is still on-going, and the ultimate source of the cyber-intrusions has yet to be determined (PBS Frontline 2006).

7.3.1 Why America Is Vulnerable to Cyber-Terrorism

Although the openness of our democratic society is one of our nation's greatest strengths, it is also one of our greatest weaknesses when it comes to cyber-defenses and protecting ourselves from cyber-terrorism. Information systems and architecture are built for efficiency, not necessarily security. Also, due to the highly competitive commercial marketplace, most companies attempt to get systems and programs out to consumers quickly, before their competition. This results in the later need for a number of software "fixes" or "patches" to correct operational problems or vulnerabilities. In addition, most companies prefer not to spend the extra time and money to enhance computer security, knowing that the average replacement cycle is three to five years anyway due to the speed at which technology develops. Ultimately, profit trumps protection.

The nature of the Internet itself also creates inherent vulnerabilities that were not anticipated when the technology moved from the government into the private sector. When the Internet was developed by analysts at the **Defense Advance Research Projects Agency (DARPA)** in the 1960s, it was designed as an open architecture network operating within a closed system (the Department of Defense). It was based on a system of trust, in which those people with access also had a "need to know" the information that would be shared. The "language" designed to allow this sharing of information packets over the Internet was referred to as Transmission Control Protocol/Internet Protocol (TCP/IP). Today, this could be considered the most widely spoken "language" in the world, as the Internet is now a major means of global communication.

Because the Internet has global connectivity, it remains highly unregulated, either by individual governments or by industry. For this reason, it is considered a truly democratic entity influencing nations and individuals around the world. It is also considered a legal "wild west" in the sense that there is little in terms of legal precedent over content, access, and issues regarding privacy rights. For example, when the USA Patriot Act became law almost immediately after the terrorist events of 9/11, a great deal of controversy arose over the right of government to monitor Internet activity, particularly in public libraries. (This provision was included as part of the USA Patriot Act because the FBI suspected that terrorists were using public library computers to communicate and do research).

Controversy still rages over any government attempt to either restrict Internet access or monitor the communication of private citizens. In 2006, President Bush admitted to authorizing the National Security Agency to monitor phone conversations to private citizens from suspected terrorists living overseas. Although the U.S. attorney general's office declared such monitoring legal, there was a large public outcry over how intrusive the government was in pursuing suspected terrorist activity. There is also some disagreement as to the extent that terrorists use the Internet for communication through the use of special coding called **steganography**, or the embedding of messages or files in computer websites. Knowing that law enforcement and intelligence officials are prevented from accessing pornography sites in the workplace, terrorists are suspected of using steganography in images on such restricted sites, thereby avoiding detection (Kessler 2004).

The same openness principle applies in the use of SCADA and DCS, as previously discussed. Because the computer commands used by this technology to manage controls and switches were originally meant for a closed system, safeguards were minimal. The designers did not expect someone to actually hack in and access these systems. However, cyber-terrorists, bent on attacking the United States using a computer and modem, clearly have the intent and capability to do so. Only since 9/11 have both private-sector and government institutions begun to seriously look at our vulnerabilities and determine ways to better defend the nation from the threat of cyber-terrorism.

7.3.2 The Impact of a Cyber-Terrorist Attack

We've already discussed the types of tools available to cyber-terrorists and what they can do with them. This section deals with the consequences of cyber-terrorism and what these acts could do to us. Being able to turn off the lights in Houston may not be that big a deal, but combine a cyber-attack on the power grid with a conventional explosives attack against a benzene storage facility at the port of Houston, and there is the potential for many more casualties and a high level of confusion. Benzene is a highly toxic chemical that can release a plume cloud. Due to prevailing winds, this would have the same effect as a chemical weapons attack on the city of Houston. If a cyber-terrorist attack occurred at the same time, cutting off power to local hospitals bracing for casualties or water supplies feeding firefighters putting out chemical fires, you can imagine the results. In this case, cyber-terrorism would become a "casualty multiplier," increasing the effect of a conventional weapon attack.

One major consequence of a potential cyber-terrorist attack is the financial impact. For example, the airline industry today is still trying to recover from the effects of 9/11. Immediately after the attacks, both passengers and air crews refused to fly. Many smaller airlines went bankrupt or were forced to merge with larger carriers to survive due to fear of a follow-up attack. Insurance companies also went bankrupt due to the large number of claims, and some smaller businesses went out of business because they couldn't afford insurance against acts of terrorism. Wall Street temporarily shut down. President Bush, in an effort to ease the economic blow of 9/11 on the U.S. economy, told the American people the best thing they could do to support their country was shop. A cyber-attack on the banking and financial sector would have an even greater financial impact because it would have also impacted the public's perception of the safety and security of their investments. This could possibly cause people to hoard money rather than spend it or place it in the bank.

Thus, another consequence of a cyber-terrorist attack is psychological. Banks today do not want to admit to the public how much money they actually lose due to computer glitches, much less criminal or terrorist cyber-robberies. (One source [Acohido and Swartz 2005] puts the annual losses to businesses alone at $48 billion.) Banks fear panic and the loss of public confidence. The government has similar concerns over the loss of public confidence in their capability to provide protection and basic human services after a terrorist incident. We are still assessing the damage done by Hurricane Katrina, a natural disaster, particularly with regard to the poor response by the New Orleans city government, as well as state and federal agencies, such as the Federal Emergency Management Agency (FEMA). When the public loses confidence in the institutions established to provide basic protective services in a crisis, such as the police or their elected officials, the inability to regain that trust can have a long-term effect. Cyber-terrorists can further exploit those seams of public confidence, creating a cascading effect by playing on public fears that are already established. The concern expressed by state and local officials over the federal government's proposed response to a possible bird flu epidemic in summer 2006 reflects just such a scenario, one in which cyber-terrorism could seriously undermine the nation's capability to respond to such a crisis.

FOR EXAMPLE

Bird Flu

The Bush administration issued the *National Strategy for Pandemic Influenza* in November 2005 in response to growing concern over a possible influenza pandemic coming from the H5N1 (bird flu) virus. The *Strategy* provides guidelines on how the United States should prepare now for such an event, and it describes the means available to mitigate the spread of the disease. A key part of the *Strategy* is the capability of our nation's health care infrastructure to respond to the demand of such a pandemic, while at the same time preventing such an event from crippling the nation's economy. The *Strategy* calls for an integrated response from federal, state, and private sector agencies, all of which could be extremely vulnerable to cyber-terrorists should they attempt to disrupt the nation's capability to respond to by attacking the health care infrastructure (Homeland Security Council 2005).

SELF-CHECK

1. Define COMPINT.

2. The use of a cyber-terrorism can be a casualty multiplier during a conventional or WMD attack. True or false?

3. What federal agency developed the Internet?

   a. DARPA
   b. DHS
   c. FBI
   d. CIA

4. Moonlight Maze investigations have determined that the source of the attacks against the Department of Defense computer systems was the former Soviet military. True or false?

7.4 Determining Defenses Against Cyber-Terrorism and Cyber-Warfare

Our nation's first attempts to protect itself in cyberspace occurred during the final days of the Reagan administration in December of 1988. At that time, DARPA provided the charter to the Software Engineering Institute (SEI) at Carnegie Mellon University in Pittsburgh, Pennsylvania, to establish our nation's first national **Computer Emergency Response Team (CERT)**. This was a result of a computer virus (the Morris worm incident) in November of that year that affected 10 percent of the entire Internet system at that time. Even then, computer experts recognized the danger posed to information systems from the effects of viruses, although the focus at the time was not necessarily on terrorist or nation-state threats due to the nature of the technology and its connectivity. They also recognized that the task of cyber-protection was beyond the scope of any one agency. For example, consider the following statement issued by DARPA:

> *Because of the many network, computer, and systems architectures and their associated vulnerabilities, no single organization can be expected to maintain an in-house expertise to respond on its own to computer security threats, particularly those that arise in the research community. As with biological viruses, the solutions must come from an organized community response of experts. The role of the CERT Coordination Center at the SEI is to provide the supporting mechanisms and to coordinate the activities of experts in DARPA and associated communities (Carnegie Mellon University 1988).*

Later, under the Clinton administration, our nation first began to organize its cyber-defenses across various federal government sectors, as a result of the findings published in the President's Commission on Critical Infrastructure Protection (PCCIP) discussed earlier in the chapter. One organization created in 1997 to meet a shortcoming identified in the report was the aforementioned National Infrastructure Protection Center (NIPC), located in the FBI building. Because it was composed of FBI, intelligence community, and Department of Defense personnel, the NIPC went beyond simply cyber-defense to providing an interagency response to cyber-attacks. The NIPC served as an indications and warning (I&W) center, providing proactive alerts and advisories intended to prevent cyber-incidents from spreading throughout government computer systems. The NIPC coordinated its efforts with the CERT at Carnegie Mellon and was also linked to Department of Defense cyber-defense efforts (discussed later).

On the policy side, President Clinton also took the initiative to establish the office of National Coordinator for Security, Infrastructure Protection, and Counter-terrorism, under Richard Clarke. In this capacity, Clarke also served as the administration's "cyber-security czar" responsible for overseeing the nation's cyber-defenses from cyber-terrorist incidents. Clarke was a hold-over when the Bush administration came into office in January 2001, though his position on the National Security Council was less visible under Condoleezza Rice, the new National Security Advisor. After the terrorist attacks of 9/11, Richard Clarke testified before the 9/11 Commission and became a popular media figure due to his pointed criticism of the Bush administration and the president's lack of response to his reported warnings of imminent terrorist threats. Clarke also accused the Bush administration of pressuring him to provide evidence of Iraqi complicity in the 9/11 incidents to justify going to war with Iraq.

In February 2003, the Bush administration issued the *National Strategy to Secure Cyberspace*. One of the first critiques of this plan came from former cyber-security czar Richard Clarke, who claimed that the administration's plan would leave a significant gap in cyber-protection. Yet, three years later, with the normal bureaucratic issues facing any massive government reorganization, the new Department of Homeland Security (DHS) now assumes many of the previously disparate cyber-security functions performed by the CIAO, NIPC, and other Clinton-era agencies under its National Cyber Security Division (NSCD). The NSCD is responsible for the implementation of the president's cyberspace strategy. Figure 7-2 displays the five priorities identified in the *National Strategy* and the correlated responsibilities by sector, both public and private.

Figure 7-2

Roles and Responsibilites in Securing Cyberspace					
	Priority 1	Priority 2	Priority 3	Priority 4	Priority 5
	National Cyberspace Security Response System	National Cyberspace Security Threat and Vulnerability Reduction System	National Cyberspace Security Awareness and Training Program	Securing Governments' Cyberspace	National Security and International Cyberspace Security Cooperation
Home User/Small Business		✗	✗		
Large Enterprises	✗	✗	✗	✗	✗
Critical Sectors/Infrastructures	✗	✗	✗	✗	✗
National Issues and Vulnerabilities	✗	✗	✗	✗	
Global					✗

National strategy roles and responsibilities (President's Critical Infrastructure Protection Board 2003, 9).

7.4.1 The Government and Private Sector Response to Cyber-Terrorism

The *National Strategy to Secure Cyberspace* (2003) further calls for a national effort to accomplish three principal strategic goals:

▲ Prevent cyber-attacks against America's critical infrastructures
▲ Reduce national vulnerability to cyber-attacks
▲ Minimize damage and recovery time from cyber-attacks that do occur

To accomplish these three goals, our nation's cyber-defenses can best be understood in the context of a model organized into four critical processes: *Protect, Detect, Restore,* and *Respond.* See Figure 7-3.

Protect

The first process in the model, *Protect,* involves proactive measures to prevent a cyber-attack, whether that attack is from terrorists or nation-states. Protection involves mainly passive measures taken to safeguard information systems and critical infrastructures. These can be both technical means and non-technical means. For example, a firewall is a technical means to protect an individual computer workstation, as well as a computer server. Computer passwords and anti-virus and anti-spyware programs are other examples of technical means to

Figure 7-3

Defending Information Systems

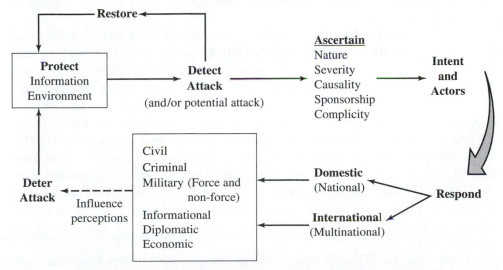

Cyber-defense model (based on Department of Defense 1998).

protect information systems. A non-technical means would be providing physical security around a computer workstation or server complex by locking doors, using cipher-locks for accessing mainframes, providing user education and awareness training, and so on. All these are means to prevent an attack from having negative consequences on individual users' systems. At the national level, prevention takes on larger significance with regard to safeguarding critical infrastructures and their associated information systems. In this case, preventive measures to protect information systems must be assessed within the larger context of the associated information environment. In other words, risk-based assessments must occur because we can't protect everything.

Detect

The next process in the cyber-defense model, *Detect*, is more complex in cyberspace than in a closed system, involving our nation's capability to even know it is being attacked by a terrorist, nation-state, teenage hacker, or possibly even a construction worker's backhoe! Former Deputy Secretary of Defense John Hamre was once quoted as stating that in cyberspace, we may not know we are under attack until it is too late and an "electronic Pearl Harbor" has occurred (Donnelly and Crawley 1999). Detection of cyber-incidents, whether they are actual cyber-attacks or not, requires 24-hour-a-day, 7-day-a-week monitoring to provide adequate indications and warning of an attack. The intelligence community maintains their indications and warnings (I&W) centers to track hostile activities by nation-states deemed to be a threat to U.S. security interests. In addition, because the source of a cyberspace attack may not be known, both the government and the private sector have established a number of **Network Operations Security Centers (NOSCs)** to provide I&W capability in cyberspace.

The Department of Defense originally established their NOSC within the **Defense Information Systems Agency (DISA)** located in Arlington, Virginia. Because this center looked at the global information infrastructure, it was called the Global NOSC, or GNOSC. As we will discuss in the next section, however, the military reorganized after 9/11 to create new command and control organizations to deal with cyber-threats. This included changing the GNOSC to the **Joint Task Force–Global Network Operations (JTF-GNO)**. Each of the military service components also established NOSCs for their own operational commands to provide immediate I&W of an attack on that particular unit's information systems. These service NOSCs were linked to regional and larger operational NOSCs, which were eventually linked to the GNOSC as a means to quickly send information both up and down the chain of command.

The civilian NOSC counterpart was initially the NIPC. It was from this location that the various government agencies could detect cyber-attacks, both on government infrastructure as well as the private sector. After 9/11 and the formation of the Department of Homeland Security (DHS), the NIPC detection function became embedded in DHS's US-CERT Command Center, which is also linked to the national CERT at Carnegie Mellon University, described earlier. These public and private sector centers serve as the conduit of information to first determine whether a cyber-attack or cyber-terrorist incident has occurred. If such an incident has taken place, the centers then ascertain the nature and severity of the attack to determine the appropriate response. But before that occurs, remedial action may be necessary to restore basic services impacted by the incident(s).

Restore

Depending on the complexity of the cyber-attack, the ability to *Restore* operational capacity could range from something as simple as shutting down and rebooting a computer to something as complex as implementing a contingency plan for restoring power, such as by rerouting the power grid. If the attack involves the use of computer viruses, the affected CERTs may issue patches or **Information Assurance Vulnerability Assessments (IAVAs)**, directing system administrators of the necessary remedial actions required to restore the affected information systems. Because incidents of cyber-warfare or cyber-terrorism could lie beneath the radar scope, meaning they may not be visible to most end-users, many remedial actions also fall within the *Restore* category, involving fixes that are made without public awareness. Cyber-warriors in both the public and private sector are charged with defending our nation's critical infrastructure from the effects of these attacks, and they pride themselves on their ability to find solutions and fix problems quickly without disruptions of basic services that put Americans at risk.

Respond

The final process in defending information systems is to determine how to *Respond* to a cyber-attack. After an attack is detected and determined to be a hostile action by either a nation-state or a terrorist organization, a decision must be made on how to respond. The first determination is often whether the incident is domestic or international and whether a U.S. or multinational response is necessary. Because there are no international boundaries in cyberspace, other nations can be affected by incidents detected on U.S. information systems. For this reason, CERTs are connected globally to facilitate communication and cooperation.

The nature of the response to a cyber-attack may further involve an interagency approach, which could include elements of national power (diplomatic, economic, or military) rather than informational power. For example, in 2001, when a U.S. reconnaissance aircraft collided with a Chinese Air Force fighter jet off Hainan Island, Chinese hackers launched an information assault on the United States, involving both overt and covert actions. The U.S. government response was diplomatic, trying to secure the release of the U.S. aircrew and assuage Chinese concern that the incident was intentional. Meanwhile, U.S. citizens, in this case "good" hackers, responded to the Chinese information assaults with "hack-backs" of their own without U.S. government complicity, targeting Chinese government websites (Wallace 2001). Although most of these attacks were simply a nuisance, aimed at defacing websites and making a political statement, they did demonstrate that when it came to cyberspace, anything goes, and the government has little capability to control the private sector. Also, the uncoordinated response to the incident further demonstrated the need for increased cooperation through influence rather than coercion. The potential for a private citizen's actions to provoke a governmental response could increase tensions and lead to physical and not just cyber-confrontation.

Because the Internet and cyberspace remain generally unregulated terrain with little governmental control, the Bush administration's *National Strategy to Security Cyberspace* recognizes that any response system must involve a public-private partnership, including solicitation of the support of "good" hackers to aid in our nation's cyber-defense. Consider the following quote from that document:

> *The National Cyberspace Security Response System is a public-private architecture, coordinated by the Department of Homeland Security, for analyzing and warning; managing incidents of national significance; promoting continuity in government systems and private sector infrastructures; and increasing information sharing across and between organizations to improve cyberspace security. The National Cyberspace Security Response System will include governmental entities and nongovernmental entities, such as private sector information sharing and analysis centers.*

Finally, the end result of any coordinated response to a cyber-incident must also focus on deterrence to prevent future attacks.

7.4.2 The U.S. Military Response to Cyber-Warfare

In the mid-1990s, the U.S. military recognized the growing threat of cyber-warfare to both its informational architecture and the nation's critical infrastructure. Because Department of Defense (DoD) installations in the United States were dependent on civilian infrastructure for communications, transportation, energy, water, and the full range of logistical support, the DoD recognized that a threat to any of these critical systems would directly impact the military's capability to deploy forces against foreign threats and actors. To make matters worse for military planners, the operational environment for these infrastructures was not a series of buildings or hard sites that could be secured with concertina wire and a guard force. Rather, these infrastructures were composed of complex information systems, which presented a whole new set of challenges for security planners. These planners were now faced with the difficult question of how to defend critical infrastructures "over here" to even begin to get military forces deployed "over there" for the next conflict.

Recognizing these new challenges, the DoD began a series of training exercises aimed at testing the vulnerabilities of our nation's critical infrastructures and the information systems on which they depended. The first operational-level exercise, which was conducted in June 1997, was called Eligible Receiver. This exercise involved using National Security Agency (NSA) "hackers" operating as an adversary to attack defense and other government information systems, while also conducting simulated attacks on civilian infrastructure (Robinson 2002). The lessons learned from the exercise showed serious problems with defending the critical information systems and infrastructures on which the DoD (and the nation) depended against cyber-attacks by adversaries who use asymmetrical means to defeat (or simply neutralize) our nation's military strength indirectly.

Later, in December 1998, the Department of Defense took the initiative to create an operational unit to specifically deal with the threat toward DoD information systems posed by cyber-warfare. The Joint Task Force–Computer Network Defense (JTF-CND) was formed as a field operating agency, based in Arlington, Virginia, at the Defense Information Systems Agency (DISA). The JTF-CND would later move to operational control of U.S. Space Command (SPACECOM) in Colorado Springs, Colorado, as a result of changes to the DoD's Unified Command Plan that took effect on October 1, 2000 (Verton 1999). The JTF-CND originally focused only on the defensive aspects of Information Operations (IO) in the military's evolving information warfare doctrine. The JTF-CND would eventually evolve into the aforementioned JTF-Global Network Operations (JTF-GNO) in May 2005, responsible for both offensive and defensive aspects of Information Operations, as part of the organization's realignment under operational control of the **U.S. Strategic Command (STRATCOM)** in Omaha, Nebraska. The JTF-GNO also integrated DISA's former GNOSC and serves as the focal point for the DoD's CERT operations. (See Figure 7-4.)

Before these operational changes took place, the DoD was moving forward with the development of military doctrine to deal with information-age cyber-warfare threats. Although individual service components began considering information warfare as a viable mission area in the mid-1990s, it was several years before the DoD recognized the need to issue joint doctrine with regard to Information Operations (IO). The DoD had previously issued IO policy guidance

Figure 7-4

JTF–GNO command center *(Courtesy of Donna Burton)*.

in the form of a classified DoD directive in 1996. Yet, it was not until the release of Joint Publication 3-13, *Joint Doctrine for Information Operations,* on October 9, 1998, that joint commands began to organize their staffs around the need for IO planning and execution, as well as education and training.

Information Operations emerged from previous joint doctrine involving command and control warfare, based on lessons learned after the first Gulf War and the effectiveness of new information-based technologies for intelligence collection and targeting. IO expanded on the traditional "pillars" of command and control warfare (psychological operations, military deception, electronic warfare, physical destruction, and operations security) by adding computer network defense and the two related activities of public affairs and civil affairs (Department of Defense 1998). IO became the means by which DoD elements would conduct cyber warfare, initially focused on defensive aspects of the cyber-threat. It later expanded to include offensive cyber-warfare planning and execution under the broader category of Computer Network Operations (CNO).

The terrorist attacks against the Pentagon and the World Trade Center in September 2001 provided the impetus for broader DoD organizational changes that impacted the military's capability to carry out and defend against cyber-warfare. The threat posed by al-Qaeda and other international terrorist groups to the U.S. homeland caused the DoD to create a new joint command, U.S. Northern Command, dedicated to the homeland defense mission of the DoD, in support of the nation's overall homeland security effort. This change to the Unified Command Plan (UCP), signed by President Bush in May 2002, further eliminated the U.S. Space Command in Colorado Springs, Colorado, moving most of the space and Information Operations roles of the military to U.S. Strategic Command (STRATCOM) in Omaha, Nebraska. Under STRATCOM, operational control for all aspects of Information Operations, including computer network attack and computer network defense, were consolidated into new organizational structures and responsibilities. The JTF-CND came under STRATCOM's control, for example. Each of the services transformed existing IO organizations into IO "commands" to provide the service components in support of the joint command structure.

The military's information-age transformation signals recognition that threats to the nation's (and military's) information systems will remain. Whether the threat of cyber-warfare comes from a terrorist organization or a nation-state, the DoD's reorganization at the joint combatant command level, as well as the service component level, will better position the military to face these information age threats. One significant problem remains, however: The DoD does not control access to, nor does it defend, the nation's critical infrastructures on which military power rides. Whether it's the nation's rail and transport system, global telecommunications architecture, or power grid, the DoD is dependent on having access to these systems. Even the DoD's logistics system cannot function in getting troops and supplies to Iraq or other future conflict areas without the help of commercial transportation and private companies such as FedEx or UPS. A cyber-attack on any of the information systems that manage these critical infrastructures would have devastating effects on our military's capability to provide for our nation's defense both here and abroad.

Because cyber-terrorism and cyber-warfare are relatively new concepts, the nature of the threat posed by terrorists or even nation-states using technology in this manner remains controversial. Some critiques argue that our nation's infrastructure is not that vulnerable to these types of attacks because the infrastructure is so complex and has multiple redundancies built into it, such as the power grid and telecommunication networks. They also contend that our economy is resilient to potential cyber-attacks and such efforts would only prove a temporary setback, as evidenced by the events of 9/11 (Ranum 2004). On the other hand, members of Congress, the military, and others charged with providing for our nation's defenses against all enemies do not take the threat lightly and continue to reassess and re-evaluate both the ability and intent of our adversaries to harm us in cyberspace (Hildreth 2001).

SELF-CHECK

1. Define CERT.

2. The three principal goals of the *National Strategy to Secure Cyber-space* include preventing cyber-attacks against America's critical infrastructures, reducing national vulnerability to cyber-attacks, and minimizing damage and recovery time from the cyber-attacks that do occur. True or false?

3. Which military command runs the JTF-GNO?
   a. U.S. Space Command
   b. U.S. Northern Command
   c. U.S. Central Command
   d. U.S. Strategic Command

4. The military's first operational-level exercise focused on the threat of cyber-warfare was conducted in June 1997 and was called Eligible Receiver. True or false?

SUMMARY

Former Secretary of Defense Donald Rumsfeld categorized the threats our nation faces in the future as "known knowns, known unknowns, and unknown unknowns" (Rumsfeld 2006). With regard to threats in cyberspace, much remains within the "unknown unknowns" category because the most significant attacks we have experienced to date may still be unknown. The consequences may only come to light after the fact or after a policy or operational decision is made based on insufficient knowledge. Such situations have happened before. However, in cyberspace, the consequences may not become "known knowns" until it is too late, and the repercussions of those actions could have far-reaching implications.

In this chapter, you learned how to assess information-based threats to our nation's critical infrastructure. You evaluated the difference between capability and intent with regard to cyber-terrorism. In addition, you appraised the consequences of cyber-terrorism and its effect on our nation's critical infrastructures; and you leaned how to judge our nation's defensive and offensive capabilities concerning cyber-warfare. Although many uncertainties about the nature of the threats we face in cyberspace still remain, our nation and others continue to develop cyber-defenses against the threats we currently face, as well as those we anticipate in the future.

KEY TERMS

C4I	The organizational architecture used by the U.S. military; stands for command, control, communications, computers, and intelligence.
COMPINT	Abbreviation for computer intelligence, or what we can learn from analyzing computer traffic, email, website hits, hard drives, and so on.
Computer Emergency Response Team (CERT)	One of several organizations that provide the supporting mechanisms necessary for researching and responding to computer security threats.
Computer Network Attack (CNA)	The offensive component of Computer Network Operations, in which the intelligence and espionage function is changed into a hostile action.
Critical Infrastructure Assurance Office (CIAO)	Federal center for coordinating the ISAC process and encouraging the private sector to cooperate with the government in protecting itself against cyber-terrorism and threats from man-made and natural disasters.
Cyberspace	The notional environment in which digitized information is communicated over computer networks.
Cyber-terrorism	The use of computer-based operations by terrorist organizations conducting cyber-attacks that compromise, damage, degrade, disrupt, deny, and destroy information stored on computer networks or that target network infrastructures.
Cyber-warfare	Conflict between nation-states using cyber-based weapons.
Defense Advance Research Projects Agency (DARPA)	Agency within the Department of Defense that created the foundations of the modern Internet in the 1960s.
Defense Information Systems Agency (DISA)	Home of the original NOSC established by the Department of Defense,

	also called the Global NOSC or GNOSC because it looked at the global information infrastructure.
Denial of Service (DOS) attack	Most common type of CNA, in which an individual computer or entire network is rendered useless, such as by the actions of a virus.
Information Assurance Vulnerability Assessment (IAVA)	An assessment issued by a CERT that directs system administrators regarding the necessary actions required to restore information systems affected by a cyber-attack.
Information Sharing and Advisory Council (ISAC)	One of a number of groups established by the federal government in 1998 to foster public-private partnerships in all sectors of the nation's critical infrastructures.
Joint Task Force–Global Network Operations (JTF-GNO)	The organization created from the Global NOSC after 9/11 to generate new military command and control capabilities for dealing with cyber-threats.
National Infrastructure Protection Center (NIPC)	Federal operations center for tracking cyber-attacks on the nation's critical infrastructure.
Network Operations Security Center (NOSC)	One of a number of centers established by government and the private sector to provide indications and warning capability in cyberspace.
Steganography	The practice of embedding messages or files in computer websites.
Supervisory Control and Data Acquisition (SCADA)	Software and hardware interface used for most of the computerized management and switching that occurs in industry, transportation, telecommunications, etc.
U.S. Strategic Command (STRATCOM)	Located in Omaha, Nebraska, one of nine regional and functional combatant commands, with responsibility for Information Operations.

ASSESS YOUR UNDERSTANDING

Go to www.wiley.com/college/kilroy to assess your knowledge of the basics of cyber-terrorism and cyber-warfare.
Measure your learning by comparing pre-test and post-test results.

Summary Questions

1. Cyber-warfare is conflict between nations using information-based weapons. True or false?
2. Threats are defined as possessing both capability and intent. True or false?
3. The Internet was developed by DARPA. True or false?
4. CERTs are located only in the United States to detect and respond to cyber-attacks. True or false?
5. Saddam Hussein was the source behind the Solar Sunrise computer hacking incidents in 1998. True or false?
6. Information Operations (IO) emerged from previous joint doctrine involving command and control warfare. True or false?
7. Which of the following is not a part of our nation's critical infrastructure?
   (a) Banking and finance centers
   (b) Water supplies
   (c) Power facilities
   (d) Manufacturing centers
8. The greatest threat, at all security levels, is posed by which of the following?
   (a) Institutional hackers
   (b) Insiders
   (c) Organized crime
   (d) Recreational hackers
9. An example of a terrorist organization using steganography would involve which of the following?
   (a) Embedding a coded message on a computer website
   (b) Hacking into a government website to deface the site
   (c) Leaving a coded message at the scene of a terrorist attack
   (d) Providing false information on captured computer files
10. The US-CERT, under the Department of Homeland Security, now coordinates the cyber-defense efforts previously performed by which of the following agencies?
    (a) CIAO
    (b) NIPC

(c) Both of the above

(d) None of the above

Applying This Chapter

1. If you were a system administrator and asked to construct a cyber-defense model for your government agency or private company, what critical processes would you include?

2. You have detected some unusual activity on your computer, such as strange characters and emails. This concerns you because your company is responsible for the computerized switches (SCADA) that control the rail tracks up and down the East Coast. To whom should your report this activity and why?

3. As a county or city manager of a small rural community in the Midwest, you may feel safe from terrorist incidents, particularly cyber-terrorism. Yet, your community depends on a number of critical infrastructures that could be impacted by cyber-attacks. Compile a list of all the critical infrastructures in your community that could be susceptible to cyber-terrorism, and select the four most essential to your community's safety and security.

4. You are a military officer assigned to U.S. Northern Command, helping to coordinate our nation's cyber-defenses. You have been asked to speak to a local Rotary Club about how the Department of Defense is organized to conduct cyber-warfare. Explain the Department of Defense contribution to fight cyber-terrorism.

Defending Cyberspace

You work at a Network Operations Security Center (NOSC) for a Department of Defense agency. You've been advised that one of your subordinate commands has been attacked by a computer virus, which is causing all the connected information systems on that base to crash and individual operators to lose critical information on their operating systems. Evaluate what you would do and how.

Cost vs. Risk at the Office

Your private company needs to update its computers and servers. You've researched a number of options and recommended a secure replacement system. Your boss tells you the computer operating system you've selected costs too much and to look for cheaper options. What do you do? Generate a policy memo to your boss explaining the cost versus risk involved in going with a less expensive operating system.

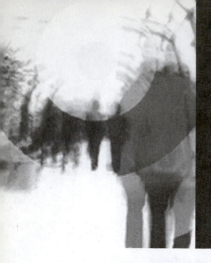

8

WEAPONS OF MASS DESTRUCTION
Understanding Weapons That Can Create a Catastrophic Event

Starting Point

Go to www.wiley.com/college/kilroy to assess your knowledge of the basics of weapons of mass destruction.
Determine where you need to concentrate your effort.

What You'll Learn in This Chapter

▲ The difference between conventional and radiological terrorist incidents
▲ The types and sources of radiation and radiological contamination
▲ The types and sources of chemical and biological weapons
▲ The consequences and management of a weapons of mass destruction event

After Studying This Chapter, You'll Be Able To

▲ Evaluate the types of chemical, biological, and radiological weapons and the nature of their employment
▲ Assess the availability and applicability of weapons of mass destruction by terrorist groups
▲ Estimate the consequences of the use of a weapon of mass destruction in creating a catastrophic event
▲ Assess the threat of terrorists using weapons of mass destruction and the potential impact on the United States

INTRODUCTION

In 2002, the National Security Strategy included the statement that "[t]he gravest danger our [n]ation faces lies at the crossroads of radicalism and technology." The reference to technology meant the ability of terrorists to obtain weapons of mass destruction (WMDs), defined as chemical, biological, or radiological weapons that can be used to create a catastrophic event. Other literature, particularly government sources, prefers to use the term CBRNE (chemical, biological, radiological, nuclear, and explosive) rather than WMD to describe the entire toolbox of weapons capable of creating a catastrophic event.

In this chapter, you will evaluate the different types of chemical, biological, and radiological weapons, as well as the nature of their employment. You will also assess the availability and applicability of WMDs by terrorist groups and estimate the consequences of the use of a WMD in creating a catastrophic event. Finally, you'll assess the threat of terrorists using weapons of mass destruction and the potential impact of such an attack on the United States.

8.1 Chemical Weapons and Their Consequences

Of the three types of WMDs (chemical, biological, and radiological) addressed in this chapter, **chemical weapons** (weapons consisting of toxic or otherwise harmful chemicals not specifically of biological origin) have been the most prolific and most readily available to armies throughout the world. Their use in conventional warfare further lends itself to a continuing concern that terrorist groups would consider them to be a low-cost, effective means to accomplish their objectives. When the U.S. military invaded Iraq during the First Gulf War in 1990, they were prepared to fight in an operational environment that would include chemical weapons because Saddam Hussein was known to possess them and had used them in previous conflicts, even against his own countrymen, the Kurds. When the U.S. military invaded Iraq during the Second Gulf War in 2003, again military planners expected that such weapons would be used by the Iraqi forces. When such weapons were not used and large stockpiles were not discovered, it raised concern that Saddam may have shipped these weapons to other nations in the region, such as Syria, with the possibility that they could end up in the hands of terrorist organizations.

8.1.1 History of Chemical Weapons Use

Chemical weapons are not new. They have existed for centuries in various forms and uses. In 423 BC, allies of Sparta in the Peloponnesian War took an Athenian-held fort by directing smoke from lighted coals, sulfur, and pitch through a hollowed-out beam into the fort. The Greeks invented Greek firs, a combination of rosin, sulfur, pitch, naphtha, lime, and saltpeter. This floated on water and was especially effective in naval operations. Defending armies in the Middle Ages used boiling oil to create blistering effects on their adversaries. Even gunpowder was invented as a result of chemical reactions to create an explosive effect.

Today, chemical weapons are typically identified by their weaponized characteristics, primarily from use in World War I. Most people are familiar with the use of mustard gas or chlorine gas, primarily by Germany beginning in 1915. From that point on, military personnel had to be prepared to fight with gas masks in a contaminated battlefield. More recently in wartime, Iraq used chemical agents, primarily mustard gas and nerve gas, against Iran in its conflict in the 1980s, as well as against its own people, including in an attack on the Kurds in Northern Iraq in 1988 that killed 5,000 (Why Files n.d.). The most recent example of the use of chemical weapons was in 1995 when the Japanese terrorist organization Aum Shinrikyo (which means "Supreme Truth") used sarin gas in a Tokyo subway, where 12 people were killed and over 5,000 injured (Beckman 2003).

8.1.2 Chemical Agents and Their Effects

Chemical agents are classified according to physical state, physiological action, and use. The broad categories of chemical agents are as follows:

▲ Pulmonary agents, such as phosgene and chlorine
▲ Blood agents, including hydrogen cyanide and cyanogen chloride
▲ Vessicants, such as mustard (H, HD), lewisite (L), and phosgene oxime (CX)
▲ Nerve agents, such as tabun (GA), sarin (GB), soman (GD), GF, and VX
▲ Incapacitating agents, such as glycolate anticholinergic compound (BZ)

The sequence of symptoms following exposure to chemical agents varies with the route of exposure. Although respiratory symptoms are generally the first to appear after inhalation of nerve agent vapor, gastrointestinal symptoms are usually the first after ingestion. Tightness in the chest is an early local symptom of respiratory exposure. Symptoms progressively increase as the nerve agent is absorbed into the circulation, whatever the route of exposure. Following comparable degrees of exposure, respiratory manifestations are most severe after inhalation, and gastrointestinal symptoms may be most severe after ingestion. The lungs and eyes absorb nerve agents especially rapidly. In high vapor concentrations, nerve agents are carried from the lungs throughout the circulatory system; widespread systemic effects may appear in less than one minute. Toxic effects of chemical agents also depend on the dose (amount or concentration) of the chemical.

Table 8-1: Toxicological Data on Several Chemical Agents

Route	Form	Effect	GA	GB	GD	VX	Dosage
Eye	Vapor	Miosis	—	<2	<2	<0.09	$mg \cdot min/m^3$
Inhalation	Vapor	Runny nose	—	<2	<2	<0.09	$mg \cdot min/m^3$
Inhalation	Vapor	Incapacitation	—	35	35	25	$mg \cdot min/m^3$
Inhalation	Vapor	Death	135	70	70	30	$mg \cdot min/m^3$
Percutaneous	Liquid	Death	4,000	1,700	350	10	mg

(Source: Federation of American Scientists, http://www.fas.org/cw/cwagents.htm)

Table 8-1 illustrates the routes of entry to the body of nerve agent chemicals, the physical form each agent takes, the agent's effect on the body, the lethal dose measure, and some of the measurement units that are used to calculate the dose. The values are estimates of the doses that have lethal effects on a 70-kilogram man. Effective dosages of vapor are estimated for exposure durations of two to ten minutes.

Because they are easier to produce, store, and disperse than biological agents, chemical agents have been the most prevalent and diverse of the group of agents available to manufacture WMDs. Researchers potentially could produce numerous variations and formulations of chemical agents much more easily than could be done with biological agents. Hiding chemical weapon production in commercial production systems can also be accomplished more easily.

As previously mentioned, chemical agents affect the body by different routes depending on the type of agent. Inhaled agents (gases, vapors, and aerosols) will impact the respiratory system. Absorption agents (liquids and solids) can affect skin, eyes, and mucous membranes, as well as the gastrointestinal tract, by being absorbed through wounds and abrasions. For this reason, military forces worldwide must be prepared to operate in a potential chemical environment.

8.1.3 The Threat of Chemical Weapons and Terrorism

Due to the documented effects of chemical weapons on the battlefield and the large numbers of chemical weapons still in existence today, nations have worked to reduce their availability and possible use through treaties and other agreements. Following World War I, many nations signed the Geneva Protocols in 1925 banning the use of chemical weapons. However, this did not stop Japan from using such weapons against China, or Italy from using them against Ethiopia in the 1930s.

FOR EXAMPLE

Chemical Weapons Training

The U.S. military prepares its forces for dealing with the effects of chemical weapons on the battlefield by various means, including the use of chemical protective equipment, such as gas masks and special uniforms with charcoal liners, as well as specialized training. Most veterans will recall their experiences in the "gas chamber" during basic training, when they are required to remove their gas masks and be exposed to CS (riot control) gas. They are also instructed on the use of atropine injectors as a means to counteract the effects of nerve agents. Military personnel are also trained to recognize the use of chemical weapons on the battlefield and to mark areas as being contaminated and by what type of agent—persistent or non-persistent. They also learn how to decontaminate themselves and their equipment. A full description of the types of measures employed can be found in the *U.S. Armed Forces Nuclear, Biological, and Chemical Survival Manual*, Appendix C, which also provides detailed information regarding specific chemical agents and effects (Couch 2003).

A more comprehensive effort to ban the use of chemical weapons was undertaken by the United Nations in 1992, when the Convention on the Prohibition of the Development, Production, Stockpiling, and Use of Chemical Weapons and on Their Destruction was adopted by the UN General Assembly. Referred to as the Chemical Weapons Convention (CWC), it went into force in 1997 with the addition of Hungary as the sixty-fifth nation to ratify the treaty. Today, over 140 nations have signed the CWC, promising to "prohibit all development, production, acquisition, stockpiling, transfer, and use of chemical weapons" (United Nations 2007).

The CWC also requires all nations that have signed the treaty to destroy existing chemical weapons, as well as any chemical weapons production facilities that may still exist. It additionally requires member states to destroy any chemical weapons they have located in other nations, such as stockpiles left by the United States in Europe or Korea after World War II. The treaty also impacts the private sector by placing controls on civilian chemical industries to ensure that they are not producing or exporting certain chemical agents that are critical for the development of chemical weapons by non-signatory states or terrorist groups. The Convention further addresses the need for member states to assist other member states when a nation violates the treaty and uses chemical weapons against that state.

The problem, however, is that terrorist groups do not abide by international law or any recognized international convention, such as the CWC. Due to these groups' desire to create a catastrophic effect, chemical weapons are ideal weapons of choice because of their continuing availability worldwide. Nations such as the United States have made a concerted effort to abide by the CWC agreements, destroying stockpiles of chemical weapons in places such as Dugway Proving Grounds in Utah, where the Department of Defense has been utilizing large incinerators since 1996 to destroy rockets with chemical warheards. However, other countries do not have the same safeguards in place, such as those nations of the former Soviet Union where accountability procedures are more lax and the documentation of chemical weapons storage, destruction, and dissemination is less rigorous. Terrorists who want to employ chemical weapons may thus be able to take advantage of existing stockpiles of weapons, or to develop their own newer and deadlier agents.

In addition to obtaining existing chemical weapons, there is also the potential for terrorist organizations to attack commercial chemical storage or production facilities. By using conventional explosives against these facilities, terrorists can create a WMD effect through the release of toxic chemical fumes into the atmosphere, which, depending on atmospheric conditions, can affect large population centers in the United States and elsewhere. Communities located near such facilities are vulnerable to these types of attacks, as evidenced by accidental explosions that have occurred in the past.

For instance, the worst industrial accident in the United States occurred on April 17, 1947, in the port of Texas City, Texas (35 miles from Houston), when a fire in the hold of a cargo ship, the *Grandcamp*, led to a series of explosions. The explosions were a result of the cargo the ship was carrying: ammonium nitrate, sulfur, and other toxic chemical products. The explosion was of such magnitude that it also destroyed nearby petroleum refining facilities and other cargo ships. The resulting physical damage, as well as fires and toxic cloud that lasted four days, eventually killed over 500 people and wounded 3,500 others (Texas City Disaster n.d.).

SELF-CHECK

1. Because chemical weapons have been banned by a United Nations treaty, they no longer exist in the world today. True or false?

2. Chemical agents include which of the following?

   a. Pulmonary agents
   b. Blood agents
   c. Nerve agents
   d. All of the above

3. Define weapons of mass destruction (WMDs).

4. Sarin is an example of a chemical agent that affects the body by exposure of the lungs. True or false?

8.2 Biological Weapons and Their Consequences

Humans have attempted to employ **biological weapons** (weapons consisting of biological or living organisms or toxins) since long before there was any factual knowledge of the causes of disease. The bodies of disease victims were used to poison water or to spread disease by contact, and bodies were even catapulted into besieged cities. In one example, the Venetian historian Gabriel de Mussis described the siege of Kaffa on the Crimean coast (the present-day city of Feodosia in Ukraine) by the Tartars in 1345. After a three-year siege, plague broke out among the Tartars, probably carried in from Asia by rats in their own ships. In 1348, Kaffa finally fell after the Tartars catapulted their plague dead over the walls and into the city. In another case, in 1422, infected cadavers and manure were catapulted into the city during the siege of Carolstein (Derbis 1996). These methods were inglorious and barbaric means of spreading death, and thus are not often reported in the documented history, poems, and songs relating battles in our past. Conventions agreed to from recent world wars ban the use of these methods of death and destruction. Of course, determined groups, such as terrorists, will readily ignore battlefield conventions if conquest or power depends on the outcome of their struggle.

8.2.1 History of Biological Weapons Use

Some epidemiologists attribute the 1352 epidemic of bubonic plague in Europe, the "Black Death," to the early crude attempt at biological warfare described in the siege of Kaffa. After the city fell, refugees fleeing Kaffa by ship may have initiated this plague pandemic that spread throughout Europe from seaport to seaport (Derbis 1996). As you will recall, during the siege of Kaffa, the Tartars flung dead plague victims into the besieged city, which spread the disease within the walls of the city. The siege was lifted by the Tartars, however, because of the huge toll the plague took on them. The besieged refugees then escaped Kaffa and landed in Genoa, spreading plague throughout Italy, and from there through the entire continent of Europe.

Transmission of disease through contaminated water, as well as through fomites (objects) such as blankets or clothing, has been another common method of warfare. For instance, the retreating U.S. Confederate forces in 1864 contaminated the water supply of their pursuers by driving sick farm animals into ponds and shooting them.

During World War I, in addition to the chemical warfare mentioned previously, soldiers on both sides tried to spread diseases of horses (glanders) to devastate the enemy cavalry. Fifty thousand horses in the French Army alone were infected with this condition. Because the mortality and morbidity of the disease rendered horses incapable of performing service, this was a serious and costly problem.

FOR EXAMPLE

Biological Warfare in the Americas

A famous story of biological weapon use is that of the Spanish conquistador Francisco Pizarro, who in 1533, during his conquest of what is now Peru, is said to have spread smallpox (an unknown disease in South America at that time) by dispensing infected clothing to the natives. This tactic was also used again in the French and Indian War in North America during the l750s. As the Native Americans gained strength in this war, a commander-in-chief of the British forces devised a plan to offer blankets from Fort Pitt's smallpox hospital to the Native American fighters besieging the fort as a peace offering. Within months, it was reported that smallpox was raging in the Ohio River Valley and the direct threat of the local Indian tribes was dissipated (Jones 2007).

Biological and chemical weapon research was extensively carried out during World War II, but neither type of weapon was used in major battles. For instance, England developed anthrax as a weapon against beef and dairy cattle in an operation called "Operation Vegetarian." The anthrax was packed in 5 million "cakes" to be dropped over grazing livestock in Germany, thus further demoralizing the already starving population. The island of Gruinard, which was used for testing the anthrax, was so contaminated that it was off limits until the late 1980s. The conventional military "Operation Overlord" during this time was so successful at hastening the end of the war, however, that Operation Vegetarian was never deployed. It is also suspected that the use of air power and the potential of seeing chemical or biological weapons rained down upon populations of soldiers or civilians kept leaders from using these weapons on each other.

More recent cases of biological weapons use since World War II have included the use of ricin as an assassination weapon in London in 1978, and the accidental release of anthrax spores in Sverdlovsk in 1979. In the London incident, the ricin was delivered via a capsule in an umbrella. The victim was injected with the tiny pellet while waiting for a bus. The assassination technology was supplied by the former Soviet Union.

Later, in 1990, the Iraqis filled 100 R400 bombs with botulinum toxin, 50 with anthrax, and 16 with aflatoxin. Other weapons were similarly prepared. In the course of an August 1991 inspection, representatives of the Iraqi government announced to leaders of the United Nations Special Commission that they had conducted research into the offensive use of *Bacillus anthracis, Clostridium botulinum,* and *Clostridium perfringens.*

In addition, a few anthrax-tainted letters mailed in the United States in late 2001 caused the evacuation of government offices and crippled our postal system for a short period of time. Even though there have not been further biological attacks on the United States, nor a massive chemical, biological, or radiological "Pearl Harbor," the U.S. government must be vigilant and investigate all reports and incidents of use of and research on these weapon types. There are endless delivery systems available, including the fomites of the past, human carriers, insect carriers, and weapons systems such as rockets, aerial bombs, and spray tanks. For instance, after 9/11, agricultural spray systems were thoroughly reviewed to prevent any other system being hijacked for terrorist purposes.

8.2.2 Biological Agents and Their Effects

There are many biological agents that exist today, both in natural form and in research laboratories throughout the world. The most commonly existing agents are typically in the form of bacteria, viruses, and toxins. A list of past and potential future biological agents is found in Table 8-2.

The effects of a biological weapon attack may not be immediately known, due to inability of medical personnel to properly diagnose the symptoms. Because smallpox has been eradicated in the United States for decades, many medical students who have not encountered the illness overseas may not immediately recognize the symptoms and may thus treat it like the common flu. Only when enough people fall sick with a disease, with common symptoms, does the medical alert system kick in, allowing for the proper diagnosis, treatment, and containment of the disease. Since 9/11, the medical profession has taken notice of the threat of biological agents being used by terrorists, and many hospitals across the country are conducting exercises for their personnel to better detect a possible biological outbreak and respond in a timely and appropriate manner.

8.2.3 The Threat of Biological Weapons and Terrorism

Just as with chemical weapons, the international community response to biological weapons has been to seek a ban on their production and use. Although the 1925 Geneva Conventional Protocols recognized the need for a restriction on the use of biological weapons on the battlefield, it wasn't until 1972 that the United Nations drafted the Biological Warfare Convention (BWC), seeking to end the production and use of such weapons. The United States signed the BWC in 1972; however, in 1969, President Nixon had already unilaterally ended the U.S. offensive biological weapon program, vowing to never use biological weapons. The United States destroyed all stockpiles of biological weapons and has since limited its work on biological agents to strictly defensive means. The **United**

Table 8-2: Biological Agents

Common Name	Scientific Name
Bacterial Agents	
Anthrax	*Bacillis anthracis*
Brucellosis	*Brucella spp*
Glanders and melioidosis	*Burkholderia mallei, Burkholderia pseudomallei*
Plague	*Yersinia pestis*
Q-Fever	*Coxiella burnetii*
Tularemia	*Francisella tularensis*
Viral Agents	
Smallpox	*Variola virus*
Venezuelan equine encephalitis	*Alphavirus*
Viral hemorrhagic fevers	*Hemorrhagic fever virus*
Biological Toxins	
Botulinum	N/A
Ricin	N/A
Staphylococcal enterotoxin B	N/A
Mycotoxins	N/A

States Army Medical Research Institute of Infectious Diseases (USAMRIID), located at Ft. Dietrick, Maryland, continues to research biological weapons and their use, maintaining small strains of agents but purely for developing defenses against such weapons.

As previously mentioned, within several weeks of the terrorist attacks on the United States in September 2001, a series of incidents caused a great deal of panic about what appeared to be follow-up biological warfare attacks. Letters containing anthrax were mailed to public officials, such as Senators Leahy and Daschle, as well as media figures like Tom Brokaw. The first victim of handling anthrax-tainted mail was a clerk at a small newspaper in Boca Raton, Florida. In the end, 5 people died and 22 were hospitalized due to inhalational anthrax. The tainted mail was traced to post offices in Florida, New York, Washington,

D.C., New Jersey, and Connecticut. Post office facilities were closed in Washington, D.C., for over a year, and Senate office buildings in Washington were evacuated (Partnership for Anthrax Vaccine Education 2003).

As a result of these incidents in 2001, people were quarantined, mail was microwaved, and radiation was used at some postal centers. The antibiotic Cipro was given to a large number of potentially exposed people in the Florida, New York, Washington, D.C., New Jersey, and Connecticut post office areas as a prophylactic against possible exposure. A USAMRIID employee was questioned about his possible link to the attacks; however, no arrests or convictions have been made in the case to date.

SELF-CHECK

1. Which of the following is not classified as a biological agent?
   a. Polonium
   b. Ricin
   c. Viruses
   d. Bacteria
2. What is the USAMRIID?
3. The United States ratified the Biological Weapons Convention in 1972, but it had already decided it would never use biological weapons as early as 1969. True or false?
4. The anthrax incidents that occurred in the United States shortly after 9/11 were found to have been caused by terrorists. True or false?

8.3 Radiological Weapons and Their Consequences

The use of **radiological weapons** (weapons consisting of radiological material) or nuclear terrorism produces more fear and outrage than the use of conventional weapons or the other WMDs discussed previously. There are several reasons for this:

▲ A nuclear weapon explosion is much more powerful than any conventional explosive.
▲ Health effects can be long-lasting and delayed.

▲ The fear factor exploited by terrorists in choosing a nuclear radiation weapon can be extremely effective.

▲ Harmful radiation following a visible and powerful explosion is invisible and undetectable by human senses. This unknown, unseen danger creates extreme stress, which adds to the complications of managing a nuclear incident.

We tend to think of nuclear incidents in terms of "accidents" at nuclear facilities during the recent history of nuclear power. The Chernobyl accident just passed its twentieth anniversary in 2006, and the effects are still very visible in the environment surrounding the Chernobyl nuclear power plant in Ukraine (see Figure 8-1). Three Mile Island, near Harrisburg, Pennsylvania, is another nuclear accident that plays a large part in our perception of nuclear power gone awry, although there were no lasting environmental effects from that incident in 1979. The other part of the nuclear terror equation is the use of a nuclear material in the production of nuclear weapons. We have less personal experience with the effects of nuclear weapons, but the pictures and stories of the effects of U.S. nuclear weapons on Nagasaki and Hiroshima in Japan at the end of World War II will always evoke horror, revulsion, and fear.

FOR EXAMPLE

The Chernobyl Nuclear Accident

The worst nuclear power accident in history occurred on April 26, 1986, in Chernobyl, Ukraine, which was at that time part of the USSR. The accident was caused by human error when engineers at the plant ignored safety procedures while going through a series of tests on reactor number 4, leading to a chain reaction in the reactor core, a massive explosion, and a partial meltdown. At least 30 people died in the initial explosion and exposure, and over 135,000 were exposed to excessive radiation as the first responders (called liquidators) tried to contain the damage. The nearby city of Pripyat (50,000 residents) had to be evacuated. Today, Pripyat remains a ghost town, and the entire area 30 kilometers around the accident site remains mostly uninhabited.

The exact health effects of the Chernobyl disaster remain in dispute. Official International Atomic Energy Agency reports state that only 56 deaths can be directly attributed to the accident, although groups like Greenpeace put the figure in the tens of thousands. Regardless of this disagreement, the accident directly impacted the growth of nuclear power sources both in the United States and abroad, as many nations considered the benefits of cheap energy to not be worth the risk of a nuclear accident.

Figure 8-1

View of the sarcophagus surrounding the reactor at Chernobyl, Ukraine, on the twentieth anniversary of the disaster (Courtesy of Cliff Hollis).

Fear and dread of accidents has effectively shut down the development of new nuclear power plants in the United States. Economic, health, and safety factors were also reasons for this slowdown. Recent improvements in designs for nuclear power plants have begun to change this perception (Global Nuclear Energy Partnership n.d.), along with rapidly increasing energy prices.

However, the deliberate sabotage of nuclear power plants is just one terrorist scenario taking advantage of current public fear, lack of adequate security at nuclear power plants, and the tremendous quantity of fissile material present in the world. The primary concern today of most security experts is the acquisition of a nuclear weapon, "the bomb," by a terrorist organization and the detonation of such a weapon in a major population center in the United States. Therefore, this section addresses this threat in more detail than the previous WMD threats of chemical or biological weapons. We will examine the complexities of nuclear and radiological weapons by discussing nuclear material and its effects, the history of nuclear weapon development, and finally the actual threat of the use of a nuclear or radiological weapon by terrorist groups today.

8.3.1 Radiological Materials and Their Effects

A relatively small amount of **highly enriched uranium (HEU)** or even less plutonium is needed to build a nuclear bomb, and obtaining this material is the difficult part of construction. It is possible, however, that terrorists could steal enough HEU to make one or more weapons. HEU theft is the most worrisome security risk because making a bomb with HEU is relatively straightforward. In addition to HEU, plutonium stockpiles are available throughout the world, although bomb construction with plutonium is more difficult.

Let's answer a few questions about nuclear material and radioactivity at this point. First, what do we mean by radioactive? Radioactive isotopes are created by nuclear fission of uranium-235 (U-235, a natural source) when it decays into other isotopes and loses particles in that decay process. The radiation is produced as particles are lost. Thus, the term "radioactive" refers to materials that give off particles and produce radiation energy at a certain rate. Soil or rock containing natural uranium at a concentration of 0.3 percent or more is considered radioactive. Table 8-3 lists the various radioactive particles given off by U-235 decay, their penetrating abilities, and their health effects.

A second factor to consider is that of **half-life**. What, exactly, does this term refer to? During the decay process of the original isotopes mentioned above, half of the material will be converted to another isotope. The length of this decay process time is called the half-life of that isotope. (The half-life for uranium-235, for example, is 704 million years.)

A third important question is, What are the health effects of nuclear material? When discussing health effects, several terms for dose are used. The most familiar one is the **Rad**, a radiation-absorbed dose. Several other units are also now being used. An online converter can be found at http://online.unitconverterpro .com/unit-conversion/convert-alpha/radiation---absorbeddose.html.

Table 8-3: Radioactive Particles Resulting from U-235 Decay

Particle	Made Of	Penetration and Health Effects
Alpha	2 protons and 2 neutrons	Travels 5–8 cm in air; does little cell damage but toxic if ingested
Beta	Electrons	Travel further than alpha rays; can be stopped by wood or metal, as can alpha particles
Gamma	Electromagnetic radiation	Most harmful and similar to toxic rays; can penetrate shields and the human body, but can be stopped by lead
Neutrons	Quarks	Consist of ionizing radiation caused by collision with other atoms; transfer energy the same as gamma rays

All exposures in humans to ionizing radiation carry a risk of biological damage. Exposure to natural background radiation is very small. However, radiological emergencies may expose people to a widely varying amount of radiation, depending upon the nature of the incident, the type of radiation involved, and even the weather.

When assessing the amount of exposure in any situation, a number of factors must be considered, including the following:

▲ The nature of the ionizing radiation
▲ The strength of the source
▲ The biological sensitivity of the exposed area
▲ Exposure factors such as time, distance, and shielding from the source

Calculating these factors is called a dose assessment.

When a nuclear bomb is exploded, the **fissile material** (uranium-235 or plutonium-239) causes a chain reaction of rapid nuclear changes, resulting in the release of several types of radiation. After the blast (explosion) energy is released, a shock wave and fierce wind are produced, and radioactive particles are spread throughout the blast area and into the air. The particles can travel worldwide from any nuclear explosion depending on winds and weather. The gamma rays remain dangerous for 704 million years. The size of the bomb can range from the size of those used at Nagasaki (21 kilotons, known as "Fat Man") and Hiroshima (15 kilotons, known as "Little Boy") to 100 mega tons, which is the size of the largest bomb ever in existence, a thermonuclear bomb tested by Soviet Union. (An interesting website to view interactive videos of the nuclear bombs Fat Man and Little Boy can be found at http://www.atomicarchive.com/movies/movie3.shtml.)

A fourth question related to nuclear weapons concerns the terrorism risk: Where would terrorists find fissile material for making a bomb? The most likely source would be "loose nukes," or unsecured nuclear weapons in Russia and its former territories. Russia still has the largest stockpile of nuclear weapons in the world, despite years of weapons treaties and weapons reduction and destruction. Unstable governments with high crime rates add to the risk of theft.

In addition to Russia, there are 40 other states in the world with about 2,070 tons of weapons-usable material, which is enough to make more than 130,000 nuclear weapons (Bunn 2002). India and Pakistan still openly produce weapons-usable material, and Russia continues to produce 1.2 tons of weapons-grade plutonium per year in its power plants. Israel refuses oversight, but it is suspected of producing nuclear material. Iran and North Korea are actively working to produce it. The U.S. stopped producing fissile material for weapons in 1992. Several countries still separate weapons-unstable plutonium from civilian reactor fuel every year.

Making enough fissile material for weapon construction (35 pounds of uranium-235 or 9 pounds of plutonium-239) is a decade-long and expensive task.

This fact in itself has limited nuclear weapon proliferation. However, the power and prestige that accompanies a "nuclear power" state leads many developing countries to spend precious resources on nuclear development. Twenty-eight states have sought nuclear weapons, and eight currently have them. Four additional states had them and gave them up. In total, there are currently approximately 22,000 nuclear weapons in the world (Bunn 2002).

8.3.2 History of Nuclear Material Discoveries and Weapons Development

Sources place the beginning of the "Atomic Age" in 1895, with the discovery of x-rays by Wilhelm Roentgen of Germany (Atomic Archive n.d.). One year later, in 1896, French physicist Antoine Henri Becquerel discovered radioactivity. In his experiments, he found that uranium could produce "rays" that would pass through paper and glass to darken a photographic plate, and that these rays possessed an electric charge. Then, in 1897, J. J. Thomson of Britain discovered the electron, and in 1899, Ernest Rutherford discovered two kinds of rays emitting from radium: alpha and beta rays. Thus, at the end of the 1890s, the "Nuclear Age" was well under way.

In the 1900s, further parts of the nuclear picture were discovered. Radioactive decay theory was published by Ernest Rutherford and Frederick Soddy, who also coined the word "isotope." The discovery of natural radioactivity won Becquerel and Pierre and Marie Curie a Nobel Prize in 1904. In 1905, Albert Einstein published the special theory of relativity ($E=mc^2$). By 1919, Rutherford was credited with inducing the first artificial nuclear reaction by bombarding nitrogen gas with alpha particles, thus obtaining atoms of an oxygen isotope along with protons. (A video animation of this reaction can be seen at http://www.atomicarchive.com/mediamenu.shtml).

By the end of the 1920s, Heisenberg, Max Born, and Schrodinger had formulated quantum mechanics and the uncertainty principle. The cyclotron was developed, and atomic transmutations (nuclear reactions) became much easier to create. In the 1930s, this equipment, along with a high-voltage accelerator, was used to discover deuterium, the neutron, and in 1934, Enrico Fermi unknowingly achieved the world's first nuclear fission using these past discoveries. By 1939, President Franklin D. Roosevelt learned that Einstein had suggested the possibility of a weapon using uranium fission. Fusion was also recognized as a source of the sun's energy in the same year.

In the 1940s, German scientists also began conducting tests of nuclear fission, with the goal to produce a fission weapon. In 1941, American physicists confirmed that a newly discovered element, plutonium, was fissionable and usable for a bomb. In December of the same year, President Roosevelt authorized the secret Manhattan Engineering Project, later to be called the Manhattan Project, to build a nuclear bomb.

By 1945, a successful test of the first atomic bomb, the Trinity test, was carried out at Alamogordo, New Mexico. In August of the same year, "Little Boy," a uranium bomb, was dropped on Hiroshima, Japan. Between 80,000 and 140,000 residents were killed. Three days later, "Fat Man," a plutonium bomb, was dropped on Nagasaki. About 74,000 people were killed. The world gasped at the news. By the end of 1946, the Atomic Energy Commission (AEC) took over the nuclear weapons program from the Army. Within a year, the Soviet Union and Britain were in the nuclear weapons club as well.

In the 1950s, hydrogen fusion bombs (thermonuclear bombs), intercontinental ballistic missiles, and atomic powered submarines were being developed. In 1957, the United Nations **International Atomic Energy Agency (IAEA)** was created. This was due to the fact that there were now enough nuclear facilities in the world to warrant inspection by a multinational group to ensure that reactors and plants were being run for peaceful purposes.

By the end of the 1960s, France and China were added to the nuclear weapons club, and the first preliminary Strategic Arms Limitation Treaty talks took place. The world had begun to see the extreme dangers of unlimited nuclear weapons proliferation. These talks would continue for years to come.

In 1979, the Three Mile Island Nuclear Power plant near Harrisburg, Pennsylvania, suffered a partial core meltdown. This was not the first nuclear power plant disaster, but it was a wake-up call to the idealist view that nuclear power would be an unlimited and totally safe source of power for the United States.

Today, energy is a central issue in many ways. Though there have been some close calls in the past (the Cuban missile crisis in 1960s, for example) nuclear weapons have not been deployed since World War II. Nuclear weapons have accumulated in the world, but no members of the original nuclear weapons group—Russia, Britain, the United States, France, and China—have seriously considered using them in an all-out war, instead maintaining a nuclear balance of power. However, possession of energy sources, particularly fossil fuels and nuclear energy, has become the new source of political power and strife in the twenty-first century.

Terrorist use of money from fossil fuel wealth in the Middle East and possession, proliferation, or illegal commerce of nuclear material by terrorist groups has become a complex web, supported by global communication and internationally connected criminal gangs. The recent radiation poisoning of a former Soviet spy, Alexander Litvinenko, by the use of polonium-210 (a rare radiological source which has a street value of approximately $2 million dollars per gram), possibly coming from Chinese sources, evinces the complex linkages in international crime syndicates, terrorist organizations, and even governments (Dastych 2006). The official version of the story coming from the investigation into Litvinenko's death involves a plot by the Russian government to have him killed due to his knowledge about President Putin's use of the successor agency to the

KGB (the FSB, or Federal Security Service) to assassinate his opposition, including Russian billionaire Boris Berezovsky. Litvinenko also described other actions by the FSB aimed at supporting Russian President Putin's rise to power in Russia. Litvinenko fell ill in London in November 2006. His death was later attributed to radiation poisoning, determined through the detection of polonium-210 in his blood.

8.3.3 The Threat of Nuclear Weapons and Terrorism

What are the forms a likely terrorist nuclear incident would take in the twenty-first century? There are several paths that a terrorist group or a rogue state could take. States such as North Korea and possibly Iran, for example, could be producing plutonium for weapons, or they could be in the process of using black-market highly enriched uranium for weapons construction. Iran's uranium enrichment plant at Natanz, for instance, purportedly for peaceful nuclear power production, has set up a series (cascades) of gas centrifuges used to enrich uranium. It was expected to have installed five cascades, each containing 164 centrifuges, but has not yet begun to operate the second and third cascades. It had informed the IAEA of its plans to install the first 3,000 centrifuges at Natanz's underground halls by the last quarter of 2006. It appears at this time that Iran will not meet this deadline. This plan has sparked an international debate over Iran's intentions in operating nuclear facilities and doing research on nuclear energy (Shire and Albright 2006).

There are suspicions that Iran may also have other undetected facilities that are being prepared for deployment of additional cascades of centrifuges needed in the production of nuclear weapons-grade fissionable material, but there is no evidence of this from IAEA inspections. Iran continues to declare that it has a right to do research in nuclear energy for peaceful purposes, or for whatever else it desires.

Even though IAEA inspections are permitted in most countries with interest in nuclear energy, including Iran, the danger of clandestine or stolen nuclear weapons proliferation adds to the uncertainty of these weapons production sources. There are numerous sources of excess weapons-grade materials vulnerable to theft in Russia and the United States. A theft or black-market sale of these ready-made materials to terrorists is probably the most serious nuclear terrorism threat to the world today.

For example, in his testimony before the U.S. House Subcommittee on Strategic Forces on July 26, 2006, Matthew Bunn reported that "[t]he biggest risks of nuclear theft are at small, vulnerable facilities with plutonium or highly enriched uranium (HEU) . . ." He continued to note that "[w]ith respect to nuclear theft and terrorism, HEU poses a somewhat greater threat than plutonium, as only HEU can be used to achieve substantial nuclear yields in the very simplest gun-type devices. Nevertheless, the possibility that terrorists could make a crude nuclear bomb from stolen plutonium cannot be ruled out." Using stolen stored HEU in an explosive device or making a nuclear bomb would be a possibility with cataclysmic results.

Bunn's report also stated that Russia, after disposing of 34 tons of excess weapons-grade plutonium, would still have well over 100 tons of this material remaining, enough to support a stockpile of over 20,000 nuclear weapons. The United States would have over 50 tons of weapon-grade plutonium remaining, enough to support a stockpile of over 10,000 nuclear weapons. The National Academy of Sciences (NAS) recommends that the process of disposing of 34 tons of excess Russian and 34 tons of excess U.S. weapon-grade plutonium be undertaken as soon as possible, with all safety, security and standards met. This would not be an assurance against nuclear theft or terrorism, but it would demonstrate a commitment to nonproliferation and would reduce the cost and danger of plutonium storage at scattered sites throughout the United States.

Storage of excess weapons-grade plutonium has been a topic of hot debate in nonproliferation talks for years. In a 2000 nonproliferation treaty agreed to by the United States and the other nuclear weapon states, one of the 13 steps in the agreement was to place excess nuclear material under IAEA monitoring and then carry out disposition. The United States has been reluctant to carry out the agreement, however.

In February 2006, the U.S. Department of Energy (DOE) Global Nuclear Energy Partnership (GNEP) announced an initiative to promote peaceful nuclear energy use worldwide. Small-scale light water reactors are preferred in this report. However, careful consideration of the risks of this technology is still needed.

Radioactive material stolen from or produced in any kind of nuclear facility, particularly in the form of shipments of radioactive material, could still be used in a **dirty bomb**, or a conventional explosive used to spread radioactive material. This could disrupt an entire city or region. It would not be as devastating as a nuclear weapon but would intimidate the public with a fear of radioactivity. Any radioactive material, including low-level waste from medical facilities, could be used in a dirty bomb. Examples are technesium-99m, iodine-131, and tritium H_3. Cleanup and re-entry after a dirty bomb explosion would be a long process. Because terrorists are interested in disrupting (if not destroying) societies, this would appear to be an ideal mechanism. It would be relatively limited in a worldwide sense, yet extremely disruptive. Stolen nuclear warheads deployment by terrorists also seems to be a remote but not unthinkable possibility in the nuclear terrorism picture. Therefore, according to the majority of experts, the most likely nuclear scenarios (from least likely to most likely) are as follows:

1. Sabotage of current nuclear power plants
2. Development of clandestine reprocessing and/or enriching facilities
3. Use of stolen black market weapons, spent fuels, and/or other low-grade radioactive material for "dirty bombs"

Prevention of such incidents and of the proliferation of weapons-grade materials in the world has taken the energy of many diplomats and policy makers over the years. Information on possible secret weapons production in non-nuclear nations has been constantly provided by surveillance networks of satellites. Political, financial, and trade sanctions have been used in instances in which nuclear production has been documented, such as in North Korea. In cases such as that of North Korea, the threat of nuclear development was a bargaining chip for the country, although one that caused tremendous suffering of the populace.

8.3.4 Managing Radiological Incidents and Their Aftermath

A bright light, tremendous explosion, high winds, heat, and "mushroom cloud" would indicate a true fission or fusion weapon attack. This is the least likely method of terrorist radiological attack according to most experts. A second and more likely attack would be the use of a conventional explosive with a "dirty" radioactive package included. Radioactive material would thus be scattered across the debris field. Victims would be killed or injured by the explosion, and people and the environment would be contaminated by the radioactive material to a distance that would depend on the size of the explosion and the weather patterns at the site. Detection of the radiation in an attack by a dirty bomb might be delayed until emergency personnel with detection devices arrived.

To prepare for either type of attack, the first defense, if there is warning, would be to seek shelter from the blast. The penetration capability of blast fire and radiation can be deflected by terrain features such as hills, mountains, fallen trees, caves, or a good foxhole. Quickly seeking the best shelter available in the case of a brief warning is the best a person can do in the case of a nuclear blast. Reinforced concrete structures offer the most protection, followed by reinforced masonry-brick houses, and finally other structures. When inside a structure, getting below ground can reduce radiation by a factor of ten (Couch 2003). The "duck and cover" drill of the 1950s remains a simple rule of action that is still pertinent today following warning of a nuclear attack.

Immediately following a nuclear attack or a radiological dirty bomb explosion (if it is detected), emergency personnel and victims must assume radioactive contamination. Covering your mouth with a wet cloth reduces the contaminants entering the body. Unfortunately, radiation sickness symptoms other than nausea and vomiting may not appear until days after exposure. However, medical, military, and HAZMAT (hazardous material) personnel may have personal dosimeters that indicate exposure levels and can be used to predict gamma radiation.

HAZMAT personnel must be relied upon in the case of a nuclear blast or a dirty bomb, to ensure isolation and decontamination of victims and to evacuate the affected area. Decontamination will involve the following process:

1. Decontamination of the individual
2. Decontamination of casualties and victims

3. Decontamination of the uninjured public
4. Decontamination of the environment (i.e., filtering drinking water)

Chemical decontamination is an emergency, but radiological contamination is not considered to be if both were to happen simultaneously. This is because life-threatening medical conditions take precedence over radiological contamination of victims (Couch 2003).

Rapid washing of the hair and skin and discarding of clothing can remove 95 percent of radiological contamination. It is seldom possible for a living patient to contaminate or threaten medical personnel; therefore, contaminated victims' wounds should be rinsed and cleaned so that particulate material is removed. Any radioactive debris material emitting alpha, gamma, or beta rays can cause extensive local damage in a wound site and could be redistributed in the bloodstream to damage internal organs as well. Usually burns will accompany wounds, and because radioactive materials can be embedded in a charred area, excision of the wound is appropriate. Burn protocols should be observed by medical personnel, except that radioactive debris and tissue should be safely handled and disposed of by radiation technical personnel.

Treatment following a radiological attack would have to include more than just physical medical care and decontamination as described above. Treatment of the aftereffects of undetected exposure would require a well-organized network of medical, emergency, public, and military communication. Mental health concerns have also recently been shown to be very important. Communication to the public to combat fear and hysteria would be of paramount importance. As in any emergency situation, whether a natural disaster, an all-out war, or a terrorist attack, a smoothly operating command and control protocol system in civilian and military organizations is critical. Communication to the public should be an integral part of this protocol.

Education of all members of society on risks, actual dangers, current personal protection actions, and family action plans is crucial in preparing against a radiological threat. Locations of local shelters, local emergency communication, medical treatment protocol in radiological emergency situations, and long-term effects are also important preparations that need to be made. Breaking through the apathy of the public regarding the likelihood of a radiological attack is a difficult task, but a critical one. Because of this apathy, the public is not very aware of the special catastrophic effects of a nuclear attack. In addition, very little information is provided to the public by any level of government. Local health departments, local emergency management offices, and other agencies are consumed with preparations for natural disasters and managing the effects of other environmental hazards. Scenarios for nuclear attack do not have a high priority in preparedness drills because the risk for nuclear attack is lower than other forms of attack. The proven unpredictability of terrorists, however, should warn us that what seems the most unlikely form of attack is potentially the one that will be next on the terrorist agenda.

SELF-CHECK

1. The threat of a terrorist organization obtaining and detonating a nuclear bomb is the most likely nuclear terrorism scenario. True or false?

2. What is fissile material?

3. Which of the following is the combination of a conventional explosive with radioactive material?
   a. Rad
   b. Half-life
   c. HAZMAT
   d. Dirty bomb

4. Alpha, gamma, or beta rays can cause extensive local damage in a wound site, and they could be redistributed in the bloodstream to damage internal organs as well. True or false?

SUMMARY

> But even as Third Wave armies hurry to develop damage-limiting precision weapons and casualty-limiting non-lethal weapons, poorer countries are racing to build, buy, borrow, or burgle the most indiscriminate agents of mass lethality ever created; chemical and biological as well as atomic. Once more we are reminded that the rise of a new war form in no way precludes the use of earlier war forms—including the most virulent weapons.
> —Alvin and Heidi Toffler, *War and Anti-War: Survival at the Dawn of the Twenty-first Century* (1993)

Even though the above passage was written in 1993, these futurist authors predicted the dawn of the terrorist age with an eerie accuracy. According to FEMA, the effect of biological, chemical, and nuclear weapons of mass destruction relies on their punch per pound. To produce the same number of deaths within a square mile, they estimate that it would take 705,000 pounds of fragmentation cluster bomb material; 7,000 pounds of mustard gas; 1,700 pounds of nerve gas;

11 pounds of material in a crude nuclear fission weapon; 3 ounces of botulism toxin type A; or half an ounce of anthrax spores. Terrorists weighing potential death and damage against the costs and invisibility of the range of weapons may choose the more costly but more concealable material. This puts biological, chemical, and nuclear materials at the top of the list of choices for mass destruction. Explosive devices of all kinds can be used in conjunction with these weapons in innumerable combinations.

In this chapter, you evaluated the types of chemical, biological, and radiological weapons and the nature of their employment. You assessed the availability and applicability of weapons of mass destruction by terrorist groups and estimated the consequences of the use of a WMD in creating a catastrophic event. In addition, you assessed the threat of terrorists using WMDs and the potential impact on the United States.

The key to terrorist success appears to be the recruitment of talented, creative, and inventive idealists who work not only on the potential use of WMD technology, but also on psychological, physical, and social means to destroy culture and human civilization. The challenge to democratic societies will be to find the means to counter the use of such weapons, in the first place, and if they are used, to recover quickly and not allow a catastrophic terrorist event using WMDs to have its intended consequences.

KEY TERMS

Biological weapons	Weapons consisting of biological or living organisms or toxins.
Chemical weapons	Weapons consisting of toxic or otherwise harmful chemicals not specifically of biological origin.
Dirty bomb	A conventional explosive used to spread radioactive material.
Fissile material	Uranium-235 or plutonium-239, the primary materials used to trigger the chain reaction involved in a nuclear explosion.
Half-life	The length of time required for half of an amount of radioactive material to be converted to another isotope during the decay process.
Highly enriched uranium (HEU)	One of the primary ingredients for building a nuclear bomb.
International Atomic Energy Agency (IAEA)	The United Nations agency charged with inspecting nuclear reactors and power plants throughout the world.

Rad	Radiation-absorbed dose; a unit used to measure exposure to nuclear material.
Radiological weapons	Weapons consisting of radiological material.
United States Army Medical Research Institute of Infectious Diseases (USAMRIID)	Institute located at Ft. Dietrick, Maryland, that researches biological weapons and their use and maintains small strains of agents for the purpose of developing defenses against them.

ASSESS YOUR UNDERSTANDING

Go to www.wiley.com/college/kilroy to assess your knowledge of the basics of weapons of mass destruction.
Measure your learning by comparing pre-test and post-test results.

Summary Questions

1. The term "weapons of mass destruction" has traditionally been used to describe the use of chemical, biological, and radiological weapons. True or false?

2. The United States still reserves the right to use biological weapons if attacked with such weapons. True or false?

3. The radiological materials required to construct a dirty bomb are difficult to obtain; thus, the possible use of such a weapon by terrorist organizations is slim. True or false?

4. Which of the following is not contained in the definition of CBRNE?
   (a) Chemical weapons
   (b) Explosive weapons
   (c) Notional weapons
   (d) Biological weapons

5. Which of the following are fissionable materials?
   (a) Plutonium-239
   (b) Uranium-235
   (c) Neither a or b
   (d) Both a and b

6. Which of the following countries currently have uranium enrichment plants potentially capable of producing weapons-grade HEU, which could be a source of weapons-grade material to terrorist organizations?
   (a) North Korea and Iran
   (b) Iraq and Syria
   (c) Indonesia and Vietnam
   (d) Cuba and Libya

7. Which of the following are not biological weapons materials?
   (a) Sarin
   (b) Anthrax
   (c) Plague
   (d) West Nile virus

8. What is the first thing you would notice in a nuclear explosion?

    (a) A terrible odor in the air

    (b) A blinding light

    (c) A loud explosion noise

    (d) A mushroom-shaped cloud

9. Which of the following ways can a chemical weapon enter the body?

    (a) Through the lungs

    (b) Through the skin

    (c) Through the blood

    (d) All of the above

10. How can you partly protect yourself from the blast wave from a nuclear explosion?

    (a) Climb a tree

    (b) Get behind a building

    (c) Get in a ravine

    (d) Put on protective clothing

Applying This Chapter

1. You are serving in the State Department on a counter-proliferation task force. What countries would you be most concerned about with regard to developing nuclear weapons in the future? What would be the "indicators" to look for when determining such a capability? What policy options exist for helping deter nations from seeking to develop nuclear weapons capability?

2. In a classroom discussion, another student makes the point that nuclear terrorism is not a serious concern in the United States because it would be virtually impossible to smuggle a nuclear weapon into the country. How would you respond? What other scenarios would you offer, other than the use of a nuclear bomb, that terrorists could use to create a WMD effect within the United States?

3. Your local community is planning a training exercise to prepare for a possible biological terrorism incident. What considerations would you recommend including for such an exercise? What local agencies and individuals would your include in this exercise? Why?

YOU TRY IT

Dirty Bomb v. Dirty Air

Provide an analysis of the effect of a conventional weapon attack on a chemical storage facility. Write a paper that explains the dangers of such an attack in terms of the capability to create a WMD effect. Research chemical storage facilities in the United States and their relative location to large urban population centers. Compare and contrast the potential damage from the "fallout" of such an attack to the use of a dirty bomb in the same location.

Radiological Sources

Analyze the availability of sources of radiological material that could be used in the construction of a dirty bomb. Identify countries where such sources exist and the safeguards that either exist or do not exist to locate and protect these sources. What policy recommendations would you make for the United States to help countries do a better job of protecting these sources of radiation?

9

DOMESTIC TERRORISM
Understanding the Nature of Domestic Terrorist Threats and Counterterrorist Responses

Starting Point

Go to www.wiley.com/college/kilroy to assess your knowledge of the basics of domestic terrorism.
Determine where you need to concentrate your effort.

What You'll Learn in This Chapter

▲ The nature of the domestic terrorist threats facing the United States
▲ The American operational environment and how it contributes to terrorist activity
▲ The nature of counter-terrorism in the United States

After Studying This Chapter, You'll Be Able To

▲ Assess the types of domestic terrorist threats
▲ Evaluate the structure and nature of terrorist threats in the United States
▲ Judge the operational environment that motivates and enables terrorism in the United States
▲ Critique counter-terrorism and how it reflects American traditions of the rule of law

INTRODUCTION

This chapter focuses on domestic terrorism and counter-terrorism. It involves learning about terrorist groups that form and/or conduct terrorist campaigns against domestic and foreign targets inside the U.S. homeland. Furthermore, we will look at recruiters for foreign terrorist groups that raise funds and enlist people for terrorist operations against U.S. or foreign interests overseas. As you may or may not expect, terrorism has a long history inside the United States, stretching back to the colonial period. Additionally, there are a wide variety of terrorist groups that have operated and/or continue to operate inside the United States. Not all of these threats are from foreign terrorists. In fact, the majority of terrorist activity inside the United States comes from domestic groups hoping to influence or change any number of political or social policies. At the same time, we do face ongoing threats from foreign terrorists attempting to penetrate the homeland security network.

Overall, what we see is a wide range of threats against American interests. Because of this variety of domestic terrorist threats, the United States is required to develop a flexible plan to secure the country. This **counter-terrorism policy** (set of laws, agencies, and programs targeted at controlling and reducing terrorist threats) must address the threat of both domestic and foreign groups. Meeting these threats means identifying the sources of threats, assigning the cases to the appropriate government agencies, and applying the best strategies to eliminate the threats. One cannot apply the same tactics and strategies to defeat domestic terrorists as one would use against foreign terrorists. Different sets of laws, criminal procedures, and strategies are needed to effectively meet these terrorist threats.

In this chapter, you will assess the types of domestic terrorist threats that impact the United States. You will also evaluate the structure and nature of terrorist threats in the United States today, as well as judge the operational environment that motivates and enables terrorism in the United States. Finally, you will critique counter-terrorism and how it reflects American traditions of the rule of law.

9.1 Analyzing the Domestic Terrorist Threat

This discussion begins with an analysis of terrorism in the United States. Terrorism in America has a long history, stretching back to the eighteenth century at about the time of the American Revolution, and it continues to the present. As an overview, note that the United States faces three types of terrorist threats:

▲ **Homegrown terrorist groups**, whose members originate within American borders and conduct operations against targets inside the United States.

▲ **Foreign terrorist groups**, whose operatives originate in countries outside the United States and conduct operations against internal targets.

▲ **Foreign terrorist organizers**, including foreign recruiters and planners who raise funds and enlist operatives for operations against U.S. and other national interests overseas.

To date, within the United States, the most prevalent domestic terrorist threat has come from homegrown terrorists. Statistics from the Worldwide Incidents Tracking System, provided by the National Counterterrorism Center (http://wits .nctc.gov/), show that between January 2004 and March 2006, there were 14 terrorist incidents inside the United States, producing nine injuries. Of these terrorist attacks, over half were committed by either the Earth Liberation Front or the Animal Liberation Front (otherwise known as ELF and ALF, respectively), domestic terrorist groups attempting to change policy regarding the environment and treatment of animals in medical testing. Although such incidents do not come close to the magnitude of the threats from foreign terrorists that occurred with the September 11, 2001 attacks, they do remind us that domestic terrorism does exist in a variety of forms and contexts.

9.1.1 Overview of Domestic Terrorism

Evaluating trends in domestic terrorism provides a picture of the types of groups in the United States and shifts in terrorist violence over time. First, however, a cautionary note is needed. Information on terrorist events is not complete. Out of approximately 518 domestic terrorist attacks from 1968 to 2006 documented by the Memorial Institute for the Prevention of Terrorism (based on the RAND/St. Andrews Chronology of Terrorist Events), only 443 are attributed to a specific group. Thus, 14.5 percent of these events can not be placed in any meaningful category. We do not know who conducted the attacks, or for what purpose. Additionally, not all terrorist events are listed as terrorist offenses. Some events, such as white supremacist attacks on immigrants or attacks on abortion clinics in the United States, are likely underreported because they are categorized as criminal offenses. Hence, the information provided here presents a reasonable picture of terrorism in the United States, but this picture is not complete.

Beginning with a broad overview of terrorism in the United States, we note the following trends.

▲ Homegrown terrorists account for the largest number of terrorist incidents in the United States. Based on statistics, homegrown terrorists account for 77 percent of all terrorist acts in the United States. There is no single decade from the 1960s through today during which foreign terrorist incidents exceeded homegrown terrorist incidents.

▲ During most decades, right-wing and religious terrorism were the dominant forms of terrorism in the United States. This trend changed in the last few years (2000–2006), during which ideological (or left-wing) terrorism became dominant. Ethno-national terrorism was also a threat from 1970 to 1990, driven by Puerto Rican nationalists and various forms of **émigré terrorism** (foreign victims killed by foreign terrorist groups). By the last decade of analysis, however, ethno-national terrorism disappears.

▲ Anti-Castro Cuban terrorism has been the most prevalent terrorist threat in the United States, accounting for 32 percent of all terrorist activity. Furthermore, because this form of terrorism was, for the most part, anti-Communist in nature, it falls into the category of right-wing terrorism. As such, anti-Castro Cuban terrorism statistically accounts for 56 percent of right-wing terrorism in the United States.

▲ Finally, in most years, terrorist activity was located in major urban cities such as New York, Washington, Miami, Chicago, Los Angeles, and San Francisco. As the ideological terrorist campaigns took off in the late 1990s, however, we observed a shift in terrorist violence away from major urban areas toward suburban and rural areas.

Summarizing this information, we can make several conclusions about broad statistical trends. Terrorism in the United States has been largely homegrown and ideological, shifting away from the urban centers toward more rural environments. Also, historically, foreign terrorist threats have not been a major problem within the United States. This does not diminish the significance of events such as 9/11 in identifying a new terrorist threat. Rather, the statistics tell us that the United States faces other terrorist threats inside our boundaries as well. Terrorist incidents do take place in the United States, and these threats are not all coming from Islamic extremists located in the Middle East and Central Asia.

One additional comparative note should be made here. Despite the terrorist events that have occurred in the United States, the number of terrorist incidents is not as high as in other countries. For instance, in the United States from January 2004 to March 2006, there were 14 terrorist events. During the same time frame, there were 156 terrorist incidents in Britain, 149 incidents in France, and 27 incidents in Saudi Arabia. Thus, when putting the data in perspective, we see terrorism is a problem in the United States, but it is not as prevalent as in other countries. Moving past the big picture into the various forms of terrorist threats (i.e., homegrown, foreign terrorists, foreign terrorist organizers), we do observe a variety of mini-trends. We now turn our attention to these subsets of terrorist activity.

9.1.2 Homegrown Terrorists

The homegrown terrorist threat consists of groups that form on American soil and conduct operations against targets in the United States. These targets may be **U.S.-based targets**, meaning that a group attacks a target that is symbolically linked to the United States, either nationally or locally (e.g., the federal building in Oklahoma City or an abortion clinic in Georgia). Additionally, groups may attack **foreign targets** located in U.S. territory. For instance, a group may attack an embassy of a different country (technically, all embassies are considered the domestic territory of that country, not U.S. territory). Terrorists may also attack foreign nationals living inside the United States or foreign business interests in the United States. A large portion of domestic terrorist attacks conducted by homegrown terrorists are against foreign targets, not U.S.-based targets. This makes the United States similar to European countries in that it serves as an operational field for terrorists. The tendency for foreign targets changes beginning in the late 1990s, when U.S.-based targets became common with the rise of the **eco-terrorism** (groups conducting terrorist operations to influence domestic policy regarding land development, environmental policy, and animal testing).

The dominant homegrown terror threats during the 1960s and 1970s were leftist groups. Many groups formed on the fringes of the American civil rights and anti-war movements. These groups barricaded various American universities, planted bombs in banks and public areas, attacked the military and police, and conducted kidnappings and prison breaks for group members (Griset and Mahan 2003). The most prominent groups were the Weather Underground (also known as the Weathermen), the Black Panthers, the Symbionese Liberation Army, and the Republic of New Africa, among others. Leftist groups were largely disorganized and fragmented, making them easy targets for infiltration and arrest. Thus, by the late 1970s, many of these organizations collapsed. The American left has revived since 1998, however, with eco-terrorist groups including the Earth Liberation Front (ELF) and the Animal Liberation Front (ALF) initiating their campaigns of terrorism throughout the American interior. The campaigns of the ELF and ALF demonstrate that the left is not dead.

During the 1990s, fear arose around the looming threat of right-wing terrorism in the form of **racial supremacy groups**, which believe the general social climate of the country is deteriorating and this condition is caused (in part or wholly) by the tolerance of different racial groups in society. In their view, restoration of the proper condition requires segregating races and the dominance of one particular race over all others. One long-time terrorist threat comes from the Ku Klux Klan, formed just after the Civil War. The KKK still exists today, but in a much less violent form than its early twentieth-century incarnations. Today, the emergent threat is that of neo-Nazi groups and the Christian Identity Movement, both of which support the racial purity programs advocated by Adolf Hitler during the 1930s and 1940s. Purity of the Aryan race (whites) is the primary goal for such groups. In their view, tolerance for African Americans and immigrants of any kind must be avoided. Black racial supremacy groups (as well as Latino-indigenous movements) exist inside the United States as well. Groups related to the Nation of Islam during the 1950s and 1960s were militant, conducting a series of assassinations and arsons to promote black supremacy (Griset and Mahan 2003). Today, the Nation of Islam has tempered its rhetoric and has no known affiliation with acts of terrorism.

The racial supremacy thread of terrorist activity moved into the militia movement in the United States during the 1990s, creating a network of potentially terrorist-like groups throughout the United States. The most direct threat from these groups came in the form of the Oklahoma City bombing in 1995, where associates of the Christian Identity Movement and the militias (Timothy McVeigh and Terry Nichols) conducted the largest single terrorist operation on U.S. soil by a homegrown terrorist cell. To date, the militia movement remains more of a potential than actualized threat, but potential does exist. Most right-wing groups remain highly fragmented and disorganized. For this reason, infiltration and arrests by law enforcement agencies have been difficult.

The United States also has its share of religious terrorism. Religious terrorism is similar to right-wing terrorism in that the groups believe society is experiencing deterioration in its social condition. They argue that this decay is caused by society's abandonment of its religious principles. These radical groups believe that recovery from this condition requires a return to religious purity. Hence, tolerance of different religions (e.g., Judaism, Islam, Hinduism, Buddhism, and so on) must be avoided. Fundamentalist Christian religious principles must be adhered to. The actions of the group take on religious meaning by invoking prophecy or aiding in the return of the messiah. Hence, violence is sanctioned as part of the process for fulfilling religious goals.

In the religious terrorist camp, we find three types of groups. First is the secular religious-based group that advances its interests and is not necessarily religious in nature. An example of this type is the Jewish Defense League (JDL). The JDL was founded by Rabbi Meir Kahane in 1968 in New York City and served primarily to protect the Orthodox Jewish population. In the 1970s, the group initiated a terrorist campaign against Palestinian Liberation Organization (PLO) targets. Their campaign expanded to include Soviet targets in the United States to protest the treatment of Soviet Jews. The JDL has officially abandoned terrorism, but incidents associated with the group have continued, and plots were uncovered as late as 2002 (Memorial Institute for the Prevention of Terrorism n.d.).

A second type of religious group is the **cult terrorist group**. Cult groups are not overtly terroristic in nature. Many have a tendency toward internal self-destruction rather than outward-oriented terrorist violence. However, some cult groups have engaged in terrorist activities against external targets or have made plans that included attacks against external targets. One notable example is Charles Manson's cult, which conducted a series of brutal murders against wealthy, white victims in California to initiate a race war in the United States. Another example is the Branch Davidians, a messianic cult in Waco, Texas, that many believed was planning to initiate God's wrath and usher in Armageddon. The exact plans of the group are disputed, as much evidence suggests they were defensive in nature and had no overt plans to conduct terrorist attacks. But the group was heavily armed, and the messianic cult around leader David Koresh provoked a confrontation with the federal government, ending with an attack that killed most of its members in 1994 (Wessinger 2000). Similarly, followers of Bhagwan Sharee Rajneesh released salmonella at local restaurants in Dalles, Oregon, in 1984 to influence local elections in favor of the cult. Examples of cult groups are rare, and the threat of a cult group becoming a major terrorist group is low, but the violence we have observed around such groups warrants monitoring nonetheless.

A third type of religious group is the single-issue group, such as those groups involved in anti-abortion terrorist violence. In the anti-abortion movement, there is no centralized organization conducting a terror campaign against abortion clinics or doctors. However, individuals and rogue groups have taken it upon themselves to advance their position on the abortion issue by bombing abortion clinics and assassinating doctors and other health care professionals associated with abortion practices. The lack of a centralized campaign by a single group or coalition of groups works against this variation of single-issue terrorism emerging as a major national threat.

The United States does not have the domestic equivalent of an Islamic fundamentalist or Christian fundamentalist group using terrorism to promote a new form of government that applies religious laws or principles. Such fundamentalist groups appear to be the province of foreign environments at the moment. This does not preclude the potential rise of such groups in the future. However, the established political climate and processes in the United States appear to allow such groups to operate satisfactorily within the conventional political framework, which is perhaps why these groups have not formed inside the United States to date.

Religious and right-wing terrorism in the United States was supplemented by the rapid spread of anti-Communist groups during the 1950s to 1980s. Most notable here is the anti-Castro Cuban terrorist groups. Placing such groups under the heading "homegrown" terrorists is problematic because such groups form within the exile Cuban communities located primarily in Miami and other major urban centers of the United States. However, the groups did not form on foreign soil. Rather, they organized inside the United States, making them domestic terrorist groups. At best, we can refer to them as cross-over groups. There are a large number of anti-Castro Cuban groups in America today, the most notable being Omega-7 based in Miami. This group consists mostly of Bay of Pigs veterans committed to overthrowing Fidel Castro's Communist regime in Cuba. Omega-7 and other anti-Castro Cuban groups conducted targeted assassinations against pro-Castro Cubans inside the United States, rival Cuban organizations, and foreign diplomats with friendly relations with Castro's regime in Cuba. As such, most activities were émigré terrorism, thus oriented toward foreign and not U.S.-based targets.

Ethno-national terrorism has not been a major threat to the United States over the years. As an immigrant-based country, most national groups are composed of people willing to reside inside the United States. Furthermore, national groups tend to be distributed throughout the United States in terms of social class and geography. Given this condition, there has been little motivation for nationalist terrorism and little ability to organize a terrorist campaign. The lone exception to this is Puerto Rican terrorist groups such as the Fuerzas Armadas de Liberación Nacional (Armed Forces of National Liberation or FALN) and Movimiento Independentista Revolucionario Armado (Independent Armed Revolutionary Movement or MIRA). FALN and MIRA were committed to establishing an independent Puerto Rico, ending its protectorate status with the United States. MIRA received aid and training from Cuba and conducted a series of operations throughout the United States (primarily in New York City) from the 1960s until the 1980s. FALN was active for about a decade (1974 to 1985) in New York and Chicago, attacking U.S.-based targets and citizens to advance the goal of Puerto Rican independence. Both MIRA and FALN are relatively inactive today. In 1998, the United States allowed a referendum on Puerto Rico's status, and the majority of Puerto Rican citizens rejected changing their status with the United States, effectively undermining the goals of MIRA and FALN.

The homegrown portion of domestic terrorism is very diverse. Right-wing and religious groups are larger in number and have been more active over the last 50 years. Ideological terrorism, however, has emerged as a major threat. In the right-wing and religious terrorist camps, fragmentation works against these groups, preventing them from becoming a major and sustained threat to homeland security. The more persistent security threat from anti-Castro Cubans is on the decline. The JDL is largely neutralized for the time being; therefore, the looming threat remains the ELF and ALF. Little has been done to this point to infiltrate these groups. Their pace of operations has waned in the past five years, but that does not eliminate them as a threat to homeland security.

9.1.3 Foreign Terrorists

The foreign terrorist threat inside the United States consists of two types of groups: émigré terrorism, where terrorist operatives infiltrate U.S. borders to conduct targeted assassinations against foreigners of the same nationality; and foreign terrorist groups that infiltrate U.S. borders to conduct operations against U.S.-based targets. The former is the more common of the two; however, the latter captures the majority of our attention today due to the events of 9/11 and the potential for catastrophic terrorist incidents conducted by these groups in the future.

Historically, émigré terrorism accounts for the highest number of foreign terrorist events and deaths inside the United States. From 1955 to 1998, there were 38 émigré terrorist deaths in the United States, accounting for 7.6 percent of all terrorism-related deaths and 48 percent of deaths related to foreign terrorist activity (Hewitt 2000). Émigré terrorism comes from people of a wide variety of nationalities, including (but not limited to) Cubans, Armenians, Haitians, Sikhs, Taiwanese, Vietnamese, Croatians, Chileans, Iranians, Libyans, Nicaraguans, Palestinians, and Venezuelans (Hewitt 2000, 5–6). For this reason, it is difficult to explain émigré terrorism. The causes or motivations for attacks are related more to the foreign environment than to the domestic environment. The United States simply became the backdrop for their terrorist activity. At the same time, the United States may be chosen as a specific environment for émigré terrorism because certain political groups enjoy a preferential status in the United States, and competitor groups that enter the United States may be perceived as a threat to their status. For instance, anti-Castro Cuban terrorism against pro-Castro foreigners is to defend the existing trade embargo and U.S. policies of isolation against Cuba, rather than risk any chance that U.S. officials or the public may change their mind on Cuba.

Today, foreign terrorism in the United States is most often linked to Islamic groups from the Middle East. Historically, activities by Islamic groups have been very low, and until 9/11, they accounted for only 11 deaths, or 2.2 percent of all terrorism-related deaths and 14 percent of all deaths related to foreign terrorism (Hewitt 2000, 5). In the 1970s, such terrorist activity was related to the PLO and Black September, but these attacks were émigré terrorism rather than foreign terrorism. During the 1990s and 2000s, Islamic terrorist activity is increasingly linked to al-Qaeda, which has been connected to two successful operations in the United States: the 1993 bombing of the World Trade Center and the 9/11 attacks. Beyond this activity, foreign terrorism inside the United States has been very rare.

However, foreign terrorist activity targeting U.S. interests overseas is not rare. A more complete global picture of terrorist activity demonstrates that the United States and U.S. interests are common terrorist targets throughout the world. Because the United States has a dominant government, military, and business presence in Europe, the Middle East, Asia, and Latin America, terrorist groups can easily attack the United States without the requirement of infiltrating U.S. homeland security. Even al-Qaeda restricted much of its terrorist campaign against the United States to American targets overseas. Examples include the Khobar Towers bombing (1996), the bombings of U.S. embassies in Kenya and Tanzania (1998), and the attack on the USS Cole in Yemen (2000).

By and large, foreign terrorism, as it relates to direct threats to the U.S. homeland, had not been a major concern prior to 9/11. The numbers of attacks were very low and most were émigré terrorism. Since 9/11, there has been a concerted effort on the part of the U.S. government to ensure that similar foreign terrorist operations have

Figure 9-1

The terrorist attacks on September 11, 2001, were the worst attacks ever carried out on American soil.

little chance of success in the future (see Figure 9-1). The fortunate side benefit of the increased homeland security effort is likely to be a reduction in all forms of foreign terrorist activity in the United States. As terrorist watch lists are improved and border security strengthens, the ability of émigré terrorists to operate inside the United States will decline as well. It is too early to tell the full impact that the post-9/11 reforms will have, but the potential benefits are great.

9.1.4 Foreign Terrorist Organizers

As we turn to foreign terrorist organizers, our attention shifts from groups and their operations to individuals and organizations that set up shop to raise funds and recruit people for terrorist operations overseas. Organizing involves two primary functions: resource mobilization, and finding individuals willing to support the cause of a terrorist group.

▲ **Resource mobilization** involves raising cash to fund operations and purchase weapons and munitions for operations.

▲ **Recruitment** is often related to finding couriers that can transfer resources into the foreign environment.

The American domestic environment is good for terrorist organizers. This is not to say that Americans are lining up to join terrorist groups all over the world. But, if an American can be recruited, the U.S. passport offers the most flexibility for free travel in and out of foreign countries. Virtually unlimited travel allows individuals from the United States to carry money all over the world to fund operations. For terrorist organizations, it is best to have people already within the organization carry out their courier functions. However, terrorist watch lists are constantly updated, making it difficult for foreign terrorists to be certain they can infiltrate U.S. border security. Furthermore, passport technology is getting more complex, making it increasingly difficult to forge passports. It is thus better to recruit Americans with U.S. passports to circumvent border security measures (Emerson 2003). Foreign terrorist organizers recruit within immigrant communities inside the United States to find people that may have sympathy for the group's causes, and they then convince these people to serve in a minor capacity, such as by transferring money. For example, Mohammed Salah, a naturalized American from Chicago, was recruited by Hamas to carry money into Israel and the Occupied Territories to support Hamas operations (Emerson 2003). Given the large and varied immigrant communities within the United States, many terrorists groups from many countries will have the potential to find recruits inside the United States. This is not to say that all immigrants are potential terrorist threats. Rather, terrorists have found a way of turning America's immigrant culture into a *potential* resource.

In addition to providing recruits, the United States provides fertile ground for raising funds. Many of the ways terrorists raise money involve illegal economic activity, such as selling forged goods such as DVDs, handbags, and t-shirts (CNN Money 2005) and engaging in identity theft. In one example, Hezbollah set up a scheme where they purchased cigarettes in outlets in North Carolina and resold them for profit in Michigan (Emerson 2003). Terrorist groups have also established legitimate businesses and invest money in stock markets. Terrorist organizations

FOR EXAMPLE

Noraid and the Provisional IRA

The sectarian violence in Northern Ireland has produced terrorist organizations such as the Provisional Irish Republican Army (IRA), which has been fighting against the British government for over 100 years. The IRA traditionally sought financial support for its cause among Irish Catholic strongholds in the United States through fundraising efforts carried out by groups such as the American-based Irish Northern Aid Committee (Noraid). Noraid was credited as being an Irish Catholic relief agency, but its founder, Michael Flannery, an outspoken IRA supporter, once commented that "the more British soldiers sent home from Ulster in coffins, the better" (Applebaum 2005).

have additionally established charitable organizations that pretend to serve the interests of women and children in war-torn regions of the world, only to collect the money and send it along to terrorist operatives. For instance, companies such as Microsoft, UPS, and Compaq have donated to the charity Benevolence International Foundation, which actually fronts al-Qaeda (Raphaeli 2003).

To move money around the world, terrorists have developed a number of schemes beyond the individual courier. One option used by terrorists is the traditional banking system. A group will establish an account, and operatives throughout the world can have money transferred from the central account into individual accounts in the bank's subsidiaries. There are also alternative funds transfer systems. Diplomatic channels have been used to transfer funds and equipment through diplomatic pouches that are free from customs inspections (Raphaeli 2003). The **Informal Funds Transfer System (IFTS)**, commonly known as the Hawala or remittance system, operates like an informal Western Union. A remitter gives money to an intermediary, who then instructs a contact in the receiving country to distribute the money to a predetermined recipient in the local currency. The transfers are all informal and do not generate paper trails or bookkeeping records of transfers (Raphaeli 2003). In this system, a terrorist organization can append its transfer to that of a remitter to move money to operational cells in the field.

In short, within the United States, foreign terrorist organizers have a plethora of opportunities available to gather resources, organize, and recruit for operations overseas. Many of the activities of foreign terrorist organizers play upon the generous civil liberties environment in the United States. Freedoms of speech, press, and assembly all make it possible to find and recruit people as needed, and to gather resources from individuals and corporations inside the United States. In addition, the liberal business environment that encourages foreign investment and the free flow of capital makes it easier for groups to move resources in and out of the United States. However, a cautionary note is required. The liberal business and political environment may be abused by foreign terrorist organizers, but it is also one of the primary barriers we have to prevent terrorist groups from establishing themselves as long-term threats to domestic security. Investigative processes have improved, and laws have been adjusted to meet the emerging terrorist threat. The activities of foreign terrorist organizers simply alert us to the existing gaps in the security network. This provides us with the opportunity to fill the gap, while balancing the interests of security against the United States' historic traditions of a generous civil liberties environment.

9.1.5 Final Thoughts on the Domestic Terrorist Threat

This analysis of the domestic terrorist threat is instructive in a number of ways. The broad trends suggest that America's primary terrorist threat, historically, has been the homegrown terrorist. Within this particular area of terrorist activity, right-wing and religious terrorists groups have been the dominant threat for much of the past 50 years. In the last ten years, ideological terrorism in the form of the ELF and ALF has become more dominant. For these groups, terrorism is moving away from urban centers to rural areas of the United States. Foreign terrorism, which dominates the public discourse on terrorism in the United States, has not been as significant of a threat in the past; however, events such as 9/11 indicate a growing threat from foreign terrorism. But if you set aside al-Qaeda's activities, most foreign terrorism has been émigré terrorism, not foreign groups infiltrating and attacking U.S. based targets.

Finally, the United States does have a problem with foreign terrorist organizers. Terrorist organizations like Hamas, Palestinian Islamic Jihad, al-Qaeda, and the Provisional Irish Republican Army (to name a few) have long used the U.S. environment to recruit, gather resources, and send those resources into operational fields overseas. Organizing activities range from illegal to legal activities. As our knowledge of the activities of foreign terrorist organizers increases, we will be better positioned to address the threat within the boundaries of our legal and political traditions. This analysis of the domestic threat does raise an important question about how terrorist groups are able to form and operate in a country like the United States. The next section analyzes the operational environment of the United States to explore the existing vulnerabilities that allow groups to form, and what prevents those groups from becoming long-term terrorist problems that threaten the political and social stability of the United States.

SELF-CHECK

1. Which of the following does not define the activities of a foreign terrorist organizer?
   a. Conducting terrorist operations against domestic U.S.-based targets
   b. Recruiting
   c. Selling forged items to raise money for terrorist operations
   d. Diverting funds from charities to support terrorist operations

2. Define resource mobilization.

3. Prior to 9/11, U.S.-based targets were the most common targets for foreign terrorists. True or false?

4. Foreign terrorist organizers find the United States to be a good environment to conduct recruitment and resource mobilization. True or false?

9.2 The Operational Environment for Terrorism

Whenever we evaluate any country's terrorist situation, we need to take some time to explore its operational environment. When talking of the **operational environment**, we are looking at "the field upon which terrorists play, and . . . a primary determinant of . . . strategy" (Long 1990, 27). The operational environment includes factors such as the physical, political, security, and resource environments that make terrorism possible. Each part of the operational environment provides terrorists with needed resources for a terrorist campaign. As such, each environment contributes to the rise of terrorism by being permissive (not establishing any barrier against the onset of terrorist activity), motivational (providing the rationale for terrorist action over other types of political behavior), enabling (giving terrorists tools necessary to conduct their campaign), or some combination of all three.

As we move through a discussion of these environments and how they relate to the United States, keep in mind that the United States has never really faced an entrenched, long-term domestic terrorist threat that had the potential to undermine the nation's political stability. This is good and indicates the operational environment may allow terrorism to exist, but it does not enable a sustained terrorist threat. As we move through the different environments, it will become clear as to how the U.S. operational environment works against terrorism. What this tells us is that the operational environment does not ensure terrorism will happen. Rather, the environment does possess characteristics that make terrorism possible. A fertile operational environment can still be terrorist-free or experience very low levels of terrorist violence, however.

9.2.1 The Physical Environment

The **physical environment** refers to the geographic conditions surrounding terrorist activity (Long 1990). Geography relates to the epicenter for action—urban or rural. The physical location shapes the form of violent activity, with rural environments more conducive to hit-and-run guerrilla tactics and urban environments more conducive to terrorist tactics. This does not mean that rural terrorist campaigns are impossible. However, terrorist tactics demonstrate greater utility in an urban environment where a group can take advantage of many available targets, transportation networks (as targets and/or escape routes), and concentrated media outlets (to broadcast actions to a larger audience). Furthermore, urban environments offer cover for criminal networks that provide weapons, falsified identity papers, and other materials needed for a terrorist campaign (Rabbie 1991). Rural environments are not immune from such criminal networks, but the criminal activities are more noticeable. Urban environments are more permissive of terrorist action than rural environments.

The physical environment of the United States is very fertile for potential terrorist activity. There are a large number of major urban centers including, but not limited to, Washington, D.C., New York, Atlanta, Miami, Chicago, Los Angeles, San Francisco, Seattle, Dallas, and so on. Currently in the United States, about 83 percent of the total population lives in metropolitan statistical areas (MSAs) containing a population of 50,000 or more people, with about 369 MSAs across the United States. This heavily urbanized environment provides terrorists with a large number of target cities to operate in or from. The importance of this is noted in section 9.1.1, showing that the majority of terrorist activity took place in major urban environments from the 1960s through the 1990s. As the campaigns of the ELF and ALF began, there was shift away from the major urban centers such as New York, Washington, and Los Angeles. However, ELF and ALF activities still take place inside the smaller MSAs.

Urban environments in the United States have multiple criminal networks, ranging from organized crime to major gangs that can provide terrorists with needed materials. At one point, for instance, the El Rukin gang out of Chicago was under investigation by the FBI for collaborating with Libya to buy and sell weapons and conduct terrorist operations inside the United States. Most major urban centers also have established media outlets that are networked throughout the United States, which ensures that a terrorist action in any city captures an attentive audience across the entire country. Furthermore, the major urban centers inside the United States are important travel centers into and out of the country. This provides terrorists with ample targets (for hijackings and bombings) and escape routes, as many airports in major urban centers have direct connection flights out of the United States. All combined, the physical environment of the United States is very fertile for terrorist activity, making our environment very permissive in this respect.

9.2.2 The Political Environment

We naturally think of the political environment as the primary source of issues or grievances that motivate terrorist action. In reality, this environment does more than generate grievances for terrorism. **Political environment** refers to the social decision-making process to include the institutions of government and rules of access (e.g., elections, political parties, interest groups) that allow issues to arise from society for debate and decision. The political environment's relationship to terrorist action has less to do with generating specific issues and more to do with maintaining legitimacy and stability for the institutions and rules of access that govern the decision-making process. At the same time, actors within the political system often form the core organizational materials that become terrorist groups.

A key issue for the political system is stability. Stable governments, regardless of regime type (democratic, authoritarian, or totalitarian), experience low levels of terrorist action. Most terrorist activity in a stable political system is episodic, a single event or small cluster of events. Rarely do we observe terrorism growing into sustained threat in a stable political system. A stable political system is defined as one where the infrastructure supporting the political system (the patterns of allegiance, access to decision-making authorities, leadership, institutionalized actors [parties and interest groups], and certainty in the rules of decision making) are routine and there is little uncertainty (Karber and Mengal 1983, 25). Political systems where the infrastructure is in flux or transition tend to experience higher levels of terrorist action.

A stable political condition is the norm for the United States. There has not been a serious or sustained challenge to the authority of the U.S. government since the Civil War (1861–1865). The American political system did experience strain during the Great Depression, but the electoral process proved useful by sweeping parties from power and bringing in new leadership as needed. During the civil rights and anti-war movements in the 1960s, the United States experienced a new period of stress. Terrorism did erupt during the late 1960s. By the early to mid 1970s, however, these movements fell apart as the political system adjusted through reforms such as the Civil Rights Act, Fair Housing Act, withdrawal from Vietnam, and changing the voting age to 18. Again, the political system proved stable and flexible as needed to adjust to the demands of society. Overall, the American political system offers enough outlets and avenues of access through political parties and interest groups to absorb political stress and pressure as it arises. This does not mean that all mobilized political groups will achieve victory in their political campaigns. But the process is deemed sufficient for addressing issues as they arise, which means that alternative behaviors, such as terrorism, are seen as extreme and unacceptable given the available alternatives.

Another major issue for the political environment is legitimacy, or the general acceptance of the political system by the population. Terrorist groups often form slowly, and they emerge as the end product of a process of deligitimization (Sprinzak 1991). This process involves three phases: crisis of confidence, conflict of legitimacy, and crisis of legitimacy.

▲ The *crisis of confidence* is when a group becomes disenfranchised by the rulers and/or policies and comes to perceive the government's reaction to new political groups as beyond the ordinary rules of society (Sprinzak 1991). In this situation, an opposition group may form against a specific policy, but leaders ignore the grievances. More importantly, the people in a political movement are treated as a general threat. The government begins information gathering, attempts to discredit group leaders, and general suppression. Issues at this point have less to do with specific political grievances and more to do with the pattern of interaction between government and the mobilized political group.

▲ The *conflict of legitimacy* emerges as group members begin to define their problem with the political system, which is now seen as manipulative and repressive (Sprinzak 1991). The evolving view in the group is that change can only occur by changing the system. New ideologies and political cultures emerge and are socialized to members of the group, and protest demonstrations become more extreme.

▲ The end phase is the *crisis of legitimacy*. In this phase the group extends the boundaries of its defined opponent to include political personnel and segments of the general population seen as supporting the state (Sprinzak 1991).

The political system thus shapes the activity of political groups by way of how it chooses to interact with mobilized political groups. What this suggests is that terrorist groups arise from broader social movements. Many terrorist groups often have a relationship to other political actors in the environment, such as political parties or interest groups (Siqueira 2005; Weinberg 1991; Weinberg and Eubank 1990). Social movements never operate with a single voice. There are many factions within a social movement drawn together by a common issue. The factions form around competing ideas on how best to achieve their goals. Competition between factions is common. Terrorist behavior, then, is typically one form of action among competing alternatives—meaning that terrorist action effectively serves as a substitute and/or complimentary activity in the dissident environment.

The deligitimization process is best observed in the evolution of leftist terrorism by groups such as the Weathermen and Symbionese Liberation Army. Both groups formed on the fringes of the New Left movement in the United States represented by the Students for a Democratic Society (SDS). SDS formed within the vortex of the anti-war movement, with particular interest in ending the U.S. involvement in Vietnam. As a student movement, the New Left and SDS were not taken seriously because many participants were not of voting age (set at 21 years during this time). The government treated the movements as immature, ill informed, and more of a threat than a legitimate political group. Political demonstrations seemed like impotent tactics, which gave fuel to fringe elements that went on to form the Weathermen and the SLA. These terrorist groups defined their political grievances in terms of a corrupt and out-of-touch political system that refused to listen to the voices of the people. Students, who formed the pool of potential draftees for the war in Vietnam, had no political voice, and they could not be taken seriously by trying to play the conventional political game. In the 1970s, however, the Twenty-fourth Amendment to the Constitution was passed, lowering the voting age to 18, and the Vietnam War came to an end. With these changes, the leftist terrorist groups also came to an end.

The political environment as a contributing factor for terrorism applies only to homegrown terrorist groups. The domestic political condition has little or no impact on foreign terrorists or foreign terrorist organizers. The established foreign policy of a country such as the United States may motivate foreign terrorists to seek out U.S. targets. However, there is no way to adapt the domestic political system to diffuse foreign terrorist threats. That is best handled through foreign policy as established by the executive branch of government.

9.2.3 The Security Environment

The security environment is deeply nested within the political environment. It is through the **security environment** (consisting of police, military, intelligence, security forces, courts, prisons, etc.) that the government responds to terrorist threats. As such, the security environment is most likely to matter because it is permissive; that is to say it does not provide a significant barrier to terrorist activity. However, in extremely repressive situations, the security environment can become a motivating factor. The optimal role security forces play is to disrupt terrorist action by providing a sufficient level of **target hardening** (physical security around likely terrorist targets like airports). By hardening targets, the cost of conducting a terrorist attack is too high, forcing terrorists to select other targets or abandon their plans altogether. Terrorist groups, even well-endowed ones, often lack the resources needed to conduct elaborate attacks that require expensive equipment and training. Terrorist targets are often selected by opportunity—what is most vulnerable at the time of the attack. Hence, terrorist operations are more opportunistic than tactfully masterful.

The optimal role for security forces is very difficult to fulfill. Terrorist groups are adaptable (Hoffman 1998). Moreover, because terrorist groups can use anything as an available target, the number of potential targets is too great to defend. In this vein, the security environment is reactive, defending targets that have been hit in the past rather than securing potential future targets. The reactive, rather than proactive, nature of the security environment generates the greatest permissive factor for terrorism. Being permissive does not mean it encourages terrorism; rather, this means that the security environment is typically ill-equipped to prevent *initial* attacks.

In response, security forces have tried to develop deterrence strategies against terrorists. Deterrence works by creating credible threats of reaction to a violent attack. The problem that confronts a government is that terrorist threats are rarely anticipated, making it difficult to develop a credible deterrent threat. Furthermore, even when a country does establish a deterrent counter-terrorist policy (e.g., no negotiations), all too often the policy is abandoned in specific cases. This weakens the security environment retaining its permissive features.

In the United States, the primary domestic security response to terrorism has been twofold. It has involved hardening common targets to make them difficult for terrorists to breach. Target hardening has taken place in phases as vulnerabilities are revealed. In the 1960s and 1970s, considerable effort went into hardening banks, the favored targets of leftist terrorists at the time. In the 1980s, airports were hardened in response to the rise in airplane hijackings. After 9/11, airports were hardened again with the nationalization of airport security, creating the Transportation Safety Administration (TSA). The mail delivery system was hardened in response to the anthrax letter attacks in October 2001. Federal buildings were also hardened after 9/11. Most recently, airline safety was hardened through the "3-1-1 policy" for liquids on board aircraft (three ounces of liquid per container, sealed in a single one-quart size bag). This policy was a response to the revealed terrorist plot to smuggle gel explosives onto aircraft en route from London to the United States. In addition, chemical and nuclear facilities are required to develop emergency plans in response to terrorist threats. Many states are developing testing programs for water safety in case of biological attacks on the domestic water supply. The target hardening reflects a response to past terrorist attacks and efforts to plan for and respond to attacks that have not happened. However, target hardening is, at best, a reactive approach to terrorism. It does not identify threats and diffuse them in advance.

The second security approach to terrorism is proactive. This involves investigations into groups and individuals that are suspected of terrorist activities and planning or that demonstrate the potential for terrorist activity in the future. Investigation into subversive activities begins with the Smith Act (1940), which made it illegal to advocate overthrowing the U.S. government. Implementation of the Smith Act led to the FBI's Counter Intelligence Program (COINTELPRO) established in 1956 (Powers 2004). Through COINTELPRO, the FBI would gather advanced intelligence on political groups in the United States to sift through those groups that had the potential to threaten the domestic security of the United States. By the 1970s, the Smith Act was revised significantly through Supreme Court decisions and congressional investigations, ultimately rendering advanced investigations politically and legally impossible. In the wake of 9/11, the U.S. government has developed various forms of investigative strategies, similar in nature to COINTELPRO. Examples include the Terrorist Surveillance Program (warrantless wiretaps on international phone calls), monitoring Internet activity, and monitoring bank account activity (above a certain level of monetary transfers). There is discussion of a return to COINTELPRO by developing secure files on people suspected of terrorist activities and affiliations. All such investigative strategies are in the early stages of development and are under review for possible revision to conform to the established civil liberties norms of the United States. What can be said, though, is that during the 1980s and 1990s, with revision and eventual suspension of COINTELPRO, investigation into terrorism in the United States became fact

FOR EXAMPLE

COINTELPRO and the Church Commission

The FBI's Counter Intelligence Program (COINTELPRO), established in 1956, was the implementation of the Smith Act of 1940, which prohibited groups and individuals from advocating an overthrow of the U.S. government. COINTELPRO initially targeted the American Communist Party. Because Communist ideology advocates violent revolution to overthrow capitalist regimes, this seemed a perfect target for monitoring. However, COINTELPRO went beyond investigations of political groups deemed potential threats to the security of the United States. COINTELPRO also investigated several social and political movements, including the New Left student movement during Vietnam and the activities of Dr. Martin Luther King, Jr., during the civil rights movement. In addition to these investigations, COINTELPRO engaged in misinformation campaigns to discredit these social groups. These aggressive, disruptive campaigns included purposely circulating rumors and dirty tricks to prevent meetings from taking place. The effort destroyed the American Communist Party and was seen as a success.

The COINTELPRO program was kept intact well into the 1970s, when it was finally revealed to the public through a Freedom of Information Act request. Upon this revelation, Congress quickly organized a commission to investigate COINTELPRO. The Church Committee investigation revealed the nature of COINTELPRO and the abuses of power associated with it. By the end of the Church Committee hearings, COINTELPRO was a shadow of what it had been. Various Supreme Court decisions required that the FBI must have evidence of subversive activity before initiating an investigation. FBI agents came to believe proactive investigations were the quickest way to kill a career. By 9/11, the FBI had all but given up surveillance of political groups because its history demonstrated abuse of power rather than good intent.

gathering and case building for prosecutions of suspected terrorists after an event took place. No program existed to provide for advanced intelligence gathering prior to an event. This is discussed in more depth in section 9.3.

9.2.4 The Resource Environment

The **resource environment** refers to a group's access to financial resources needed to build an organization and conduct terrorist operations. All groups need materials, recruits, training, and equipment. After all, rebels cannot rebel without the means to do so (Weinstein 2005; Lichbach 1995). Moreover, resource availability ultimately shapes the character and conduct of the terrorist group (Weinstein 2005; Crenshaw 1990). The classical perception of a terrorist organization is that it lives hand-to-mouth off donations from supporters or by engaging in illegal activities such as bank robberies, extortion, and kidnappings for ransom (Adams 1987, 393). The extended view is that many terrorist groups have expanded their resource base through external state sponsors. These perceptions are not wrong, but they are incomplete. Many terrorist groups have built large networks of legitimate and illegitimate enterprises, investments, and charitable fronts to generate independent, self-sustaining, resource bases (Adams 1987; Raphaeli 2003).

The independent finance systems for terrorist organizations reflect Raphaeli's (2003) description of an octopus with arms that reach across political and economic boundaries (59). The entire system involves a complex of legal and semi-legal activities designed to enhance terrorist operations. Resource-generating activities involve a combination of legitimate and illegitimate businesses, extortion rackets, and kickback business arrangements that generate hundreds of millions of dollars every year for various terrorist groups. The **extortion rackets** are most common as they combine the skills of terrorists with money generation. In simple form, the organization provides security or protection to a business, farmer, or other organization. Business enterprises come in various forms that involve legitimate, criminal, and quasi-legitimate practices. On the criminal side, groups such as Hezbollah have immersed themselves in the production and sale of counterfeit items like DVDs, handbags, and t-shirts (as noted earlier in this chapter). Kickback arrangements are often the most intricate and unique. Take, for example, the more simple system for the PLO. The Arab Bank is the primary center of PLO financial operations. The Bank accepts PLO funds and invests them in markets in the United States and Europe. At the same time the Bank makes large loans to building contractors, it also recommends the recipient of the loan use PLO front companies to do subcontracting work (Adams 1987). An emerging source of revenue is the non-profit charity. Various groups throughout the world have established or linked into charities with public missions to aid people in war torn regions of the world (typically in the group's region of operations). Many wealthy people and businesses in the United States and Europe have made donations to the charities. The charity front in turn donates the money to front nongovernmental organizations that use the money to fund operations in Chechnya, Lebanon, the Israeli Occupied Territories, or other places (Raphaeli 2003).

The important thing to note in relation to the resource environment as it applies to the United States is that many foreign terrorist groups take advantage of the United States to fund terrorist operations overseas. By and large, homegrown terrorist groups remain of the variety that live hand-to-mouth or off the donations of supporters. On the other hand, Latin American terrorist organizations from Colombia and Peru are linked to the drug trade in the United States to fund terrorist activities back home. Middle Eastern groups have used charitable enterprises and illegal business activities to fund operations in Lebanon, the West Bank and Gaza, and Chechnya. Charitable enterprises like Noraid are used to raise money for the Provisional Irish Republican Army in Northern Ireland. As such, the American resource environment, while wealthy, is not used as much by home-grown groups. Homegrown groups are more self-reliant. These groups run smaller operations and have fewer resource needs.

9.2.5 Final Thoughts on the Operational Environment

The operational environment for the United States is one that has a number of permissive factors. This would indicate that terrorist threats are plentiful; however, it does not seem to be the case for the United States. Certainly there are terrorist threats, and active terrorist groups operating inside the United States, and infiltrating the border security systems. At the same time the United States has experienced fewer terrorist incidents than many other countries around the world. This is due, in part, to its political environment. The political environment is very stable and has high levels of legitimacy. There are a number of ways citizens can access the political system to address grievances. The political environment works against the rise of terrorist groups. The United States does experience terrorist activity, and mostly from homegrown groups, but much of it is episodic in nature, not a long-term threat to national security. Sustained terrorist campaigns from anti-Castro Cubans or the JDL were conducted primarily against foreign targets inside the United States. Only the ELF and ALF have conducted extended terrorist campaigns inside the United States against U.S.-based targets. Despite this seemingly benign operational environment, the United States does have to deal with terrorist threats. The next section explores the ways in which the United States is dealing with these threats.

SELF-CHECK

1. Terrorist activity can occur as a result of a permissive operational environment. True or false?

2. Define political environment.

3. Which of the following is a permissive environment for terrorism?

   a. The security environment
   b. The political environment
   c. The resource environment
   d. The university environment

4. Charity fronts have been used to take money away from terrorist groups. True or false?

9.3 The U.S. Response to Terrorism

The variety of terrorist threats the United States faces (homegrown terrorists, foreign terrorists, and foreign terrorist organizers) means the United States must operate a flexible counter-terrorist policy. This section explores elements of this flexible response. Because this chapter is primarily about domestic terrorism, the majority of the discussion is centered on domestic responses to terrorism. This involves the criminal justice system as the centerpiece of our system. The Posse Comitatus Act of 1878 prohibits the use of federal troops (the military) to conduct police and security operations inside the boundaries of the United States. This act has been loosened somewhat over the years to allow for the military to participate in limited terrorist response situations, employing what is called Military Aid to Civilian Authorities (MACA) (Wilkinson 2000). In such cases, the military may serve temporarily as airport security or help with disaster recovery (as they did following 9/11). For the most part, the United States has forsaken the use of the military as the primary counter-terrorist tool, thus eliminating the war model and opting for the criminal justice model.

▲ The **war model** refers to militarization of a terrorist conflict.
▲ The **criminal justice model** refers to the use of police, courts, laws, and prisons to respond to a terrorist threat.

Still, employing the criminal justice model is difficult. Numerous government agencies come into play, and many state governments may be involved. To sort out this jurisdictional problem, the United States has opted for the **lead agency approach**, where the agency with authority over a terrorist case is determined by the source (domestic or international) of the threat, combined with the Department of Homeland Security and the National Counterterrorism Center to ensure some level of order and accountability.

9.3.1 The Lead Agency Approach and Counter-terrorism

Inside the United States, there are over 20 federal agencies, as well as 50 states, that potentially hold jurisdiction over any single terrorist event. Managing all the involved parties is difficult. Given that all federal agencies are under direction of the president of the United States, this would seem to be one way to control the situation. However, President Eisenhower once lamented that the biggest problem of being president was that he spent most of his time trying to convince people to do what they ought to be doing anyway. Federal agencies have their own interests. This may include participating in or avoiding counter-terrorism. Budgetary concerns, jurisdiction, and mission all influence the decisions of agencies to get involved with terrorism. If bureaucratic leaders believe there is a positive budgetary payoff, they will likely join in the effort. However, if taking on counter-terrorist duties means doing more with the same budget, leaders may balk to defend their own agencies' interests. Budgets are one excuse. The gist of this situation is that there may often be too many agencies trying to get involved or avoiding responsibility, making it difficult to manage counter-terrorism operations.

To provide some order to the process, a vice presidential commission led by George H. W. Bush established the lead agency approach to handle terrorist threats. Under the lead agency system, the federal agency with jurisdiction over the terrorist situation is determined by the location of the event. Domestic terrorism falls to the Department of Homeland Security, Federal Bureau of Investigation (FBI), Bureau of Alcohol, Tobacco, and Firearms (ATF), and Drug Enforcement Agency (DEA). Foreign terrorist threats are assigned to the U.S. Department of State and the Department of Defense. Aviation terrorism (e.g., hijackings) is assigned to the Federal Aviation Administration.

In the post-9/11 world, the United States has reworked much of its organization to combat terrorism. One feature missing before 9/11 was any single agency or bureaucratic leader with clear responsibility and accountability over terrorism and counter-terrorism. The lead agency approach provided some coordination for activities related to terrorism and counter-terrorism. However, for most the 1980s and 1990s, there was no clear authority. Under the Reagan and G. H. W. Bush administrations, counter-terrorism was a collective responsibility of the National Security Council (NSC). Under the Clinton administration, a specific individual, Richard Clarke, was identified within the NSC to oversee counter-terrorism. However, this National Coordinator for Security did not have an independent secretarial portfolio, meaning he had no budget, no personnel, and no real authority to order agencies to cooperate for counter-terrorism.

Following 9/11, the George W. Bush administration established two new bureaucratic entities to provide accountability and clear authority for counter-terrorism. The first and most prominent was the Department of Homeland Security (DHS). The role of DHS is to manage border security against foreign terrorists attempting to gain entry into the United States. In addition to this function, DHS is assigned the duty of managing rescue and recovery efforts in the wake of a terrorist attack. In addition to DHS, the National Counterterrorism Center (NCTC) was created in 2004 to provide the larger picture on existing, and emerging terrorist threats domestically and globally. This agency's primary duties are to collect all available intelligence on terrorist activities, and to coordinate and direct strategic operational planning in response to terrorist threats. Combined, DHS and the NCTC provide a more unified command and clearer accountability in relation to counter-terrorism, and response and recovery efforts inside the United States. These federal entities, though, are not the very front line of counter-terrorism in the United States. These agencies simply provide leadership and accountability. The front line for domestic counter-terrorism is the criminal justice system at both the federal and state level.

9.3.2 The Criminal Justice Approach

The United States prides itself in being a nation based on the rule of law. As such, a conscious decision was made long ago to address terrorism as a criminal activity and to apply the rule of law to govern counter-terrorist efforts. By utilizing the criminal justice model (the system of laws, police, courts, and prisons), the United States is making a clear statement about terrorism: Terrorists are still criminals. The United States has been slow to develop new laws that deal with terrorism specifically. The approach from the 1960s until 1990s was to apply existing laws on murder, kidnapping, public endangerment, property damage, etc., to acts of terrorism. Generally, the federal government held the position that crafting special legislation on terrorism redundantly outlaws these same behaviors (Donohue and Kayyem 2002). Special legislation against terrorism raises the treatment of the crime as political motivation, and this becomes an aggravating factor yielding special sentencing rules (Walker 2000). Such legislative measures run up against First Amendment protections on free speech and assembly (Donohue and Kayyem 2002). Moreover, by making a special case for terrorism as a distinct crime, the courtroom is transformed into a public forum for a terrorist or terrorist group to espouse their ideology.

The United States began amending its legal approach to terrorism in the 1990s. The change reflected a growing concern over foreign terrorists conducting operations against domestic U.S.-based targets. In 1996, the Anti-Terrorism and Effective Death Penalty Act (AEDPA) paved the way for the United States to designate a list of foreign terrorist organizations (FTOs), criminalizing any contribution to an organization associated with FTOs. The government is also allowed to deny entry to any person affiliated with a designated FTO, and it may freeze the assets of any person or group affiliated with an FTO (Donohue and Kayyem 2002).

In addition to the AEDPA, the United States altered its laws regarding investigations and prosecution of suspected terrorists. Such measures amend rules on search and seizure, detention of suspects, admissibility of evidence, and confessional statements (Wilkinson 2000, 116; Chalk 1995, 18). The FBI Access to Telephone Subscriber Information Act (1993) gave the FBI access to telephone subscriber information without the need of a court order. New laws were crafted to aid investigations by tagging materials that could be used in terrorist operations. For instance, the Chemical and Biological Weapons Control and Warfare Elimination Act (1991) allows the Secretary of Commerce to maintain a list of goods and technology that can be used by terrorist organizations and requires such materials to include strict tracking systems for police and federal investigators to quickly follow the trail of a terrorist and identify suspects (Donohue 2001).

In the wake of 9/11, Congress passed the Uniting and Strengthening America by Providing Appropriate Tools Required to Intercept and Obstruct Terrorism Act of 2001 (commonly called the USA Patriot Act) as a supplement to existing anti-terrorism legislation. The USA Patriot Act provides wide discretion to the executive branch to institute measures necessary to combat terrorism and eliminate the threat posed by al-Qaeda in particular. Through the USA Patriot Act, the G. W. Bush administration has implemented several new investigative strategies and prosecutorial rules to supplement the criminal justice approach to terrorism. Most are directed toward foreign terrorist threats, and include the following:

- ▲ Warrantless wiretaps on international phone calls
- ▲ Regulation of foreign bank accounts that maintain correspondent accounts inside the United States (i.e., money laundering)
- ▲ Creation of the "enemy combatant" status for foreign terrorists as a special class of criminal not subject to traditional civil liberties protections

Many of these programs have come under scrutiny for their potential violation of civil liberties. Negotiations are underway to define court proceeding rules for enemy combatants.

Finally, the USA Patriot Act includes a sunset provision that allows Congress to revisit and reauthorize or amend the legislation every five years. This ensures accountability and oversight between the executive and legislative branches to prevent an excess of power by the executive.

In addition to the federal statutory record, many states have adopted corresponding legislation applied at the state level. Much of the legislation is redundant to the federal counterpart, causing potential jurisdictional battles in the future. However, state governments correctly argue that a majority of terrorism takes place within states, and many groups, such as eco-terrorists (ELF), are not a major concern of the federal government, leaving states with the primary responsibility to deal with the local terrorist threats. The states have been on the frontline of passing laws to deal with "school terrorism," ecoterrorism, gang activity, and narcotics regulation, all of which are increasingly defined as "terroristic offenses" (Donohue and Kayyem 2002).

Overall, the legal approach to terrorism has proven useful. Between 1980 and 1996, about 327 cases were brought against individuals suspected of terrorist activities. Of these, 255 were domestic terrorists and 72 were international (Donohue 2001). These numbers reflect the success of the legal system absent special terrorism legislation initiated in the 1990s. As new anti-terrorism legislation passed and was used in terrorism cases, we observe a surge in defendants using their political motivation as a defense. Immediately there were a number of acquittals and mistrials for cases involving domestic terrorism. However, allowing political motivation to arise in court cases has also proven useful for the prosecution (Donohue 2001).

Supplementing anti-terrorism legislation, the United States has developed a variety of security measures that effectively harden likely terrorist targets or enhance the rights of victims of terrorist offenses. The Transportation Security Act (1974) requires air carriers to develop new security measures aboard aircraft. Supplementing this act, the FAA introduced the "sky marshal" program to place armed guards aboard aircraft to prevent hijackings. Compensation programs have been established for the families of terrorist victims. The Foreign Sovereign Immunities Act allows U.S. citizens to bring civil suits against foreign countries involved with or sponsoring terrorist acts. To build domestic preparedness, the Clinton administration issued Presidential Decision Directive 39, requiring the Marine Corps to develop a chemical and biological incident response force. Similar measures have branched out into the Department of Health and Human Services, FEMA, the Department of Defense, and the Department of Justice (Donohue 2001).

The biggest area of missing coverage in the United States is a specially designated security service that collects intelligence on suspected terrorists and dispenses it to local and federal instigative authorities to pursue. The United States has opted more for traditional local law enforcement in this area. Police units typically have an advantage in community intelligence. Over time, police personnel develop networks of informants who provide information that directs investigation and surveillance. This community intelligence is needed to focus the counter-terrorism effort at the terrorists and away from the community. However, the localized and compartmentalized nature of the information does little overall, as the goal is to neutralize a terrorist organization, not just individuals. The challenge is how to centralize all the information into databases, accessible by many, to maintain focus on the broader terrorist threat.

To facilitate centralization for counter-terrorism, many countries have developed specialized security services that are specifically designed to collect and disseminate information to meet terrorist challenges (Chalk and Rosenau 2004). Examples include Direction de la Surveillance du Territoire (DST) in France; MI5 in Britain; Bunderkriminalant (BKA) and Persone, Institutionen, Objekte, Sachen (PIOS) in Germany; Cesid Gaurdia Civil, Policia Nacional in Spain; and ASIO in Australia (Chalk 1995). The security service collates intelligence data and disseminates it to international intelligence services and local police (Wilkinson 2000). Moreover, the agency does not have a law enforcement or military role. Rather, the security services provide information to direct police action (Chalk and Rosenau 2004). The role for the security services is very narrow in definition: preemptive information gathering designed to prevent new groups from emerging or entrenching in society. In addition to this narrow role, the security services also provide information directed at specific homeland threats, which helps with target hardening by directing resources to the most vulnerable targets.

Given the U.S. experience with COINTELPRO in the past, the tendency inside the U.S. government is to avoid repeating past mistakes. However, the need is still present. To fill this gap, the United States created the National Counterterrorism Center and the Director of National Intelligence, which ideally will provide a nexus point where all intelligence, foreign and domestic, is combined. After the intelligence is combined, it can then be distributed to the appropriate local or federal agencies to guide counter-terrorism efforts. The system is still very new, and time is needed to coordinate the activities of agencies that were previously independent.

9.3.3 Final Thoughts on the U.S. Response to Terrorism

Summarizing U.S. counter-terrorism, we can say that policies are in a state of flux. The United States has made drastic changes to its laws and policies regarding counter-terrorism over the past 50 years. From the 1960s to the 1990s, terrorism was treated exclusively as a local crime issue, especially for homegrown terrorists. This tactic has been very effective. As homegrown and foreign terrorist threats mounted, laws and policies changed to reflect the rising importance of the issue. The uncoordinated efforts of the federal government were first reorganized in the 1980s with the rise of international terrorism. New laws were implemented in the 1990s to define terrorist offenses and apply new sentencing requirements for terrorist offenses. In the post-9/11 world the federal government mounted a major reorganization to meet the terrorist threat, placing counter-terrorism policy as a major national policy. The Department of Homeland Security was created, along with the National Counterterrorism Center. The Director of National Intelligence is a new addition to the intelligence community to better serve national interests by combining all available intelligence to direct counter-terrorism efforts. The rights of terrorist victims are now secured.

In all countries, counter-terrorism responses tend to reflect the most recent attack. In the United States, a decision was made to think proactively about terrorism, not just react. At the state level, governments are passing new laws to define terrorist offenses to supplement their battles against homegrown terrorists. Gaps still exist, and many gaps we may not even be aware of. The test is always the ability of the government to diffuse terrorist threats before they manifest. To date, the United States, in cooperation with its allies, has diffused terrorist plots to bomb airplanes in route from London, and a major plot to bomb the New York City subway and tunnel system has been discovered. At the same time, the ELF and ALF continue to operate relatively unchecked inside the United States. The counter-terrorist system today is better and more comprehensive than in the past, but it is still an evolving system.

SELF-CHECK

1. Which of the following government bureaucracies is not involved in domestic counter-terrorism?

   a. Department of Homeland Security
   b. Department of Defense
   c. Federal Bureau of Investigation
   d. Bureau of Alcohol, Tobacco, and Firearms

2. The Foreign Sovereign Immunities Act allows individuals to pursue civil suits against state sponsors of terrorism. True or false?

3. The Posse Comitatus Act of 1878 prohibits which of the following?

   a. Terrorism
   b. The FBI from harassing political groups
   c. Federal troops from performing police and security operations inside the United States
   d. The federal court system from being used in terrorism cases

4. Define the lead agency approach to counter-terrorism.

SUMMARY

In this chapter, you assessed the types of domestic terrorist threats that impact the United States. You also evaluated the structure and nature of terrorist threats in the United States today, as well as the operational environment that motivates and enables terrorism in America. Finally, you critiqued U.S. counter-terrorism efforts and how they reflect American traditions of the rule of law

By analyzing terrorism inside the United States, we revealed the long and varied history of domestic terrorism. Historically, homegrown terrorists have represented the dominant threat to the United States. However, there are numerous foreign terrorist threats, including émigré terrorism, foreign terrorists using the United States as a base of operations against foreign targets, and foreign terrorists conducting operations against domestic targets. We learned that the United States has a fairly permissive condition toward terrorist activity, meaning there are few institutionalized barriers to prevent terrorist groups from operating. The highly urbanized nature of American society, our reactive security posture, and the rich resource environment are all conducive to the formation of terrorist threats. At the same time, the United States historically experiences comparatively low levels of domestic terrorism. This is due in part to our stable political system that can absorb demands from many mobilized political groups and eliminate the usefulness of terrorist action. Additionally, foreign terrorists wanting to attack the United States can more readily hit targets abroad than targets inside U.S. boundaries.

The United States shows a strong tendency to use the criminal justice system for counter-terrorism. We pride ourselves on being a nation of laws, and we rely on this approach to deal with domestic terrorist threats. Counter-terrorist policy has been very fragmented, however, as many homegrown terrorists were treated as regular criminals and prosecuted at the local level. This policy suited the United States very well until the 1980s and 1990s. The growth of international terrorist threats against the homeland prompted a variety of government reorganizations and new laws to better address terrorist threats. Gaps may still exist in the counter-terrorism shield, but to date, the system has proved to work very well. In time, we may see if new vulnerabilities exist. No nation can completely eliminate its exposure to terrorism, but as of this point, the United States appears to have done a good job in minimizing the risk.

KEY TERMS

Counter-terrorism policy Set of laws, agencies, and programs targeted at controlling and reducing terrorist threats.

Criminal justice model Use of the system of police, courts, laws, and prisons to address a terrorist threat.

Cult terrorist group Type of group that conducts terrorism with the intent or goal of initiating religious prophecy, such as bringing forth a new millennium or messiah.

Eco-terrorism Form of terrorism in which a group attempts to influence domestic policy regarding land development, environmental policy, and animal testing.

Émigré terrorism Form of foreign terrorism in which a foreign victim is killed by a foreign terrorist group inside the boundaries of a different country.

Extortion rackets Scheme in which a group provides security or protection to a business, farmer, or other organization in exchange for materials and resources, most often money. Protection is often from the group offering the protective services.

Foreign targets Terrorist targets located in U.S. territory but symbolically linked to a different country; examples include embassies, foreign nationals, and foreign businesses.

Foreign terrorist group	Type of terrorist group whose operatives originate outside the United States and penetrate homeland security to plan and conduct operations against internal targets.
Foreign terrorist organizers	Foreign terrorist recruiters and agents that raise funds and recruit operatives from inside the United States for operations against U.S. and other national interests overseas.
Homegrown terrorist group	Type of terrorist group whose members originate within the United States and conduct terrorist operations against targets inside the United States.
Informal Funds Transfer System (IFTS)	A foreign remittance system in which a person gives money to an intermediary, who then instructs a contact in the receiving country to distribute the money to a predetermined recipient in the local currency.
Lead agency approach	A counter-terrorism policy in which the federal agency with jurisdiction and accountability over a threat is determined by the loci of the threat (domestic, international, or aviation).
Operational environment	The location of a terrorist group and its primary field of activity, determined by available resources and the ability to recruit members and survive against other political competitors.
Physical environment	The geography surrounding terrorist activity, typically considered as either urban or rural, which determines the epicenter of the activity.
Political environment	The social decision-making process of a society, including its government institutions and rules of access, which allow issues to arise for discussion and decision.
Racial supremacy groups	Type of terrorist group that believes the general social climate of a country is deteriorating and that this condition is caused by the tolerance of different racial groups in society.
Resource environment	The ability of a terrorist group to access necessary financial resources to build an organization and conduct terrorist operations.

Resource mobilization Raising money and other materials to fund terrorist operations, including purchasing weapons and munitions.

Security environment The combination of police, military, intelligence, security forces, courts, and prisons that enforce law and ensure domestic security.

Target hardening Increasing the physical security around likely terrorist targets to prevent an attack.

U.S.-based targets Local or national terrorist targets symbolically linked to the United States.

War model Militarization of a terrorist-related conflict.

ASSESS YOUR UNDERSTANDING

Go to www.wiley.com/college/kilroy to assess your knowledge of the basics of domestic terrorism.

Measure your learning by comparing pre-test and post-test results.

Summary Questions

1. Historically, the domestic terrorism problem in the United States was primarily a result of foreign terrorists operating on American soil. True or false?

2. After 9/11, the United States reorganized its counter-terrorism administration by creating the Department of Homeland Security and the National Counterterrorism Center. True or false?

3. U.S. counter-terrorism policy is based in the criminal justice model, which uses laws, courts, police, and prisons to handle terrorists, rather than the war model, which primarily uses the military. True or false?

4. Under the George W. Bush administration, a specific individual, Richard Clarke, was identified within the NSC to oversee counter-terrorism and was given an operational budget and authority to direct the nation's counter-terrorism effort after 9/11. True or false?

5. Which of the following is **not** an example of a homegrown terrorist group?
   (a) Weather Underground
   (b) Black Panthers
   (c) Al-Qaeda
   (d) Animal Liberation Front

6. Which group has accounted for 32 percent of all terrorist incidents and 46 percent of all right-wing terrorist incidents in the United States?
   (a) Jewish Defense League
   (b) Anti-Castro Cubans
   (c) Earth Liberation Front
   (d) Symbionese Liberation Army

7. The Foreign Sovereigns Immunity Act allows Americans to do what?
   (a) Sue state sponsors of terrorism for damages and losses caused by a terrorist attack
   (b) Conduct terrorist operations in foreign countries
   (c) Hold the same privileges as an ambassador
   (d) Conduct rendition raids in any country in the world to capture suspected terrorists

8. From the 1950s through the 1990s, the majority of foreign terrorist acts in the United States were of what type?
   (a) Islamic extremist
   (b) Communist
   (c) Émigré
   (d) Animal rights

Applying This Chapter

1. You are asked to explain why terrorism takes place in the United States. Beyond simple motivating issues, such as animal rights or opposition to abortion, what can you use to explain why terrorism exists in the United States? How would you discuss the impact of the political environment on the rise of terrorism? How does the political environment work against terrorism?

2. You are serving in the National Counterterrorism Center. Information appears on your desk from an FBI Field Office in Boulder, Colorado, to suggest a group plans to burn down an animal import and quarantine facility. Who do you dispense the information to? What additional information would you disclose to the officials with jurisdiction? What measures would you suggest to disrupt the event and/or capture the perpetrators?

3. A terrorist attack has taken place in the United States, and you hear people arguing that is it time to bring out the military to deal with these foreign terrorists. How would you respond and why?

4. You are serving in the U.S. attorney general's office. A terrorist attack by al-Qaeda has killed dozens of Americans and caused millions in economic damage. What remedies would you recommend to the families of the victims and owners of the property damaged or destroyed by the attack?

YOU TRY IT

Terrorism in America

Provide an analysis of the operational environment in the United States. Write a paper that explores the political environment of the United States, focusing on the New Left and Students for a Democratic Society. Explain how the Weathermen grew out of this organization, but at the same time failed to gain much support to sustain their campaign in the United States.

Counter-terrorism

Analyze the nature of American counter-terrorism policy. Assess the lack of proactive intelligence gathering to identify potential terrorist threats. Explain why this intelligence gathering ability is absent. If the United States were to develop this capacity now, what safeguards must be put in place to ensure compliance with the civil liberties norms of the United States?

10

ENABLERS OF MASS EFFECTS
How Terrorists Benefit from the Information Age

Starting Point

Go to www.wiley.com/college/kilroy to assess your knowledge of the basics of enablers of mass effects.
Determine where you need to concentrate your effort.

What You'll Learn in This Chapter

▲ The ways information and ideas are transmitted in the information age
▲ The role the media plays in shaping perceptions
▲ The ways terrorists can use the Internet to further their aims
▲ The role of educational institutions in shaping generational views toward terrorism

After Studying This Chapter, You'll Be Able To

▲ Evaluate why the information age benefits terrorist organizations in communicating their messages to domestic and international audiences
▲ Propose different media sources for an informational requirement
▲ Evaluate the role of ideas in the international battle against terrorism
▲ Assess the impact of the Internet on terrorist capabilities and threats

INTRODUCTION

The word **enabler**, as it appears in the title of this chapter, can have several different meanings. It can mean anything that assists in the creation of mass effects—an institution or process that makes it possible for the mass effect to occur when it would not have occurred otherwise. Or, the word can mean an institution or process that allows the mass effect to have a greater effect than it would have had otherwise. "Enabler" could also mean an institution or process that is utilized by those who might cause a mass effect.

The institutions and processes we will discuss in this chapter include the media, the Internet, and educational institutions. All of these can make it easier for mass effects to happen, they can help mass effects become larger than they might have been otherwise, and they all have also been used by terrorists and others to further their aims. Before looking at these institutions and processes, however, we'll look at the roles that information and ideas play in mass effects. In this discussion, it is important to remember that the all-hazards approach to emergency and disaster management is heavily dependent on information to assist first responders in determining actually what is happening, who (if anyone) might be responsible for the act, and what can be done to address the situation.

Thus, in this chapter, you will assess the role of the information age in facilitating the spread of terrorists' messages both domestically and internationally. You'll also become familiar with the role of ideas and values in modern world culture and evaluate the role of decision-making rules-of-thumb in assessing the likelihood of potential disastrous events in the United States. Finally, you'll evaluate the assets and limitations of the Internet as a tool for terrorists.

10.1 The Power of Information and Ideas

We live in a global society. Today, the world is linked together through a variety of mass media that make it possible for virtually everybody on the planet to be able to witness an event within a few minutes or hours of its occurrence. For example, more than 300 million people—nearly one in every 20 people on Earth—watched live as Italy beat France in the 2006 World Cup soccer final match in June (and remember that the match didn't draw a particularly large audience in the United States, and we are one of largest television-watching markets in the world!). Other sporting events—the Olympics, the Super Bowl, and so forth—draw somewhat smaller but still impressive audiences. Breaking news also captures people's attention, especially when that news has a sensationalistic aspect to it. For example, some 58 percent of the American public reported watching news of the Asian tsunami in December 2004. The number of people who receive breaking news also seems to be increasing, although finding accurate numbers globally is difficult because it involves aggregating information from over 200 countries around the world.

Although this is a global society, there is also a tremendous amount of local variation in how people view problems, solutions, and so on. For example, religion plays a much more important role in determining how people in some parts of the world (e.g., the Middle East and Latin America) view social and political reality than it does in other parts of the world (e.g., northern Europe). As a result of this disparity, political scientist Ronald Inglehart has developed a series of questions in which he attempts to measure individuals' value orientations across the globe. He classifies these on a materialist–post materialist dimension.

▲ **Materialists** are people who are concerned with personal survival: providing for themselves or their families, making a good salary, and all the "perks" that come along with that salary.

▲ **Post materialists** are those who are more concerned with what some call "higher goals," such as preserving and protecting freedom of speech and other more self-expression-type values.

In addition, Inglehart and others (Inglehart and Baker 2000) have described more traditional values as compared to values associated with change and "modernism." The map in Figure 10-1 (Inglehart Values Map 2006) shows more than 65 nations around the world arrayed on these two dimensions. Countries in the lower left corner of the map are those where the populations (as measured by answers to questions in the World Values Survey) are more traditional and materialistic, while countries in the upper right corner are those where the populations are more post-materialistic and less traditional. One can see the United States' position as high on self-expression values, but also somewhat more traditional than other English-speaking countries like Canada, New Zealand, or Great Britain. When it comes to the importance of religion in one's life or fairly conservative social values, the United States is very different than Great Britain, Canada, Italy, Germany, Japan, or France. Some 59 percent of Americans say religion is very important in their lives, while much smaller percentages (ranging from 11 percent to 33 percent) in Europe say religion is very important. These statistics make the United States fairly similar to Chile or Turkey in this dimension. In terms of economic development and commitment to freedom of speech, however, the United States is similar to countries in Europe and much different than either Chile or Turkey (Starobin 2006).

This focus on values and the way they influence one's view of the world should not surprise anybody—information and ideas are extremely powerful in determining what happens in our world. As Victor Hugo, the nineteenth-century French writer said, "Nothing is as powerful as an idea whose time has come." But how do we know that an idea's time has actually come? The contest over the control of information, the interpretation of information, and the role of ideas

Figure 10-1

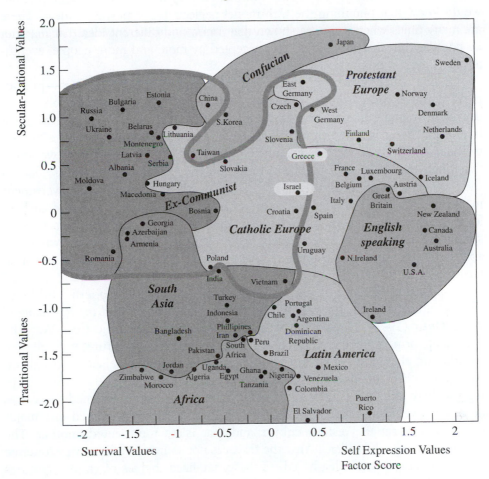

Inglehart Values Map (Source: World Values Survey).

is one that is never-ending. When two people who do not have a shared world-view discuss controversial issues, it often seems they are talking past each other. This is because they do not share a common frame of reference through which the issues can be debated.

For many years, the dominant model of American politics has been the plural-ist model. This model assumes that various groups compete in the political arena using money, numbers of members, leadership, and so on as resources in group competition. As early as the writing of the U.S. Constitution, James Madison described the U.S. government as an attempt to cure "the mischief of faction" (Federalist Paper 10). This political model is so deeply engrained in American society that it is difficult at times to think that it may not be entirely accurate. But we do know that one thing the U.S. model neglects is the power of ideas. There are many times when it can be shown that a new and different idea that may not be popular (but that may be right) is accepted by more and more people, eventually becoming a dominant worldview.

In this different type of competition—the competition of ideas—politics plays a much more complicated role than it does in the simpler pluralistic universe. If money or numbers of adherents or other resources are the most important things in determining success in any political competition, the "haves" in the world have a tremendous advantage over the "have nots." Yet, we know that often the "have nots" can win based on the power of their ideas, not on their own innate political power. For example, while the apartheid government in South Africa had almost a monopoly on political force, the anti-apartheid forces had a much more positive idea: that people should not be separated simply because of the color of their skin. This idea eventually won when the apartheid government was replaced in 1994 by a government composed of all races.

The classic reference in discussing the battle of ideas in modern world culture is Samuel Huntington's book *The Clash of Civilizations and the Remaking of World Order* (1996). Huntington wrote that with the end of the Cold War, the dominant form of conflict had changed from ideology to culture and religion. Huntington also wrote that Western civilization was at an intellectual disadvantage in this clash, because it assumed that liberal democracy was the only remaining ideology after the end of the Cold War, and so simply assumed there was no alternative. Huntington thought that Chinese culture represented one major intellectual threat to Western culture and that Islam represented another. The major point here, however, is that the threat is not so much military or economic as it is intellectual and idea-based, as the generalized themes of various cultures compete for large-scale popular adoption.

How does this happen? How does one set of ideas supplant another? Malcolm Gladwell (2000) describes one such process in his book *The Tipping Point*. Gladwell and others (Grodzins 1958, Schelling 1978) have developed a model in which ideas influence a few people, who influence a few more, and so on, until at some point, one additional person adopts the new idea and then, suddenly, everybody does. The environment thus turns from one state to another. Think of an avalanche. In one place, when a small amount of snow and ice breaks loose in the mountains, nothing happens. In a different place, a small amount of snow and ice breaks loose and begins to slide, picking up additional snow and ice. At some point, the amount of snow and ice is enough to let the whole side of the mountain come down, taking trees, houses, and unfortunate people with it.

10.1.1 Ideas and Terrorism

In the recently published *National Strategy to Combat Terrorism* (2006), President George W. Bush said, "In the long run, winning the War on Terror means winning the battle of ideas. Ideas can transform the embittered and disillusioned either into murderers willing to kill innocents, or into free peoples living harmoniously in a diverse society." This battle of ideas involves creating a positive alternative to the image of world society that terrorists would like people to believe. Examine the map of political values described earlier. Look for countries that we might think are places where terrorism could arise. In which section of the map do these countries tend to be clustered? Many are in the lower left section—where traditional and survival values dominate. In other words, these are countries in which there are a large number of poor people who at the present time seem to have little hope that they can better themselves. This may partially be the result of poor education, poor economic development opportunities, or a worldview that ignores physical accomplishments in the current world but instead focuses on rewards that may be granted in the afterlife. When people lack education, they have a hard time succeeding in a world where education is valued. Where economic development opportunities are lacking, even educated people may not succeed because there are few venues to exercise one's education. And when people's worldview replaces physical, material rewards in the current world with promises of rewards in the afterlife, those same people may focus on all kinds of actions that make them worthier for those promised rewards rather than taking actions to improve their current material conditions.

What is the positive alternative that the United States and the Western world can offer to the have-nots of the Middle East and other areas that may be hotbeds of potential terrorism? Certainly one thing is material comfort—it is absolutely true that the nations of North American and Europe have the highest standards of living of all nations in the world. Yet, if one does not think that such material comfort is important or if one thinks that it is beyond one's possible reach, what does this promise mean? Indeed, one might ask why a person might want to continue his or her life if there is no promise for improvement in the current life but a possibility of reward in the afterlife.

If this battle of ideas is framed as a battle between true believers and a decadent Western culture, true believers have an upper hand. By describing to a conservative, traditional people the ways that Western societies glorify semi-nude public display of the human body—at beaches and nightclubs, on television, and in films—the "true believer" side in the battle of ideas seizes the moral high ground. By portraying this same thing as an exercise in freedom of expression, Western societies can attempt to blunt the attack by demonstrating that simply because people *can* act in such ways doesn't mean that everybody *does* act in those ways, and that the freedom that such activity exemplifies is worth more than any excess that might be its result. "I may disagree with everything you say, but will defend unto death your right to say it," a quotation commonly attributed to the French philosopher Voltaire, best sums up this Western attitude of freedom of expression and tolerance for differing opinions. But this is a difficult point to make to people who have not been raised with norms of tolerance or freedom of expression.

Many times, this battle of ideas takes the form of choosing the proper term to describe a thing or event that carries with it certain connotations. President George W. Bush's unfortunate choice of words immediately after the 9/11 attacks—"'this crusade, this war on terrorism'—brought up images of European knights invading Muslim strongholds over several hundred years in the Middle Ages" (Ford 2001). Moqtada al-Sadr—an Iraqi Shiite cleric—organized a militia in 2003 that he called the Mahdi Army. This term carried heavy spiritual connotations to Muslims. According to Islamic scripture, the Mahdi is a figure who will assist the believers in defeating the anti-Christ in apocalyptic times. By using this term to describe this army, U.S. and other Western forces play into the hands of this clever cleric in furthering his claim to be on a religious mission. Likewise, the United States has had a difficult time in describing who the terrorists actually are. The Bush administration has used several terms to describe these groups: radical Islamists, Islamic fascists, radical Islam, Islamic terrorists, Jihadists, and so on. Each of these carries with it a somewhat different connotation; each risks alienating certain subgroups in the Muslim world; and none of these terms has particularly resonated with the American public. In addition, both American political leaders and the media have had difficulties in coming up with a term to describe the Iraqi opposition. The term "rebel" implies legitimacy, while "resistance" implies patriotism and protection of one's country against invaders. Even the nature of the conflict has been difficult to correctly title. "Sectarian violence" does not adequately describe the extent of the fighting. On the other hand, the term "civil war" implies two legitimate sides contesting over who should rule the country— something the U.S. government does not want to imply—so it is also used sparingly. This contest over what words to use to describe items and events is an example of the larger battle of ideas: Choose the wrong term, and you risk being on the wrong side of history in opposition to an idea whose time has come.

10.1.2 Ideas and the All-Hazards Assessment

The all-hazards assessment of emergency and disaster management has been described in Chapters 3 and 4. Risk assessment models and matrices help evaluate hazards on the basis of their probability and the extent of the potential damage they might cause. Large-scale terrorist attacks, which could cause huge amounts of damage, are generally considered to be low probability events, while hurricanes, floods, tornadoes, and earthquakes are much higher probability events in areas where they have occurred before (e.g., hurricanes in East and Gulf Coast areas, tornadoes in the Midwest, and so on). The all-hazards assessment places the probability of an event occurring partially on the basis of how frequently that event has occurred in the past. Five-hundred year floods cause much more damage than 100-year floods, but 500-year floods are also much less probable than 100-year floods, so the preparation for each is different.

One way that ideas become involved in the all-hazards assessment process is in the evaluation of the probability of various types of events occurring. There are many ways that these probabilities can be estimated; the most common is through experience as stated above. But assessing the probability of an event through how commonly it has occurred in the past means that the probability of events that are new cannot be assessed at all. This can be the situation with nuclear, biological, chemical, or radiological terrorist events, described in Chapter 8. Because these have never occurred in the United States and have occurred only extremely rarely elsewhere, figuring out their likelihood is problematic, to say the least. With these types of events, even sophisticated decision makers often resort to using **heuristics** (rules of thumb). Among these are the representativeness heuristic, the availability heuristic, and the vividness heuristic.

▲ **Representativeness heuristic:** This involves assessing the probability of an unknown event on the basis of how it represents an event we know.

▲ **Availability heuristic:** Here, the probability of an event is assessed by how clearly we can imagine events like it.

▲ **Vividness heuristic:** With this heuristic, events that contain vivid descriptions or images are often viewed as more probable than those that are more abstract (Kahneman and Tversky 1973; Nisbett and Ross 1980).

These heuristics often work well, but sometimes their use can result in wrong conclusions. The following are examples of how each heuristic can lead to a potential wrong conclusion:

▲ *Representativeness heuristic:* Consider the following series of potential events: XXXXXOOO and XXOXXOOXX. Which series of events is more probable? Many people will say the second one, because it looks "more random" than the first. However, the correct answer is that they are both equally probable, because they both contain six Xs and three Os.

▲ *Availability heuristic:* Imagine that people are asked what they believe the probability of dying in a plane crash is. After there has actually been a plane crash, people will generally say the probability is higher than they would if asked during a period when there hasn't been a recent plane crash.

▲ *Vividness heuristic:* Say that on the basis of the National Highway Traffic Safety Administration (NHTSA) ratings of automobiles, you decide to buy the safest rated car. Your best friend then calls you and says, "Don't buy that car—a friend of mine almost died in a crash when she was driving that make of car!" How does this new piece of information change your decision? If you are like many people, this vivid piece of information will dramatically affect your decision, but it really shouldn't, because this is only one case compared to the many involved in developing the NHTSA ratings.

You can see how each of these heuristics would work in estimating the probability of natural disasters or terrorist events. Even sophisticated disaster managers might not correctly estimate probabilities if they are working in areas where there are few pre-existing cases.

FOR EXAMPLE

Hurricane Katrina

The Federal Emergency Management Agency (FEMA) developed a report in 2001 that concluded that a major hurricane hitting New Orleans was one of the three most likely disasters that might occur in the United States (the other two were an earthquake along the San Andreas fault in California and a major terrorist event in New York City). So it should have come as no surprise when Hurricane Katrina hit New Orleans in 2005. But emergency management officials at the federal, state, and local levels were slow in responding to Katrina partially because they could not imagine the consequences of such a storm (availability). People along the Gulf Coast thought that if they moved their cars inland of the CSX railroad tracks that ran near the coast through Mississippi and Louisiana, their cars would not be flooded. This natural berm had protected cars when Hurricane Camille hit in 1969 (representativeness). After Katrina, aerial photos of the Gulf Coast showed some 10,000 flooded cars that had been parked just north of the CSX tracks (Allen 2006). The vivid depiction of the destruction from Hurricane Katrina and the disorganized governmental response to this storm led to the appointment of U.S. Coast Guard Admiral Thad Allen as the Principal Federal Officer (PFO) on the scene. Allen's success in organizing the relief effort in New Orleans led to the appointment of Coast Guard Admiral Brian Peterman to spearhead possible relief efforts before Hurricane Ophelia hit the North Carolina coast later in 2005, even though Ophelia caused relatively little damage to coastal North Carolina (vividness).

SELF-CHECK

1. Define enabler.
2. Post materialists are people who are concerned with personal survival. True or False?
3. List examples of heuristics.
4. Prior to 9/11, what did FEMA believe were the three most likely disasters to occur in the United States?

10.2 The Role of the Media in the Global War on Terrorism

Media have a major role in creating the effects mentioned above. In Zen Buddhism, there is a famous **koan** (a question that cannot be answered) that asks, "If a tree falls in a forest and nobody is there to hear it, does it make a sound?" We can ask the same kind of question here—if a terrorist attack occurs anywhere in the world and it is not covered by the media, did it actually happen? We know that media coverage affects personal reactions to terrorism and natural disasters. For example, a major study of the incidence of post-traumatic stress disorder (PTSD) after the 9/11 terrorist attacks found that the most important predictors of higher levels of PTSD were as follows:

1. Living in the New York City area
2. Having family, friends, or coworkers who were killed or injured in the attacks
3. Being in the military or having close friends or family in the military
4. Perhaps most interestingly, the number of hours of watching coverage of the 9/11 attacks on television (Schlenger et al. 2002)

The authors of this report also built an index of television graphic content of the 9/11 attacks. The survey respondents reported how many of seven different graphic events (for example, seeing at least one of the planes hit the towers) they had seen. The larger the number of events a respondent reported seeing *indirectly via television*, the more likely it was that he or she would have reported suffering from PTSD two months after the attacks (vividness again).

Media also frame the events they cover. In their coverage of different kinds of stories, media provide meaning to the people who are watching, listening, or reading. For example, when TWA flight 800 crashed into the ocean just off Long Island in 1996, television news at first reported the story as if it were a terrorist attack. Stories were framed such that the key issues were who might have done this, what their motives may have been, why they chose this flight, and so on. Later, when the probable cause of the crash was identified as frayed wires in a fuel tank that caused the tank to explode, the framing of the stories changed. However, the initial media stories were so strong that there is a continued focus on the terrorism link, even to the point that many believe the plane was brought down by a missile fired from the ground. This framing of stories can result in incorrect conclusions but, more subtly, it influences the way we think about potential terrorist events. In the wake of the 9/11 attacks, some 1,200 Middle Eastern or South Asian undocumented male aliens were taken into custody in the United States, their major offense being that they were Muslim men who were in the country illegally (Amnesty International 2002). Law enforcement officials around the country were on the lookout for Arab- or Muslim-looking men who might also be terrorists, partially as a result of media stories focusing on the ethnicity of the 9/11 terrorists. While it is certainly the case that all of the 9/11 terrorists were Middle Easterners, it is not the case, by a long shot, that all terrorists are Middle Easterners. However, many of the news reports on the 9/11 attacks did not make this point clear, leaving a false impression in the minds of many viewers and framing the story differently than it might have been. Public confusion over 9/11 is widespread—for example, in 2003, a *Washington Post* poll (USA Today 2003) found that some 70 percent of Americans surveyed thought that Saddam Hussein was somehow involved in the 9/11 attacks, while three years later, a U.S. Senate panel found that there actually was no connection between Saddam, al-Qaeda, and the attacks (United States Senate Select Committee on Intelligence 2006).

Media provide a tremendous amount of information to both average citizens and to government officials. It was said that President Lyndon Johnson had a special television set with three screens built for the White House so that he could watch the CBS, ABC, and NBC evening news at the same time. The advent of cable television reduced the power of the television network news shows, and they are not nearly as strong as they were in the 1960s, but television media remains the means by which most people around the world get their news about current events.

10.2.1 The Use of Media by Terrorist Groups

Osama bin Laden releases a videotape that condemns American involvement in Iraq and Afghanistan. This tape is somehow delivered to **al-Jazeera**, the Arabic language news network headquartered in Qatar. The broadcast is watched by many in the Middle East and also recorded by CNN and Fox News in the United States, who then rebroadcast the tape with commentary. What has happened here?

▲ First, this is a news event—most speeches by bin Laden are covered heavily by the news media, because there is a fascination with him by many people around the world (for a variety of reasons).

▲ Second, this is an intelligence event—the U.S. and other Western intelligence agencies will examine the tape closely to see if it provides any information on bin Laden's whereabouts, health, clues of future intentions, or changes in his political agenda.

▲ Third, it is a publicity event. Al-Qaeda uses these tapes as a way of demonstrating that they are still a force to be reckoned with, to reinforce support for the group among those who already support it, and to win new converts among those who do not already support it. Even the horrible images of kidnapped victims being threatened with beheading by hooded terrorists that seem all-too-common on television in recent years have a publicity focus. These latter tapes are designed to demonstrate that the kidnappers are serious—they are willing and able to take the actions they are graphically describing unless their demands are met. The tapes are also designed to show that the kidnappers will take similar actions in the future if their demands are not met in this specific case.

▲ Fourth, the tapes "introduce" previously unknown terrorist groups to the world, showing that even though they may not be known, they are capable of dramatic action.

▲ Fifth, the tapes show sympathetic people that there are groups that are willing and able to take radical action in support of some political agenda.

▲ And sixth, the tapes provide a warning to unsympathetic people that they may be the target of future action if they become too vocal in their opposition to the terrorist group.

So, as you can see, these tapes have a number of different meanings. It is interesting, to say the least, to see the reaction that the most recent al-Qaeda or other group's tape gets from Western media, Western governments, Middle Eastern governments, the public, and so on. Each different group reacts to the tapes differently, stemming from their own positions on the underlying issues. But very rarely do such tapes fail to create a sensation throughout the world. As Ayman al-Zawahiri, Osama bin Laden's second in command of al-Qaeda, wrote in 2005, "We are in a battle and more than half of this battle is taking place in the battlefield of the media . . . [W]e are in a media battle for the hearts and minds of our **umma** [the community of the faithful]" (quoted in Lynch 2006, 50).

SELF-CHECK

1. Explain how the media frames an event.
2. Describe how terrorist organizations use the media to their advantage.
3. List an example of an Arabic media source in the Middle East.
4. Videotapes broadcast via television news are rarely used as a way to introduce new terrorist groups to the world. True or false?

10.3 The Internet and Other Global Communications Means

In the 1990s, when the Internet and the World Wide Web became widely popular as methods of communication, the designers of this new communication medium worried that it was not achieving its full potential because it did not create instantaneous many-to-many communication. Some fifteen years later, we can see that these early concerns were largely unwarranted. Recent estimates of Internet users around the world run to over 1 billion, or about one in every six people on Earth (Internet World Stats n.d.). Growth in the number of Internet users has begun to level off in the Western world as the number of users approach saturation. However, 2000–2006 growth rates of over 600% in Africa, 400% in the Middle East, and 300% in Latin America show that larger numbers of people are just now being introduced to the Internet in many parts of the world.

The Internet is an anarchic, decentralized environment. There is little external regulation of the content and procedures that take place in this virtual environment, and almost anybody can contribute. The Internet is also easy to use. Plus, the Internet allows for almost complete anonymity in communications—individuals can make themselves known by screen names or aliases or they may simply be known only by their IP (Internet protocol) addresses. (And even in this instance, users can work through proxy servers to disguise their IP addresses, or they can "spoof" another user's profile and send out materials as if they were coming from the second user's computer.) While external monitors (government, university web administrators, corporate supervisors, and so on) can trace where individual users have gone on the Internet and where they currently are, this monitoring is very resource-intensive and for the majority of cases, it makes little sense. Only in a totalitarian society or when there is a known threat does it make sense to monitor one's Internet usage.

Figure 10-2

Image from an al-Qaeda website (Source: Weimann 2004b).

And even though it is possible to monitor where users go on the Internet, it is much less possible to control what they post on the Internet. Researchers and students both have fallen victim to inaccurate or false information posted on Internet websites—often with humorous results. But the use of the Internet by terrorist groups is not humorous; it is instead powerful, dangerous, and widespread.

Gabriel Weimann, a researcher at the United States Institute of Peace, has conducted a six-year research project on how modern terrorism uses the Internet. In Weimann's view, the "Internet is in many ways an ideal arena for activity by terrorist organizations" (Weimann 2004a, 3). Many terrorist groups have their own websites—a screen shot from one of the al-Qaeda websites is shown in Figure 10-2.

While a great deal of attention has been paid to the possibility of cyber-terrorism, Weimann writes that terrorist groups can also use the Internet in more mundane ways that can be just as dangerous. These ways include psychological warfare, publicity and propaganda, data mining, fundraising, recruitment and mobilization, networking, sharing information, and planning and coordination. Let's examine these one at a time.

▲ *Psychological warfare*: Terrorism is a form of **psychological warfare**, which the Department of Defense defines as "the use of propaganda and other psychological actions having the primary purpose of influencing the opinions, emotions, attitudes, and behavior of hostile foreign groups in such a way as to support the achievement of national objectives" (2003). The Internet, because of its attributes described above, is almost the perfect venue to carry out this type of warfare. Weimann discusses the threat of cyber-terrorism—or more accurately, "cyber-fear." This occurs when "concern about what a computer attack could do (for example, bringing down airliners by disabling air traffic control systems, or disrupting national economies by wrecking the computerized systems that regulate stock markets) is amplified until the public believes than an attack will happen" (Weimann 2004a, 5).

▲ *Publicity and propaganda:* Television, radio, and print media have some form of editorial control; at some point in the publication process, editors make decisions about what the media will carry. The Internet does not have this—terrorist websites carry anything the terrorist groups want to post there. Part of this is an act of self-creation as the underdog. Terrorist groups use websites partially because, they claim, they are being excluded from traditional media. They use words like "martyr" and "genocide" on their websites to frame issues in the way they want. They claim that they are the victims of state violence and only resort to violence in self-defense. They portray themselves as weak but also portray their cause as inherently "right."

▲ *Data mining:* **Data mining** can be defined as the use of the Internet for open source information, which when pieced together, provides information of intelligence value for an organization. As a result of laws and policies developed in the 1980s and 1990s, a great deal of information about government agencies in the United States has been posted on the World Wide Web. For example, laws collectively known as "community right to know" laws required companies that stockpiled hazardous chemicals to notify residents of surrounding neighborhoods what chemicals the companies were using. Local fire departments also needed to have this information in case a fire broke out in the company facilities. When the World Wide Web became popular in the mid-1990s, many companies and government agencies concluded that it would be more efficient for them to comply with these laws and regulations by listing the hazardous chemicals they were working with on their websites. After the 9/11 attacks in the United States, different U.S. government agencies—the Environmental Protection Agency, the Department of Energy, and so on—began advocating the removal of this kind of information from these websites because they thought potential terrorists were collecting sensitive data from them. Gellman (2002) reported that the FBI had tracked multiple casings of websites for nuclear power plants, dams, and gas facilities to computers outside the United States. Later, in 2002, laptop computers seized from al-Qaeda contained some of the information that had been collected from those websites. Just after the 9/11 attacks, Steven Aftergood, the director of the

Project on Government Secrecy of the Federation of American Scientists (a group that had continually advocated more openness in U.S. government websites) was quoted as saying, "I had to come to terms with the fact that government secrecy is not the worst thing in the world . . . There are worse things" (Toner 2001, B4).

▲ *Fundraising:* Related to publicity and propaganda, fundraising is also an aim of terrorist websites. Weimann (2004a) writes that the Irish Republican Army (IRA) website allows visitors to make donations by credit card. Often terrorist groups gather information from website users to develop a demographic profile of people they can approach for donations. Then a sympathetic front group approaches the user and asks for money for seemingly legitimate uses. This money is then forwarded to the terrorist organization. After 9/11, the U.S. government seized the assets of several charities operating in the United States, claiming they were front groups for Hamas and al-Qaeda.

▲ *Recruitment and mobilization:* Many terrorist websites have pages that are headed "What You Can Do" or "Help in the Struggle." These webpages often are recruitment devices by which the terrorist group is seeking individuals who are more devoted to their cause than the casual web browser. The user who goes to one of these pages may get an anonymous email asking if he or she would like more information or directions on how to use an anonymous chat room where details of upcoming events may be discussed. Often, training manuals are distributed to the user who can prove that he or she is genuinely interested in the terrorist group's cause or mission. These manuals might teach users how to build bombs, purchase satellite phones, and so on. Interested users are also provided with propaganda and information on the group's ideology or religious beliefs. Using information gathered from the pattern of how the individual user accesses the group's website, the group can customize the information provided to the user—different information for men and women, older people or younger, people from different countries, and so on.

▲ *Networking:* Modern terrorist organizations do not often resemble the hierarchical type of structure described by Max Weber (the nineteenth-century German sociologist who coined the word "bureaucracy") in his classic works on organizations. Instead, these new type organizations look something like amoebae—the organization can change its shape when it is confronted by a threat or presented with an opportunity. After Afghanistan was invaded by U.S. and other troops in late 2001, al-Qaeda morphed into what Peter Bergen (2002) has called "al-Qaeda version 2.0," a virtual organization that maintains contacts via the Internet rather than in person. Rather than being an organization with Osama bin Laden at its head, the new al-Qaeda is composed of highly trained operatives around the world who keep in touch with each other via the Internet and who know that they can take action on their own to maximize their opportunities. This has been entitled the "leaderless resistance" by some analysts (Wallace-Wells 2006).

▲ *Information sharing:* A great deal of information on the fundamentals of terrorist activity can be found on the Internet. Guides to bomb making, chemical weapons, poisons, assassinations, and so on are readily available from a variety of websites. These guides are not only good for potential terrorist organizations but also for the lone, disaffected individual who may be looking for revenge to compensate for perceived insults. Many of the more common guides—*The Terrorist's Handbook, The Anarchist Cookbook*, and so on—are available from a number of websites, so when one website is shut down or convinced to stop carrying the information, users can find it elsewhere. Weimann (2004a) reports that a Google search for the words "terrorist" and "handbook" found nearly four thousand hits.

▲ *Planning and coordination*: After 9/11, the U.S. government seized a laptop computer from Abu Zubaydah, the al-Qaeda operative who is commonly thought to have planned the attacks. This computer contained a large number of encrypted messages, many dated just before the September attacks. At times, the codes used in messages are very elaborate—for example, some use steganography (embedding messages in graphic files)—but at other times, the codes are fairly simple. Mohammed Atta, one of the 9/11 terrorists, described the buildings targeted by the terrorists as the faculties of fine arts, law, urban planning, and engineering. And the scenario described by Gellman in the "Data Mining" section above shows that al-Qaeda and other terrorist groups were gathering information to plan to combine conventional and cyber-terrorism attacks. A facility's website containing evacuation information could be jammed at the same time the physical facility was attacked, thus presumably maximizing casualties (this effect is developed more fully in Chapter 7).

Partially to address the use of the Internet by terrorist groups, Western and other anti-terrorism forces have recently been waging a war against terrorist websites. Intelligence agencies do this by putting pressure on web hosting companies to shut down websites that are associated with terrorism, by taking direct action themselves, or by relying on outside groups and individuals to take action. Alneda.com (the word *alneda* means "the call" in Arabic), for example, was an al-Qaeda associated website on which encrypted information was posted that directed users to other websites and where users could see videos of Osama bin Laden and other information on al-Qaeda, its programs, and goals. Alneda.com

---

FOR EXAMPLE

Irhabi 007

The story of Irhabi 007 is also instructive (Labi 2006; Levine 2006). Irhabi first surfaced on terrorist associated websites in 2003. He became a regular on the website al-ansar.com—the website on which in 2004 the late Iraqi terrorist al-Zarqawi posted the video of the beheading of American contractor Nicholas Berg. Irhabi posted sensitive information on the al-ansar website—maps of Israel, guides on how to be a sniper, and so on. He was also looking for personal information on U.S. soldiers that he could provide to al-Qaeda or other terrorist groups (Cutler 2006). Eventually, he came to the attention of several independent agencies that track terrorist type Internet activity. One of these agencies—the Terrorist Research Center in northern Virginia—took notes and described him as one of "a new and growing terrorist vanguard" (Labi 2006, 103). Other individuals with computer knowledge and vested interests in anti-terrorism also were working to stop Irhabi's efforts. One of these was Aaron Weisburd, who developed a website called Internet Haganah (a Hebrew word meaning "defense") that kept close watch on Irhabi. After tracking Irhabi's exploits for more than a year, Weisburd announced on Internet Haganah in September 2005 that he thought Irhabi was located in Ealing, England. Eventually British police arrested Younis Tsouli in an apartment near Ealing and charged him under British anti-terrorism laws with being Irhabi 007. At the time of his arrest, Tsouli was finishing a webpage entitled "You Bomb It," containing videos of how to make a car bomb and potential sites in Washington, D.C. (Levine 2006). Additional evidence found in Tsouli's apartment led to the arrest of two other men, Waseem Mughal and Tariq al-Daour. Some anti-terrorist Internet watchers have noted that Irabi's efforts were too widespread to be the work of one person. Rita Katz, the director of the Search for International Terrorist Entities (SITE) Institute, does not think that Irhabi was one person but instead the name for a group of terrorists (Labi 2006), meaning that the arrest of Tsouli, Mughal, and al-Daour may not have ended the Irhabi 007 threat.

---

was hosted by the Internet service provider Malaysia Technology Development Corporation. The site was attacked many times in 2002 by different actors using what is known as Denial of Service (DoS) attacks (explained in Chapter 7), but it was not until later in the year that it was finally shut down by an individual independent of the U.S. government.

In the United States, the Terrorist Research Center, the SITE Institute, Internet Haganah, and others monitor terrorist websites with varying degrees of interactivity—some groups only monitor those websites to see what is going on; other groups monitor and report suspicious activity; still other groups seek to shut down terrorist websites using DoS or other type attacks. Similar efforts are also being conducted in other countries, both in the West and in the Middle East. A recent interview by Mahan Abedin with Saad al-Faqih, the head of a group opposed to the current Saudi regime, contained the following interchange:

> [D]o you think that the jihadis now see the Internet as the most important battle space?
>
> Only the jihadis in Iraq.
>
> Why?
>
> Because the only place on earth where the jihadis feel safe is Iraq. The Internet used to be awash with jihadi material but this is becoming less so for two reasons. Firstly, Western intelligence services are now aggressively targeting jihadi websites and are showing a greater determination to close them down completely. In the past they would allow some of the more interesting ones to remain in operation so that they could covertly gather intelligence on the web masters and the contributors. Dozens of websites have been closed in recent months.
>
> Secondly, Western governments have provided software and other expertise to the Saudi regime to trace individual contributors to web forums. But the jihadis in Iraq feel safe and secure because they have satellite Internet connections and they can set up temporary websites and upload files very easily. The invasion of Iraq has boosted the fortunes of jihadis in many respects, and the Internet is no exception (Abedin 2005).

SELF-CHECK

1. List some of the uses of the Internet by terrorist organizations.
2. Define cyber-fear.
3. Terrorists use psychological warfare to influence the opinions, emotions, attitudes, and behavior of people in such a way as to support the achievement of their objectives. True or false?
4. What is the value of data mining?

10.4 The Role of Educational Institutions

In the worldwide contest of ideas, what role do educational institutions play? For the most part, Western educational institutions have been the home of liberal democracy. It is in Western universities, for example, that students learn the history of Western intellectual thought from Plato to the post-modern theorists. The term "liberal arts" is often used to describe this set of humanistic values that students study in Western universities.

10.4.1 Alternative Educational Institutions

In recent years, alternative educational models have arisen both in the West and in other parts of the world to compete with the liberal Western university. The media have focused a great deal of attention on the growth of **madrassas** (religious schools in Islamic countries which teach traditional Islamic ideas) and the role that these schools may have in recruiting members of terrorist organizations. A recent analysis done for the Congressional Research Service (Armanios 2003) summarizes the growth of madrassas in the Middle East and South Asia. In countries such as Pakistan, Indonesia, and Qatar, interest in madrassas increased in the early 2000s.[1] There are both economic and religious reasons why madrassas are attractive to Muslims. Most madrassas are free to those who attend; the schools are supported by alms given by Muslim faithful and, at least in the past, by wealthy Saudi international charities like al-Haramayn.[2] Also, and most likely as important as financial considerations, many Muslims prefer that their children be educated in a religious institution because some "view its traditional pedagogical approach as a way to preserve an authentic Islamic heritage" (Armanios 2003, 3). Only a small number of madrassas have been linked to terrorist groups—the United States Agency for International Development (USAID) reported that such links are "rare but worrisome" (Benoliel 2003, 12), but the larger question of the effect of the type of education being offered at madrassas is murkier. Although the schools were financed by Saudi charities, the focus of the curriculum was often on Wahabbism, a strict form of Sunni Islam. In this type of curriculum, "students are often instructed to reject the 'immoral' and 'materialistic' Western culture" (Armanios 2003, 3). Graduates of madrassas are not particularly prepared to compete for western or international corporate jobs, thus many find employment in the religious sector in their home countries or become educators in madrassas themselves.

---

[1] A recent survey conducted by Tahir Andrabi, Jishnu Das, Asim Ijaz Khwaja, and Tristan Zajonc (2005) of Harvard University questions the growth of enrollment in madrassas in Islamic countries. Based on published data made available by the Pakistani government, this study estimates that only 1 percent of students in Pakistan are enrolled in madrassas.

[2] As a result of pressure put on the Saudi government by the United States, such international charity work was banned by the Saudi authorities in 2003.

10.4.2 International Students in the United States

Since the early part of the twentieth century, U.S. universities have accepted large numbers of foreign students. Today, U.S. universities house the largest number of international students (in excess of 500,000) of any country in the world, although as a percentage of all university students, the percentage of international students in the United States remains low (on the order of 1 percent). Universities in the United States like to accept international students for a variety of reasons—at times, they are even better prepared to pursue university courses than U.S. educated students are. Students who do not speak English as a first language but who have had formal training in English often know more about the English language than native-born English speakers who have picked up the language naturally. Training in math and science in many parts of the world is more rigorous than it is in the United States, so students coming to this country to pursue university education in those fields often are better prepared than U.S.-educated students.

The U.S. government assists in the education of international students in American institutions of higher learning. For example, the Muskie/Freedom Support Act—passed after the dissolution of the Soviet Union—provides full tuition, fees, an allowance for books and professional development, and a monthly stipend to highly qualified graduate students from the former Soviet Union and eastern Europe. These students study curriculum in fields such as law, public administration, public policy, business administration, and education. When the students have completed their studies in the United States, they are required to return to their home countries to work, and they must agree not to apply for immigration to the United States for at least two years. The idea behind this program and others like it is multifaceted: to contribute to the economic and political development of other countries; to expose U.S. students to excellent foreign students with the hope that such exposure will stimulate the American students to better performance; and so on. But one goal of the program should be clear: It is in the interests of the U.S. government to attempt to spread American values to other countries, especially those where values are currently changing. Investing resources in university students seems to be a particularly good way of doing this because, upon returning home, many of the U.S.-educated students take positions of political, economic, and educational leadership.

The general openness of the American system to international students does come at some cost. Several of the 9/11 terrorists entered the United States with legitimate student visas. This led the federal government to a major re-examination of visa requirements for students studying in the United States. One problem with pre-9/11 regulations was the lack of monitoring of what foreign students studying in U.S. universities were actually doing—some enrolled in classes, dropped them, and then disappeared for the remainder of the semester or academic year. Others graduated from the programs to which they applied and then disappeared into the American shadow economy, working as undocumented aliens. The problem of "visa overstaying" is probably larger (in terms of numbers of people) than the problem of people sneaking across the border from Mexico or Canada—a recent General Accounting Office (GAO) report estimated that there were some 2,000,000 people in the United States who had overstayed legitimate business, tourist, or student visas or border control crossing cards.

After 9/11, the federal government began to address the question of tracking international students in the United States for study more seriously. Since 2002, international students who enter the United States have been required to register with **SEVIS** (Student and Exchange Visitor Information System), a computerized registry of international students studying in the United States. The fee for complying with SEVIS is paid by the individual student and is typically $100. Partially as a result of increased fees and regulations on international students (as well as increased tuition and fees in the United States), the number of such students requesting visas to study in the United States declined dramatically immediately after 9/11 and has continued to decline for the years following that, although at a much lower rate. At the same time, however, the number of international students attending universities in Europe, Australia, and China has increased dramatically.

Although the U.S. government hopes that international students who study in the United States will return to their countries to spread American values, this may not always be the case. International students studying in the United States face discrimination in local rentals, education of children, and even in their interactions with other students. The goal of most international study programs is to expose foreign students to their American colleagues, but international students often wind up living and socializing with people from their home countries or with other international students. For students who do not speak English as a first language, living and socializing with somebody "from home" may mean speaking a language that is much more comfortable than English. This, of course, means that their exposure to and immersion in U.S. culture is diminished. An evaluation of the first ten years of the Muskie/Freedom Support Act graduate program found, however, that alumni of the program had a more democratic outlook toward the work environment, greater communication skills, and were more likely to think they could influence the direction that their own society was taking in comparison to a similar group of students who had not enrolled in U.S. graduate programs (Bureau of Educational and Cultural Affairs 2002). All of these outcomes argue that exposure to U.S. graduate programs has very positive outcomes on these international students who returned to their home countries.

10.4.3 Education of Domestic Students in Security

The broad field of homeland security or security studies has become a major growth area in academia over the last few years. After 9/11, it became apparent to some academics that new programs that spanned the fields of international relations, public administration, criminal justice, emergency planning, and the

FOR EXAMPLE

Homeland Security Education

The area of homeland security education is becoming increasingly popular in U.S. universities, but those universities are taking very different approaches to this new area of education and training. Some universities are organizing new, more practically oriented programs in homeland security or security studies; others are attempting to integrate the study of security into courses throughout the curriculum. The methods for offering courses in these new programs also differ. Some courses are offered in the traditional manner—on campus for one semester. Others are offered "off-model" via the Internet, on weekends, or as block courses offered for several weeks or months. The following are examples of the ways different universities are answering the challenge of educating students for homeland security:

▲ Texas A & M University's Integrative Center for Homeland Security website (http://homelandsecurity.tamu.edu) states that "[t]he serious study of homeland security is hampered by the lack of formal structure to provide content and connectivity between issues." The program offers on-campus graduate instruction for any Texas A&M student who is interested and a graduate certificate via distance education.

▲ Ohio State University offers the Program in International and Homeland Security (http://homelandsecurity.osu.edu) under its Office of Research. The overall goal of this program is to "help improve the security of the nation, while preserving our values, freedoms, and economy." The program sponsors both undergraduate and graduate courses, but does not offer a specific academic program. The thinking is that security-consciousness should be spread throughout the Ohio State University curriculum.

▲ East Carolina University (http://www.ecu.edu/securitystudies) offers an interdisciplinary graduate certificate in security studies, and an interdisciplinary undergraduate minor in security studies. The university is also working toward the establishment of an interdisciplinary Master of Security Studies degree. The mission of the program stresses the development of new thinking toward national security; the development of an integrated view of homeland security by taking an interdisciplinary approach to the subject; and the creation of core competencies in students through development of knowledge, skills, and abilities in security-related fields of study.

sciences were necessary for students who were interested in working to combat terrorism and to deal with natural disasters. The **Homeland Security/ Defense Education Consortium (HSDEC)** is a cooperative arrangement of universities and research centers in the United States, Canada, and Mexico that is seeking to develop the academic field of homeland security. Housed in Colorado Springs, HSDEC has already developed guidelines for graduate certificates in homeland security, and is working on guidelines for undergraduate degrees in the field (see http://www.hsdec.org). Homeland security programs are inherently interdisciplinary and thus do not often fit the traditional departmental structure of American universities. Different institutional arrangements are being developed to cope with this and many programs around the country are under development.

Students entering the field of homeland security need to know both the basics of security and emergency management, but also need to have the larger skills of a university-educated person. These are the ability to write, think, do basic mathematics, be familiar with computer programs, and communicate verbally, in writing, and in the new multimedia environment. Knowledge of American government, the international environment, and some expertise in a foreign language are particularly useful. The ability to manage projects and people successfully are also great assets for those entering this field.

SELF-CHECK

1. Explain why the United States has the largest number of international students and why this is a concern to security planners.

2. What is SEVIS?

3. What are the advantages and disadvantages of the increased number of international students in the United States?

4. All U.S. colleges and universities have taken the same approach in creating homeland security programs of study. True or false?

SUMMARY

In this chapter, we examined the broad topic of enablers of mass effects and the many variations on how this term can be applied in the context of homeland security today. Clearly, in the information age, the diverse forms of media and communication available to terrorist organizations can have multiplier effects in helping them win the war of ideas. The Internet, print, and broadcast media have all contributed to the spread of information about terrorism, and, at the same time, serve as a means of propagating terrorist messages throughout the world. Islamic schools called madrassas also serve as a means of propagating radical Islamic teachings to Muslim youth.

Within the United States, colleges and universities serve multiple educational purposes by providing the means by which international students can learn U.S. democratic values and pluralism, or they can serve as recruiting grounds for disenfranchised groups who face discrimination or profiling, particularly Middle Eastern students. The same schools may also serve to educate students about homeland security and provide academic programs that will better enable future generations of security managers, planners, and leaders the tools to effectively combat terrorism through knowledge of the threat. At the same time, these new programs of study can lead to new research methods and policy choices that will aid in confronting the threat of terrorism, yet without alienating nations and peoples who share the same desires for peace, security, and more democratic ways of life.

In this chapter, you examined the role of the information age in facilitating the spread of terrorists' messages both domestically and internationally. You also became familiar with the role of ideas and values in modern world culture and considered the role of heuristics in assessing the likelihood of potential disastrous events in the United States. In addition, you evaluated the assets and limitations of the Internet as a tool for terrorists.

KEY TERMS

Al-Jazeera	An Arabic-language news network headquartered in Qatar.
Availability heuristic	Assessing the probability of an event by how clearly we can imagine events like it.
Data mining	The use of the Internet for open source information, which when pieced together provides information of intelligence value for an organization.
Enabler	Anything that assists in the creation of mass effects. Can be an institution or process that makes it possible for the mass effect to occur when it would not have occurred otherwise; an institution or process that allows the mass effect to have a greater effect than it would have had otherwise; or an institution or process that is utilized by those who would cause a mass effect.

Heuristics	Rules of thumb.
Homeland Security Defense Education Consortium (HSDEC)	A cooperative arrangement of universities and research centers in the United States, Canada, and Mexico that is seeking to develop the academic field of homeland security.
Koan	A question that cannot be answered.
Madrassas	Religious schools, primarily located in Muslim countries, that teach radical Islamic ideas and are often considered a potential breeding ground for terrorists.
Materialists	People who are concerned with personal survival: providing for themselves or their families, making a good salary, and all the "perks" that come along with that salary.
Post materialists	People who are more concerned with what some call "higher goals," such as preserving and protecting freedom of speech and other more self-expression-type values.
Psychological warfare	The use of propaganda and other psychological actions having the primary purpose of influencing the opinions, emotions, attitudes, and behavior of hostile foreign groups in such a way as to support the achievement of national objectives.
Representativeness heuristic	Assessing the probability of an unknown event on the basis of how it represents an event we know.
SEVIS	Acronym for "Student and Exchange Visitor Information System," a computerized registry of international students studying in the U.S.
Umma	In Islam, a term used to describe those called to the community of the faithful.
Vividness heuristic	Assessing the probability of an event based on how vividly it is described or portrayed.

ASSESS YOUR UNDERSTANDING

Go to www.wiley.com/college/kilroy to assess your knowledge of the basics of enablers of mass effects.
Measure your learning by comparing pre-test and post-test results.

Summary Questions

1. Enablers of mass effects refer only to the Internet. True or false?

2. Terrorist organizations are aware of the role the media plays in helping them frame their story. True or false?

3. Psychological warfare is a term used only to describe means of interrogation. True or false?

4. Universities can play an important role in educating students about the nature of threats today and the all-hazards nature of homeland security by offering courses and programs of study in this new academic discipline. True or false?

5. Which of the following is not a current use of the Internet by terrorist organizations?
   (a) Propaganda
   (b) Planning and coordination
   (c) Data mining
   (d) Widespread cyber-warfare against U.S. government institutions

6. Schools that propagate radical Islamic teachings are called:
   (a) ummas.
   (b) materialists.
   (c) heuristics.
   (d) madrassas.

7. Of all regions of the world, Internet growth is occurring most rapidly in:
   (a) Africa.
   (b) Latin America.
   (c) Europe.
   (d) the Middle East.

8. Which of the following heuristics are applicable in understanding the power of ideas and communication?
   (a) Representativeness
   (b) Vividness
   (c) Availability
   (d) All of the above

Applying This Chapter

1. You are serving as a counter-terrorism analyst at the Department of Homeland Security. Your boss asks you to explain how terrorist groups are using the Internet today. She is concerned about the threat of cyber-warfare. How would you respond? Provide specific examples of how terrorists are using the Internet today.

2. During a college class on the politics of terrorism, a student makes a comment that due to the potential threat of terrorists using student visas as a means of entering the United States legally, your university should stop accepting international students. How would you respond? Explain your reasons for supporting or not supporting such a position.

3. You are a staffer for an influential member of the U.S. Congress (pick your local representative) who holds a key vote in a tough new anti-terrorism law. Conduct a web search on the Internet for information about this member of Congress. Using data mining, see what you can find out about that individual that would help enable a terrorist organization better understand how to influence his or her vote using the enablers identified in this chapter. Only use open source, accessible information available over the Internet or other known media sources. Prepare a report back to that member of Congress.

4. Conduct a survey on campus of how many students have seen al-Jazeera TV broadcasts or visited the network's website. Record their responses as favorable, unfavorable, or neutral with regard to its reporting on the war on terrorism.

YOU TRY IT

Terrorism and the Media

Review a number of different media sources in the United States and overseas reporting on terrorism. Compare similar stories in the different media outlets and how each source frames the argument. Determine the heuristic the reporter may be assuming in his or her reporting on the subject. Also consider the source within the Inglehart Values Map for content analysis and perspective.

Homeland Security Education

Do a web search on colleges offering programs of study related to homeland security. Categorize them on the basis of the predominant academic discipline under which they fall (e.g., which academic department) and their main focus (terrorism, emergency management, all-hazard, interdisciplinary, etc.). Also determine who you think their main target audience is for this type of degree (e.g., full-time student, adult learner, resident vs. distance learning, and so on).

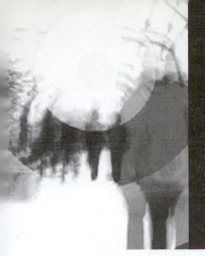

BIBLIOGRAPHY

Chapter 1 Works Cited

Barnett, T. P. M. 2004. *The Pentagon's new map: War and peace in the twenty-first century.* New York: Putnam.

———. 2005. *Blueprint for action: A future worth creating.* New York: Putnam.

Brower, C. 2002. The commander-in-chief and TORCH. Address given at the Franklin D. Roosevelt Presidential Library, Hyde Park, New York, November 12. http://www.fdrlibrary.marist.edu/cbtorch.html (accessed June 23, 2006).

Foley, H. 1969. *Woodrow Wilson's case for the League of Nations.* New York: Kraus.

Gaddis, J. L. 1990. *Strategies of containment: A critical appraisal of postwar American national security policy.* New York: Oxford University Press.

Griffith, J. 1997. In pursuit of Pancho Villa, 1916–1917. *Journal of the Historical Society of the National Guard of Georgia* 6 (3–4).

Hamilton, A., J. Madison, and J. Jay. 1961. *The Federalist Papers.* New York: New American Library.

Hammes, T. X. 2004. *The sling and the stone: On war in the twenty-first century.* St. Paul, MN: Zenith.

History Guide. n.d. George Kennan: The sources of Soviet conflict (1947). http://www.historyguide.org/europe/kennan.html (accessed March 22, 2007).

Jentleson, B. 2004. *American foreign policy: The dynamics of choice in the twenty-first century.* 2nd ed. New York: Norton.

Jordan, A. A., W. J. Taylor, Jr., and M. J. Mazarr. 1998. *American national security.* 5th ed. Baltimore: Johns Hopkins University Press.

Kagan, D. 2001. *While America sleeps: Self delusion, military weakness, and the threat to peace today.* New York: St. Martin's.

Kagan, R., and W. Kristol, eds. 2000. *Present dangers: Crisis and opportunity in American foreign and defense policy.* New York: Encounter.

Morganthau, H. J. 1978. *Politics among nations: The struggle for power and peace.* 5th ed. New York: Knopf.

Siasico, R. V., and S. Ross. 2006. Japanese relocation centers. http://www.infoplease .com/spot/internment1.html (accessed March 13, 2007).

Snow, D. M. 2004. *National security for a new era: Globalization and geopolitics.* New York: Pearson Longman.

Tuchman, B. 1966. *The proud tower: A portrait of the world before the war, 1890–1914.* New York: Macmillan.

White, M. 2003. Historical atlas of the twentieth century. http://users.erols.com/ mwhite28/coldwar1.htm (accessed July 18, 2006).

Williams, W. A. 1978. *Americans in a changing world: A history of the United States in the twentieth century.* New York: Harper and Row.

Chapter 2 Works Cited

Anderson, J. E. 2000. *Public policymaking.* 4th ed. Boston: Houghton Mifflin.

AT&T. 2006. AT&T government markets: Government solutions—Homeland security. http://www.att.com/gov/solution/integrated_solutions/homeland_security/ (accessed July 5, 2006).

Barrett, J. 2006. Makes no sense. *Newsweek,* June 2. http://www.msnbc.msn.com/id/ 13106435/site/newsweek/ (accessed July 5, 2006).

Crossett, K., T. Culliton, P. Wiley, and T. Goodspeed. 2004. *Population trends along the coastal United States: 1980–2008.* Silver Spring, MD: National Oceanic and Atmospheric Administration.

Department of Homeland Security. 2006a. Homeland Security Grants Program. http:// www.ojp.usdoj.gov/odp/grants_hsgp.htm (accessed July 14, 2006).

———. 2006b. National Infrastructure Protection Plan. http://www.dhs.gov/interweb/ assetlibrary/NIPP_Plan.pdf (accessed July 15, 2006).

Dye, T. 2005. *Understanding public policy.* 11th ed. Upper Saddle River, NJ: Pearson Education.

Gellman, B. 2005. The FBI's secret scrutiny: In hunt for terrorists, Bureau examines records of ordinary Americans. *Washington Post,* November 6.

Hobijn, B. 2002. What will homeland security cost? *Federal Reserve Bank of New York Economic Policy Review* (November).

Lictblau, E. 2005. At FBI, frustration over limits on an antiterror law. *New York Times,* December 11.

Mohammed, A. 2006. Google refuses demand for search information: Government asked four firms for data in effort to revive anti-porn law. *Washington Post,* January 20.

Nexia Biotechnologies. 2004. Press release, December 14. http://www.nexiabiotech .com/pdf/2004_12_14_Nexia%20Results.pdf (accessed July 8, 2006).

Office of Homeland Security. 2002. *National strategy for homeland security.* Washington, DC: Author.

Plano, J., and M. Greenberg. 1985. *The American political dictionary*. 7th ed. New York: Holt, Rinehart, and Winston.

Reese, S. 2005. State and local homeland security: Unresolved issues for the 109th Congress. Congressional Research Service report RL 32941, June 9.

Risen, J., and E. Lictblau. 2005. Bush lets U.S. spy on callers without courts. *New York Times,* December 16. http://www.nytimes.com/2005/12/16/politics/16program.html?ei =5090&en=e32072d786623ac1&ex=1292389200.

Sylves, R. 1998. *The political and policy basis of emergency "management."* Emmitsburg, MD: Federal Emergency Management Agency Emergency Management Institute.

United Nations Population Division. 2002. Future world population growth to be concentrated in urban areas of the world. Report POP/815, March 21. http://www .un.org/esa/population/publications/ (accessed June 30, 2006).

United States Environmental Protection Agency. 2004. *National coastal condition report II.* EPA-620/R-03/002. Washington, DC: Author.

Waugh, W., Jr. 2000. *Public administration and emergency management.* Emmitsburg, MD: Federal Emergency Management Agency.

Chapter 3 Works Cited

1900 Storm. n.d. The 1900 Storm. http://www.1900storm.com/facts.lasso (accessed January 15, 2007).

Bea, K. 2006. Federal Stafford Act disaster assistance: Presidential declarations, eligible activities, and funding. Congressional Research Service report RL 33093, April 28.

Broughton, E. 2005. The Bhopal disaster and its aftermath: A review. *Environmental Health* 4(6). http://www.pubmedcentral.nih.gov/articlerender.fcgi?tool=pub med&pubmedid=15882472 (accessed January 19, 2007).

Carrns, A., and B. McKay. 2005. New Orleans levee system has been key to survival. *Wall Street Journal,* August 31.

Center for Chemical Process Safety. n.d. About CCPS. http://www.aiche.org/CCPS/About/index.aspx (accessed January 19, 2007).

CNN. 2006. Apex mayor: Fire fizzling, evacuees can't go home yet. October 6. http://www.cnn.com/2006/US/10/06/plant.fire/index.html (accessed January 19, 2007).

Department of Homeland Security. 2006. DHS introduces new regulations to secure high-risk chemical facilities. Press release, December 22. http://www.dhs.gov/xnews/releases/pr_1166807052891.shtm (accessed January 19, 2007).

England-Joseph, J. 1998. Disaster assistance: Information on federal costs and approaches for reducing them. Testimony before the U.S. House of Representatives Subcommittee on Water Resources and Environment, March 26.

Epic Disasters. n.d. The United States' worst earthquakes. http://www.epicdisasters.com/deadlyusearthquake.php (accessed January 15, 2007).

Federal Emergency Management Agency. n.d. FEMA history. http://www.fema.gov/about/history.shtm (accessed January 15, 2007).

Gannon, M. 2005. AIR Worldwide estimates total property damage from Hurricane Katrina's storm surge and flood at $44 billion. http://www.iso.com/press_releases/2005/09_29_05.html (accessed January 15, 2007).

Glasser, S. B., and J. White. 2005. Storm exposed disarray at the top. *Washington Post,* September 4.

Global Security. n.d. Weapons of Mass Destruction Civil Support Teams. http://www.globalsecurity.org/military/agency/army/wmd-cst.htm (accessed January 19, 2007).

Infoplease. n.d. America's worst disasters. http://www.infoplease.com/ipa/A0005349.html (accessed January 15, 2007).

Lowder, M. W. 2006. FEMA disaster response operations and cross border events for Trilateral Conference on Preparing for and Responding to Disasters in North America. Presentation given in San Antonio, Texas, November 7, 2006.

Miskel, J. F. 2006. *Disaster response and homeland security: What works and what doesn't.* Westport, CT: Praeger Security International.

National Oceanic and Atmospheric Administration. 2002. Hurricane Andrew: Ten years later. http://www.noaa.gov/hurricane andrew.html (accessed January 15, 2007).

National Park Service. n.d. A roar like thunder. http://www.johnstownpa.com/History/hist19.html (accessed January 22, 2007).

Organization for Economic Cooperation and Development. n.d. Chemical accidents. http://www.oecd.org/about/0,2337, en_2649_34369_1_1_1_1_1,00.html (accessed January 19, 2007).

Ortmeier, P. J. 2005. *Security management: An introduction.* 2nd ed. New York: Pearson Prentice Hall.

Pocock, E. n.d. Disasters in the United States: 1650–2005. http://www.easternct.edu/depts/amerst/disasters.htm (accessed January 19, 2007).

Sylves, R. 2006. President Bush and Hurricane Katrina: A presidential leadership study. *Annals of the American Academy of Political and Social Science* 604: 1, 26–56.

Tiwari, J., and C. Gray. n.d. U.S. nuclear weapons accidents. http://www.cdi.org/Issues/NukeAccidents/accidents.htm (accessed January 19, 2007).

United States Environmental Protection Agency. 2006. Kanawha drill to test local responders. http://yosemite.epa.gov/opa/admpress.nsf/93216b1c8fd122ca85257018004cb2dc/3f8af06ebf12afca852571ed006d5d94!OpenDocument (accessed January 22, 2007).

United States Geological Survey. n.d. Mississippi Valley: Whole lot of shakin' goin' on. http://quake.wr.usgs.gov/prepare/factsheets/NewMadrid/ (accessed January 15, 2007).

Chapter 4 Works Cited

Anderson, J. 2000. *Public policymaking.* 4th ed. Boston: Houghton Mifflin.

Bates, F. L., and W. G. Peacock. 1993. *Living conditions, disasters, and development: An approach to cross-cultural comparisons.* Athens, GA: University of Georgia Press.

Bolin, R. C. 1982. *Long-term family recovery from disaster.* Boulder: University of Colorado Institute of Behavioral Science.

———. 1993. *Household and community recovery after earthquakes.* Boulder: University of Colorado Institute of Behavioral Science.

Caruson, K., and S. MacManus. 2006. Mandates and management challenges in the trenches: An intergovernmental perspective on homeland security. *Public Administration Review,* August, 522–537.

Committee on Disaster Research in the Social Sciences. 2006. *Facing hazards and disasters: Understanding human dimensions.* Washington, D.C.: National Academies Press.

Department of Homeland Security. 2004. *National response plan.* Washington, DC: Author.

———. 2006a. Hurricane Katrina: What the government is doing. http://www.dhs .gov/interweb/assetlibrary/katrina.htm (accessed July 15, 2006).

———. 2006b. National Infrastructure Protection Plan. http://www.dhs.gov/interweb/ assetlibrary/NIPP_Plan.pdf (accessed July 15, 2006).

———. 2006c. *Notice of change to National Response Plan.* Washington, DC: Author.

———. 2006d. Securing our nation's rail systems. http://www.dhs.gov/dhspublic/ display?content=5749 (accessed September 26, 2006).

Dynes, R., E. L. Quarantelli, and G. Kreps. 1972. *A perspective on disaster planning.* Columbus: Ohio State University Disaster Research Center.

Emergency Management Institute. 2006. *Fundamentals of emergency management.* Washington, D.C.: Federal Emergency Management Agency.

Energy Information Administration. 2005. Indian Point nuclear power plant. http://www.eia .doe.gov/cneaf/nuclear/page/at_a_glance/reactors/in_point.html (accessed March 23, 2007).

Federal Emergency Management Agency. 1997. *Multi-hazard identification and risk assessment: A cornerstone of the national mitigation strategy.* Washington, D.C.: Author.

———. 2006a. FEMA: HAZUS. http://www.fema.gov/plan/prevent/hazus/ (accessed August 4, 2006).

———. 2006b. NFIP: What we do. http://www.fema.gov/plan/prevent/floodplain/How_the_ NFIP_works.shtm (last modified May 5, 2006).

———. 2006c. What we do. http://www.fema.gov/about/what.shtm (last modified April 5, 2006).

Lyman, E. 2004. Chernobyl on the Hudson?: The health and economic impacts of a terrorist attack at the Indian Point nuclear plant. http://www.ucsusa.org/global_security/

nuclear_terrorism/impacts-of-a-terrorist-attack-at-indian-point-nuclear-power-plant.html (last modified September 2004).

Mileti, D. S. 1999. *Disasters by design: A reassessment of natural hazards in the United States.* Washington, DC: Joseph Henry Press.

Miskel, J. F. 2006. *Disaster response and homeland security: What works and what doesn't.* Westport, CT: Praeger Security International.

National Oceanic and Atmospheric Administration. 2006. Vulnerability assessment techniques and applications (VATA). http://www.csc.noaa.gov/vata/intro2.html (last modified June 13, 2006).

Perry, R., and M. Lindell. 2003. Preparedness for emergency response: Guidelines for the emergency planning process. *Disasters* 27 (4): 336–350.

Pitchford, P. 2006. Air ban on liquids lightened. *Press-Enterprise,* September 25.

Smith, S. K., J. Tayman, and D. A. Swanson. 2001. *State and local population projections: Methodology and analysis.* New York: Kluwer.

Sylves, R. 2006. U.S. disaster policy and management in an era of homeland security. In *Disciplines, disasters, and emergency management: The convergence and divergence of concepts, issues, and trends from the research literature,* ed. D. A. McEntire. Emmitsburg, MD: Federal Emergency Management Agency Emergency Management Institute.

White, G. F., and J. E. Haas. 1975. *Assessment of research on natural hazards.* Cambridge, MA: MIT Press.

Wisner, B., P. Blaikie, T. Cannon, and I. Davis. 2004. *At risk: Natural hazards, people's vulnerability, and disasters.* 2nd ed. London: Routledge.

United Nations Office for the Coordination of Human Affairs. 2005. Disaster reduction definitions and distinctions. http://www.irinnews.org/webspecials/DR/Definitions.asp (accessed September 26, 2006).

Chapter 5 Works Cited

Achin, K. 2006 Libya nuclear deal may be a model for North Korea. *Voice of America News,* May 25. http://www.voanews.com/english/archive/2006-05/2006-05-25-voa35.cfm.

Arendt, H. 1970. *On violence.* San Diego: Harvest.

Asimov, L., and F. Homer. 1988. Democracies and the role of acquiescence in international terrorism. In *Terrible beyond endurance?: The foreign policy of state terrorism,* ed. M. Stohl and G. A. Lopez. New York: Greenwood Press.

Badey, T. J. 1998. Defining international terrorism: A pragmatic approach. *Terrorism and Political Violence* 10 (1): 90–107.

BBC News. 2004. U.S. House calls Darfur "genocide." *BBC News,* July 24. http://news.bbc.co.uk/2/hi/africa/3918765.stm (accessed July 13, 2006).

———. 2005. Iran leader defends Israel remark. *BBC News,* October 28. http://news.bbc.co.uk/1/hi/world/middle_east/4384264.stm (accessed July 12, 2006).

Bushnell, P. T., V. Shlapentokh, C. K. Vanderpool, and J. Sundram. 1991. *State organized terror: The case of violent internal repression.* Boulder, CO: Westview Press.

Claridge, D. 1996. State terrorism? Applying a definitional model. *Terrorism and Political Violence* 8 (3): 47–63.

Cline, R. S., and Y. Alexander. 1986. *Terrorism as state-sponsored covert warfare.* Fairfax, VA: Hero Books.

Combs, C. 2000. *Terrorism in the twenty-first century.* 2nd ed. Upper Saddle River, NJ: Prentice Hall.

Cunningham, W. G. 2003. *Terrorism definitions and typologies.* In *Terrorism: Concepts, causes, and conflict resolution.* Fort Belvoir, VA: Defense Threat Reduction Agency.

Cusimano Love, M. 2003. *Beyond sovereignty: Issues for a global agenda.* Belmont, CA: Wadsworth.

Department of State. 2004. Patterns of global terrorism 2003. www.state.gov/s/ct/rls/crt/2003/31880.htm (accessed March 15, 2007).

———. 2006. *Country reports on terrorism 2005.* Washington, DC: Author.

Federal Bureau of Investigation. 2001. Terrorism 2000/2001. www.fbi.gov/publications/terror/terror2000_2001.pdf (accessed July 15, 2006).

Glover, J. 1991. State terrorism. In *Violence, terrorism, and justice,* ed. R. G. Frey and C. W. Morris. Cambridge: Cambridge University Press.

Held, D. 1993. *Political theory and the modern state.* Cambridge: Polity Press.

Hoffman, B. 1998. *Inside terrorism.* New York: Columbia University Press.

Jenkins, B. 1986. Defense against terrorism. *Political Science Quarterly* 101 (5): 773–786.

Joyner, C. C. 2004. The United Nations and terrorism: Rethinking legal tensions between national security, human rights, and civil liberties. *International Studies Perspectives* 5: 240–257.

Kegley, C. W., T. V. Sturgeon, and E. R. Wittkopf. 1988. Structural terrorism: The systemic sources of state-sponsored terrorism. In *Terrible beyond endurance?: The foreign policy of state terrorism,* ed. M. Stohl and G. A. Lopez. New York: Greenwood Press.

Kelleher, A., and L. Klein. 1999. *Global perspectives: A handbook for understanding global issues.* Upper Saddle River, NJ: Prentice-Hall.

Levitt, M. 2002. *Targeting terror: U.S. policy toward Middle Eastern state sponsors and terrorist organizations, post-September 11.* Washington, DC: Washington Institute for Near East Policy.

Mahbubani, K. 2003. The United Nations and the United States: An indispensable partnership. In *Unilateralism and U.S. foreign policy,* ed. D. M. Malone and Y. Foong Khong. Boulder, CO: Lynne Rienner.

Menjívar, C., and N. Rodríguez. 2005. *When states kill: Latin America, the U.S., and technologies of terror.* Austin: University of Texas Press.

Murphy, J. F. 1989. *State support of international terrorism: Legal, political, and economic dimensions.* Boulder, CO: Westview.

Nacos, B. 2006. *Terrorism and counterterrorism: Understanding threats and responses in the post-9/11 world*. New York: Columbia University Press.

O'Sullivan, M. L. 2003. *Shrewd sanctions: Statecraft and state sponsors of terrorism*. Washington, DC: Brookings Institution.

Peed, M. J. 2005. Blacklisting as foreign policy: The politics and law of listing terror states. *Duke Law Journal* 54 (2): 1321–1354.

Perdue, W. D. 1989. *Terrorism and the state: A critique of domination through fear*. New York: Praeger.

Pillar, P. 2003. *Terrorism and U.S. foreign policy*. Washington, DC: Brookings Institution.

Rummel, R. J. 2006. *Death by government*. New Brunswick, NJ: Transaction Publishers.

Schmid, A. P. 1991. Repression, state terrorism, and genocide: Conceptual clarifications. In *State organized terror: The case of violent internal repression,* ed. P. T. Bushnell, V. Shlapentokh, C. K. Vanderpool, and J. Sundram. Boulder, CO: Westview Press.

Silverstein, K. 2005. Official pariah Sudan valuable to America's war on terrorism. *Los Angeles Times,* April 29. http://www.globalpolicy.org/empire/terrorwar/analysis/2005/0429sudan.htm

St. John, R. B. 2006. Decision on Libya marks shift in Bush foreign policy. *Foreign Policy In Focus Commentary,* May 27 (available at www.fpif.org).

Stohl, M. 1984. International dimensions of state terrorism. In *The state as terrorist: The dynamics of governmental violence and repression,* ed. M. Stohl and G. A. Lopez. Westport, CT: Greenwood Press.

Stohl, M., and G. A. Lopez, eds. 1984. *The state as terrorist: The dynamics of governmental violence and repression*. Westport, CT: Greenwood Press.

———. 1988. *Terrible beyond endurance? The foreign policy of state terrorism*. New York: Greenwood Press.

Sullivan, M. P. 2005. Cuba and the state sponsors of terrorism list. Congressional Research Service report. Available at http://www.fas.org/sgp/crs/terror/RL32251.pdf.

Tucker, D. 2001. What is new about the new terrorism and how dangerous is it? *Terrorism and Political Violence* 13 (3): 1–14.

White, J. R. 2003. *Terrorism: An introduction*. 4th ed. Belmont, CA: Thomson/Wadsworth.

Wilkinson, P. 1981. Can a state be a terrorist? *International Affairs* 57 (3): 467–472.

———. 1986. *Terrorism and the liberal state*. 2nd ed. New York: NYU Press.

———. 2000. *Terrorism versus democracy: The liberal state response*. London: Frank Cass.

Chapter 6 Works Cited

Abercrombie, N., S. Hill, and B. S. Turner. 1988. *The Penguin dictionary of sociology*. London: Penguin.

Badey, T. J. 1998. Defining international terrorism: A pragmatic approach. *Terrorism and Political Violence* 10 (1): 90–107.

Carlton, D. 1979. The future of political substate violence. In *Terrorism: Theory and practice,* ed. Y. Alexander, D. Carlton, and P. Wilkinson. Boulder, CO: Westview.

Combs, C. 2000. *Terrorism in the twenty-first century.* 2nd ed. Upper Saddle River, NJ: Prentice Hall.

Crenshaw, M., and M. Cusimano Love. 2007. Networked terror. In *Beyond sovereignty: Issues for a global agenda,* ed. M. Cusimano Love. Belmont, CA: Wadsworth.

Cunningham, W. G. 2003. Terrorism definitions and typologies. In *Terrorism: Concepts, causes, and conflict resolution.* Fort Belvoir, VA: Defense Threat Reduction Agency.

Dale, S. 1988. Religious suicide in Islamic Asia: Anticolonial terrorism in India, Indonesia, and the Philippines. *Journal of Conflict Resolution* 32 (1): 37–59.

Fromkin, D. 1975. The strategy of terrorism. *Foreign Affairs* 53: 683–698.

Hoffman, B. 1998. *Inside terrorism.* New York: Columbia University Press.

Hoffman, B., and G. McCormick. 2004. Terrorism, signaling, and suicide attack. *Studies in Conflict and Terrorism* 27 (4): 243–281.

Jenkins, B. M. 1978. International terrorism: *Trends and potentialities. Journal of International Affairs* 32 (1): 115–123.

———. 1982. Statements about terrorism. *Annals of the American Academy of Political Science* 463: 11–23.

———. 1986. Defense against terrorism. *Political Science Quarterly* 101 (5): 773–786.

———. 1987. The future course of international terrorism. *The Futurist* 21 (4): 8–13.

———. 2001. Terrorism and beyond: A twenty-first century perspective. *Studies in Conflict and Terrorism* 24: 321–327.

Jensen, R. B. 2004. Daggers, rifles, and dynamite: Anarchist terrorism in nineteenth century Europe. *Terrorism and Political Violence* 16 (1): 116–153.

Juergensmeyer, M. 2001. The logic of religious violence. In *Inside terrorist organizations,* ed. D. Rapoport. Portland, OR: Frank Cass.

———. 2003. *Terror in the mind of God.* Berkeley: University of California Press.

Kegley, C. W., T. V. Sturgeon, and E. R. Wittkopf. 1988. Structural terrorism: The systemic sources of state-sponsored terrorism. In *Terrible beyond endurance?: The foreign policy of state terrorism,* ed. M. Stohl and G. A. Lopez. New York: Greenwood Press.

Laqueur, W. 1987. *The age of terrorism.* Boston: Little, Brown, and Co.

Mannes, A. 2004. *Profiles in terror: The guide to Middle East terrorist organizations.* Lanham, MD: Rowman and Littlefield.

Memorial Institute for the Prevention of Terrorism. n.d. MIPT Knowledge Base entry: Hamas. http://www.tkb.org/Group.jsp?groupID=49 (accessed March 28, 2007).

Nacos, B. 2006. *Terrorism and counterterrorism: Understanding threats and responses in the post-9/11 world*. New York: Columbia University Press.

Pape, R. A. 2003. The strategic logic of suicide terrorism. *American Political Science Review* 97 (3): 1–19.

——— 2005. *Dying to win: The strategic logic of suicide terrorism*. New York: Random House.

Rapoport, D., ed. 2001. *Inside terrorist organizations*. Portland, OR: Frank Cass.

Rotberg, R. I. 2006. *Israeli and Palestinian narratives of conflict: History's double helix*. Bloomington: Indiana University Press.

Sisk, T. D. 1996. *Power sharing and international mediation in ethnic conflict*. Washington, DC: United States Institute of Peace.

Sprinzak, E. 2000. Rational fanatics. *Foreign Policy* 120: 66–73.

Stern, J. 2003. The protean enemy. *Foreign Affairs* 82 (4): 27–40.

Tucker, D. 2001. What is new about the new terrorism and how dangerous is it? *Terrorism and Political Violence* 13 (3): 1–14.

United Nations. n.d. The question of Palestine. http://www.un.org/Depts/dpa/qpal/index.html (accessed March 25, 2007).

White, J. R. 2003. *Terrorism: An introduction*. 4th ed. Belmont, CA: Thomson/Wadsworth.

———. 2006. *Terrorism and homeland security*. 5th ed. Belmont, CA: Thomson/Wadsworth.

Wilkinson, P. 1986. *Terrorism and the liberal state*. 2nd ed. New York: NYU Press.

———. 2000. *Terrorism versus democracy: The liberal state response*. London: Frank Cass.

Chapter 7 Works Cited

Acohido, B., and J. Swartz. 2005. Cyber crooks break into online accounts with ease. *USA TODAY*, November 11. http://www.usatoday.com/money/industries/technology/2005-11-02-cybercrime-online-accounts_x.htm (accessed October 2, 2006).

Anderson, R. 1996. The day after . . . in cyberspace: An exploration of cyberspace security R&D investment strategies for DARPA. RAND Monograph Report. Washington, DC: RAND Corporation.

Armistead, L., ed. 2004. *Information operations: Warfare and the hard reality of soft power*. Dulles, VA: Potomac Books.

Astahost. 2006. Computer glitch causes massive budget shortfalls in Indiana. February 11. http://www.astahost.com/info.php/computer-glitch-causes-massive-budget-shortfalls-indiana_t10545.html (accessed May 10, 2006).

Bayles, W. 2001. The ethics of computer network attack. *Parameters: The U.S. Army War College Quarterly* 31 (Spring): 44–58.

Carnegie Mellon University. 1988. DARPA establishes Computer Emergency Response Team. Press release, December 13. http://www.cert.org/about/1988press-rel.html (accessed May 17, 2006).

Cebrowski, A., and J. J. Gartska. 1998. *Network centric warfare: Its origins and its future*. Annapolis, MD: U.S. Naval Institute. http://www.usni.org/Proceedings/Articles98/PROcebrowski.htm (accessed January 6, 2006).

Denning, D. 2004. Information technology and security. In *Grave new world: Security challenges in the twenty-first century*, ed. M. E. Brown, 91–112. Washington, DC: Georgetown University Press.

Department of the Army. 2003. *Information operations: Doctrine, tactics, techniques, and procedures*. Field manual 3-13. Washington, DC: Author.

Department of Defense. 1998. *Joint publication 3-13: Joint doctrine for information operations*. Washington, DC: U.S. Government Printing Office.

Dick, R. L. 2001. Testimony before the Senate Committee on the Judiciary, Subcommittee for Technology, Terrorism, and Government Information, May 22. http://www.fbi.gov/congress/congress01/ron-dick2.htm (accessed May 17, 2006).

Donnelly, J., and V. Crawley. 1999. Hamre to Hill—We're in a cyber-war. *Defense Week*, March 1. http://jya.com/dod-cyberwar.htm (accessed May 17, 2007).

Gellman, B. 2002. Cyber-attacks by Al Qaeda feared. *Washington Post*, June 27.

Global Security. n.d. Solar sunrise. http://www.globalsecurity.org/military/ops/solarsunrise.htm (accessed May 11, 2006).

Gross, G. 2003. Former Bush official blasts government cybersecurity. *Computer World*, April 9. http://www.computerworld.com/action/article.do?command=viewArticleBasic&articleId=80183&pageNumber=1 (accessed May 17, 2006).

Hildreth, S. 2001. Cyberwarfare. Congressional Research Service report for Congress, June 19.

Homeland Security Council. 2005. *National Strategy for Pandemic Influenza*. Washington, DC: The White House.

Kessler, G. C. 2004. An overview of steganography for the computer forensics examiner. *Forensic Science Communications* 6-(3). http://www.fbi.gov/hq/lab/fsc/backissu/july2004/research/2004_03_research01.htm (accessed May 15, 2006).

Liang, Q., and W. Xiangsui. 1999. *Unrestricted warfare*. Beijing: PLA Literature and Arts Publishing House.

Office of the Undersecretary for Defense Acquisition and Technology. 1996. *Report of the Defense Science Board Task Forces on Information Warfare—Defense (1W-D)*. Washington, DC: Department of Defense.

PBS Frontline. 2006. Cyberwar! Warnings! http://www.pbs.org/wgbh/pages/frontline/shows/cyberwar/warnings/ (accessed May 12, 2006).

President's Critical Infrastructure Protection Board. 2003. *National Strategy to Secure Cyberspace*. Washington, DC: The White House.

Ranum, M. 2004. Myths of cyberwarfare. *Information Security,* April. http://infosecu ritymag.techtarget.com/ss/0,295796,sid6_iss366_art692,00.html (accessed May 19, 2006).

Robinson, C. 2002. Military and cyber defense: Reactions to the threat. Center for Defense Information, Nov. 8. http://www.cdi.org/terrorism/cyberdefense-pr.cfm (accessed September 10, 2005).

Rumsfeld, D. 2006. Remarks by Secretary Rumsfeld at Southern Center for International Studies, Atlanta, Georgia. Department of Defense news transcript, May 6. http://www .defenselink.mil/transcripts/ 2006/tr20060504-12979.html (accessed May 19, 2006).

Shalikashvili, J. 1995. *Joint Vision 2010: Department of Defense and Office of the Joint Chiefs of Staff.* Washington, DC: U.S. Government Printing Office.

Shelton, H. H. 2000. *Joint Vision 2020: Department of Defense and Office of the Joint Chiefs of Staff.* Washington, DC: U.S. Government Printing Office.

Sherman, M. 2006. Consultant hacked FBI chief's password. *The Eagle,* July 7. http://www .theeagle.com/stories/070706/nation_20060707024.php (accessed October 2, 2006).

Sizer, R. A. 1997. Land information warfare activity. Military intelligence bulletin 1997-1. http://www.fas.org/irp/agency/army/tradoc/usaic/mipb/1997-1/sizer.htm (accessed January 6, 2006).

Song, J. 2006. Five nations left off tsunami warning list. Associated Press/Yahoo News, May 5. http://news.yahoo.com/s/ap/20060505/ap_on_re_us/tonga_earthquake_ warning&printer=1;_ylt=Alj21h9cZbEFwGtf8TV6PElH2ocA;_ylu=X3oDMTA3MXN1b HE0BHNlYwN0bWE- (accessed May 10, 2006).

Sullivan, B. 2005. Bank crime theft on rise. MSNBC, June 26. http://msnbc.msn .com/id/3078568/ (accessed May 11, 2006).

Times of India. 2000. I Love You virus hits 45 million PCs. May 8. http://www .k7computing.com/NewsInfo/45million_May00.htm (accessed May 12, 2006).

U.S. Strategic Command. 2006. Functional components. http://www.stratcom.mil/ organization-fnc_comp.html (accessed January 6, 2006).

Verton, D. 1999. DoD boosts IT security role. *Federal Computer Week,* Oct. 9. http://www .fcw.com:8443/fcw/articles/1999/FCW_100499_7.asp (accessed January 9, 2006).

Wallace, R. 2001. It's an all-out cyber war as U.S. hackers fight back at China. *Fox News,* May 1. http://www.foxnews.com/story/0,2933,19337,00.html (accessed May 18, 2006).

White House. 1998. *Presidential decision directive 63: Critical infrastructure protection.* Washington, DC: Author.

Chapter 8 Works Cited

Atomic Archive. n.d. Timeline of the atomic age. http://www.atomicarchive .com/Timeline/Timeline.shtml (accessed January 8, 2007).

Beckman, A. 2003. Death cults of war. *National Review Online.* http://www .nationalreview.com/comment/commentbeichman062003.asp (accessed January 7, 2007).

Bunn, G., and L. Zaitsera. 2001. Guarding nuclear reactors from terrorists and thieves. In *Proceedings of the Symposium on International Safeguards: Verification and nuclear material security*. Vienna: International Atomic Energy Agency.

Bunn, M. 2002. Nuclear Threat Initiative Center for Non-Proliferation Studies. http://www.nti.org/e-research/cnwm/threat/global.asp (accessed Sept. 15, 2006).

Cirincione, J., J. B. Wolfsthal, and M. Rajkumar. 2005. *Deadly arsenals: Nuclear, biological, and chemical threats*. 2nd ed. Washington, DC: Carnegie Endowment for International Peace.

Couch, D. 2003. *U.S. armed forces nuclear, biological, and chemical survival manual*. New York: Basic.

Dastych, D. 2006. The nuclear assassins. *Journalismus Nachrichten von Heute,* November 27. http://oraclesyndicate.two-day.net/stories/2988318/ (accessed January 8, 2007).

Derbis, V. J. 1996. De Mussis and the Great Plague of 1348: A forgotten episode of bacteriological warfare. *Journal of the Amercian Medical Association* 19 (1): 180.

Federation of American Scientists. n.d. Types of chemical weapons. http://www.fas.org/cw/cwagents.htm (accessed January 6, 2007).

Global Nuclear Energy Partnership. n.d. Global Nuclear Energy Partnership home page. http://www.gnep.gov/ (accessed January 8, 2007).

Jones, D. 2007. *Poison arrows: North American Indian hunting and warfare*. Arlington: University of Texas Press.

Luczkovich, J., and D. B. Knowles. 2002. *ECU students review guide to accompany "Environmental science: Earth as a living thing."* Hoboken, NJ: Wiley.

Partnership for Anthrax Vaccine Education. 2003. U.S. anthrax attacks 2001. http://www.gwu.edu/~cih/anthraxinfo/public/publicthreat_attacks.htm (accessed January 8, 2007).

PBS Nova. 2006. The ghost particle. http://www.pbs.org/wgbh/nova/neutrino/ (accessed September 15, 2006).

Shire, J., and D. Albright. 2006. ISIS issue analysis: Iran's response to the EU—Confused but sporadically hopeful. http://www.isis-online.org/ (accessed September. 15, 2006).

Texas City Disaster. n.d. Texas City Disaster. http://www.local1259iaff.org/disaster.html (accessed January 8, 2007).

Thomas, E. 2006. Terror now. *Newsweek,* August 21, 43–60.

Union of Concerned Scientists. 2005a. Fat Boy and Little Boy bombs. http://www.ucsusa.org/global_security/nuclear_terrorism/40-50kilograms (accessed Sept 15, 2006).

———. 2005b. Global security, nuclear terrorism. http://www.ucsusa.org/global-security/nuclearterrorism (accessed Sept. 15, 2006).

———. 2005c. Improving government oversight. http://www.ucsusa.org/clean-energy/nuclear safety/(accessed September 15, 2006).

United Nations. 2007. United Nations chemical weapons convention. http://www.un.org/Depts/dda/WMD/cwc/ (accessed January 8, 2007).

Why Files. n.d. Chemical reaction. http://whyfiles.org/025chem_weap/3.html (accessed January 6, 2007).

Chapter 9 Works Cited

Adams, J. 1987. The financing of terror. In *Contemporary research on terrorism,* ed. P. Wilkinson and A. Stewart. Aberdeen: Aberdeen University Press

Applebaum, A. 2005. The discreet charm of the terrorist cause. *Washington Post,* August 3, A19.

Carlson, J. R. 1995. The future terrorists in America. *American Journal of Police* 14 (3/4): 71–91.

Chalk, P. 1995. The liberal democratic response to terrorism. *Terrorism and Political Violence* 7 (4): 10–44.

Chalk, P., and W. Rosenau. 2004. *Confronting the "enemy within": Security intelligence, the police, and counterterrorism in four democracies.* Santa Monica, CA: RAND Corporation.

CNN Money. 2005. Hezbollah pushes Prada? *CNN Money,* May 26. http://cnnmoney .com/pt/cpt?action=cpt&title=Prada%27s=%27hezbollah (accessed May 27, 2005).

Crenshaw, M. 1990. The logic of terrorism: Terrorist behavior as a product of strategic choice. In *Origins of terrorism: Psychologies, theories, states of mind,* ed. W. Reich. Cambridge: Cambridge University Press.

Donohue, L. K. 2001. In the name of national security: U.S. counterterrorist measures, 1960–2000. *Terrorism and Political Violence* 13 (1): 15–60.

Donohue, L. K., and J. N. Kayyem. 2002. Federalism and the battle over counterterrorist law: State sovereignty, criminal law enforcement, and national security. *Studies in Conflict and Terrorism* 25: 1–18.

Emerson, S. 2003. *American jihad: The terrorists living among us.* New York: Free Press.

Enders, W., and T. Sandler. 2000. Is transnational terrorism becoming more threatening? *Journal of Conflict Resolution* 44 (3): 307–332.

Griset, P. L., and S. Mahan. 2003. *Terrorism in perspective.* Thousand Oaks, CA. Sage.

Hewitt, C. 2000. Patterns of American terrorism, 1955–1998: A historical perspective on terrorism-related fatalities. *Terrorism and Political Violence* 12 (1): 1–14.

Hoffman, B. 1998. *Inside terrorism.* New York: Columbia University Press.

Karber, P. A., and R. W. Mengla. 1983. Political and economic forces affecting terrorism. In *Managing terrorism: Strategies for the corporate executive,* ed. P. J. Montana and G. S. Roukis. Westport, CT: Quorum Books.

Lichbach, M. I. 1995. *The rebel's dilemma.* Ann Arbor: University of Michigan Press.

Long, D. E. 1990. *The anatomy of terrorism.* New York: Free Press.

Memorial Institute for the Prevention of Terrorism. n.d. MIPT Knowledge Base. http:// www.tkb.org/home.jsp (accessed December 7, 2006).

National Counterterrorism Center. n.d. Worldwide Incidents Tracking System. http://wits .nctc.gov (accessed November 27, 2006).

Powers, R. G. 2004. A bomb with a long fuse: 9/11 and the FBI "reforms" of the 1970s. *American History,* December: 43–47.

Rabbie, J. M. 1991. A behavioral interaction model: Toward a social-psychological frame-work for studying terrorism. *Terrorism and Political Violence* 3 (4): 134–163.

Raphaeli, N. 2003. Financing of terrorism: Sources, methods, and channels. *Terrorism and Political Violence* 15 (4): 59–82.

Schiller, D. T. 1987. The police response to terrorism: A critical overview. In *Contemporary research on terrorism,* eds. P. Wilkinson and A. Stewart. Aberdeen: Aberdeen University Press.

Sequoias, K. 2005. Political and militant wings within dissident movements and organizations. *Journal of Conflict Resolution* 49 (2): 218–236.

Sprinzak, E. 1991. The process of deligitimation: Towards a linkage theory of political terrorism. *Terrorism and Political Violence* 3 (1): 50–68.

Walker, C. 2000. Briefing on the Terrorism Act 2000. *Terrorism and Political Violence* 12 (2): 1–36.

Weinberg, L. 1991. Turning to terror: The conditions under which political parties turn to terrorist activities. *Comparative Politics* 23 (4): 423–438.

Weinberg, L., and W. Eubank. 1990. Political parties and the formation of terrorist groups. *Terrorism and Political Violence* 2 (2): 125–144.

Weinstein, J. M. 2005. Resources and the information problem in rebel recruitment. *Journal of Conflict Resolution* 49 (4): 598–624.

Wessinger, C. 2000. *How the millennium comes violently: From Jonestown to Heaven's Gate.* New York: Seven Bridges.

Wilkinson, P. 2000. *Terrorism versus democracy: The liberal state response.* London: Frank Cass.

Chapter 10 Works Cited

Abedin, M. 2005. New security realities and al-Qaeda's changing tactics: An interview with Saad al-Faqih. *Spotlight on Terror* 3: 12. http://www.jamestown.org/terrorism/news/article.php?articleid#69847.

Allen, T. 2006. Leadership in disaster. Comments made at the annual Federal Emergency Management Agency Emergency Management Institute, Emmitsburg, MD, June 6. http://training.fema.gov/EMIWeb/edu/06conf/Conference%20Agenda%202006.doc.

Amnesty International. 2002. United States of America: Amnesty International's concerns regarding post–September 11 detentions in the USA. http://web.amnesty.org/library/pdf/AMR510442002ENGLISH/$File/AMR5104402.pdf.

Andrabi, T., J. Das, A. I. Khwaja, and T. Zajonc. 2005. Religious school enrollment in Pakistan: A look at the data. Faculty working paper RWP 05-024, Kennedy School of Government, Harvard University.

Armanios, F. 2003. Islamic religious schools/madrassas: Background report. Congressional Research Service report #RS21654, October 29.

Benoliel, S. 2003. Strengthening education in the Moslem world. Issue paper #2, United States Agency for International Development.

Bergen, P. 2002. *Holy war, inc.: Inside the secret world of Osama bin Laden*. Boston: Free Press.

Bureau of Educational and Cultural Affairs. 2002. Evaluation summary: Edmund S. Muskie/FSA graduate program. http://exchanges.state.gov/education/evaluations/onepagers/Muskie-FSA.pdf (accessed March 16, 2007).

Cutler, A. 2006. Web of terror. *Atlantic Monthly,* June 5. http://www.theatlantic.com/doc/200606u/labi-interview.

Department of Defense. 2003. *Joint Publication 3-35: Doctrine for Joint Psychological Operations*. Washington, DC: Author.

Ford, P. 2001. Europe cringes at Bush "crusade" against terrorism. *Christian Science Monitor,* September 19. http://www.csmonitor.com/2001/0919/p12s2-woeu.html

Gellman, B. 2002. Cyber-attacks by al-Qaeda feared: Terrorists at the threshold of using Internet as tool of bloodshed, experts say. *Washington Post,* June 27, A01.

Grodzins, M. 1958. *The metropolitan area as a racial problem*. Pittsburgh: University of Pittsburgh Press.

Huntington, S. 1996. *The clash of civilizations and the remaking of world order*. New York: Simon and Schuster.

Inglehart, R., and W. Baker. 2000. Modernization, cultural change, and the persistence of traditional values. *American Sociological Review* 65 (1): 19–51.

Internet World Stats. n.d. Internet usage statistics: The big picture. http://www.internetworldstats.com/stats.htm (accessed September 18, 2006).

Kahneman, D., and A. Tversky. 1973. On the psychology of prediction. *Psychology Review* 80: 237–251.

Labi, N. 2006. Jihad 2.0. *Atlantic Monthly* 298 (6): 102–109.

Levine, B. 2006. The man who put Al-Qaeda on the web. *News Factor,* July 29. http://www.newsfactor.com/story.xhtml?story_id=13200C4PE9Z0.

Lynch, M. 2006. Al-Qaeda's media strategies. *National Interest* 83: 50–56.

Nisbett, R., and L. Ross. 1980. *Human inference: Strategies and shortcomings of social judgment*. New York: Prentice Hall.

Schelling, T. 1978. *Micromotives and macrobehavior*. New York: W. W. Norton.

Schlenger, W., J. Caddell, L. Ebert, B. K. Jordan, K. Rourke, D. Wilson, L. Thalji, J. M. Dennis, J. Fairbank, and R. Kulka. 2002. Psychological reactions to terrorist attacks: Findings from the national study of Americans' reactions to September 11. *Journal of the American Medical Association* 288 (5): 581–588.

Starobin, P. 2006. Misfit America. *Atlantic Monthly* 297 (1): 144–149.

Toner, R. 2001. Reconsidering security, U.S. clamps down on agency web sites. *New York Times,* October 27, B4.

United States Senate Select Committee on Intelligence. 2006. *Postwar finding about Iraq's WMD programs and links to terrorism and how they compare with prewar assessments.* Washington, DC: U.S. Government Printing Office.

USA Today. 2003. Poll: 70% believe Saddam, 9-11 link. http://www.usatoday.com/news/washington/2003-09-06-poll-iraq_x.htm.

Wallace-Wells, B. 2006. Annals of terrorism: Private jihad. *New Yorker* 82 (15): 28–33.

Weimann, G. 2004a. *www.terror.net: How modern terrorism uses the Internet.* Special Report #116, United States Institute of Peace.

———. 2004b. Terrorists and their tools—Part II: Using the Internet to recruit, raise funds, and plan attacks. In *Terror on the Internet: The new arena and the new challenges,* ed. G. Weimann. Washington, DC: United States Institute of Peace.

GLOSSARY

Accident An unintentional incident that causes damage, injury, or loss of life, but on a lower scale than a disaster.

Agricultural vulnerability Agricultural plant and animal vulnerability to environmental extremes; the ability of livestock and crops to withstand disasters.

Al-Jazeera An Arabic-language news network headquartered in Qatar.

All-hazards approach An approach to homeland security that addresses impacts, disruptions, and cascading effects of both natural disasters and man-made incidents.

Anarchists People or groups who seek to abolish all governments because they believe that governments act against the interests and rights of people to behave as they wish.

Anarchy Absence of a central government or overarching authority regulating the relations between states.

Asymmetrical warfare The use of non-conventional warfare tactics and techniques by a less powerful force against a more powerful adversary.

Availability heuristic Assessing the probability of an event by how clearly we can imagine events like it.

Axis Powers The alliance among Germany, Japan, and Italy during World War II.

Biological weapons Weapons consisting of biological or living organisms or toxins.

Bipolar system A relationship among countries in the international system in which two countries dominate and other nation-states tend to align themselves with either of the two, such as the United States and the USSR during the Cold War.

Bretton Woods Agreements   Series of post–World War II agreements that created key economic institutions intended to promote international economic stability and trade, such as the International Monetary Fund (IMF) and the International Bank for Reconstruction and Development (World Bank).

Bureaucracy   The sum of all federal departments, agencies, and offices that implement laws under the authority of the president. By definition, bureaucracies are hierarchical organizations that are highly specialized, and they operate with very formal rules.

C4I   The organizational architecture used by the U.S. military; stands for command, control, communications, computers, and intelligence.

CBRNE   Abbreviation for chemical, biological, radiological, nuclear, and explosive weapons.

Central Powers   The alliance between Germany, Austria-Hungary, the Ottoman Empire, and Bulgaria in World War I.

Chemical weapons   Weapons consisting of toxic or otherwise harmful chemicals not specifically of biological origin.

CI/KR   Abbreviation for critical infrastructure and key resources.

Circular error of probability (CEP)   Term that describes the accuracy with which nuclear weapons strike their targets.

Civil defense   The protection of the nation against threats within the United States.

Civil war   War that occurs within a state.

Clandestine and covert operations   Clandestine operations are secret efforts to gather information, while covert operations are intended to influence how governments behave. Covert operations could include bribes, subversion and psychological operations, and support for insurgent forces.

Collective security   An agreement among countries to unite against any aggressor.

COMPINT   Abbreviation for computer intelligence, or what we can learn from analyzing computer traffic, email, website hits, hard drives, and so on.

Composite Exposure Indicator (CEI)   A hazard assessment model that ranks potential for losses in a given region for single or multiple hazards by assigning a numeric value to the exposure potential for communities. FEMA has used this approach to quantify 14 variables in 3,100 U.S. counties, with rankings based on the amount of each variable present.

Computer Emergency Response Team (CERT)   One of several organizations that provide the supporting mechanisms necessary for researching and responding to computer security threats.

Computer Network Attack (CNA)   The offensive component of Computer Network Operations, in which the intelligence and espionage function is changed into a hostile action.

Containment   Principal national security policy pursued during the Cold War to prevent the spread of Communism and Soviet influence.

Correlation of forces   A measure of comparative military power between the United States and the USSR during the Cold War, based on the combined resources of the nations that were aligned with each superpower.

Counter-terrorism policy   Set of laws, agencies, and programs targeted at controlling and reducing terrorist threats.

Criminal justice model   Use of the system of police, courts, laws, and prisons to address a terrorist threat.

Critical infrastructure   Systems and assets, whether physical or virtual, so vital to the United States that the incapacity or destruction of such systems and assets would have a debilitating impact on security, national economic security, national public health or safety, or any combination of those matters.

Critical Infrastructure Assurance Office (CIAO)   Federal center for coordinating the ISAC process and encouraging the private sector to cooperate with the government in protecting itself against cyber-terrorism and threats from man-made and natural disasters.

Criticality   The impact of loss on an individual or company.

Criticality assessment   Process that identifies and evaluates an organization's assets based on a variety of criteria.

Cult terrorist group   Type of group that conducts terrorism with the intent or goal of initiating religious prophecy, such as bringing forth a new millennium or messiah.

Cyberspace   The notional environment in which digitized information is communicated over computer networks.

Cyber-terrorism   The use of computer-based operations by terrorist organizations conducting cyber-attacks that compromise, damage, degrade, disrupt, deny, and destroy information stored on computer networks or that target network infrastructures.

Cyber-warfare   Conflict between nation-states using cyber-based weapons.

Data mining   The use of the Internet for open source information, which when pieced together provides information of intelligence value for an organization.

Defense Advance Research Projects Agency (DARPA)   Agency within the Department of Defense that created the foundations of the modern Internet in the 1960s.

Defense Information Systems Agency (DISA)   Home of the original NOSC established by the Department of Defense, also called the Global NOSC or GNOSC because it looked at the global information infrastructure.

Demographic impacts   Effects on a community's population after a disaster.

Denial of Service (DOS) attack   Most common type of CNA, in which an individual computer or entire network is rendered useless, such as by the actions of a virus.

Department of Homeland Security (DHS)   Federal department created in 2002 with the primary mission of protecting the United States against terrorist threats.

Détente   Literally, a "relaxation of tensions"; refers to the efforts of the Nixon administration to promote diplomatic compromise with the USSR.

Direct democracy   A system of government in which people represent themselves and vote directly on legislative matters.

Dirty bomb   A conventional explosive used to spread radioactive material.

Disaster   An unintentional event that causes extensive damage, injury, and loss of life.

Disaster impact process   The way to examine the effects a disaster will have on a community. The first step of the disaster impact process is the pre-impact phase, which includes planning and mitigation efforts. The second phase is the actual disaster event, which includes specific hazard conditions and community response. The third phase is the emergency management intervention phase, which includes response, recovery, and program evaluation.

Disaster response   The reaction individuals have when faced with the onset of a disaster.

Domestic terrorism   Terrorism directed by a group against the specific state within which they reside.

Dual function of violence   Refers to the fact that terrorist violence is both externally directed (directed against a specific target) and internally directed (intended to solidify a support base).

Economic impacts   Changes in asset values after a disaster that are measured by the cost of repair or replacement.

Eco-terrorism   Form of terrorism in which a group attempts to influence domestic policy regarding land development, environmental policy, and animal testing.

Émigré terrorism   Form of foreign terrorism in which a foreign victim is killed by a foreign terrorist group inside the boundaries of a different country.

Enabler   Anything that assists in the creation of mass effects. Can be an institution or process that makes it possible for the mass effect to occur when it would not have occurred otherwise; an institution or process that allows the mass effect to have a greater effect than it would have had otherwise; or an institution or process that is utilized by those who would cause a mass effect.

Entente Powers   The alliance between the United States, Britain, France, Russia, and Italy in World War I.

Environmental impact statement   Statement of the hazards posed by a building project to the local community. Such statements are required under the National Environmental Protection Act for all major building projects or legislation that will impact the environment both positively and negatively.

Environmental Protection Agency (EPA)   The lead federal agency for assuring compliance with U.S. codes and statutes related to industrial plant safety and security.

Ethno-nationalist/separatist terrorism   Use of terrorism by a sub-state, ethnic, or national group in order to change its access to power either by taking over the state or by forcing secession to form its own independent state.

Externally directed state terrorism   The abuse of state power against citizens/ governments from other states in order to motivate the target state to make policy changes in line with the political objectives of the "aggressor" state.

Extortion rackets   Scheme in which a group provides security or protection to a business, farmer, or other organization in exchange for materials and resources, most often money. Protection is often from the group offering the protective services.

Federal Coordinating Officer (FCO)   The single individual, usually the head of the lead federal agency, designated to work under the PFO for coordinating the federal response to a domestic situation.

Federal Emergency Management Agency (FEMA)   Agency created in 1979 to provide a coordinated federal response to local communities' disaster needs.

Federalist Papers   Essays authored by James Madison, Alexander Hamilton, and John Jay in 1787–1788 that argued the need for a U.S. federal government strong enough to provide for national security while also protecting states' rights and individual liberties.

Federal system   A vertical division of power found in the United States in which the national government has some exclusive powers, state and local governments have some exclusive powers, other powers are shared by all levels of government, and some powers are reserved to state and local governments.

Fissile material   Uranium-235 or plutonium-239, the primary materials used to trigger the chain reaction involved in a nuclear explosion.

Force multiplier   That which increases the appearance of strength.

Foreign Intelligence Surveillance Court (FISC)   Court that can issue search warrants that are not public record and therefore not required to be released.

Foreign targets   Terrorist targets located in U.S. territory but symbolically linked to a different country; examples include embassies, foreign nationals, and foreign businesses.

Foreign terrorist group   Type of terrorist group whose operatives originate outside the United States and penetrate homeland security to plan and conduct operations against internal targets.

Foreign terrorist organizers   Foreign terrorist recruiters and agents that raise funds and recruit operatives from inside the United States for operations against U.S. and other national interests overseas.

Geopolitics   The political impact of geographical relationships.

Globalization   The increasing economic and social interdependence among countries.

Global War on Terrorism   (GWOT) Military campaign launched after 9/11 that targets terrorist groups in multiple countries.

Half-life   The length of time required for half of an amount of radioactive material to be converted to another isotope during the decay process.

Hazard assessment   The process by which we identify new and existing threats and assess the level of risk to a population.

Hazard exposure   The likelihood that specific disasters will occur; the probability of occurrence of a given event magnitude.

Hazard mitigation   Sustained action to alleviate or eliminate risks to life and property from natural or man-made hazard events.

HAZMAT   Abbreviation for hazardous materials.

Heuristics   Rules of thumb.

Highly enriched uranium (HEU)   One of the primary ingredients for building a nuclear bomb.

Homegrown terrorist group   Type of terrorist group whose members originate within the United States and conduct terrorist operations against targets inside the United States.

Homeland security   Those activities that protect people, critical infrastructure, key resources, economic activities, and our way of life.

Homeland Security/Defense Education Consortium (HSDEC)   A cooperative arrangement of universities and research centers in the United States, Canada, and Mexico that is seeking to develop the academic field of homeland security.

Human vulnerability   Individual vulnerability to environmental extremes.

Ideological terrorist groups   Groups that challenge the fabric of existing liberal democratic states from either a left-wing or a right-wing political framework.

Ideology   A tightly knit body of beliefs organized around a few central values; examples include communism, fascism, and variations of nationalism.

Informal Funds Transfer System (IFTS)   A foreign remittance system in which a person gives money to an intermediary, who then instructs a contact in the receiving country to distribute the money to a predetermined recipient in the local currency.

Information Assurance Vulnerability Assessment (IAVA)   An assessment issued by a CERT that directs system administrators regarding the necessary actions required to restore information systems affected by a cyber-attack.

Information Sharing and Advisory Council (ISAC)   One of a number of groups established by the federal government in 1998 to foster public-private partnerships in all sectors of the nation's critical infrastructures.

Interests   The human (individual or group), environmental, political, or economic components of society that we seek to protect through homeland security programs.

Internally directed state terrorism   The use of force by the state apparatus against its own population.

International Atomic Energy Agency (IAEA)   The United Nations agency charged with inspecting nuclear reactors and power plants throughout the world.

International terrorism   Terrorism that relies on an increasing link between groups from different states as well as an increasing internationalization of targets in order to speak to a wider audience.

Inter-state war   War between two or more states.

Isolationism   A foreign policy based on avoiding alliances with other countries.

Joint Task Force–Global Network Operations (JTF-GNO)   The organization created from the Global NOSC after 9/11 to generate new military command and control capabilities for dealing with cyber-threats.

Key resources   Individual targets whose destruction would not endanger vital systems, but could create local disaster or profoundly damage our nation's morale or confidence. Key resources can be publicly or privately controlled resources essential to the minimal operations of the economy and government.

Koan   A question that cannot be answered.

Lead agency approach   A counter-terrorism policy in which the federal agency with jurisdiction and accountability over a threat is determined by the loci of the threat (domestic, international, or aviation).

Lead federal agency   A single federal agency designated as having overall responsibility for coordinating federal response to a domestic situation, such as a natural disaster or terrorist incident.

Madrassas   Religious schools, primarily located in Muslim countries, that teach radical Islamic ideas and are often considered a potential breeding ground for terrorists.

Marshall Plan   Plan that provided U.S. funds to help rebuild non-Communist countries after World War II.

Materialists   People who are concerned with personal survival: providing for themselves or their families, making a good salary, and all the "perks" that come along with that salary.

Matrix   A tool for decision making that uses a grid design to weigh the frequency of an event against its severity to rank potential costs or damage.

Monroe Doctrine   A regional security policy proposed by President James Monroe in 1823 that sought to limit European influence in the Americas.

Multiple independently targeted reentry vehicle (MIRV)   Device that allows a missile to carry more than one nuclear warhead.

Multipolar system   A relationship among countries in the international system in which no country dominates, with a number of nation-states possessing military power and capable of acting independently.

Narcoterrorism   Terrorist violence used to guarantee continued profit from the drug trade.

National Flood Insurance Program (NFIP)   FEMA-administered program that features three major components: flood insurance, floodplain management, and flood hazard mapping.

National Infrastructure Protection Center (NIPC)   Federal operations center for tracking cyber-attacks on the nation's critical infrastructure.

Nationalism   The belief that political communities share common characteristics such as language, religion, or ethnicity, and that a state only gains legitimacy by representing these shared characteristics.

National security   Protecting the United States, its citizens, and its interests through the threatened and actual use of all elements of national power.

National Security Letter (NSL)   Letter issued by an FBI field supervisor without a prosecutor, grand jury, or judge. An NSL receives no review after the fact by the Department of Justice or by Congress. Federal laws expanded by the USA Patriot Act give anti-terrorism and counter-intelligence investigators access to an array of consumer information through NSLs.

Natural disaster   The effect of a naturally occurring phenomenon, usually referred to by the insurance industry as an "act of God." Examples of natural disasters include hurricanes, tornados, floods, and forest fires due to natural causes.

Network Operations Security Center (NOSC)   One of a number of centers established by government and the private sector to provide indications and warning capability in cyberspace.

Neutrality Acts   Laws passed by Congress in the 1930s forbidding American support for or involvement with countries at war.

Non-governmental organization (NGO)   An organization that provides a service to a community free of charge or for a minimal cost that is required to defray the cost of the service furnished. NGOs usually hold special non-profit federal tax-exempt status and receive financial support through donations, contracts, and grants.

Non-intervention   The principle that no one outside of a state can interfere in the internal affairs of that state.

Non-state actors   People or organizations that exercise political influence either domestically or internationally, such as al-Qaeda.

Non-state terrorist actor   Term that applies to a variety of groups with different aims and identities but that all share two elements: (1) they don't have access to state power, and (2) they believe that they can achieve their goals only through violence.

Operational environment The location of a terrorist group and its primary field of activity, determined by available resources and the ability to recruit members and survive against other political competitors.

Operation Enduring Freedom (OEF) Military operations in Afghanistan, the Philippines, and the Horn of Africa against terrorist groups believed to be associated with al-Qaeda.

Organization for Economic Cooperation and Development (OECD) International economic organization whose goals include developing common principles and policy guidance on prevention of, preparedness for, and response to chemical accidents.

Physical environment The geography surrounding terrorist activity, typically considered as either urban or rural, which determines the epicenter of the activity.

Physical vulnerability The ability to prepare for, cope with, and withstand disasters; includes human vulnerability, agricultural ability, and structural vulnerability.

Pluralism A system of government in which many groups or institutions share power in a complex system of interactions, which involves compromising and bargaining in the decision-making process.

Political environment The social decision-making process of a society, including its government institutions and rules of access, which allow issues to arise for discussion and decision.

Political impacts Changes in the political structure of a community after a disaster.

Political violence The use of force in the pursuit of political objectives.

Post materialists People who are more concerned with what some call "higher goals," such as preserving and protecting freedom of speech and other more self-expression-type values.

Preemption Taking action against a state or non-state actor before it becomes too dangerous a threat.

Preparedness actions Pre-impact actions that provide the human and material resources needed to support active responses at the time of hazard impact.

Prepositioning Establishing bases and supplies in foreign countries to prepare a rapid response to future crises.

Principal Federal Official (PFO) The single lead federal representative with overall responsibility for the federal response to a domestic situation, such as a natural disaster or terrorist incident. This individual may or may not be the head of the lead federal agency.

Probability   The likelihood of suffering loss due to potential risks.

Proliferation   The supplying of other countries with the technology to build their own nuclear weapons.

Psychological warfare   The use of propaganda and other psychological actions having the primary purpose of influencing the opinions, emotions, attitudes, and behavior of hostile foreign groups in such a way as to support the achievement of national objectives.

Psychosocial impacts   Effects on mental health and the ability to get treatment after a disaster.

Racial supremacy groups   Type of terrorist group that believes the general social climate of a country is deteriorating and that this condition is caused by the tolerance of different racial groups in society.

Rad   Radiation-absorbed dose; a unit used to measure exposure to nuclear material.

Radiological weapons   Weapons consisting of radiological material.

Recovery   The period of time after a disaster. It can be of immediate, short term, or protracted duration.

Religious terrorism   Terrorism with the primary motivation of furthering a particular religious set of ideas.

Representative democracy   A system of government in which the ultimate political authority is vested in the people, who elect their governing officials to legislate on their behalf.

Representativeness heuristic   Assessing the probability of an unknown event on the basis of how it represents an event we know.

Resource environment   The ability of a terrorist group to access necessary financial resources to build an organization and conduct terrorist operations.

Resource mobilization   Raising money and other materials to fund terrorist operations, including purchasing weapons and munitions.

Risk   The combination of vulnerability and the consequence of a specified hazardous event.

Risk assessment   Identifying and evaluating risks based on an objective analysis of an organization's entire protective system.

Risk management   A process involved in the anticipation, recognition, and appraisal of a risk and the initiation of action to eliminate entirely or reduce the threat or harm to an acceptable level.

Risk reduction   An examination of the actions necessary to decrease detected or projected levels of danger and to identify the resources required for implementing those actions.

Rummel's power principle   "Power kills and absolute power kills absolutely"; in other words, the more power that is concentrated in a few hands, the more likely it is that this power will be abused.

Secondary and tertiary effects   Consequences that are compounded during a natural or accidental disaster due to man-made errors.

Security environment   The combination of police, military, intelligence, security forces, courts, and prisons that enforce law and ensure domestic security.

Self-help   The idea that each state has to rely on its own strength and that it cannot wait for others to help it in a situation of crisis; assumed to be the key behavioral characteristic of sovereign states and explains how in international relations the use of force is sometimes considered acceptable (as in the case of self-defense).

Separation of powers   System through which governmental power is divided between the executive, legislative, and judicial branches of the national government.

SEVIS   Acronym for "Student and Exchange Visitor Information System," a computerized registry of international students studying in the United States.

Sneak-and-peek search   A special search warrant that allows law enforcement officers to lawfully enter areas in which a reasonable expectation of privacy exists, to search for items of evidence or contraband and leave without making any seizures or giving concurrent notice of the search.

Socialists   People or groups who want to control the state apparatus so as to redistribute wealth and ensure the rights of the people.

Social vulnerability   A person's or group's ability to anticipate, prepare for, or cope with disasters.

Sovereignty   The idea that there is a final and absolute authority in the political community.

Stafford Act   Originally passed by Congress in 1985 as the Robert T. Stafford Disaster Relief and Emergency Assistance Act, this act provides the means by which the president can declare a state of emergency, authorizing federal funds for disaster relief to both public agencies and private persons.

State   A distinct political community that spans a definable geographical territory, acknowledges one form of authority over that territory and population, and is recognized by other sovereign states.

State of emergency   A declaration by the president in response to a disaster, making the affected area of the country eligible for increased federal support and funding.

State terrorism   When a state's legitimate use of force/power is abused.

Steganography   The practice of embedding messages or files in computer websites.

Structural vulnerability   A building's ability to withstand extreme stresses or features that allow hazardous materials to infiltrate the building.

Suicide terrorism   Method of attack in which the attacker does not expect to survive.

Superpowers   The dominant military powers during the Cold War: the United States and USSR. After the demise of communism, the United States remained the world's lone superpower.

Supervisory Control and Data Acquisition (SCADA)   Software and hardware interface used for most of the computerized management and switching that occurs in industry, transportation, telecommunications, etc.

Target hardening   Increasing the physical security around likely terrorist targets to prevent an attack.

Terrorism   Use or threat of use of seemingly random violence against nontraditional targets in order to instill a climate of fear so that the fear will induce political acquiescence and/or a political change in favor of those instigating the violence.

Threat   Natural or man-made event that can destroy or damage human, environmental, political, or economic components of society.

Threat assessment   Process that identifies and evaluates threats based on various criteria.

Umma   In Islam, a term used to describe those called to the community of the faithful.

Unipolar system   An international system characterized by one superpower.

United Nations (UN)   International organization established after World War II to resolve disputes and stop aggression through collective security.

United States Army Medical Research Institute of Infectious Diseases (USAMRIID)   Institute located at Ft. Dietrick, Maryland, that researches biological weapons and their use and maintains small strains of agents for the purpose of developing defenses against them.

U.S.-based targets   Local or national terrorist targets symbolically linked to the United States.

U.S. Strategic Command (STRATCOM)   Located in Omaha, Nebraska, one of nine regional and functional combatant commands, with responsibility for Information Operations.

Vividness heuristic   Assessing the probability of an event based on how vividly it is described or portrayed.

Vulnerability   Exposure to risk in general.

Vulnerability assessment   Process that identifies weaknesses in a structure, individual, or function.

War model   Militarization of a terrorist-related conflict.

Weapon of mass destruction (WMD)   Device such as a chemical, biological, radiological, nuclear, or explosive weapon that can inflict widespread damage when used.

Weapons of Mass Destruction Civil Support Teams (WMD-CSTs)   Teams within the Army National Guard that have personnel trained to operate in contaminated areas due to potential terrorist attacks involving hazardous materials.

White House Office of Homeland Security   An executive agency that advises the president on homeland security issues and works with the Office of Management and Budget to develop and defend the president's homeland security budget proposals.

Writ of habeas corpus   The constitutional guarantee that accused persons will be brought before a judge to hear charges against them.

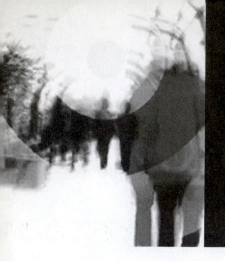

INDEX